# THE GENDERED
# LYRIC

# Purdue Studies in Romance Literatures

# THE GENDERED LYRIC

Subjectivity and

Difference in

Nineteenth-Century

French Poetry

Gretchen Schultz

Purdue University Press
West Lafayette, Indiana

03   02   01   00   99                    5   4   3   2   1

∞The paper used in this book meets the minimum requirements of
American National Standard for Information Sciences—Permanence of
Paper for Printed Library Materials, ANSI Z39.48-1992.

Printed in the United States of America
Design by Anita Noble

**Library of Congress Cataloging-in-Publication Data**
Schultz, Gretchen, 1960–
      The gendered lyric : subjectivity and difference in nineteenth-
century French poetry / Gretchen Schultz.
            p.   cm. — (Purdue studies in Romance literatures ; v. 17)
      Includes bibliographical references and index.
      ISBN 1-55753-135-8  (cloth : alk. paper)
      1. French poetry—19th century—History and criticism. 2. Sex
role in literature. 3. Authorship—Sex differences. I. Title. II. Series.
PQ433.S33 1999
841'.709—dc21                                            98-55268
                                                              CIP

**For my parents—**
Pamela Macpherson Schultz
and William Schultz

# Contents

*Contents*

# Preface

Gender played a determining role in the aesthetic and ideological values associated with the dominant poetic tendencies of nineteenth-century France. From Romanticism through Symbolism, both the sex of the author and textual inscriptions of gender shaped poetic doctrine and practice in inextricably related ways. Men manipulated "woman" as a poetic symbol and, in turn, women poets on the edges of nineteenth-century French poetic communities challenged dominant poetic discourses with strategies ranging from assimilation to satire and outright defiance. Female poetic production was thus shaped by its milieu, but succeeded in questioning the very foundations of its own context.

*The Gendered Lyric* juxtaposes male- and female-authored poetry in order to explore the reciprocal influence of dominant and marginal poetic traditions. It questions prevailing assumptions that women writers (whether through poor education, innate incompatibility, or disinterest) were somehow at odds with this elite and difficult genre, or that the lyric provided a poor medium for the translation of feminine subjectivity. While forming a decided minority, women did in fact participate in predominantly male poetic communities. They produced fascinating texts, largely unread today, that illuminate the play of sexual difference in canonical poetry.

I contend that nineteenth-century critics and poets rebuffed women poets' attempts to become writing subjects because the prevailing conception of lyric poetry was predicated upon the objectification of woman. Indeed, the analysis of poetic subject positions through the optic of gender shows that sexual difference functioned symbolically to define lyricism itself. From the fictional representation of the poet to the articulation of poetic voice and choice of trope and form, gender is intricately connected to the production of poetic meaning.

This study traces the chronological development of lyric poetry through the three major movements of the nineteenth century: Romanticism (Part 1), Parnassianism (Part 2), and Symbolism (Part 3). I focus on the critical and literary production of the chief poetic schools and the works of women poets in relation to them. In this I follow Nancy K. Miller's insistence on temporal and cultural context: "it is important to locate any

*Preface*

poetics of feminist writing in relation to a historicized national and cultural production; [. . .] a 'poetics of location' is the only way to work against the universalizing tendencies of a monolith of 'women's writing'" ("Men's Reading, Women's Writing" 44). My introduction serves two contextualizing functions, first sketching out the nineteenth-century poetic environment in France, and then situating the problematic of the gendered lyric within the context of contemporary theories of the subject, of poetics, and of feminism.

The relationship between gender and lyric poetry creates a fabric of unfolding, intertwining stories. The story spun out in time starts with the rebirth of lyric poetry with Romanticism. I begin in chapter 1 by retracing the terms of this poetic renaissance. The first to provide a vocabulary for the Romantic experience was Germaine de Staël, who described the new aesthetics of spontaneity and emotive effusion. Her work points to a poetic revolution in expression, the desire to break out of constraints by privileging unrestrained, forward-rolling narratives of the self.

Indeed, literary historians define French Romanticism in terms of a small number of male poets whose work involves the exploration of the self and the liberation of sentiment. The canonical poets Lamartine, Vigny, Hugo, and Musset consistently proffered masculine lyric subjects and spoke to masculine ambition, and yet their very emotiveness suggests both implicitly and explicitly the exploration of femininity. Although Romanticism invariably represented a male, heterosexual poet, this figure underwent a curious feminization during the period. Even the most robust of the Romantics, Victor Hugo, describes the "soft" qualities of the poetic persona.

The Romantic construct of the poet offers the best gauge of the gendering of lyric expression and helps explain why stories of female Romantic poets often go untold. In chapter 2, I focus on the works of Desbordes-Valmore, one of a number of Romantic women poets who enjoyed popular success during their lifetimes. Although these women confronted significant cultural obstacles, these were less considerable than for women poets of other eras, since the reigning Romantic style, associated with passionate effusion and spontaneity rather than formalism, accorded relatively easily with the myth of the Eternal Feminine. The very acceptability of Desbordes-Valmore indicates her collusion with such myths. And yet my analyses of the metaphoric and prosodic features of her work, as of her manipulation of subject positions, reveal her attempts to write as a woman within a context that appropriated the female voice for masculinity.

By the middle of the century, neoclassical Parnassian poets (those issuing from *l'art pour l'art* and presaging *la poésie pure*) began to view Romantic verse as weak and feminine or, more simply stated, as low literature. Poets and critics questioned the positive valuation of femininity and characterized elegiac poets as lacking in muscular qualities. For example, Baudelaire called Musset "féminin et sans doctrine," and Leconte de Lisle bemoaned Lamartine's "absence de virilité." The rigorously formalist aesthetic of the poets identified with the Parnassian movement, then, depended on Romantic spontaneity and looseness as a foil against which to cast their poetry as "high" or "pure," concurrently defining a masculine poetic stance of hardness.

Formalist Parnassians, the most self-consciously virile poets of the nineteenth century, disturbed Romantic trends and ridiculed the softness of their predecessors. I examine the significance of this reaction in chapter 3, where I focus on the work of Leconte de Lisle, one of the Parnasse's most distinguished elders and uncompromising theoreticians. His repudiation of subjective poetry, his formalist aesthetic, and his metaphors of hardness all functioned to evacuate the lyric of any trace of what was perceived to be feminine. In chapter 4, I broaden my scope to consider how other Parnassians elaborated upon the poetic obsessions articulated by Leconte de Lisle, paying particular attention to Théophile Gautier, among other male poets who exploited the sculpture metaphor that dominated Parnassian representations of women. The movement located its exploration of femininity in the classical figure of Venus, resulting in the immobilization of sexuality and the consolidation of the male poetic subject. Moreover, Parnassians pursued their poetics of constraint through the resurrection of the sonnet, one of the "hardest" and most intricate of fixed forms.

Chapter 5 closes my Parnassian section by considering the work and status of the few women poets who managed to integrate the movement. Coming from diverse backgrounds and exhibiting a broad variety of approaches to form and subjective expression, these women practiced strategies ranging from assimilation to parody in order to secure a place among their male poetic contemporaries.

The final section on Symbolism attests to the complexity with which sexual difference was played out in the poetry of the late-nineteenth century. In the increasingly non-narrative and opaque poems of Symbolism, one encounters lyric voices that often defy the inscription of a centralized male subject. With the Symbolists, the tension becomes more manifest between, on one hand, the ideological self-representation of the male Poet and, on the other, the dissolution of constituted identities that occurs in the process of writing.

In chapter 6, I read Baudelaire as a transitional figure with links to each of the movements studied here, but one fairly universally considered responsible for the inscription of the modern poetic subject. Although most current work on Baudelairian modernity focuses on his prose poetry of the city and his art criticism, I find his most novel contribution to the representation of subjectivity in his heterometric verse. While the fragmented urban subject of his prose is implicitly masculine, Baudelaire's manipulation of poetic forms, and of these sinuously metered pieces in particular, created a setting for variously gendered subjects by surpassing the dogmatic cleavage of both Romantic and Parnassian aesthetics.

In my seventh and final chapter, I take the work of Paul Verlaine and Marie Krysinska as exemplary of new inscriptions of sexuality and gender made possible by the re-evaluation of French prosody and subject positions. Like Baudelaire, these poets looked to poetic rhythm as a metaphor for difference. Verlaine coupled his homoerotic poetry with the manipulation of rhythm and meter. He placed himself in the tradition of Desbordes-Valmore by using the hendecasyllabic line to represent his double departure from conventional versification and normative sexuality. Krysinska, a relatively unknown and under-appreciated Symbolist, reread lyric femininity within the context of the new practice of free verse. Claiming the invention of free verse as her own, Krysinska defied contemporaries who denigrated her accomplishments and, more boldly than her Romantic and Parnassian sisters, challenged the male poetic establishment with her specifically feminine, and often feminist, language.

# Acknowledgments

Since the work that would coalesce into this book dates back to my graduate studies at Cornell University and beyond, I have over a decade of appreciation to express and many people to thank for the intellectual exchanges and human kindness that nurtured my research.

I would like to thank these professors, mentors, friends, for their guidance and for teaching me so much and so well about poetry and feminism: Anne Berger, Phil Lewis, Nelly Furman, Philippe Hamon, Patsy Baudoin, and Domna Stanton. To the other members of my Ithaca family, Brigitte Mahuzier and Katrina Perry, I am always and in every way beholden.

I extend my appreciation to Brown University for its generous support of my work, and particularly for granting me a semester's research leave with a Henry Merritt Wriston Fellowship. Thanks go to my colleagues in French Studies at Brown, and especially to Lewis Seifert, whose solidarity and intelligence have meant so much to me. For critiquing chapters with sharp insight and good humor I am indebted to Elizabeth Francis and Tamar Katz.

Thanks go to the editors at Purdue Studies in Romance Literatures for supporting my project and for their expert guidance in assisting me to see this book through to its final form, and to the anonymous reviewers for their extremely helpful feedback. I would also like to thank Seth Whidden for his invaluable research assistance and buoyant enthusiasm for French poetry.

For their encouragement and hand-holding, I extend my deep appreciation to my family: my admirable grandmothers, my sister Karen Iverson, and my parents, to whom I dedicate this book. Loving thanks go to my dear friends Evie Lincoln, Jill Pipher, and Amy Remensnyder for their support and companionship. Carolyn Dean, buddy and brilliant colleague, has my affectionate appreciation for the serious and silly ways she helped me see this project through to its end. Finally, I would like to express my warm gratitude to Henry Majewski, who generously read nearly every word of my manuscript, gently offered his invaluable criticism, and sustained me with his devoted friendship.

*Acknowledgments*

Sections of this book were previously published in slightly different form: "Gender and the Sonnet: Marceline Desbordes-Valmore and Paul Verlaine," in *Cincinnati Romance Review* 10 (1991): 190–99; "Loathsome Movement: Parnassian Politics and Villard's Revenge," in *Moving Forward, Holding Fast: The Dynamics of Nineteenth-Century French Culture,* ed. Barbara T. Cooper and Mary Donaldson-Evans (Amsterdam: Rodopi, 1997), 169–81; and "Sexualités de Verlaine," in the *Revue Verlaine* 5 (1997): 46–59.

# Introduction

## Does Poetry Have a Gender?

*The Gendered Lyric* aims to fill a rather astonishing gap in existing criticism. While feminist scholars have devoted considerable attention both to the nexus of femininity and the French novel, and to the role of gender in Anglo-American lyric traditions, there exist no equivalent studies of gender and modern French poetry.[1] Thanks to the work of such prominent critics as Joan DeJean, Nancy K. Miller, and Naomi Schor, we can trace female authorship and the play of gender back to the origins of the novel in France.[2] Interest in the relationship between femininity and the French novel shows no signs of abating, and is particularly strong in nineteenth-century studies.[3]

Feminist neglect of poetry appears to be a particular problem in the context of the French tradition, since English and American literary studies are rich in works on gender and the lyric, beginning with Sandra Gilbert and Susan Gubar's groundbreaking collection *Shakespeare's Sisters: Feminist Essays on Women Poets* (1979). Indeed, as Yopie Prins and Maeera Shreiber point out in their introduction to *Dwelling in Possibility: Women Poets and Critics on Poetry* (1997), their recent anthology "continues the work of several generations of feminist critics. It is a substantial body of work" (9).[4] There is no comparable body of scholarship on gender and the modern French lyric. The dialogue in this realm, while probing, remains limited to article-length studies.[5]

How can we explain the delay in introducing modern French poetry to gender studies? It would seem that our acceptance of the equation opposing the "feminine novel" to "masculine poetry" has been too hasty. The dearth of work on women poets and on the function of gender in the lyric indicates a tacit agreement that poetry in France belongs to a masculine domain. While the model of sex-segregated genres is particularly helpful in describing the homosocial organization of poetic communities and the historical conditions of women's access to poetic production, it is less useful in the analysis of the symbolic structures of poetry. This study demonstrates that while masculinity dominates lyric production, femininity is always present as a foil, an appropriation, or a threat.

It has been convincingly argued that the sexual segregation of genres is historically and culturally produced. Michael Danahy describes the gendered hierarchy of genres: "the novel was trivialized and feminized in relation [. . .] to all forms of poetry and the lyric in particular" (*Feminization* 62). Critics have attributed the novel's association with femininity to the relative newness of the genre and consequent malleability of style,[6] the greater ease that prose-writing affords to the presumably less-educated woman writer, its domestic and sentimental themes, and subsequent appeal to a female reading public. DeJean likewise asserts that "French women writers were [not] likely [. . .] to explore forms other than the novel. It is as if the French female tradition had come into existence in order to create the modern novel" (*Tender Geographies* 8). While the association of femininity and the novel often served to denigrate women's writing, it also rendered fictional prose more available than other genres to women. The woman novelist was simply more acceptable to the French reading public and literary milieu than the woman poet.

All women authors have confronted very real social barriers, including limited access to education, closed literary communities, and lack of physical and intellectual autonomy. Feminist writers since Christine de Pizan have pointed to poor education as a barrier that discourages women from becoming writing subjects. Closer to our period, in 1811, Stéphanie-Félicité de Genlis recognized this as an enduring and considerable obstacle: "le manque d'études et l'éducation [ont] dans tous les temps écarté les femmes de la carrière littéraire" (iii). It was not until 1850 that the Falloux law required primary schools for girls, which consisted of "moral and religious instruction" under the aegis of the Catholic church. And not before the second decade of the Third Republic, in the early 1880s, did free and secular primary education become available and even mandatory in France.[7] At all points during the century, the curriculum in girls' schools was less rigorous than that in boys' schools and did not provide the opportunity to prepare for the baccalauréat.[8] The "democratization" of education therefore gave middle-class women the basic linguistic tools previously available only to the wealthy, a result evidenced by the proliferation of bourgeois names on the rosters of women writers during the nineteenth century and beyond. It was, however, far from complete and was consistently class-based. The illiteracy rate for poor women continued to be high, and only the wealthy could afford a rigorous, private education for their daughters.

It has been suggested that the rigors of French versification compounded the educational obstacles faced by women writers in general. Without a solid foundation in the classics, French literature, and prosody, women poets were at a disadvantage working in a genre that relied so heavily on precedent. Still, although poetry requires the mastery of more formal rules than prose, a number of informally or self-trained women (including Marceline Desbordes-Valmore, the subject of my second chapter) wrote and published volumes of verse.

Women were also marginalized from the "fraternity of poets" whose literary education stretched beyond formal schooling and continued through informal social networks, such as salons and café culture.[9] Hampered by the threat of social condemnation or ridicule in their negotiation of the public sphere, women were necessarily side-lined from the inauguration of and participation in poetic *cénacles* and movements. As Genlis pointed out, men alone (critics, writers, male literary institutions) possessed the power and authority to define literariness and to confer legitimacy on writers: "Les hommes [. . .] assignent les rangs dans la littérature, [. . .] ils en dispensent les honneurs et en distribuent les places, dont toutes les femmes sont exclues [. . .]" (viii). Nineteenth-century critics who wrote on women poets did not take their subjects for serious writers, but rather amateurs whose purely emotional poetic production lacked profundity, originality, and compositional rigor. In his 1910 study *Les muses d'aujourd'hui,* Jean de Gourmont (Rémy's younger brother) asserts that:

> [L]eur art, et ceci est un des caractères de la poésie féminine,
> sait éliminer ce qui serait trop nouveau pour s'adapter à la
> sensibilité du public. [. . .] J'ai lu presque tous les livres de
> vers des jeunes femmes poètes [. . .], mais, souvent, malgré
> le rythme et la rime, ce n'est pas encore de l'art, c'est trop
> près de la sensation directe. (26, 27)

As Paul Gaston de Molènes inadvertently suggested in his 1842
article "Les femmes poètes," male writers functioned in complicity with critics in their condemnation of women's poetry:
"Tous les hommes qui ont reçu du ciel une verve originale et
un esprit vigoureux [. . .], tous [l]es francs écrivains, au hardi
parler et aux énergiques boutades, ont été d'accord pour condamner les tentatives des poètes femelles" (75). Men of letters viewed *la poésie féminine* as low literature or as a minor
genre, with a specific and negligible audience. This perception
more often than not relegated the works of Romantic women
poets to the feminine press, which trivialized women's literature with titles such as *Almanach des dames* and *Chansonnier
des grâces*.[10] The very notion of the yearly almanac presented
women's poetry under the sign of the ephemeral or temporary,
rather than that of permanence (if life is short, women's poetry
is shorter still).

Significant differences between reading practices of the lyric
poem and of prose texts have intensified the objectification of
woman in poetry and the silencing of women poets. There exists
to this day a certain mystification of poetry as an elite, necessarily opaque language, a notion that must be deconstructed
in order to render femininity and poetry compatible. At stake
here is the perception that poetry, or at least "good" poetry, is
difficult, rarefied, and hermetic. Such definitions of literariness
go to the heart of normative canon formation; one of the central goals of *The Gendered Lyric* is to question these definitions
in order to show how poetic composition has been construed
as an unattainable practice for women.

Tangible cultural obstacles existed alongside symbolic barriers that hindered and shaped women's access to poetic production in a number of ways. Constructs imbedded in the long
tradition of lyric poetry proved equally forceful in contributing to the anomaly of the "woman poet." The notion of genius
upon which the creation of poetry depended presumed a mas-

culine identity. Romantic poetry (from the Greek *poiein,* meaning to make or create) figured its maker as a solitary prophet having extraordinary insight and creative powers. The pervasive association of poetic genius with masculinity left no room for women poets: "Une existence passée tout entière dans cette solitude où la royauté du génie vous relègue [. . .], une existence sans les plaisirs réglés, le bonheur intime, les affections fidèles et familières, peut-elle convenir à une femme?" (Molènes 50). The figure of the poet, often construed as the conflation of the poem's maker and the beloved's suitor—that is, of creative genius and of aspiring seducer—was invariably portrayed as male.

Lyric conventions fixed stock characters in strictly gendered roles, historically locking the terms *man* and *woman* in a relationship of subject to object. Nancy Vickers's ground-breaking work on the Petrarchan tradition, "Diana Described," illustrates that the first-person love lyric depends on a mute feminine object. It is important, moreover, to recognize that the nearly exclusive heterosexuality of this tradition reinforced the paradigm of female objectification by fixing the relationship between "I" and "you" into an intimate opposition of masculine to feminine. Although identified as other, "woman" occupied a central position in the lyric text: if the poet and the lyric persona are inevitably masculine, female roles are played by those silent creatures, Muse and beloved and often, metaphorically, by the poem itself.

We must go back to the pre-Romantics, and especially to Rousseau, to understand how the speaking subject of the poem and the biographical author eventually became conflated in the figure of the male poet. Rousseau's autobiographical *Confessions* and his lyric *Rêveries du promeneur solitaire* inaugurated a new vision of the writer, whom Dennis Porter aptly describes as "someone who puts his or her private self on display for the purpose of personal witness, self-affirmation, and sociopolitical emancipation, and whose writings address themselves directly to humanity at large" (12). In chapter 1, I describe in detail how the Romantic hero, initially seen in first-person prose texts positing this transparent vision of literature, gave way to the figure of the deified poet. Romantic lyric poetry depended on the idea of poetry as personal expression and consequently was often construed as autobiography. The persistence of Romantic reading habits that conflate author and lyric subject has left the dividing line between the textual and the extra-textual insistently hazy in poetry.[11] Although narratology has, with a precise descriptive vocabulary, clarified relations in the novel between the historical person, the writer, and the first-person narrator, the same cannot always be said of the distinction between the historical person, the writer of poetry, and the lyric subject. The figure of the poet permits this slippage and, consequently, reserves the positions of speaking subject and poet for male voices through the pretense of transparency.

External criticism, specifically the analysis of the socioeconomic and cultural situation of women writers in the context of male poetic production and, more generally, of nineteenth-century social realities and beliefs, convincingly explains the association of masculinity and poetry. It shows as well that topoi created by the lyric tradition were reinforced by literary men who alone held the authority to define "good" poetry. But if we accept this scenario without probing further, we limit ourselves to a normative view of the lyric tradition that freezes women in the silent position of object and tends to homogenize the exceptional few who did compose verse. A more probing question than "What is the gender of the lyric?" would therefore be: "How is the lyric gendered?" This latter question moves beyond extant scholarship and provokes a more complex analysis of the relationship between gender and the lyric, one that permits the study of changing inscriptions of gender on various levels of the poem at disparate moments in nineteenth-century France. As feminist scholars of the novel have problematized and deconstructed the "feminine novel," we might begin in a similar way to question the "masculinity" of poetry, and of the lyric in particular.

## Gendered Forms, Lyric Subjects

In the following pages, I underscore the complexity of gender's relationship to the lyric by focusing in particular on the symbolic and compositional parameters of poetic language. We shall see how, across the different movements of nineteenth-century France, poets—regardless of their gender—defined themselves and their practices in explicitly and implicitly gendered terms. The study of generic and movement-linked traits and readings of specific poems, whether they defy or reinforce conventions, demonstrate how women and men have, during specific moments in the history of the lyric, manipulated poetic language sometimes to conform to and sometimes to seek a way out of gendered binarisms.

While it is true that binarisms such as poetry/prose and masculine/feminine do as much to limit as to illuminate the fields of literary and gender studies, I rely on a specific duality to illuminate my findings: the relationship between constraint and diffusion is consistently descriptive of the gendering of the lyric. These two opposing values coincide with other terms that have defined sexual difference in the larger context of Western discourses. As Hélène Cixous has indicated in "Sorties," the couple Man/Woman is only the most literal instance of the hierarchical oppositions that evaluate gender for phallocentric thought (*La jeune née* 115 ff). To this pair she adds activity/passivity and a number of other coupled terms that carry the weight of gender imbalance. I would suggest that constraint and diffusion function oppositionally within the same paradigm, with constraint carrying associations of virility, intelligence, centrality, verticality, control, and hardness. Diffusion, on the contrary, is marked as feminine, corporeal, dispersed, horizontal, spontaneous, and soft.

In the context of poetic production, this opposition maps out the play of gender in a number of overlaying categories (formal, rhetorical, ideological, and subjective) that define the lyric experience. By exploring the specific ways in which sexual difference functions on all levels of the lyric, we can see how poets open and close themselves to "feminine" (diffuse) practices in order to define themselves and their relation to their métier.

The vagaries of form—ranging over the course of the nineteenth century from Romantic expansionism, to Parnassian obsessions with clearly drawn borders, to the Symbolist war against poetic barriers—supply the most tangible topography of constraint and diffusion. In my readings, I pay particular attention to trope and prosodic structure in order to demonstrate that poets manipulate even the least referential aspects of poetic language to create gendered meaning. Poeticians have identified rhetorical figures, meter and rhythm, repetitive sound structures (including rhyme, alliteration, refrain), and stanzaic form as elements definitive of verse poetry. While failing separately to do so, each of these aspects is a constitutive feature of the lyric poetry of the period. And all, I suggest, are susceptible to gender coding. Some pertinent examples of gendered form that I will explore in the following pages include the fixed and regular sonnet and alexandrine, both aligned with masculinity, which Decadent and Symbolist poets would eventually challenge with less inhibited forms, including nonstanzaic verse and prose poetry, uneven meters, *vers libéré,* and *vers libre.*

The parameters of constraint and diffusion, while contributing to the shape of poetry, also explain the ideological positions that define different poetic tendencies by qualifying the tension between neoclassical and innovative approaches to lyric composition. The more conventional or traditional the movement, the more likely it is to associate masculinity with poetry and to valorize difficulty and constraint. Hence more women poets flourished during the Romantic period than during the Parnassian era. Similarly, Symbolism began to deconstruct the opposition between constraint and diffusion, permitting a new search for female and "other" subjectivities. Although poetry is so frequently associated with masculinity and heterosexuality, it becomes increasingly obvious toward the end of the century—for example, in the appearance of homoerotic poetry—that these associations are not essential.

Constraint and diffusion also provide terms with which to describe the manifold representations of subjectivity in lyric poetry. The self-questioning of the poetic "I" is one of the *raisons d'être* of the lyric experience, and poetic communities implicitly viewed these poles as indexes of the gendering of lyric subjects. One of the most subjective and "personal" of genres, first-person literature by definition, the lyric offers rich possibilities for the inscription of various and specific voices. Philippe Hamon has characterized lyricism as a broad field having subjectivity at its center: "C'est une certaine 'question du Sujet' qui forme, par delà les oppositions stylistiques vers/prose, littéraire/non littéraire, narratif/non narratif, élégiaque/lyrique, etc., l'unité du champ lyrique et des textes, très divers, qui le constituent [. . .]" (*Expositions* 185). Although, as we have seen, poetic institutions and conventions hampered women poets' access to lyric production and subject positions, the genre's focus on the "question of the subject" would seem to invite the exploration of alterity and provide a vehicle for the literary articulation of female voices.

As the basis for my readings of poetic voice, I depend on a model of subjectivity in language that avoids slippage between the positions of author, poet, and lyric persona, which Romanticism's pretense of transparency and enduring Romantic reading habits often maintain in uncertain relationship to one another. Work by structuralist linguists and poststructuralist philosophers, semioticians, and psychoanalysts has clarified relationships between person, voice, and text. My critique of the Romantic conflation of the lyric "I" and the biographical person depends upon this body of criticism, which takes to task the belief in a coherent, unchanging written subject. While I will not presume here to summarize the enormous body of writing on subjectivity in language,[12] I shall highlight a few important aspects of this question as it relates to the present study and indicate some theorists whose thinking has guided my own.

The work of linguist Émile Benveniste illustrates the grammatical foundations of subjective enunciation in language and is essential to contemporary theories of the subject.[13] Although he does not address gender, his distinctions open the door to a feminist critique by clarifying the functioning of linguistic categories, which often prove to be implicitly gendered. (I refer for the moment, of course, to social rather than grammatical categories of gender.) Benveniste suggests that subjectivity depends on articulation: "C'est dans et par le langage que l'homme se constitue comme *sujet;* parce que le langage seul fonde en réalité, dans *sa* réalité qui est celle de l'être, le concept d''ego'" (1: 259). The gesture of voicing an "I" serves a multiple purpose: it designates the speaker as subject and locates that speaker in time and space, assuring her or his identity.

Benveniste elaborates on the intersubjective implications of the first-person singular pronoun, suggesting that the sound of the vibrating vocal chords also implicates the speaker in a symbolic relationship with another or others, since to say "I" is to presuppose a "you." Tzvetan Todorov would later describe this phenomenon as "la loi sémiotique générale selon laquelle 'je' et 'tu' [. . .] sont toujours solidaires" (*Qu'est-ce que le structuralisme?* 67). The "I" can therefore never be purely isolated, since it implies, by its very utterance, another person. The intersubjective space of the poem similarly invites representations of relations between self and other, between "I" and "you," whose explicit or implicit gender I will question.

The specificity of pronouns lies in this: "ils ne renvoient ni à un concept ni à un individu" (Benveniste 1: 261). The signifier "I" belongs to no single speaker, and "Chaque *je* a sa référence propre, et correspond chaque fois à [un] être unique, posé comme tel" (1: 252). Similarly, possessives, demonstratives, and adverbs, belonging to the category of deictics or shifters, have changing referents, which depend upon the moment of utterance: "Ce sont les indicateurs [. . .] qui organisent les relations spatiales et temporelles autour du 'sujet' pris comme repère: 'ceci, ici, maintenant,' et leurs nombreuses corrélations [. . .]" (1: 262). Deictics are particularly preponderant in subjective language that aims to capture a sense of immediacy and presence (*I am now caressing my cat Hubert as I type this sentence here at my desk*).

The implications of Benveniste's and Todorov's work for the study of gender in poetry are multiple. Who is the lyric "I," and to what extent is its referent male or female, masculine or feminine? Just how subjective is this lyric subject, and when does *his* subjectivity hide behind the third person's pretense of objectivity?[14] What relationship of proximity or distance exists between the lyric subject and others with whom it shares the space of the poem; put another way, how is intersubjectivity represented? All these questions relate to the gendering of the lyric subject: could one even imagine positing subjects uninhabited by gender? Is it possible to write of *her* subjectivity, or must we accept as sex-specific Benveniste's definition that "c'est dans et par le langage que *l'homme* se constitue comme sujet"?

Writing is a specific linguistic phenomenon that destabilizes conclusions based on the ephemeral experience of spoken language. While like Benveniste they overlook the category of gender, narratologists Gérard Genette and Todorov have supplied a vocabulary for the analysis of literary texts and opened the way to questioning gender ideologies imbedded in positivist structuralism.[15] Genette has paid considerable attention to narrative voice and the narrator's relations to novelistic events and characters. Indebted to Benveniste's work, Genette maintains his category of discourse, but focuses on narration instead of enunciation. Although his *Discours du récit* and much of his other work analyze the novel in particular, certain aspects of his theory and lexicon can be transferred to the poetic text.[16] We might consider the speaking subject in poetry to be analogous to Genette's autodiegetic narrator, who as hero relates his or her story in the first person ("Personne" [*Figures III* 251–59]).

Although the first-person singular pronoun "I" designates the speaker, in written discourse, the immediacy of the relationship between the writing subject and the utterance itself is lost. According to Roland Barthes, "l'écriture est destruction de toute voix, de toute origine" (*Bruissement* 61). Consequently in the written text, where there is no fixed referent and no marker imbedded in the pronoun "I" to locate an empirical person, much less to designate the sex of the referent, there exists no guarantee of a direct relationship to a clearly defined and unified subject. The words are re-created each time a text is read, but an original voice no longer speaks to indicate physical presence or to claim responsibility for the words. The temporal and spatial discontinuity of the written text distances the enunciator from the utterance, the author from his or her words, and renders ambiguous the relationship between the two.

Since the 1960s, poststructuralist theory has, of course, displayed much more interest in the written text than in empirical speech. Jacques Derrida's ground-breaking *De la grammatologie* articulated the philosophical basis for the study of writing. A fundamental aspect of Derridean theory is its critique of presence, the refutation of a centered Cartesian subject, the "subject with a locked-inside consciousness that is bounded, self-possessed" (Wesling and Slawek 11). Although Derrida's work privileges writing over orality, other theorists such as Henri Meschonnic and Julia Kristeva have pursued the study of rhythm as the trace of physical presence (articulation and drives) in written texts. While aspects of their work are debatable, their approach carries important implications for a feminist analysis of poetry, since they both study the relationship between the physical body and the poetic text. Poetic language holds a privileged position in the theory of voice and subjectivity, due not only to the presence of the lyric "I," but also to its origins in orality, the musical and rhythmic aspects of prosody.

The poet and critic Meschonnic, while relatively unknown in the US, has contributed a vast body of work on poetics and, in particular, on rhythm.[17] Meschonnic suggests that rhythm is indissociable from subjectivity and meaning: "Si le sens est une activité du sujet, si le rythme est une organisation du sens dans le discours, le rythme est nécessairement une organisation ou configuration du sujet dans son discours" (*Critique* 71). He argues that orality is not confined to spoken language, but also leaves its subjective traces as rhythm in writing and, particularly, in poetry: "[La poésie . . .] est un mode de signifier qui expose plus que tous les autres que l'enjeu du langage [. . .] est le sujet. [. . .] [L]a poésie [. . .] est une pratique spécifique du rythme" (*Critique* 35). Refuting the notion that "le passage à l'écrit soit la perte de la voix [et] du geste [. . .]," he pursues the study of "le primat du rythme et de la prosodie dans le sémantique" (Meschonnic, "Qu'entendez-vous?" 16, 18).

Meschonnic acknowledges that his interest in the relationship between the body and language has points of convergence with feminist theory,[18] and yet (typically polemical) he takes pains to distance himself from it. Although he is particularly dismissive of Kristeva, her work on physical drives and rhythm is not far from his. Like him, she studies unquantifiable aspects of poetry that reveal traces of physical presence.[19] In *La révolution du langage poétique,* Kristeva distinguishes between what she identifies as two inseparable aspects of the signifying process, relying and expanding upon the psychoanalytic categories of Jacques Lacan. She defines the symbolic as "un produit social du rapport à l'autre," while the semiotic is pre-oedipal and therefore pre-verbal, "antérieu[r] ou transcendan[t] au langage" (*Révolution* 29, 26). The semiotic is structured in relation to the mother's body, springing from a time when "le signe linguistique n'est pas encore articulé comme absence d'objet et comme distinction entre réel et symbolique" (25). Kristeva refers here to Lacanian terminology, specifically to his notion of the imaginary, presymbolic stage, taking issue with the transcendental ego ("toujours déjà dialectique" [18]; that is, defined by intersubjectivity) assumed in Benveniste's description of the "sujet de l'énonciation." For Kristeva, the semiotic derives from presubjective remains of psychic drives, which persist and signify as "ruptures" in language.

Kristeva is particularly interested in "le démantèlement du symbolique par le sémiotique dans la poésie," a task she undertakes by studying the poetry of Lautréamont and Mallarmé. Elsewhere she defines the "semiotic disposition" of poetic language as

> the various deviations from the grammatical rules of the language: articulatory effects which shift the phonematic system back towards its articulatory, phonetic base and consequently towards the drive-governed bases of sound-production; the over-determination of a lexeme by multiple meanings which it does not carry in ordinary usage but which accrue to it as a result of its occurrence in other texts; syntactic irregularities such as ellipses, non-recoverable deletions, indefinite embeddings, etc. [. . .][20]

Kristeva's poetic subject is therefore a "subject-in-process," one divided between its conscious and its unconscious.

Before pointing to the pitfalls of Kristevan theory, I would like to indicate her uses for my project. Her exploration of the multiplicity of poetic language and its relation to subjectivity leads the way to a more complex understanding of the lyric. Obviously, her elaboration of the divided subject refutes the transparency of Romantic discourse. But it also challenges Parnassian pretenses of transcendental subjectivity and offers insight into Symbolist poetry, which finally begins to acknowledge the divided nature of lyric subjectivity. Kristeva is, moreover, one of the first poeticians to explore gender and form through the analysis of rhythm. Without sanctioning her conclusions, I would suggest that the link she establishes between maternity and poetry is not unfounded, if only because so many men seem to work through issues relating to origins and separation in their poetry (as we shall see, for example, in Baudelaire).

Nonetheless, Kristeva's theory of poetic language is not particularly feminist, since the "subject" of primary interest to her in fact precedes subjectivity and therefore gender difference. When she does posit post-oedipal subjects, and this is the most troubling aspect for a feminist critique of her work, she relies consistently on masculine models. Her investigation of femininity focuses primarily on the mother in her relationship to the implicitly male child. It is not by chance, then, that she locates the semiotic in male-authored texts, since her prescriptive definition of femininity as diffuse materiality and source of drives precludes female participation in the "radical" and "transgressive" language of Symbolist poetry. As Judith Butler points out, "Kristeva thus alternately posits and denies the semiotic as an emancipatory ideal" (*Gender Trouble* 80). Butler further suggests that "What for Kristeva is a pre-paternal causality [the semiotic] would then appear as a *paternal* causality under the guise of a natural or distinctively maternal causality" (91).

While the work of Cixous has many points of disagreement with Kristeva's, they have both explored the link between poetic language and unconscious feminine constructs. Cixous, in contrast with Kristeva, calls on women as subjects to explore their difference through writing in her manifesto, "Le rire de la méduse." Her notion of *écriture féminine* can be defined as texts that recognize and inscribe sexual difference or articulate feminine subjectivity. For Cixous, femininity and subjectivity coincide above all in poetry, whose language is structured like the unconscious.[21] Poetry would then be a privileged site for the inscription of sexual difference, since in its multivalence one finds the echo of a repressed feminine unconscious: "Il y a eu des poètes pour faire passer à tout prix quelque chose d'hétérogène à la tradition. [. . .] Les poètes parce que la poésie n'est que de prendre force dans l'inconscient et que l'inconscient, l'autre contrée sans limites est le lieu où survivent les refoulés: les femmes [. . .]" ("Le rire" 42–43). Cixous thus specifically addresses the female rather than the male unconscious, and in so doing provides a useful model for the analysis of sexual difference in women's poetry. More generally, Cixous's work applies to all poetry that questions normative characterizations of gender and sexuality. I am thinking in particular of gay and lesbian poetry, which, like *écriture féminine,* necessarily opposes dominant sexual conventions and seeks new languages with which to represent the previously unrepresentable. As Cixous includes Jean Genet in her study of *écriture féminine,* so I explore the relationship between gay male and women's writing in my final chapter on Paul Verlaine and Marie Krysinska.

The French feminist theorist Luce Irigaray has produced one of the most rigorous bodies of work devoted to feminine subjectivity. Although she does not address poetic language in particular, her notion of *parler-femme* echoes Cixous's *écriture féminine* by focusing on the repressive effects of dominant discourses and seeking a way to express feminine difference in language. In *Speculum,* she describes and deconstructs philosophical and psychoanalytic discourses that have relegated woman to the position of nonrepresentable "other." Butler recapitulates the functioning of phallocentric discourses succinctly: "The economy that claims to include the feminine as the subordinate term in a binary opposition of masculine/feminine excludes the feminine, produces the feminine as that which must be excluded for that economy to operate" (*Bodies* 36). Irigaray aims to redress this exclusion and to correct masculine projections of femininity by focusing on "la spécificité [du] rapport [de la femme] à l'imaginaire" (*Speculum* 165), upon which she elaborates in the essays of *Ce sexe qui n'en est pas un*.[22] She formulates a model for sexuality that opposes multiple feminine sexuality to unitary masculinity. As much a model for discursivity as for sexuality, the embrace of multiplicity promises to release women from what Irigaray terms "the return to the same," to subvert phallocentrism, and to allow for the articulation of feminine specificity.

Since the 1980s, American feminists have questioned whether French feminists have reproduced the same binarisms that they propose to deconstruct. Irigaray in particular has been accused of reappropriating cultural stereotypes of femininity defined in terms of the body, maternity, fluidity, and irrationality. The charge of essentialism, first leveled by proponents of social construction theories, challenged much of French feminist thought on the relationship between the body and the articulation of feminine subjectivity.[23] This critique is extremely useful in keeping at the forefront the issue of culturally determined representations and asking to what extent Irigaray herself relies on constructed notions of sexual difference in her analyses of femininity. Critics of essentialism have nonetheless tended to treat her work in a vastly reductive manner, literalizing categories that she herself employs metaphorically.[24] At the same time, such critics often challenge the very metaphoricity of deconstructive feminism, which tends to universalize femininity and erase the specific historical contexts that determine gender identities adopted by living persons. Irigaray, among others, has come under attack for proposing a monolithic definition of femininity that does not account for the empirical reality of women's oppression, nor for cultural, racial, sexual, and class differences that variegate gender oppression.

The debate between essentialism and social construction, now dated, reproduced a conflict long at the heart of the feminist Anglo-French divide, in which French theories of difference and American materialism collided. The contradictions between identity politics and deconstructive feminisms created still-unresolved quandaries in dealing with women's literature. Many feminist critics questioned whether the French notion of *écriture féminine* was not based on the belief in an innately feminine style that they found essentialist. Deconstructionists in turn often considered the American focus on women authors to be a positivistic engagement in phallocentric discourse that ultimately effaced sexual difference. My own sense is that deconstruction and other language-based approaches need not be seen as in conflict with materialist or cultural criticism; that, in fact, such divergent viewpoints have a lot to teach each other.

The discussion around female authorship provides one example of an American feminist challenge to French poststructuralist thought. Roland Barthes first posed the question of authorial identity when he proclaimed "La mort de l'auteur," in this 1968 essay (*Bruissement*). Michel Foucault elaborated upon this claim in his article "Qu'est-ce qu'un auteur?" which he closed by insisting: "Qu'importe qui parle?" (95). Although the landmark "discovery" of the author's death was first and foremost a poststructuralist response to biographical criticism and the cult of the author, it carries important consequences for the study of female-authored and "minority" literatures. Nancy K. Miller, for one, suggests that "[Barthes's] model of reading and writing by definition excludes the question of an identity crucial to feminist critical theory."[25] While my analyses of the gendered aspects of textual subjectivity do not presuppose native styles attributable to the gender or the sexuality of the author, I do hold that the study of women's writing or gay and lesbian writing is meaningless without a knowledge of the author's identity. Historical perspectives provided by Foucault contribute a theory of gender and sexual identity that accepts socially constituted categories such as "woman" and "homosexual" as politically necessary. With increasingly weakening voices, deconstructionists maintain that these terms are continually diminished and essentially unknown or unsayable within the context of phallocentric discourse.

In their grappling, both French and Anglo-American feminists shed light on the intricate relations between gender, discursivity, and subjectivity, topics that lie at the heart of my study of poetry. I would suggest, as have many others, that the utopian aim of celebrating femininity evident in writers such as Cixous and Irigaray does not necessarily prevent them from recognizing and repudiating confining social constructions. Many of the women poets I study in the following pages do just that, in a variety of ways and based on a variety of definitions, conventional and otherwise, of femininity. My own task will be to untangle the complex knot of assimilation, repudiation, reappropriation, and reimagination at work in poetry by women, so as to illuminate the variability of poetic identities. In doing so, it becomes clear that the poetry itself addresses tensions between identities and essences, which are sometimes imposed, sometimes embraced, sometimes recast, and sometimes simply cast aside.

On the level of conscious representation, the subject of poetry of interest to feminist criticism must be defined first in terms of access to the first-person pronoun: to whom does "I" refer? The second aspect of my analysis explores the nature of male and female lyric subjects. Do they reiterate "the same" and reproduce femininity as projected by dominant discourses, or do they successfully represent woman's specificity? And where can we locate instances of intersubjective equality? Cixous terms representations of non-objectifying sexual difference "l'autre bisexualité": "celle dont chaque sujet non enfermé dans le faux théâtre de la représentation phallocentrique, institue son univers érotique" ("Le rire" 46). Donald Wesling and Tadeusz Slawek propose a similar description of nonbounded language, which I take as a model for feminist poetics: "an intersubjective account that makes much of the role of alterity, the equal-to-self role of others in the constitution of subjectivity" (6). Contemporary critics often see alterity as a gauge for the modern (post-Baudelairian) subject in poetry, but just as often base their discussions on a masculine subject whose quest for alterity rarely manages to surpass his gender. "Non pour se contempler dans le narcissisme du moi, mais pour s'accomplir *soi-même comme un autre*" (Collot 32–33): this too would be a fine definition for an inclusive poetics if it did not elide gender in the pursuit of masculine self-exploration.

My approach is unabashedly interdisciplinary: I rely on French deconstructionist theories of feminine subjectivity, Anglo-American materialist work on women writers and context, and more recent American theories positing gender as a category of analysis. My close readings depend on the fields of poetics, linguistics, and narratology. It is my inclination to take lessons from such theoretical sources, but to "apply" theory with a light hand.[26] The reader will therefore find me taking a step back from the abstract theoretical framework I present here, and giving priority in the following pages to discussions that concentrate on the lyric texts in question as they illuminate the work of gender in poetry. I will show how some of these poems themselves question the ascendancy of the critical act. Many of the women poets I study in the following pages refused to adopt theoretical and critical stances that have been used against them to construct their work as weak and anti-intellectual. They question literary and educational institutions that both valorize metapoetic discourse as a masculine endeavor and justify the systematic exclusion of women from the writing of poetry. It is therefore by listening to their voices that I pursue the critique of dominant poetic structures, which often emerges implicitly from the language of women's poetry.

# Part 1
# Romanticism's Genders

*Homme, il est doux comme une femme.*
Victor Hugo
"Fonction du poète"

*Oui, le vrai féminin, c'est bien de se cacher éternellement.*
Charles Maurras
"Le romantisme féminin"

*Le poète qu'on n'écoute pas finit par se taire.*
Louise Ackermann
"Ma vie"

**Chapter One**

# Femininity and the Renewal of the Lyric

A return to the beginnings of what would become a reflowering of poetry in nineteenth-century France leads us to a critical curiosity: Romanticism, which inaugurated a major poetic renaissance and prepared the way for later Symbolist poetry considered among the most original of the French tradition, has long been the object of suspicion. Since the mid-nineteenth century, critics of Romanticism have accused its poets of verbosity, insipidity, self-indulgence, sentimentality, and a lack of compositional rigor. Paradoxically, an explosive and influential rebirth of lyric production came to be colored by the suggestion of mediocrity. Strength or weakness, vigor or impotence: how are we to describe this era so important to the history of lyric poetry?

Although opponents of Romanticism trivialized or dismissed poetry they considered unrestrained as "feminine," the movement is, of course, diverse enough to defy generalizations about its practitioners' manipulations of gender. The forceful voices of Vigny and Hugo, whether misogynist or chivalrous, provide a strikingly different impression from those of Lamartine and Musset, the most notable proponents of sentimental Romanticism. Next to Hugo's powerful poetic persona we find the plaintive voice of Lamartine's *Méditations poétiques* (1820), one of the first Romantic collections. And Musset's long-suffering Poet contrasts distinctly with Vigny's philosophical and stoic, if melancholic, voice.

Despite their differences, the Romantics participated in a historical moment that reimagined the author as one having access to a wide range of gendered attributes.[1] Their implicit flirtation with culturally attributed femininity had very much to do with both the renewal of the lyric and the negative backlash of the following generation. A comprehensive study remains to be written that would show how French Romanticism came to be constructed as the sentimental discourse of the self and how this subjective poetry implicitly entailed an inquiry into femininity. My intentions are more modest in this chapter. I shall investigate the sexual politics of male Romantic poets and their detractors in order to illustrate the circumscribed position women poets held in Romanticism's literary communities, a position that depended on both deference to "feminine" insight and the concomitant reassertion of poetry as a masculine sphere.

## The Lyrical Lexicon

In order to unravel the role of gender in the origins of the modern lyric, we must begin by recalling the context and the terms of the debate. It is perhaps ironic to find a woman, Germaine de Staël, as French Romanticism's first theoretician; she was, nonetheless, instrumental in defining French Romantic discourse and articulating the emerging lyric experience. Staël's two chapters on poetry in her vast study *De l'Allemagne* (1813) provide the movement's first theoretical elaboration in France. With this text, she introduced the German vocabulary of Romanticism to a French readership and created the framework for its discussion. Writing of the movement begun over a generation earlier in Germany, she announces the renewal of lyricism: "Le nom de *romantique* a été introduit nouvellement en Allemagne pour désigner la poésie dont les chants des troubadours ont été l'origine [. . .]" (2: 127–28). She describes the conflict between the new Romantic sensibility and the classical quest for formal perfection, signaling emotionality as a marker of the new, for which the French poetic tradition is a particularly inhospitable breeding ground. Central to her vocabulary of Romanticism are the words *enthusiasm, inspiration,* and *imagination,* all positioned in opposition to formal constraint: "les difficultés de la langue et de la versification française s'opposent presque toujours à l'abandon de l'enthousiasme" (2: 117). Staël posits the aesthetic value of the natural as the bedrock of poetry: "Un homme d'un esprit supérieur disoit *que la prose étoit factice, et la poésie naturelle*" (2: 114).

Staël's language is implicitly gendered and aligned with feminized characteristics, such as diffusion and fecundity. Although Staël herself did not acknowledge this association, later critics made it plain by deprecating values considered positive during the Romantic era. Théophile Gautier would anticipate both the Parnassians and the Decadents in turning the tables on these values, praising artifice and inveighing against naturalness, which Charles Baudelaire later equated with femininity: "la femme est *naturelle,* c'est-à-dire abominable" (*Œuvres complètes* 1: 677). Baudelaire's criticism of Romantic spontaneity and effusion consistently equates these terms with femininity, a disorderly force that carries the poet away from mastery: "Tout ce qui est beau et noble est le résultat de la raison et du calcul" (2: 715).

The classics and the Romantics engaged in a struggle on both prosodic and subjective grounds, which implicitly pitted masculine against feminine terms. In the first instance, mastery and constraint defined the classical relation to form, to which Romantics reacted with disdain and greater formal liberty. In the second case, classical universality gave way to individual and intimate voices. Romanticism's new literary program privileged the investigation and expression of the self. Dennis Porter has suggested that Rousseau assisted in the creation of the modern individual in literature: "it is with Rousseau that 'the writer' appears virtually fully formed on the European scene as a cultural hero of a new age of revolution [. . .] turning himself into both subject and object of his writing in the cause of a new openness among men" (8–9). After Rousseau, prose writers created characters that would become prototypes for the Romantic hero, a solitary, introspective figure of which Chateaubriand's René provides an early example.[2] The Romantic hero was "poetic," whether or not a poet. Staël herself points to prose writers as the inaugurators of the new lyric stance: "Un nouveau genre de poésie existe dans les ouvrages en prose de J-J Rousseau et de Bernadin de Saint-Pierre; c'est l'observation de la nature dans ses rapports avec les sentiments qu'elle fait éprouver à l'homme."[3] The terms *romantisme* and *poésie* were nearly synonymous designations for subjective expression, indicating a certain fluidity in the literary terminology of the era.[4] The study of related signifiers, particularly the definition of the word *poëme,* exemplifies this poetic shift toward the first-person voice, thus illuminating early-nineteenth-century lyric values and their relation to masculinity and femininity.

The difficulty of defining such central terms as *lyrique* and *poëme* for the early-nineteenth century attests to the movement and change that characterized this period's renewed poetic production. The exact meaning of lyricism cannot easily be pinned down, since over the two millennia of its existence as a genre, the lyric has undergone continual modification. Although it is etymologically and classically associated with music and song and therefore with mode of performance, modern definitions of the lyric based on written poetry rely instead on textual indicators of form and subjective stance, with rhythmic and phonic structures remaining as echoes of orality and musicality.

The very meaning of the word *poëme* migrated from the general to the specific during the Romantic period, signaling a refashioned hierarchy of poetic genres, ultimately a shift from a third-person to a first-person poetics. In the lyric's glory days of the sixteenth century, Joachim Du Bellay defined the *poëme* as an "ouvrage en vers d'une assez grande étendue."[5] This was initially a generic term that, when modified by an adjective, described a whole range of poetic production, traditionally grouped under three categories, *poème épique, poème lyrique,* and *poème dramatique.*[6] During the lyric's low tide of the seventeenth and eighteenth centuries, *poème* referred more specifically to epic verse, an association that persisted in the work of the early Romantics, especially in Alfred de Vigny's *Poèmes antiques et modernes* (1826). After the first wave of Romanticism, however, this word came to be more narrowly synonymous with the lyric, once again the preferred mode of poetic expression after three centuries of neglect. Romanticism, then, re-evaluated poetic genres to privilege the lyric over the epic and dramatic.

Laurence Porter has suggested that the first Romantics in fact returned to classical lyric subgenres, the plaintive elegy, the joyous ode, and the epiclike *poème,* all longer and nonfixed verse forms: "before 1830 the leading French Romantic poets conceived of their achievements in the lyric as, in effect, a culmination of Neoclassicism, preserving traditional literary forms while regenerating them with new inspirations [. . .]" (*Renaissance* 12). While these subgenres relied on divergent content and tone, formally they were similar and, even, lacking in distinction. These poems looked alike and, thanks to their length and lack of architectural structure, they favored narrativity. They all told stories, whether of loss, struggle, or triumph.

Of these three modes of expression, it was the melancholic, subjective elegy that emerged to be the privileged vehicle for intimist lyric expression and, subsequently, the focus of anti-Romantic scorn. Porter's description of early Romantic forms shows a continuum from a weak subject to a heroic and unified one:

> The elegy depicts [. . .] a lyric self inferior to his surroundings, helpless and passive, [. . .] unable to resist the loss or destruction of what he loves [. . .]. The "Poëme" presents a hero ultimately inferior in physical might, but superior in courage and resolve [. . .]. The ode [. . .] depicts a lyric self representative of humanity, buoyed up by solidarity, and superior to his circumstances. (L. M. Porter, *Renaissance* 16)

Not surprisingly, those considered the most "feminine" of the Romantics, represented by Lamartine and his followers, privileged the elegy, while Vigny's *poème* and Hugo's odes fortified their masculine heroism.

The elegy in particular was therefore to become the *bête noire* of the following generation's anti-Romantic criticism, which condemned its obsession with suffering and tears. After about 1850, ambivalent and negative criticism of elegiac and intimist poetry employed a completely different set of metaphors suggesting imprecision, anti-intellectualism, and softness. Writers of all kinds participated in the critique of sentimentality, including Parnassian and Symbolist poets, realist authors, literary and cultural critics of both nineteenth and twentieth centuries, and blatant misogynists as well as self-professed experts of *la littérature féminine*.

In his recent study, *La matière-émotion* (1997), Michel Collot has shown to what extent emotion is "désastreuse en poésie" (9); few critics, however (Collot included), have analyzed the role played by gender in this assessment. Indeed, such valuations attest to the often unconscious manner in which metapoetic discourse describes and evaluates literary movements and qualities in terms of gender. Barbara Johnson has suggested that

"Lamartine's association with lacks, lakes, and laments had ended up feminizing *him,* so that literary history's ambivalence toward Lamartine may very well itself be an expression of ambivalence toward femininity" ("Lady" 631). I would broaden Johnson's conclusion about Lamartine and suggest that literary history's ambivalence toward Romantic affect expresses an ambivalence toward the femininity revealed in works of many of its authors.

In his essay "Le romantisme féminin: Allégorie du sentiment désordonné" (1904), the right-wing literary critic Charles Maurras provides the most extreme and sweeping example of condemning the movement for its femininity. This royalist, pro-Catholic founder of the Action française combined virulent misogyny with nationalist, antirevolutionary rhetoric to blame Romanticism for the decline of French values: "Au lieu de dire que le romantisme a fait dégénérer les âmes ou les esprits français, ne serait-il pas meilleur de se rendre compte qu'il les effémina?" (189). The traits of this effeminate movement, according to Maurras, include lack of discipline, anarchy and antitraditionalism, perversity and neurosis, excessive sentiment, and obsessive subjectivity. He derides the focus on interiority with particular virulence: "Bulle écumeuse ou sphère en flamme, le moi crève et se rompt" (189). Since Rousseau, this feature of Romanticism was responsible for feminizing French literature: "Dire *moi* fait presque partie du caractère de la femme" (191).

Maurras used the term *romantic* indiscriminately to refer to subjective, "effeminate" literature, rather than to the literature of the first half of the nineteenth century. Indeed, the four poets he uses to exemplify feminine Romanticism were the Symbolists Renée Vivien, Mme de Régnier,[7] Lucie Delarue-Mardrus, and Anna de Noailles. Maurras claims that these twentieth-century women took effeminate men as their guides: "elles ne faisaient guère que reprendre leur bien. Leurs modèles les avaient, plus ou moins, volées de sexe" (190). Their models included Rousseau, Chateaubriand, Lamartine, Musset, and even Hugo: "Hugo lui-même, qui nous fut donné pour le type de l'homme sain et de la nature virile, n'échappe pas à ce caractère [féminin . . .]" (189–90). Nor did his invective spare the Parnassians ("romantiques adoucis, corrigés" [184]) or the Symbolists: "Baudelaire, Verlaine ressemblaient à de vieilles coureuses de sabbat" (190).

Maurras was an extremist who saw femininity everywhere and condemned it indefatigably: "Tout s'est efféminé, depuis l'esprit jusqu'à l'amour. Tout s'est amolli. [. . .] on ne songe plus qu'à subir."[8] While Maurras's rhetoric is certainly excessive, others before and after him engaged in the same associations between Romantic femininity and sentimental softness, if in a less virulent fashion. Jean Larnac's *Histoire de la littérature féminine en France* (1929), a mild-mannered but patronizing survey, has anti-intellectual feminine sentiment fairly pouring out of the floodgates during the Romantic period: "Le romantisme, déclenché par Mme de Staël, avait réveillé, chez les femmes, une sensibilité comprimée par deux siècles de raison" (194).

Authors seemed equally invested as critics in repudiating excessive, feminine emotion, and Musset and Lamartine provided the most ready targets for those scornful of Romantic effusion. Henry Murger, the author of *Scènes de la vie de bohème* (1851), lumped them and their followers together as "des poètes pleurards dont la muse a toujours les yeux rouges" (81). Baudelaire lambasted Alfred de Musset as "féminin et sans doctrine" (*Œuvres complètes* 2: 110), and Arthur Rimbaud railed against him in these terms: "Musset est quatorze fois exécrable pour nous, générations douloureuses et prises de visions, —que sa paresse d'ange a insultées! Ô! les contes et les proverbes fadasses!" (253). Tearful, feminine, atrocious, lazy, insipid: similar accounts of the weakness of both Musset and his work persist today.[9]

The late-nineteenth-century literary historian Gustave Lanson couched his critique of Alphonse de Lamartine's weakness in praise:

> Ni dans la langue, ni dans le vers, ni dans les thèmes [de Lamartine], il n'y avait là *rien de bien nouveau.* Ce qui était nouveau, c'était *cette intense spontanéité, cette sincérité* qui, à chaque page, découvrait l'homme. [. . .] Il fut poète, comme plus tard orateur et homme d'État, par *inspiration,* par besoin du cœur: ce fut une fonction de sa vie morale, d'ennoblir par le vers *ses émotions intimes;* jamais il ne voulut en faire un exercice professionnel, jamais même un pur jeu d'artiste. [. . .] Et voilà pourquoi *cette poésie fut si peu travaillée.* (949; emphasis mine)

While commending the poet's self-portraiture, Lanson nonetheless attributes to him a lack of compositional rigor and uses a vocabulary of transparency often employed to describe women's poetry. Like women poets, always imitators and never original, Lamartine offers "rien de nouveau." The strength of feminine poetry lies in the expression of sentiment and emotion ("[l]es émotions intimes"), rather than the carefully crafted poetic line. Critics of Romanticism characterize the uncontrolled, spontaneous, and sincere outpouring of the inner self as a feminine poetic method. Gustave Flaubert's correspondence, for example, harshly condemns Lamartine's writing while casting aspersions on his virility: "La vérité réclame des mâles plus velus que M. de Lamartine" (2: 397).

The anti-Romantic reaction associated the elegy not only with feminine emotion, but with female verbosity as well. The sheer length of Romantic poetry is attributed to undisciplined feminine outpouring; emotion creates tears, and both pour forth in unrestrained effusion, as evidenced in this citation from the Goncourt journals: "Les femmes ont le bavardage des larmes" (1: 212).[10] Post-Romantics opposed this movement from the self toward the exterior by privileging self-possession through mastery of form. Critics since Edgar Allan Poe proposed concision as a requirement for the lyric ("I hold that a long poem does not exist" [91]), and in so doing repudiated the longer, narrative forms of Romantic poetry.[11] Indeed, the relation between length and subjective expression must not be overlooked in order to understand the Romantic value of effusive sentiment. The Romantic lyric, then, had a propensity for lengthiness, diverging from shorter lyric forms introduced during the Middle Ages (the ballade, virelai, and rondeau), the Renaissance (the sonnet and dizain), and the Symbolist period (nonfixed shorter poems, prose poetry). The length and openness of the Romantic lyric, fueled by anticlassicism,[12] pointed to a certain disdain for formalism, concision, and architectural symmetry. Although exploiting ancient forms, Romantic poets imbued them with a new subjective style. While the Parnassians would later favor concision in their conception of the poetic act, Romantic poetry enjoyed an almost prosaic formal permissiveness in its poetic exploration of subjectivity. The lack of compositional tightness came to signal femininity, as did the lack of emotional restraint and focus on personal expression.

Indeed, Staël's references to Rousseau and Saint-Pierre suggest that form was a secondary consideration in the Romantic rebirth of poetry. For the French Romantic lyric, subjective expression appears to be more definitive than a clearly delineated compositional program. Different values can and have been placed on such expression. Romanticism might be considered to have produced one of the more egocentric of literatures ("Romantics are strangely self-involved") or, conversely, one of the most sincere.[13] Questions of style aside, then, Romantic poetry participated in the revaluation of the exploration of the self, a constant aspect of the modern lyric, whether short or long.

## The Poet's Masculinity

Staël's work exemplifies the conflation of author and speaking subject touched upon in my introduction. Her focus on the person of the author confirms and illustrates the Romantic belief in a transparent relationship between the "I" of the poem and the person of the poet. Her assessment of lyric poetry points to the glorification of the poetic subject, at the same time summarizing the Romantic equation of author and first-person subject: "La poésie lyrique s'exprime au nom de l'auteur même; ce n'est pas dans un personnage qu'il se transporte, c'est en lui-même qu'il trouve les divers mouvements dont il est animé" (*De l'Allemagne* 2: 117).

Even though Staël herself did not directly evaluate this battle in gendered terms in *De l'Allemagne,* a consideration of a broader selection of her work reveals the ambiguity of her position as, on one hand, a universalizing social critic oblivious to her sex and, on the other, a woman writer painfully aware of personal and cultural obstacles. It must be said that Staël, as a woman who shaped the theoretical discourse of nineteenth-century literature, was a singular figure. Did her gender influence her perception and definitions of the new Romantic literature? Or did the nature of Romanticism, more than other movements, allow for critical incursions by female authors? While her novel *Corinne* offers the most in-depth reflection on the position of the woman poet, her chapter "Des femmes qui cultivent les lettres," in the nonfictional *De la littérature,* addresses in a more direct fashion the conflicts inherent in this position. In the latter text she defines woman's "premier intérêt" as "les sentiments du cœur," a phrase that resonates throughout her discussion of the Romantic poet. "Woman" and "poet" emerge as nearly synonymous terms when we compare her essay on literary women to her definition of the lyric endeavor: "Le don de révéler par la parole *ce qu'on ressent au fond du cœur* est très-rare; il y a pourtant de la poésie dans tous les êtres capables d'affections vives et profondes [. . .]. Le poëte ne fait pour ainsi dire que dégager *le sentiment prisonnier au fond de l'âme*" (*De l'Allemagne* 2: 114; emphasis mine). And in *De la littérature,* she proposes that "la littérature proprement dite devînt le partage des femmes," leaving philosophy as a masculine domain (335). The very first definition of the Romantic poet, then, relied on emotional qualities culturally associated with femininity.

The cult of the poet, which took hold during the early part of the century, grew out of the Romantic assimilation of author and speaking subject. This complicated figure hovers on the boundaries of the poem, identified at once with the biographical writer and the speaking subject of the poem. The Poet (I use the capital henceforth to indicate the archetype) relies on several associative categories, largely related to exceptionality and emotionality. The first, I contend, assured the masculinity of the lyric voice, while the second permitted forays into femininity. Exceptionality suggests both singularity and isolation, hence the ready metaphors of other solitary occupations (the Poet as priest) and the focus on the experience of exile (whether physical, moral, or intellectual). On the other hand, the poetics of effusion turns on the elaboration of interiority and the expression of sentiment (a movement from within to without), on an aesthetics of fluidity unavoidably associated with femininity.

Since the role played by both masculinity and femininity in the makeup of the Poet was not stable, the task of untangling gender assignations can be a difficult one. Numerous works by Romanticism's literary fathers describe the Poet's role and explore his double nature, both his feminine effusiveness and his masculine exceptionality. Physical and psychological representations of the Romantic hero and of the Poet in particular frequently focus on his delicacy. Like Balzac's Lucien de Rubempré, he is effeminate; like Vigny's Chatterton, he is mel-

ancholic and frail.[14] While with Chatterton, Vigny offered a
fictionalized representation of a historical poet, other Romantic poets curiously embodied this fictional type, and consequently their work was all the more esteemed.

Although cutting a more masculine figure than these fictional
characters, the extravagant Lord Byron encouraged the Romantic cult of personality, and his tempestuous life and early death
undoubtedly contributed to his French success. Baudelaire wrote
that "Byron [. . .] avait [. . .] ce qui fait les poètes: une diabolique
personnalité" (*Œuvres complètes* 2: 232), an opinion shared by
Paul Bénichou, who named Byron "[l']actualisation prestigieuse
de la grandeur et de l'infortune du poète" (*Le sacre* 334). Byron's
long narrative poem *Childe Harold's Pilgrimage,* which follows the wanderings of a misunderstood, outcast Poet, blurs
the line between fictional representation and autobiography,
since here the searchings of the speaking subject echo the life
of the man. Charles de Leconte de Lisle would also notice the
impact of Byron's person on his contemporaries, disparaging
Romantic poetry as "[le] reflet confus de la personnalité fou-
gueuse de Byron" (*Articles* 116).

Other French Romantics represented their vocation in self-
reflexive poetry by inscribing figures with complex gender
attributes. Hugo's "La fonction du poète" (1839), for example,
describes the Poet as an exceptional creature, misunderstood
and yet necessary for the redemption of the common man. This
poem confirms the image of the solitary Poet in the privileged
stance of separation and interiority, or *recueillement,* from which
he finds inspiration:

> Ô rêveur, cherche les retraites,
> Les abris, les grottes discrètes,
> Et l'oubli pour trouver l'amour,
> Et le silence, afin d'entendre
> La voix d'en haut, sévère et tendre,
> Et l'ombre, afin de voir le jour!
> . . . . . . . . . . . . . . . . . . . . . . .
> Dieu t'attend dans les solitudes [. . .].
> (*Poésie* 1: 421, lines 25–30, 35)

Hugo's poets are at once "philosophes," "sages," "lutteurs,"
"hommes de persévérance," and "chercheurs." Set apart from

the corrupt masses, they are men of vision and of hope: "l'homme des utopies." While these occupations suggest masculinity, feminine delicacy complements the Poet's more forceful characteristics: "Homme, il est doux comme une femme." And yet Hugo never leaves the maleness of the Poet in doubt, apostrophizing him in clearly masculine terms: "Ô poète, ô maître, ô semeur." The metaphor of insemination identifies Hugo's Poet as paternal in origin. The Poet-as-father is confirmed by the reproductive function that Hugo imparts to his visionary Poet:

> Une utopie est un berceau!
> De ce berceau, quand viendra l'heure,
> Vous verrez sortir, éblouis,
> Une société meilleure. [. . .]
>
> (1: 422, lines 110–13)

This Poet's mastery grants him an authority that could not be intoned in a woman's voice, while at the same time he appropriates birth imagery for masculinity.

Like "La fonction du poète," Musset's "Les nuits" (1835–37) describe a male Poet in the throes of a conflict that defines both his superiority and his task.[15] And like Hugo, in "La nuit de décembre" Musset employs a gendered simile to describe the Poet's emotional expressiveness: "J'ai [. . .] sangloté comme une femme" (41). Lamartine's Poet goes farther than the simple imitation suggested by Hugo's and Musset's comparisons. The speaking subject of "La prière de femme" passes as an emotive subject with a feminine voice rather than simply adopting her mannerisms. This poetic transgendering is, however, unveiled in the final stanza where the "je" reveals that his femininity is merely borrowed for expressive purposes:

> Moi, j'emprunte une voix de femme
> Pour porter à Dieu mes accents;
> Mes soupirs, passant par ton âme,
> Ont plus de pleurs et plus d'encens!
>
> (*Recueillements* 290)

Softness, sobbing, sighs, and tears are thus all represented as feminine attributes called upon by the male Poet to convey his feelings. One might even consider this a kind of ploy on the part of the fictive Poet to enhance the believability of his emotion and further the illusion of the text's transparency. Given the tendency to read women writers autobiographically (a tendency that persists to this day), we can see the femininity of these male voices functioning to validate the sincerity of the Romantic lyric.[16] It is as if the male Poet were saying: "I speak from my heart with affect, as does a woman; the voice and the sentiment that travel to you through this poem are therefore my own."

These examples point to the liberality that Romanticism afforded its poets in the investigation of "otherness" through the expression of sentiment. The poetry of other Romantics often confirms the Poet's femininity, although it rarely represents a female poet.[17] For male poets, the era was one of inclusion that invited representations of femininity as well as of masculinity in the service of self-examination. While subsequent generations have blamed some strains of Romanticism for self-indulgence or naïveté, the readers of this period welcomed revelations of interiority and gave poets free reign to probe femininity.

Although presented as a subject sounding the gendered boundaries of the self, the construct of the Poet nonetheless excluded the possibility of female authorship and of feminine lyric subjectivity, ultimately affirming the identification of poetry with masculinity. Irigaray's project in *Speculum* and in subsequent works suggests that the scrutiny of "femininity" in phallocentric discourse necessarily erases feminine subjectivity: "Car parler *de* ou *sur* la femme peut toujours revenir ou être entendu comme une reprise du féminin à l'intérieur d'une logique qui le maintient dans le refoulement, la censure, la méconnaissance" (*Ce sexe* 75). Romantics delved into the "other" of femininity by projection. Their exclusively male and heterosexual Poet never became a woman and relied on heroic qualities inaccessible to female voices. Although rarely downright misogynist (with the exception, perhaps, of Vigny), Romantics alternately idealized feminine emotive qualities and infantilized women with paternalistic protectionism.

Traditional literary critics have aptly described the Poet's masculine qualities, although without proceeding to a critique of this figure, in essence adopting rather than analyzing Romantic constructs. In Bénichou's *Le sacre de l'écrivain* (1973), this eminent historian of Romanticism describes the divinization of the figure of the Poet, who was assumed to be capable of higher feelings, deeper insight, a more profound intelligence than the common man.[18] Like the priest who mediates between God and humanity, the Poet was seen as an intercessor whose poetry translated the world and the experiences of common people in nobler terms. Poetic language thus often doubled for metaphysical discourse. Bénichou uses the word *mission* to describe the Romantics' poetic quest: "c'est à partir de l'unité romantique qu'a pris forme définitive en France l'idée de la *mission* du poète" (*Le sacre* 330). Implicit in this notion is a double position for the Poet, who was seen as both a practicing artist (one who writes poems) and a visionary (one who speaks truths). Bénichou's uncritical analysis of the Romantic Poet finally reiterates the Romanticized version of language and subjectivity. By accepting the conflation of the empirical author and the lyric subject, he participates in the double project of reappropriating femininity while asserting masculine superiority.

Hugo personifies the most robust episode in this history, and his monumental oeuvre invites metaphors of strength and grandeur. Historians of Romanticism since Gautier have chronicled the premiere of Hugo's play *Hernani,* which marked 1830 as the beginning of French Romanticism's heyday, in militaristic terms. Gautier, himself a colorful player on the scene, described this event as a battle that placed an army of young poets in the heat of combat, fighting for recognition and glory against a fading and bigoted regime of moldy, impotent classicists. The masculine metaphor of the poet as soldier recurs often enough to become a stock figure in texts by Baudelaire, among others: "Il n'existe que trois êtres respectables: le prêtre, le guerrier, le poète. Savoir, tuer et créer" (*Œuvres complètes* 1: 684). Like priest and soldier, poet was an occupation open only to men; femininity threatened the homosocial world of poets as, to this day, it threatens the army and the church.[19] Both Byron and Vigny were soldiers, representing a virile strain of Romanticism. In "La colère de Samson," for example, Vigny offered a starkly tragic worldview of masculine strength undone by corrupt femininity:

> Une lutte éternelle en tout temps, en tout lieu
> Se livre sur la terre, en présence de Dieu,
> Entre la bonté d'Homme et la ruse de Femme.
> Car la Femme est un être impur de corps et d'âme.
> (*Poèmes* 179, lines 35–38)

This piece stands for both heroic masculinity and the fatalism that lies at the heart of many of Vigny's poems, in sharp opposition to the masculine fragility of his Chatterton. All too evident in "Samson" is an antifeminism that, however, was not characteristic of the period. On the contrary, much Romantic poetry tended to praise and defend (and occasionally even mimic) a virtuous and empathetic femininity in the name of humanitarianism. Hugo's masculine voice, for instance, was a protective one, often speaking on woman's behalf: "Oh! n'insultez jamais une femme qui tombe!" (*Poésie* 1: 342).

Even Lamartine, who was among those associated with the elegiac strain of Romantic poetry, employs images of masculine valor. His "Le génie" contains a metaphor uncharacteristic of his more celebrated poems (such as "Le lac" or "Le vallon") and associates masculine genius with physical prowess:

> Toi donc, des mépris de ton âge
> Sans être jamais rebuté,
> Retrempe ton mâle courage
> Dans les flots de l'adversité!
> Pour cette lutte qui s'achève,
> Que la vérité soit ton glaive,
> La justice ton bouclier.
> Va! dédaigne d'autres armures;
> Et si tu reçois des blessures,
> Nous les couvrirons de laurier!
> (*Méditations* 85, lines 101–10)

Although negative criticism of Romanticism involved the perception of its femininity, Romantic poets themselves called upon images of masculine vigor as ably as those of feminine sensitivity. Proponents often marshaled virile metaphors to defend Romanticism, operating like the anti-Romantics in the name of masculinity. For Romantics, tragic melancholy, sublimity and transcendence, mastery, and monumentality provided the vocabulary of affirmation. By representing the poet in terms of heroic models, they secured their profession as a masculine domain. Their critics simply feminized the terms of sentimentality, intimacy, spontaneity, naturalness, morbidity, and the lack of formal rigor.

Ultimately, therefore, the boundaries of the gendered self were fluid only in one direction. While male poets pursued variegated representations of interiority and looked to women as passive exemplars of sensitivity, they did not afford women poets their own forays into circumscribed gender categories. Exceptionality and genius, like voyages into the realm of the other, remained the domain of male poets. The practice of inclusion entailed a politics of containment, since the Romantic spotlight on femininity relied on the reassertion of masculinity. The imbuing of poetic values with gender assignments governed the content of Romantic women's work and relegated it to the status of minor poetry. So although women poets had a more receptive audience during the first part of the century than thereafter, their position was nonetheless constrained by expectations of conformity to the virtues of domesticity.

## The Exclusion of Femininity

Femininity, so forceful a conveyor of feeling, reveals its weakness before the task of assuming the Poet's role. Affect, woman's strength, ends up being her worst enemy when she confronts masculinist criticism. Jules Barbey d'Aurevilly roundly condemned women with literary and intellectual aspirations as masculine: "la prétention subsiste, la prétention au génie, cette immense virilité!" (*Les bas-bleus* xvii). It is this pretension of genius, while accompanying the Romantic Poet's pretensions of femininity, that forestalls the possibility of feminine poetic subjectivity. The very characteristics of this figure—centrality, exceptionality, solitude, and divinization—render it incompatible with femininity. These qualities, which define the lyric endeavor, prompted Molènes to ask: "Comment [. . .] concilier l'idée que nous avons de l'existence du poète avec celle qu'on doit se faire de la vie des femmes?" (49).

The blurring of the lines between the speaking subject of a poem and its author, mediated by the Poet as fictive incarnation of both, posed added barriers for the woman poet who was acceptable no more as writing subject on the literary scene than as the lyric subject of poetry. Staël describes public opinion as the greatest barrier to the woman writer: "quand les femmes écrivent [. . .] le public leur accorde difficilement son suffrage. [. . .] Quand une femme publie un livre, elle se met tellement dans la dépendance de l'opinion, que les dispensateurs de cette opinion lui font sentir durement leur empire" (*De la littérature*

334). By parading in the public sphere such characteristics as genius and individual autonomy, the woman writer debased or rejected her femininity, seen as ideally modest, retiring, and dependent.[20]

Such characteristics were perhaps even less acceptable as definitive of the struggles of a feminine writing subject; metaphors of nudity were repeatedly used to describe the self-exposing woman poet. A great danger for a respectable nineteenth-century woman was to exhibit herself in public: to find herself in an inappropriate place, to offer herself to the eyes of men, to reveal a wrist or an ankle. Sometimes more dangerous, even obscene, was the immodesty of a woman writer grappling with issues of identity in writing. For this, women poets were frequently accused of a figurative kind of exhibitionism, summed up by the epithet *monstre,* derived from the Latin *monstrare,* meaning "to show."[21] Therefore, for a woman to publish, to place herself in public view, was either a monstrous or an indecent act. Jean de Gourmont has written:

> *Toute femme poète* fait un peu le geste de Phryné qui *se dé-nude devant ses juges* [. . .], le geste de l'amante qui *se déshabille pour son amant.* Mais c'est *une impudeur* plus complète, puisque ces femmes porte-lyres nous révèlent ce que l'amant le plus perspicace, le plus curieux ne saurait découvrir: les secrets mouvements de leur horlogerie senti-mentale. (28; emphasis mine)

Molènes particularly abused the clothing metaphor, using it not only to ridicule women ("je ne sais rien de plus laid [. . .] qu'un chapeau d'homme sur une tête de femme" [69]), but also to detail their incompatibility with the poetic act. Women are not fit for literary battle: "n'est-il point des femmes qui savent conquérir parmi les écrivains une place honorable sans avoir changé jamais la robe traînante en tunique de combat?" (53).[22] They lack originality and seriousness: "Ce qui caractérise tous les talen[t]s féminins [. . .] c'est une incroyable promptitude à répudier pour le costume de l'année nouvelle le costume de l'an passé" (63).

Some women poets, perhaps fearful of such accusations, authorized this metaphor themselves. Louise Ackermann, for example, wrote that "Mon mari n'eût pas souffert que sa femme se décolletât, à plus forte raison lui eût-il défendu de publier des vers. *Écrire, pour une femme, c'est se décolleter;* seulement il est peut-être moins indécent de montrer ses épaules que son cœur" (*Pensées* 53; emphasis mine). Ackermann describes her short marriage as "exquis," nonetheless avowing that during it she abandoned her own work to become "une aide précieuse" for her husband in his. Furthermore, she concealed her past poetic activity out of "consideration" for him: "Mon mari a toujours ignoré que j'eusse fait des vers" (*Œuvres* xii). Fortunately for Ackermann's readers, her husband's premature death left her free to write.

Although Romantics thought of expressivity as a feminine quality, subjectivity and femininity were seen as essentially incompatible, and so women had no place in the lyric endeavor. Female writing subjects, like a woman in masculine dress, defied both public opinion and that of the literati. Although male Romantics were free to act feminine, the critical invective goes to show that they did not accept masculinity in women. Disparate nineteenth-century critics and poets, among them Molènes, Gautier, Baudelaire, and Barbey d'Aurevilly, adamantly regulated femininity, confirming the incompatibility of femaleness with the qualities of individuality and exceptionality. Their writings are at once startling and predictable in their vehement condescension toward women who write poetry. The incursions of women into the poetic arena must have desecrated a particularly hallowed ground for them to have been condemned so strongly.

What is perhaps more surprising than the misogyny of nineteenth-century critics is the number of contemporary critics who quietly subscribe to the same belief that "woman poet" is an oxymoron, by excluding women poets from in-depth studies of Romanticism. The following quotation appeared as recently as 1979: "On a tort de ne pas relire les poétesses qui soignent leurs vers aussi coquettement que leurs toilettes, il leur arrive de réussir un beau sonnet entre deux coiffures et deux sorties mondaines. [. . .] Il nous a paru utile de montrer à nos oublieux contemporains le beau décolleté de Mme Colet [. . .]" (Somoff and Marfée 75, 95).

Let me illustrate the scope of the problem of exclusion with another example from the present day, one perhaps more sobering than amusing. This entails returning to Bénichou's quartet of studies on Romanticism, which so painstakingly and convincingly portrays the divinization of the Poet. Given his desire to trace and record Romanticism as a story of masculine accomplishment, does it surprise us that Bénichou's masterful studies overlook such women poets as Louise Ackermann, Marceline Desbordes-Valmore, Amable Tastu, Louise Colet, and Elisa Mercœur? In the 2,000 meticulously-researched pages of his four volumes, Bénichou does not mention Ackermann, only footnotes Colet (whose novel *Lui* provides testimony of Sand and Musset's affair), notes Tastu and Desbordes-Valmore once each as addressees of poems by male poets, and refers in passing to Mercœur as the "Muse armoricaine." Thus are these writers sidelined (literally, in Bénichou's footnotes) and displaced from the position of writer or subject of poetry to that of gossip, muse, or object in poetry. Because they did not contribute to the making of a movement as literary historians understand it, nor fit with the image of the Poet, Bénichou erased them from literary history.

During their lifetimes, these women were in fact not the obscure figures that they are today and, indeed, had greater popular success than some of the minor Romantic men treated by Bénichou (Petrus Borel and Philothée O'Neddy, for example). A detailed study remains to be done on the place of women poets in the Romantic movement, of their dialogues both with male poets and among themselves. One significant barrier to the discussion of these women's works is their unavailability. For this reason, Tastu (1798–1885), Mercœur (1809–35), and Ackermann (1813–90) are names still unfamiliar to many readers of nineteenth-century French literature. Colet (1810–76) comes to mind primarily as Flaubert's once-lover and correspondent. Desbordes-Valmore (1786–1859) alone approaches canonical status, thanks to the republication of her *Œuvres poétiques* in 1973 and the discussion of her work that has ensued. Although the biographies of these women are as different as their poetry, each began her career as a poet during the Romantic era.

Given the definition of those who devote themselves to the writing of poetry, what position remained for such women who aspired to do so? What were the specific obstacles they confronted?

The work of these Romantic women offers a variety of answers to such questions. Before turning to Desbordes-Valmore in the next chapter, let us take the time to listen to some of the voices of her lesser-known peers. Why do they not share Desbordes-Valmore's relatively more privileged status?

Perhaps the careful and restrained Tastu, although crowned several times by the Academy of the *Jeux floraux* (the Toulouse poetry festival dating to 1324, whose winners include Hugo), effaced herself too much. After the success of her first collections (*Poésies* [1826] and *Poésies nouvelles* [1835]), she abandoned poetry and wrote mostly educational tracts for children. Her poem "L'ange gardien" speaks to female poetic ambition and lost opportunity (see appendix). It presents a woman's life-long dialogue with a guardian angel, beginning in the speaking subject's childhood and ending on her deathbed. At each stage of her life, the poem's voice searches for meaningful avenues of self-expression. An ambitious child, she looks to the future with eagerness: "Avide d'un espoir qu'à peine j'entrevois, / Mon cœur voudrait franchir plus de jours à la fois!" The adolescent would write poetry: "Ne puis-je [. . .] / M'élancer seule, libre, et ma lyre à la main?" As a young woman she seeks permission for poetic introspection: "Oh! laissez-moi charmer les heures solitaires; / Sur ce luth ignoré laissez errer mes doigts, / Laissez naître et mourir ses notes passagères [. . .]." The mother wants to continue growing with her child: "Je puis forcer la gloire à tenir sa promesse; / Recueillis pour mon fils, ses lauriers seront doux." The old woman wonders at the lost aspirations for which she no longer has time, and then despairs of the emptiness of her approaching death:

> Mais quoi! ne rien laisser après moi de moi-même!
> Briller, trembler, mourir comme un triste flambeau!
> Ne pas léguer du moins mes chants à ceux que j'aime,
> Un souvenir au monde, un nom à mon tombeau!

To each pleading intervention of the speaking subject, the guardian angel responds with cautionary advice: "Des vœux confus d'une âme ambitieuse, / [l'ange sait] réprimer l'impétueuse ardeur." The moral of the poem is that moderation and conformity make for a happy life ("crois-moi, je conduis au bonheur").

Instead of poetic ambition, the angel counsels humility, modesty, devotion to the home, soothing memories of domesticity, and the promise of heavenly grace. The poem's last words belong to the angel:

> La tombe attend tes dépouilles mortelles,
> L'oubli tes chants; mais l'âme est au Seigneur.
> L'heure est venue, entends frémir mes ailes:
> Viens, suis mon vol, je conduis au bonheur!

And yet the vivacity and disappointment of the female voice are not quickly quieted. The reader is left wondering, perhaps like Tastu herself, which path is best to follow: the freedom of self-expression, with its risks of danger, or the calm emptiness promised by a cautious life.

Mercœur, Lamartine's protégée, succumbed to these storybook dangers of celebrity and freedom.[23] Poor but ambitious, she was published by age seventeen and subsequently lauded by prominent writers. Nonetheless, after her move to Paris, she met with obscurity instead of poetic glory. She died at age twenty-six and, although published posthumously, her poetry shared the obscurity of her tomb. Colet's life was not so tragic, and she found literary, political, and social outlets for her ambitions. But her renowned beauty attracted more attention than her writing and, typecast as Flaubert's muse, she finds few readers or editors today for her poetry (I return to Colet's second incarnation as a Parnassian below).

Male critics did not know how to read the decidedly unfeminine Ackermann. Although the preceding quotations from her prose works exemplify her lapses into wifely devotion, she largely avoided the sentimental floweriness of her contemporaries. The cynical boldness of her opinionated, positivist poetry kept critics divided between respect and ridicule.[24] While she has been derided for her "voix mâle" (Somoff and Marfée 95), in fact she wrote works that offered new representations of femininity. "Mon livre" (see appendix) provides a powerful antidote to Tastu's "L'ange gardien." Its speaking subject forcefully opposes all barriers to expression: "Je ne vous offre plus pour toutes mélodies / Que des cris de révolte et des rimes hardies." She adopts a militant tone and does not shy from metaphors of war:

Comment? la Liberté déchaîne ses colères;
Partout, contre l'effort des erreurs séculaires,
La Vérité combat pour s'ouvrir un chemin;
Et je ne prendrais pas parti dans ce grand drame?

This survey, while rapid, points to the diverse strategies and styles present in the work of "ces êtres deux fois mystérieux qui sont en même temps poètes et femmes" (Barbey, *Poètes* [1862] 147). It also illustrates a number of internal contradictions in the work of women poets. In the next chapter, I will consider Marceline Desbordes-Valmore as a case study of the woman poet, addressing both the obstacles she confronted and the strategies she employed to gain a relative renown. Within her work we will encounter a variety of stances that betray some incongruities and elicit a great deal of critical ambivalence. This ambivalence provides the first focus of my inquiry into Desbordes-Valmore's work and critical reception.

# Chapter Two

# "Women's Poetry"

## The Case of Marceline Desbordes-Valmore

Marceline Desbordes-Valmore's career as a published poet spanned nearly fifty years.[1] It began in 1813 with the appearance of solitary pieces in various almanacs (*Almanach des muses, Chansonnier des grâces*), a popular forum for women's poetry at the beginning of the century. In 1819 she published her first collection, *Élégies, Marie et romances*. While this received little attention, those to follow were widely read, bringing to Desbordes-Valmore a new popularity and literary associations with prominent Romantic poets. During the next decade, several augmented editions of her poetry rode the wave of interest in elegiac poetry unleashed by Lamartine's *Méditations poétiques* (1820).[2] After *Les pleurs* (1833), Desbordes-Valmore's popularity declined, a fate shared by most women poets after the first Romantic period: "aux environs de 1840, il se faisait une réaction contre la littérature des femmes. [. . .] On se détournait de la poésie sentimentale, plaintive et personnelle" (Jasenas, *Critique* 62). *Pauvres fleurs* (1839) and *Bouquets et prières* (1843) did not successfully maintain her literary renown. Beginning in the mid-1830s, in the face of critical failure and financial need, she devoted much of her writing to novels and children's literature, more profitable genres. Increasing poverty accompanied her advancing age, and in her final sixteen years, she published no poetry, having tried in vain to find a publisher for her last collection (*Poésies inédites* appeared posthumously in 1860).

We can reconstruct one version of Desbordes-Valmore's personal life from an autobiographical interpretation of her poetry. She writes nostalgically about childhood, a time of innocence and hope. She celebrates her parents, her sisters, and her children, making of the family a central theme in her poetry. She chronicles the private tragedies, including the loss of four of her children, that punctuated her life. We see her too as an impassioned lover, a devoted friend, the defender of the disenfranchised, and a woman of letters whose poems communicate with both male and female poets of her day. But Francis Ambrière's massive biography of Desbordes-Valmore (*Le siècle des Valmore*) reveals still other aspects of her life not always evident in her poetry. Several of her children were illegitimate, and she took lovers while married. She scraped by, supporting her family, including her husband, through a life of constant movement and various careers, most notably as an actress. This biography gives the impression of tenacity and independence rather than frailty, and suggests that the poet's familial devotion did not rule out an extramarital quest for pleasure and companionship.

Several readers have suggested that Desbordes-Valmore manipulated her image in her poetry. Christine Planté contends that she conformed to prescribed notions of feminine modesty, piety, and domesticity out of self-preservation: "Dans cette modestie féminine, il y a peut-être une bien habile pirouette, une révérence faite au bon goût, aux autorités littéraires et morales et aux règles des censeurs pour mieux se concilier leur indulgence et leur protection" ("L'art sans art" 174). Planté's "peut-être" leaves room for doubt, illustrating once more the uncertainty surrounding Desbordes-Valmore's poetry. Éliane Jasenas's analysis of Desbordes-Valmore's self-packaging gives her somewhat less credit in suggesting that she altered her tone because she could not bear negative criticism. Jasenas relates the story of a critic who "avait fait le reproche, jugé fort grave, de profaner la religion en mêlant Dieu à l'amour." She proposes that Desbordes-Valmore, whose poetry subsequently became more pious, responded with fear and acquiescence: "elle s'est empressée de faire pénitence. Elle se dit que peut-être elle a trop parlé" (*Critique* 56).

Barbara Johnson brings the question of sincerity to the forefront of her study on Desbordes-Valmore. She suggests that Desbordes-Valmore engaged in conscious rather than ingenuous self-packaging, styling herself as a faithful wife and virtuous mother to cultivate "the absolute voice of the native informant from the field of the 'eternal feminine.'"[3] After destroying this myth with the help of Ambrière's painstaking biography, Johnson suggests that Desbordes-Valmore tailored her poetic image and output to conform to contemporary expectations and to project "an unthreatening poetics of sincerity" ("Gender" 170). Given critics' stubborn insistence on reading women's poetry literally, Johnson argues, Desbordes-Valmore's sincerity has gone unquestioned, and her poems have been accepted as transparent representations of her lived experience, while her male contemporaries are seen as engaging in convention or poetic pose. As all these critics have suggested, whether they attribute discrepancies between Desbordes-Valmore's life and work to artless self-protection or concerted image-making, the literal interpretation of her poetry does not do it justice. In my reading of her poems to follow, I focus on their contradictions and moments of opacity in order to shed light on her manipulation of the Romantic aesthetic and her strategies for inscribing female subjectivities in a genre hostile to femininity.

## Critical Ambivalence

The authorities of the literary world have consistently greeted Desbordes-Valmore's poetry with ambivalence. Although many of her contemporaries (including Lamartine, Vigny, Hugo, Sainte-Beuve) honored her work, as did poets of the following generation (Baudelaire, Verlaine), and Aragon and Bonnefoy in the twentieth century, such praise has often been two-faced. It tends to compliment Desbordes-Valmore's poems for the feminine passion and motherly devotion they represent, thereby reading her work as a transparent reflection of the woman herself. At the same time such criticism frequently calls her art as a poet into question. We can summarize nineteenth-century criticism of Desbordes-Valmore in the following way: Marceline Desbordes-Valmore, the woman, is exemplarily feminine; her poetry, consequently, is necessarily minor. Even Sainte-Beuve, her editor and purportedly her greatest admirer, relegated her to the category of minor poet: "L'avenir, nous le croyons, ne l'oubliera pas; tout d'elle ne sera pas sauvé sans doute; mais, dans le recueil définitif des *Poetæ minores* de ce temps-ci, un charmant volume devra contenir sous son nom quelques idylles, quelques romances, beaucoup d'élégies; *toute une gloire modeste et tendre*" (19; emphasis mine).[4] Thus she owes her glory to the feminine virtues of modesty and tenderness rather than to her poems themselves, whose future is less certain. Sainte-Beuve's appraisal does not stray from the universal equation that identified "women's poetry" as a lyrical subgenre with characteristic content and tone (charm, modesty, tenderness, elegiac sorrow). Defined in this manner, women's poetry is inevitably relegated to the position of footnote to the dominant tradition.

Baudelaire's assessment of Desbordes-Valmore's work is emblematic of her uneasy reception by subsequent generations. In 1861, two years after her death, he published an article bearing her name. While ostensibly laudatory, "Marceline Desbordes-Valmore" nonetheless begins with Baudelaire's confession that his appreciation for her poetry is "en complet désaccord avec toutes [mes] autres passions et avec [ma] doctrine" (*Œuvres complètes* 2: 146).[5] In the passage that follows, where Baudelaire offers his characterization of Desbordes-Valmore's poetry, the contradictions born of a woman undertaking what was perceived to be a man's métier become evident. He produces a series of oppositions between an ideal male poetics and the kind practiced by Desbordes-Valmore:

> Si le cri, si le soupir *naturel* d'une âme d'élite, si l'ambition désespérée du cœur, si *les facultés soudaines, irréfléchies,* si tout ce qui est gratuit et vient de Dieu, suffisent à faire le grand poète, Marceline Valmore est et sera toujours un grand poète. Il est vrai que si vous prenez le temps de remarquer tout ce qui lui manque de ce qui peut s'acquérir par *le travail,* sa grandeur se trouvera singulièrement diminuée; mais au moment même où vous vous sentirez le plus impatienté et désolé par *la négligence,* par le cahot, par le trouble, que vous prenez, *vous, homme réfléchi et toujours responsable,* pour un parti pris de paresse, une beauté soudaine, inattendue, non égalable, se dresse, et vous voilà enlevé irrésistiblement au fond du ciel poétique. Jamais aucun poète ne fut plus *naturel;* aucun ne fut jamais moins artificiel. Personne n'a pu imiter ce charme, parce qu'il est tout original et *natif.* (2: 146; emphasis mine)

Baudelaire begins and ends this passage with reference to the "natural" qualities of Desbordes-Valmore's poetry. Whereas here he praises her "natural art," let us recall that in his *Journaux intimes* he voices disdain not simply for nature, but specifically for woman's essential link to it. In his article ostensibly devoted to praising Desbordes-Valmore, Baudelaire includes a digression on the pretensions of women writers and calls their works "une désolation pour leur famille, pour leur amant même" (2: 146). A masculine poetics would instead be artificial and the product of diligent toil. Baudelaire describes the consistent work habits necessary to form *l'homme de génie,* and in the present article judges meritorious "ce qui peut s'acquérir par le travail," at the same time charging Desbordes-Valmore with negligence in her work. Reflection is clearly the domain of man and spontaneity the modus operandi of the woman poet, for while this article is addressed to and written by an "homme *réfléchi,*" it describes the "facultés soudaines, *irréfléchies*" of Desbordes-Valmore.

The marks of equivocation are apparent in Baudelaire's language ("Si," "Il est vrai que si"). Was Desbordes-Valmore a privileged exception for him, or did he couch his contempt for her work in faint praise? Baudelaire's correspondence to his editor, Crépet, who originally commissioned the article for his anthology *Les poètes français,* provides reason to doubt Baudelaire's sincerity. He begins their collaboration with good intentions, writing "Mon cher Crépet, j'ai fini vos sept notices, toutes conçues dans le style et suivant la méthode demandés" (*Correspondance* 1: 590). But soon Baudelaire's indulgence turns to juvenile anger when Crépet demands revisions: "Je ne veux plus en faire du tout, du tout, du tout!!!!!!" (1: 615). He writes later that "J'ai déjà, pour lui complaire, *abîmé* trois notices. Il paraît que TOUTES sont à refaire" (2: 45), and finally yields completely to Crépet's demands: "J'ai consenti à supprimer dans toutes les notices tout ce qui était trop âpre et pouvait blesser les gens" (2: 173). While the specific changes requested by Crépet are not spelled out, it is clear that he asked Baudelaire not simply to tone down his invective, but to maintain a positive tone. Let us recall that Baudelaire lived most of his adult life in rather dire financial straits, and that he depended on journalistic publications for income. Given such a quandary for a writer like Baudelaire, for whom literary truth, however unpleasant, was a violent imperative, it is easier to imagine him making a game of praising Desbordes-Valmore under the cover of an oppositional rhetoric than to simply bow down before the demands of an editor he considered "mou" (*Correspondance* 2: 166). Indeed, Baudelaire hints at the violence he does himself in praising her work: "J'aime cela [la poésie de Desbordes-Valmore . . .] probablement à cause même de la violente contradiction qu'y trouve tout mon être" (*Œuvres complètes* 2: 146).

Baudelaire's appreciation for Desbordes-Valmore's poetry thus appears to be only an insincere exception to his abhorrence for and dismissal of women writers. Perhaps, in addition, the suffering she projected in her poems renders her an unsuitable object of attack for Baudelaire and others. She was one of the more palatable exceptions, since she never stepped out of her feminine role to encroach on what Baudelaire insisted was the exclusively masculine domain of reasoned judgment: "Mme Desbordes-Valmore fut femme, fut toujours femme et ne fut absolument que femme" (*Œuvres complètes* 2: 146–47). As Johnson has pointed out, she was perceived as less threatening than other women poets because she pretended not to be one. This might also explain why so many male poets and critics have seen fit to praise her work, for in addition to respecting conventional definitions of femininity, she refused the position and the aspirations of the Poet.

Barbey d'Aurevilly suggests as much, writing that "Mme Desbordes-Valmore n'est pas une femme de lettres, puisqu'il y a de ces monstres qu'on appelle maintenant *femmes de lettres*" (*Poètes* [1862] 145). Gustave Kahn would later concur:

> il y a vraiment dans ces vers [de Desbordes-Valmore] une absence de cabotinage charmante, et des notes féminines avec une partie seulement des défauts des œuvres féminines, soit de la mièvrerie et trop de petits gestes, mais jamais la grosse caisse et les ouragans des Amazones qui montent sur les grands chevaux de l'autre sexe. (141)

It is interesting to note how often admirers of Desbordes-Valmore employ the word *charm* and its variations to describe the woman and her poetry. Male critics appear charmed by her in direct proportion to their perception of her femininity.

Baudelaire also relies on the notion of femininity presented in his prose writings to define his own practice. Desbordes-

Valmore serves as a foil against whom he sketches his ideal Poet: she is all that the *homme de génie* is not, and vice versa. So even while Desbordes-Valmore won Baudelaire's cynical praise, she remains relegated to the position of outsider to the world of letters. The question of influence is therefore moot: Baudelaire consistently opposed her poetic practice to his own, locating the appeal of her work in its dissimilarity and never opening his theory or practice of poetry to include hers. For Baudelaire, poetry prevails as a masculine domain from which Desbordes-Valmore is categorically barred.

Twentieth-century critics are more direct in their *ad feminam* criticism of Desbordes-Valmore's poetry: the attacks against her poetic corpus do not spare the woman who penned them. They lament her poetry's perceived lack of rigor, thus echoing their nineteenth-century predecessors. But they also criticize the sentimentality of her poems, which often represent private and domestic scenes from a variety of feminine viewpoints, including those of mother, daughter, lover, and friend. I would attribute such attacks to both old-time antifeminist dismissal of women authors and a more recent impatience with sentimental literature. Henri Peyre condemns Desbordes-Valmore quite virulently, all the while minimizing her importance. In *Qu'est-ce que le romanticisme?*, he names her only once as "la détestable femme-poète que fut Marceline Desbordes-Valmore" (226). In which of her roles, *femme* or *poète*, she is most detestable, Peyre does not specify. Although Barthes does not share Peyre's blatant misogyny, he too writes condescendingly of Desbordes-Valmore's poetry while commenting on Nadar's 1857 photograph of her: "Marceline Desbordes-Valmore reproduit sur son visage la bonté un peu niaise de ses vers" (*Chambre* 159). With his accusation of simple goodness (*niaiserie*), Barthes illustrates that even the most sophisticated of contemporary critics occasionally lapse into predictable evaluations of women's poetry.

Critics from Romanticism to the present have thus tended to evaluate Desbordes-Valmore using similar terms: they agree on the central role that the author's sex plays in her work, which they read literally as a true portrait of the woman holding the pen. In its femininity lies either the greatness of her work, for it speaks forcefully from a woman's soul, or its failure, for it is thus specific and sentimental, never universal. Contemporary feminist criticism exhibits equal ambivalence toward her work. Johnson describes a scenario of critical reception wherein Desbordes-Valmore is more often than not praised by the guardians of the male poetic tradition who condemn or simply ignore other women poets, while largely dismissed by feminist critics. At the same time, she continues, Desbordes-Valmore's "very success in constructing an unthreatening poetics of sincerity [. . .] has tended to render her unusable and invisible for feminism" ("Gender" 170).

It is true that Desbordes-Valmore's most steadfast admirers have been and remain male critics, editors, and biographers, from Sainte-Beuve to Bertrand, Bonnefoy, and Ambrière.[6] We have their work to thank for her present visibility and their praise with which to counter the voices of her detractors. But why Desbordes-Valmore and not the "masculine" Ackermann or the "ambitious" Delphine de Girardin?[7] To what extent does Desbordes-Valmore's visibility spring from an over-investment in her reassuring representation of femininity? Anne Berger describes a maternal cult among nineteenth-century poets that might just extend to twentieth-century critics: "[Desbordes-Valmore] enjoyed great popularity among the poets who celebrated in her a universal mother" ("The Maternal Idol" 136). Johnson's equivocation ("it is hard to like a woman who inspires such praise" ["Gender" 165]) is understandable in light of such unrelenting and problematic fervor. But it also, I would argue, is indicative of the renewed, if ambivalent, interest in Desbordes-Valmore's work by feminist critics, rather than of the poet's unusability for feminism.

Indeed, recent feminist critics have also contributed to the renewed interest in Desbordes-Valmore's poetry, although they do not always agree in their assessment of her work. While Danahy and Planté portray her as a feminist poet writing against the expectations of a male tradition, Domna Stanton does not include Desbordes-Valmore in her collection of French feminist verse, *The Defiant Muse*. Johnson never quite makes up her mind, pointing to the difficult position of the feminist critic who wants to claim a woman poet as her own while remaining suspicious of a strategy of feminine acquiescence. Ambivalence thus reigns in both feminist and traditionalist criticism of Desbordes-Valmore's poetry, such that there is no consensus even on the nature of her reception: was she overly privileged and accorded more popularity than she merited or unfairly relegated to the ranks of minor poet? Is the femininity represented in her poetry exemplary or exaggerated, subversive or conventional, natural or carefully packaged?

As Johnson suggests, the ambivalence *toward* Desbordes-Valmore's work is mirrored by the irresolution *in* her work: "Desbordes-Valmore [. . .] is no less ambivalent toward the female voice. Her voice is a voice that struggles to write its way out of the silences assigned to it by poetic tradition" ("The Lady" 630). This is the hesitant voice of a woman writing in a tradition dominated by images of the male Poet. Such overwhelming uncertainty, on the part of both writer and reader, points to a conflict that is played out in Desbordes-Valmore's poetry. In addition to conventional images, Desbordes-Valmore reveals in her work a tendency to resist the very tradition that adopted her as its own foil.

Desbordes-Valmore's resistance is most evident in her response to critics and the institutions they represent. While refusing herself to engage in metapoetic discourse (she did not write critical essays), her poetry reveals impatience with masculine censure. In particular, her two final collections (*Bouquets et prières* [1843] and *Poésies inédites* [1860]), written after her fall in popularity, retain traces of her resentment. In "Jeune homme irrité . . . ," Desbordes-Valmore's female speaking subject adopts a condescending tone to mock male scholarship that is critical of women writers. She lambastes the exclusionary pride of male writers and critics as if scolding a pretentious schoolboy:

> Jeune homme irrité sur un banc d'école,
> Dont le cœur encor n'a chaud qu'au soleil,
> Vous refusez donc l'encre et la parole
> À celles qui font le foyer vermeil?[8]

> (lines 1–4)

In criticizing male rejection of female writers, she refuses to engage in the privileging of intellect over sentiment, or of erudition over experiential wisdom. The rigid repudiation of the woman writer suggests that masculine standards, which vaunt the acquisition of knowledge, cover for misplaced aggression.

> Savant, mais aigri par vos lassitudes,
> ...........................
> Vous portez si haut la férule altière,
> Qu'un géant plierait sous son docte poids.
> Vous faites baisser notre humble paupière,
> Et nous flagellez à briser nos doigts.
> Où prenez-vous donc de si dures armes?
> Qu'ils étaient méchants vos maîtres latins!
>
> (5, 11–16)

She finally suggests that eloquence is the product not of diligent study, but of interpersonal sensitivity:

> Ce beau rêve à deux, vous voudriez l'écrire.
> On est éloquent dès qu'on aime bien:
> Mais si vous aimez qui ne sait pas lire,
> L'amante à l'amant ne répondra rien.
>
> (21–24)

Here Desbordes-Valmore questions the value of erudition and points to its misuse as a weapon of exclusion. Elsewhere she employs scholastic metaphors that treat the published word with less-than-poetic reverence, and which speak to the importance of knowledge acquired from other sources, including daily living. In "Laisse-nous pleurer," addressed to a "philosophe distrait" critical of women's ignorance, she rejects the written word for the book of life: "Nous n'allons point usant nos yeux au même livre; / Le mien se lit dans l'ombre où Dieu m'apprend à vivre" (*OP* 2: 528). This metaphor appears frequently in Desbordes-Valmore's work: "Ce livre, c'est ma vie et ses mobiles pages / Où le cyprès serpente à chaque ligne" ("L'ange gardien" [2: 382]). Desbordes-Valmore questions not only the value of erudition and its elitist abuses, but also the quest for permanence and glory implicit in the masculine poetic stance. Her writing, she acknowledges, will not necessarily outlive her or become a monument to her memory. The pages of her book are mobile, and the book itself is *périssable*.

Desbordes-Valmore's critique of nineteenth-century critical elitism, which punished women for their inadequate access to education and cultural production, still resonates in contemporary feminist criticism that questions the phallic investment in knowledge. This type of hypercritical assault, which greets inadequate knowledge or insufficient production—both highly subjective concepts—with categorical condemnation, more often than not derives from visceral disagreement rather than from measured consideration. The fervor of antifeminist criticism springs from opposing ideology and a quest for power, and yet such writers as Baudelaire and Barbey d'Aurevilly argue with pretended objectivity. Desbordes-Valmore is merely pointing out that erudition does not completely clothe the emperor and, in so doing, reveals a stronger bite than she is usually given credit for.[9]

These poems suggest that Desbordes-Valmore, and the woman poet in general, engage in writing practices that are very different from those of the male Poet, whose sights are set on recognition. There are, of course, two interpretations of this "feminine stance," which associates writing with immediacy rather than permanence. A poetics of ephemerality might first be considered a defensive reaction to negative criticism that rendered monstrous the ambitious woman writer. We could criticize such a retreat as demurring to interdiction or, instead, appreciate it as a strategy to circumvent censure. A second interpretation suggests a positive difference rather than a negative reaction. In this case, the woman writer's investment in her product is quite different from a man's. Her work is not intellectual property whose value can be measured by the laurels of posterity, or by the cultivation of a reputation through the propagation of her name. Desbordes-Valmore's poetry sets little store by the proper name: "Que mon nom ne soit rien qu'une ombre douce et vaine" (*OP* 2: 547). There was, of course, nothing "proper" (*proprius,* "one's own") about her hyphenated name, which combines those of her father (Desbordes) and her husband (Valmore). By refusing to write poems as a monument to it, she shows her relationship both to her name and to the act of writing to be significantly different from that of many male poets who sought recognition for their greatness:

> Ton nom au plus distrait donne de la mémoire,
> Poète! autant chéri qu'amoureux de la gloire.
> Elle a rendu visite à chacun de tes jours,
> Et t'a si bien aimé qu'on t'aimera toujours!
> ("À M. Bouilly," *Poésies inédites, OP* 2: 564)

Like Bouilly, the addressee of this poem whose name failed to fulfill Desbordes-Valmore's generous promise, Baudelaire's poetic persona betrays the wish for glory beyond the grave: "que mon nom / Aborde heureusement aux époques lointaines" ("Je te donne ces vers . . .").[10] Ironically, Baudelaire's verb *aborder* contrasts with *déborder,* which resonates in Desbordes-Valmore's name. Baudelaire wants his name to reach a future time intact, whereas Desbordes-Valmore, in name as in her poetry, suggests a spilling over and subsequent loss in diffusion. Her gesture suggests not only less investment in the social identity that a proper name confers, but a different motivation for picking up the pen as well. Clearly this stance occasionally broaches feminine self-abnegation, as in this stanza from "La pauvre fille":

> À toi le monde! à toi la vie!
> À toi tout ce que l'homme envie!
> Mais dans l'ombre et sans me nommer,
> À moi le ciel! à moi le bonheur de t'aimer!
>
> (*OP* 2: 575)

And yet let us not jump as readily as Marc Bertrand to this conclusion: "'La pauvre fille,' c'est Marceline" (*OP* 2: 767). Desbordes-Valmore's sixty-five years (her age when she composed this poem) are enough to distinguish her from her poem's youthful voice. While feminine self-effacement is hardly foreign to her work, neither is the renunciation of imposed models for poetic identity.

Desbordes-Valmore questions the intellectual elitism employed to belittle her work by calling into question both the Poet and the critic. While her poetry reveals traces of her critical stance and poetic tendencies, she herself wrote no literary essays. She also largely abstained from the writing of prefaces, with which so many poets position their work. This reticence reflects her refusal to engage in critical discourse and theorizing, abstract activities she identified as typically male: "philosophe distrait, amant des théories" is how she identifies the book-toting Poet, ignorant of and antagonistic to woman's experience (*OP* 2: 528). The preface, normally a short prose essay signed by the author, offers the opportunity to contextualize the collection to follow. The choice to theorize one's writing, to lend a hand to the interpretation of the work, is telling, and some writers are more inclined to do so than others. Hugo, for example, was an avid writer of prefaces, penning a new one for each of the five editions of *Odes et ballades* published between 1822 and 1828. And, as we shall see below, Leconte de Lisle's prefaces helped to launch the Parnassian school. Literary critics lavish attention on prefaces for the keys to reading they provide, the poetic stances they reveal, and for the manifestos they sometimes become.[11] They represent theoretical writing that contextualizes the collection (poetically, historically, politically, personally, and so forth) as it pleases the author.

Because Desbordes-Valmore abstained from writing prefaces, other preliminary parerga,[12] including the dedication and the prologue, become particularly interesting segments of her work, often substituting poetic commentary for metapoetic discourse.

## Tearful Beginnings

*Bouquets et prières* is the exception rather than the rule in her work: here, Desbordes-Valmore offers her only preface. Of her five major collections, the only preliminary text written in her own hand (Alexandre Dumas prefaced *Les pleurs,* her second collection) appears here under the title "Une plume de femme." It is followed by a poem entitled "À celles qui pleurent" with which, like Baudelaire with his "Au lecteur," she identifies and addresses an imagined audience. "Une plume de femme" and "À celles qui pleurent" (*OP* 2: 689–90 and 444, respectively) both raise the question of gender in writing, and from the perspective of the reader as well as of the author. One might wonder why Desbordes-Valmore chose to begin the last poetic collection published during her lifetime on such a self-reflexive note, thus countering her image as a poet of spontaneity rather than of reflection. These two texts reveal a clear awareness of sexual difference in writing, at the same time offering Desbordes-Valmore's interpretation of what constitutes that difference.

As prefaces go, "Une plume de femme" is unusual: although written in prose, it is punctuated by a refrain repeated after each of its four paragraphs (see appendix). Bertrand calls it "une sorte de poème en prose" (*OP* 2: 689), but lying as it does on the margins of the collection, it seems to exist on the borders between fiction and nonfiction. Its most striking poetic element is its direct address to and personification of the author's pen, a device that structures the text and its punctuating refrain: "Courez, ma plume, courez: vous savez bien qui vous l'ordonne." Like other prefaces, "Une plume de femme" sketches a portrait of the author and offers an indication of her poetic principles. But thanks to its poetic language, the typically objective stance of the preface gives way to a subjective voice that pretends sincerity while actually contributing to the fictionalization of the author as Woman Poet.

The piece begins by calling on a muse to veil in fiction the scene and the source of her writing: "Je prie un génie indulgent de répandre sur votre travail le charme mystérieux de la fiction, afin que nul ne sache la source de vos efforts et de la fièvre qui vous conduit" (*OP* 2: 689). The "vous" in question is the pen onto which Desbordes-Valmore displaces the poet's work. She projects both her labor and her motivation onto her writing utensil ("votre travail," "la fièvre qui vous conduit"). The image of "la plume conduite" returns in a later passage:

> c'est vous, que personne ne m'apprit à conduire; c'est vous, que sans savoir tailler encore, j'ai fait errer sous ma pensée avec tant d'hésitation et de découragement; c'est vous, tant de fois échappée à mes doigts ignorants, vous, qui par degrés plus rapide, trouvez parfois, à ma propre surprise, quelques paroles moins indignes des maîtres, qui vous ont d'abord regardée en pitié. (*OP* 2: 690)

Although here Desbordes-Valmore comes closer to acknowledging her agency in the pen's movement, she does so with a negative gesture: "personne ne m'apprit à [vous] conduire." While conceivably reflecting the pride of an autodidact, the passage goes on to betray the author's hesitation and discouragement, for which she apologizes with the pretense of ignorance. The game of displacement continues, for here the ignorance belongs to the author's fingers, which hold the pen ("mes doigts ignorants"). And any success—albeit unexpected—is attributed to the pen's, rather than to the author's, ability to find the *mot juste:* "vous [. . .] trouvez parfois, à ma propre surprise, quelques paroles moins indignes des maîtres, qui vous ont d'abord regardée en pitié."

The appearance of these unnamed "maîtres" reveals Desbordes-Valmore's design in distancing herself from the product of her writing, for in so doing she distances herself from the criticism of the masters as well. This crafty maneuver ultimately contradicts the portrait of the ingenuous poetess painted by the text. Desbordes-Valmore, knowing what she was up against, artfully protected herself with the image of artlessness.[13] *Bouquets et prières,* let us recall, coincided with its author's drop in popularity and an era of renewed hostility toward women's writing in general. Desbordes-Valmore responded with a renewed pretense of false humility, but most likely with a sharper appreciation for the barriers that impeded her acceptance as well.

While in "Une plume de femme" she speaks of the woman writer, with "À celles qui pleurent" she addresses the woman reader:

Vous surtout que je plains si vous n'êtes chéries:
Vous surtout qui souffrez, je vous prends pour mes sœurs:
C'est à vous qu'elles vont, mes lentes rêveries,
Et de mes pleurs chantés les amères douceurs.        4

Prisonnière en ce livre une âme est contenue:
Ouvrez, lisez: comptez les jours que j'ai soufferts:
Pleureuses de ce monde où je passe inconnue,
Rêvez sur cette cendre et trempez-y vos fers.        8

Chantez: un chant de femme attendrit la souffrance.
Aimez: plus que l'amour la haine fait souffrir.
Donnez: la charité relève l'espérance;
Tant que l'on peut donner on ne veut pas mourir!        12

Si vous n'avez le temps d'écrire aussi vos larmes,
Laissez-les de vos yeux descendre sur ces vers;
Absoudre, c'est prier. Prier, ce sont nos armes:
Absolvez de mon sort les feuillets entr'ouverts.        16

Pour livrer sa pensée au vent de la parole,
S'il faut avoir perdu quelque peu sa raison,
Qui donne son secret est plus tendre que folle:
Méprise-t-on l'oiseau qui répand sa chanson?        20
(*OP* 2: 444)

The poem's verbs and pronouns place its female audience in the foreground. Its speaking subject addresses "vous" five times in the first three lines, and in the central three stanzas she invokes her female addressees with no less than ten imperatives.

These readers are immediately placed in a relationship of equality with the speaking subject, who presents herself as author of the book in hand: "je vous prends pour mes sœurs." This recalls the sardonic final line of Baudelaire's "Au lecteur": "Hypocrite lecteur, —mon semblable, —mon frère!" (*Œuvres complètes* 1: 6). Although both these addresses rely on a gesture of association, Baudelaire's mocking irony and his poem's accumulation of sordid images lend an antagonistic tone to the fraternal relationship. On the contrary, Desbordes-Valmore's appeal to her "sisters" summons them as allies and as mediators. Rather than writing for men, as did Baudelaire and his confreres, she addresses her work to the women she would have as readers and critics.

Underlying the poem's clichéd images and apologetic tone is a call for aid in the poet's defense and a condemnation of the negative criticism she received. Desbordes-Valmore's poetry consistently sets this strategy in motion: she presents an "appropriate" picture inoffensive to dominant sensibilities, at the same time addressing, in a much more subtle and ambiguous manner, questions of gender difference in writing. "À celles qui pleurent" carries all the marks of a woman tortured in love: the verb "souffrir" appears three times, the noun "souffrance," once. The excessive weeping of both the speaking subject ("mes pleurs chantés") and her addressees ("celles qui pleurent," "pleureuses"), along with the numerous exhortations to dream, sing, love, give, pray, would seem to catalogue fairly completely the activities expected of women and their poetry (only the maternal function, which generally pervades her work, is lacking here). A chirping bird in the final line graces the decor with yet another innocuous image. At this point one yearns for the invective of Baudelaire.

And yet this hackneyed picture of lovesickness and its wholesome antidotes, which seems to confirm the worst accusations made against women's poetry, can be read from two sides. Lost among the soft and stereotypic images is a vocabulary of war. The first stanza serves both as a dedication ("C'est à vous qu'elles vont, mes lentes rêveries") and to align reader and writer in the experience of suffering ("*vous* surtout qui souffrez," "les jours que *j'ai* soufferts"). This poem and the entire collection is addressed to other women as a call for solidarity and support, rather than from the simple desire for commiseration. We must assume that Desbordes-Valmore knew who her friends were.

In the second stanza the speaking subject asks for witnesses to her suffering, and here begins the language of confrontation. Captivity is the torment in question, not lovesickness: "Prisonnière en ce livre une âme est contenue." The image of a book as a place of confinement is countered by the freedom of thought evoked in line 17: "livrer sa pensée au vent de la parole." It is thus neither thought nor words that constitute the prison, but rather the book that contains (holds captive) the poems in which these thoughts take shape. Once again we find an indication of the constraint Desbordes-Valmore felt before the published form. Presumably by opening the prison/book, one would free the captive poems. The two imperatives ("ouvrez, lisez") equate reading with the liberating act of opening. But the poet calls on a specifically female audience to free her, as if their reading or rereading would correct the interpretation responsible for confining her in the first place.

The final stanza indirectly supplies a clue about the responsible agent by positing a singing bird as an object of scorn: "Méprise-t-on l'oiseau qui répand sa chanson?" If "l'oiseau qui répand sa chanson" can be taken as a metaphor for the poet exercising her craft, the referent to "on" is at first more opaque. Who might disapprove of a female poet's freedom of speech or accuse her of folly ("avoir perdu quelque peu sa raison") for giving her thought free reign? The unspoken tenor of this implicit metaphor becomes quite clear: Desbordes-Valmore's apology aims to justify herself before those critics (like the "maîtres," "jeune homme," and "philosophe distrait" of other poems) who condemn women's writing and banish (confine) it by leaving it ignored and unread in a closed book. Desbordes-Valmore's female *destinataires* not only save her poetry from obscurity by reading it with a sympathetic eye, but they are called upon as well to defend the poet with words from the charges against her work ("Absolvez de mon sort les feuillets entr'ouverts"). Their words become weapons ("prier, ce sont nos armes") in the critical war, and she offers her text as a forge in this call-to-arms: "Rêvez sur cette cendre et trempez-y vos fers."

In a previous poem from *Les pleurs* to the sixteenth-century poet Louise Labé, Desbordes-Valmore placed these opening lines from Labé's third elegy as an epigraph:

> Quand vous lirez, ô dames lionnoises!
> Les miens écrits pleins d'amoureuses noises;
> Quand mes regrets, ennuis, dépits et larmes
> M'orrez chanter en pitoyables carmes,
> Ne veuillez point condamner ma simplesse,
> Et jeune erreur de ma folle jeunesse,
>     Si c'est erreur!
>
> ("Louise Labé," *OP* 1: 228)[14]

From its dedication to women readers to its defense against the charge of written folly, these lines resonate in "À celles qui pleurent." This citation also carries the seed of the metaphor traversing Desbordes-Valmore's work that equates weeping with writing.[15] In "À celles qui pleurent," the speaking subject tells of her own "pleurs chantés" and exhorts other women to "écrire aussi vos larmes." Rather than a reductive expression of excessive feminine emotion, tears function in Desbordes-Valmore's work to define women's poetry not as a discourse whose sources lie in the fixed and dusty confines of a book, but as one that is rooted in experience and the material world. They also function to elicit an empathetic reaction by calling forth the tears of her readers. If dominant criticism valued above all the end result of the published poem on the printed page, divorced from the scene and the act of writing, Desbordes-Valmore's poetry would seem to privilege, on the contrary, the moment of emanation. As such, Desbordes-Valmore can be said to write under the sign of expenditure rather than of concentration, the preferred pose of "masculine" poetry.

Just as reader and writer are associated in the act of weeping, reading and writing become reciprocal functions: "Si vous n'avez le temps d'écrire aussi vos larmes, / Laissez-les de vos yeux descendre sur ces vers." While anticipating twentieth-century feminist calls-to-writing from Woolf to Cixous,[16] these lines also present reading as a creative and liberating act. Through the intermediary of the song, the passive act of reading becomes a performance in itself. The imperative of line 9, "Chantez!," gains new meaning when we remember that Desbordes-Valmore intended many of her poems to be set to music. Weeping does not necessarily refer to a solitary lament, but rather to the act of giving voice, an outpouring like singing. Because of her experience as an actress and a singer, the lyric practice of Desbordes-Valmore was perhaps closer to its ancient origins than was that of her contemporaries. In "À celles qui pleurent" as in many other poems, Desbordes-Valmore identifies abundant tears as an aspect of a specifically feminine poetics that relies on the all-pervasive and multivalent image of fluidity.

## A Watery Landscape

The theme of liquidity is as vast as the sea and, as Gaston Bachelard has shown in *L'eau et les rêves,* reverberates in mythology and literature since the beginning of recorded history. While Bachelard's associations to bodies of water are as diverse as narcissism, suicide, and violence, his chapters on femininity and purity are most interesting for the present study. His descriptions of water as a hidden, primeval element evocative of both maternal activities (lactation, rocking) and female sexuality provide cogent philosophical and psychological explanations for the Romantic obsession with the sea.

Of all the watery vistas that dominate the Romantic landscape, there is one in particular that seems to have captured the imagination of its male poets. Charles Hugo's photograph of his father, "Victor Hugo sur un rocher à Jersey, été 1853," represents a scene that, by the middle of the century, had become formulaic: Hugo, in a thoughtful pose, seated high on a cliff, gazes out onto the expanse of water below him. Here again is the Romantic image of the reflective and solitary Poet who contemplates the waters as he would infinity or Woman. Lamartine's "Le lac" provides the most famous version of this posture:

> Ô lac! l'année à peine a fini sa carrière,
> Et près des flots chéris qu'elle devait revoir,
> Regarde! Je viens seul m'asseoir sur cette pierre
> Où tu la vis s'asseoir!

This passive attitude of contemplation from afar—the distantiation and differentiation between the speaking subject atop his rocky perch and the vast, fluid, and incomprehensible object of his gaze—suggests a certain male fascination before the enigmatic and powerful female body, whose force lies, above all, in its fecundity.[17]

The representations of natural waters in Desbordes-Valmore's poetry, however, carry specific meanings that cannot be subsumed under the general category of Romantic imagery. Where is the poet and the woman Desbordes-Valmore in such panoramic images? Bachelard's insistence on a universalizing masculine viewpoint does not account for her. Since the role of the Romantic Poet is forbidden to Desbordes-Valmore, rather than objectifying her own sexuality by assuming his stance, she rejects it. This is a double rejection, both of the conventional value of the Poet (as thinker) and of the passive distancing produced by this posture. On the contrary, Desbordes-Valmore's work is shaped by a poetics of proximity, which she associates with femininity. While retaining liquidity as a metaphor for feminine sexuality, Desbordes-Valmore recasts the metaphor and, in so doing, rewrites the patterns of subject positions offered by Romanticism.[18] Consequently, I believe that she must be defended from the charge of having, with too much credulity, adopted masculine images of femininity. A reading of her "L'eau douce" will demonstrate that, underlying an apparently normative allegorical tale, the poet subtly traces a second, less conventional image of feminine sexuality.

"L'eau douce" would appear to be a direct response to the Romantic scenario sketched above, since it entails an interaction between a male poet and a feminized body of water. In this poem, the subject speaks as a freshwater stream, which struggles in vain to retain its identity after an encounter with the salty sea:

> *L'eau qui a rencontré la*
> *mer ne retrouve jamais sa*
> *première douceur.*
> Un poète persan

Pitié de moi! j'étais l'eau douce;
Un jour j'ai rencontré la mer;
À présent j'ai le goût amer,
Quelque part que le vent me pousse.     4

Ah! qu'il en allait autrement
Quand, légère comme la gaze
Parmi mes bulles de topaze
Je m'agitais joyeusement.                    8

Nul bruit n'accostait une oreille
D'un salut plus délicieux
Que mon cristal mélodieux
Dans sa ruisselante merveille.               12

L'oiseau du ciel, sur moi penché,
M'aimait plus que l'eau du nuage,
Quand mon flot, plein de son image,
Lavait son gosier desséché.                  16

Le poète errant qui me loue
Disait un jour qu'il m'a parlé:
"Tu sembles le rire perlé
D'un enfant qui jase et qui joue.            20

Moi, je suis l'ardent voyageur,
Incliné sur la nappe humide,
Qui te jure, ô ruisseau limpide,
De bénir partout ta fraîcheur."              24

Doux voyageur, si ta mémoire
S'abreuve de mon souvenir
Bénis Dieu d'avoir pu me boire,
Mais défends-moi de revenir.                 28

Mon cristal limpide et sonore
Où s'étalait le cresson vert
Dans les cailloux ne coule encore
Que sourdement, comme l'hiver.               32

L'oiseau dont la soif est trompée
Au nuage a rendu son vol,
Et la plume du rossignol
Dans mon onde n'est plus trempée.            36

Cette onde qui filtrait du ciel
Roulait des clartés sous la mousse . . .
J'étais bien mieux, j'étais l'eau douce,
Et me voici traînant le sel.                 40
                    (*Poésies inédites, OP* 2: 511)

This poem presents two distinct descriptions related temporally as are the two pictures of a before-and-after set. The first quatrain, which rephrases the epigraph in the lyric (that is, first person and poetic) mode, serves to introduce a relationship that can be summarized by this simple proposition: "l'eau douce" meets the sea and is changed for the worse. It gives the broad lines of two opposing self-portraits that the anthropomorphized speaking subject details in the remainder of the poem. The next five quatrains develop the "before" picture, listing stanza-by-stanza the stream's qualities: light and joyous movement (stanza 2), melodious sound (stanza 3) and refreshing waters (stanza 4). The two central quatrains find a rather conventional male Poet praising the stream that he describes as fresh and childlike. After addressing the Poet and warning him of her fall from purity (stanza 7), the last three quatrains finally paint the "after" picture, showing the degradation of each of the qualities detailed above. The drama of the anthropomorphized stream's metamorphosis is mirrored in the abrupt switch of rhyme scheme, until now in *rimes embrassées,* suddenly changing to *rimes croisées* in the seventh and eighth stanzas.

The stream functions as an extended metaphor for female sexuality. The delicious, gurgling water, described in terms of its purity ("limpide" appears twice), encounters the ocean and is left sullied and hardened: "J'étais bien mieux, j'étais l'eau douce, / Et me voici traînant le sel." It is perhaps too easy to read in this poem a story of defloration (which would, curiously, render "la mer" male). If this is the pretext of the poem, the subtext that contradicts it surely lies in the pleasure experienced by "l'eau douce" before her fall. Above all, her delight in movement ("Je m'agitais joyeusement") suggests that this privileged state of innocence encompasses sexual activity. Moreover, she shares her pleasure on two accounts: her song graces the ear of the listener and the birds bathe and drink in her water. This complicitous enjoyment would seem to represent an unproblematic sexuality, which is halted rather than initiated by the confrontation with the sea. In contrast with the stereotype of the chaste Romantic heroine undone (and done in) by her own passions, Desbordes-Valmore presents an unapologetic picture of a robust feminine sexuality. Such a picture, although often presented indirectly, recurs frequently in the poet's work and is nearly always accompanied by the presence of water.

If Desbordes-Valmore's representation of femininity hides behind the veil of normative models, her relationship to her craft appears in an even more problematic light. The central two stanzas on which the poem turns introduce a male poet and describe his relationship with the speaking subject. The Poet is at first relegated to the third-person position, effecting a reversal of the conventional subject-object relation: here "l'eau douce," as speaking subject, controls the flow of words. But if the point of view is new, the roles certainly are not: the Poet's task is to praise the feminized speaking subject ("l'eau douce" is feminine in grammatical gender as well as by the qualities attributed to her), and the stream finds herself, once again, the *object* of this attention. The grammatical reobjectification of the stream is made complete when the Poet speaks within quotation marks, saying "moi" and "je." This poem thus presents a curious *mise-en-abyme* wherein the male Poet is objectified but permitted to praise that which gives him voice. The "je" that speaks without quotation marks is not identified as a poet, but rather as she who holds the power to let the Poet speak. Would not the Poet fall silent without the water, or the woman, to praise?

The contradictions and jumbled subject positions represented in this poem are inherent and unavoidable. We can attribute them both to the incongruity of a female speaking subject in the French poetic tradition and to Desbordes-Valmore's ambivalent, slippery treatment of the female subject who finds herself the object of poetic language after relinquishing the speech act to the Poet. The very uncertainty of this relationship betrays Desbordes-Valmore's uneasy attitude toward the role and the métier of the Poet. Her self-distancing from that role is evidenced by the representation of the Poet as grammatical other to a female speaking subject; her reserve with respect to the métier itself becomes clear when we consider the registers of language in "L'eau douce." For when the Poet speaks in the two central stanzas, his language is more classically poetic than that of the rest of the poem, indeed more so than that of the Desbordes-Valmorian oeuvre generally, as if here she aimed to mimic him. This suggests not that Desbordes-Valmore could not manipulate poetic figures, but rather that she preferred to do so with restraint, opting deliberately to manipulate the melodic and rhythmic, rather than the rhetorical, possibilities of language.

When allowed to speak, the male Poet begins with a simile compounded by the figurative sense of "perlé" (ordinarily a visual or tactile quality made over, by synesthesia, into sound): "Tu sembles le rire *perlé* / D'un enfant qui jase et qui joue." In general, Desbordes-Valmore avoids such densely metaphoric language. In these same lines the alliteration of "qui jase et qui joue" reinforces the onomatopoeic "jaser" to capture the sound of the babbling brook. While sound repetitions play an important part in Desbordes-Valmore's poetry, they tend to function on the level of the word or phrase as in a refrain, rather than through such alliterations as this. Another example of conventional poetic language placed in the mouth of the male Poet, which Desbordes-Valmore herself normally uses sparingly, is the apostrophe: "ô ruisseau limpide." This figure, whose etymological roots lie in the Greek verb meaning "to turn away," normally assumes that the addressee is distant or absent. Let us recall the apostrophe that begins Lamartine's poem ("Ô lac!") and the distancing it implies. But Desbordes-Valmore's preferred form of direct address is the imperative that, in the second person, lends itself to greater immediacy and intimacy than apostrophe, as in the seventh stanza: "Bénis Dieu d'avoir pu me boire, / Mais défends-moi de revenir." Unlike apostrophe, the imperative relies on the presence of the other. Like the imperative, the great number of deictics found in Desbordes-Valmore's poetry contributes to her poetics of presence (here, "cette onde," "me voici"). She captures proximity both grammatically and on the representational level. In "L'eau douce," the speaking subject's days of happy purity are marked by encounters with this Poet-voyager and passing birds who stop to quench their thirst. These interactions, unlike the distance maintained in the conventional Romantic scenario, place the body of water in direct and active contact with other creatures.

But the problem remains of the overwhelmingly harmful contact between "l'eau douce" and the sea, whose salt water recalls the bitter tears of other poems. Although crucial to the narrative of the poem, and a literally central mediator between the two moments (before and after) that the poem captures, this tragic event is cast to its margins. The epigraph of an unknown Persian poet encapsulates the story of the poem, telling of the meeting of stream and sea: "L'eau qui a rencontré la mer ne retrouve jamais sa première douceur." After the first stanza, this encounter receives no further mention: it remains like a hole in the middle of the poem's narrative. Stated but never described in the detail accorded to the other interactions represented by the poem (between stream and bird, stream and Poet), after the second line, the sea disappears, to be indicated only synecdochically by the effects produced by its encounter (for example, "j'ai le goût amer"). The elision of this scene is most apparent in the poem's final reprise where the speaking subject describes her two states, fair and foul, but leaves out the circumstance productive of her change: "J'étais bien mieux, j'étais l'eau douce, / Et me voici traînant le sel."

Although this event of supposedly central importance, both for the chronology of the poem and for the story represented therein, is relegated to the poem's margins, there is another event that takes its place: the poem turns on the encounter with the Poet. This meeting, related in the poem's central stanzas, falls between the description of the pure stream (stanzas 2–4) and that of the polluted stream (stanzas 7–10), effectively usurping the narrative position at first assigned to the encounter with the sea. Let us read in this new narrative the same causal relationship: the encounter with the Poet precipitates—precedes and thus causes—the pollution of the stream who after this meeting is, in the chronology of the poem, irreversibly changed. To rediscover the stream in her state of purity would be to return to the beginning of the poem, before the intrusion of the male Poet. It is he who spoils her, even while preserving the vision of her purity in his poetry. While his work profits from the portrait he draws of her, she is lessened above all in her poetic qualities: movement and sound ("mon cristal mélodieux [. . .] sonore"). Sound is the essence of poetry, and the movement of the stream re-creates its melodic line. By capturing and freezing these very qualities in the images and the language of his poetry, the Poet leaves the stream itself, and the woman it represents, dull, used, and no longer desirable.

Although couched in terms of finality and loss, this poem's ending presents instead an ostensible starting point for poetic endeavor, which becomes a *pis-aller* for pleasure lost. "L'eau douce" concludes by invoking the natural ingredients that else-where Desbordes-Valmore identifies as staples for her poetic artifice: the feather and tears that serve as pen and ink. The bird is the privileged animal in the Desbordes-Valmorian bestiary as much for the writing utensil its plumage provides ("la plume du rossignol") as for its melodic song. And once again tears, salty as sea water ("Et me voici trainant le sel"), double for ink, as in the refrain of "Une plume de femme": "trempée d'encre ou de larmes, courez, ma plume, courez."

"L'eau douce," under the guise of a conventional story of innocence lost, instead ends by telling a very different tale that would seem to valorize unmediated pleasure over the second-ary work of the male Poet who, in his telling, has recourse to his memory alone ("Doux voyageur, si ta mémoire / S'abreuve de mon souvenir [. . .]"). Writing, like memory, assumes the loss of the original scene that finds itself preserved on the page or in one's thoughts. Hence, perhaps, the bitterness, in Desbordes-Valmore's schema, and the bitter tears, of poetic production. Tears mourn the lost presence that is necessarily victim to the writing endeavor. This is the absence—of physical contact, as of the sound of the voice—that Desbordes-Valmore strives to overcome with her poetics of presence, which functions both on the representational level (in the stories told by her poems) and in the play of the signified. At the same time, these tears mark by their written presence that which was lost—the mate-riality of poetic production, the physicality present at the scene of writing—and is forgotten in the dissemination of the printed page. In the image of tears streaming from eyes we hear words emitted by a mouth and see the movement of a hand racing across a page.

I would like to linger, for the time it takes to read one more poem, on the rich and diversified figuration of water in Desbordes-Valmore's poetry. In the flowing and overflowing of water, we glimpse again the inscription of the poet's name—Desbordes, *débordement*—which elsewhere she silences. We have seen a stream, an ocean, and tears falling in abundance. "La jeune fille et le ramier" adds to this collection of flowing liquids the image of the storm, whose violence readily translates an eager and barely concealed sexuality, describing an atmosphere of growing erotic tension as a young woman and a dove wait and watch for a storm to break:

Les rumeurs du jardin disent qu'il va pleuvoir;
Tout tressaille, averti de la prochaine ondée;
Et toi qui ne lis plus, sur ton livre accoudée,
Plains-tu l'absent aimé qui ne pourra te voir?          4

Là-bas, pliant son aile et mouillé sous l'ombrage,
Banni de l'horizon qu'il n'atteint que des yeux,
Appelant sa compagne et regardant les cieux,
Un ramier, comme toi, soupire de l'orage.          8

Laissez pleuvoir, ô cœurs solitaires et doux!
Sous l'orage qui passe il renaît tant de choses.
Le soleil sans la pluie ouvrirait-il les roses?
Amants, vous attendez, de quoi vous plaignez-vous?  12
                    (*Poésies inédites, OP* 2: 510)

Although a storm vocabulary dominates this short poem ("pleu-voir," "l'orage," "la pluie," "l'ondée," "mouillé"), the future tense in line 1 ("il *va* pleuvoir") signals that the rain has not yet come. This is a poem of anticipation, but of a double anticipation. Its title speaks not of expected rains, but rather of two creatures known for their preoccupation with matters of love. The vocabulary of wetness and the mood of expectancy heighten the poem's undercurrent of sexual arousal. Watching for the storm, the young woman and the dove search for their absent mates. This anticipatory stance is at first displaced onto the quivering of the garden: "tout tressaille." The first stanza describes the young woman's disappointment at the absence of her lover; the second evokes the longing of the dove, following its eyes, which scan the horizon for its mate. Line 8 ("un ramier, comme toi, soupire de l'orage") compares these two subjects, who are both occupied with waiting and sighing.

The anticipated storm has now arrived to drench the dove. In the third stanza the speaking subject invokes it, unleashing the torrent and a series of metaphors linking it with sexual activity. Line 10 describes its fecund nature: "Sous l'orage qui passe il renaît tant de choses." Line 11 suggests that such a blossoming results only from the happy union of the (grammatically and symbolically) masculine "soleil" and feminine "pluie." The poem's rhythms reinforce its anticipatory theme and the languorous setting that heightens the expectant mood.

Although this squared piece, composed of twelve alexandrines (12 x 12), presents a symmetrical front, the tendency is for its lines to be unbalanced, such that initial hemistichs read more slowly than the rhyming side of the poem. Five lines (2, 5, 8, 9, and 12) contain commas preceding the caesura; in no instance is a final hemistich marked with such a heavy pause. Consequently, the reader unavoidably lingers on these halting line beginnings whose second measures flow much more rapidly. This device is used in the initial and final lines framing both the second and third stanzas, setting a languid beat for their internal lines. Desbordes-Valmore calls upon the related technique of the internal *contre-rejet,* which Jean Mazaleyrat describes as "un procédé d'*anticipation* de la phrase sur le mètre" (122), as in line 9: "Laissez pleuvoir, ô cœurs / solitaires et doux!" She employs syntactic suspension as a final delaying technique. In the central stanza, the reader waits through three lines and five qualifying phrases (dependent on the participles "pliant," "mouillé," "banni," "appelant," "regardant") before arriving at the subject and the main verb of the sentence: "Un ramier, comme toi, soupire de l'orage."

The play of presence and absence, whose importance for Desbordes-Valmore's poetry I have already noted, necessarily relates to the theme of anticipation: presence of those who wait, absence of those expected. Deictics ("là-bas"), direct address ("et toi"), and present tense of main verbs ("plains-tu l'absent aimé") all conspire to establish the here-and-now. The future tense in line 4 points to the absent one, the source of anticipation ("qui ne pourra te voir"). Such emphasis on the present of waiting would seem to cut off the anticipated future: it is the rain that falls like a dividing wall between these two moments and forestalls reunion plans.

In this present time of pure anticipation, what fills the void of waiting? A vocabulary of communication signals the dominant activity: "dire," "avertir," "plaindre," "appeler," "soupirer." These verbs of speech are conjugated with various subjects, animate and otherwise: "les rumeurs du jardin," "tu," and "un ramier." Curiously, the only human being in this landscape, "tu," is the subject of only the least articulatory of verbs ("plaindre" and "soupirer"), while those verbs that generally carry a message ("dire," "avertir," "appeler") are attributed to the bird and the surrounding environment itself. The animate but nonhuman bird would seem to serve as an intermediary between the young woman and her natural surroundings, sighing with the former but sending messages like the latter. In this reversal of the normal distribution of communicative skills, the "tu" has renounced more than just articulate speech, she has rejected a second communicative activity as well: reading ("Et toi qui ne lis plus, sur ton livre accoudée"). In fact, this casual negligence of the book, which recalls its problematic status elsewhere in Desbordes-Valmore's oeuvre, is countered by the abundant verbal production, articulate or otherwise, of the poem's different characters.

One of Desbordes-Valmore's critics has described this poem as a "petite vignette sentimentale" (*OP* 2: 736). A small poem it certainly is, and a sentimental one as well. But the trivialization inherent in this doubly diminutive characterization does not do the poem's reflections on language justice. Rather than privileging the book, the final resting place for a poem after it has been divorced from its origin in orality, Desbordes-Valmore aims here to capture the immediacy of the voice, of sound even before meaning. Sound itself would not need to rely on words in order to mean. "La jeune fille et le ramier" invests meaning in the most seemingly inarticulate of places: the confused, incoherent noises of nature, "les rumeurs du jardin."

These poems help us to understand Desbordes-Valmore's poetics of effusion and tears as something more than stereotypic feminine excess and emotion. While her style and images are indebted to Romantic conventions and her explicitly female voices answer to certain expectations for conventional femininity, Desbordes-Valmore's work nonetheless stands its ground among the poetry of the dominant tradition. She engages with her contemporaries, responds in her poetry to misogynist criticism, and offers a corpus that speaks to and with women poets and readers. Her poetics of *débordement* relies, as we have seen, on several related elements: the multivalent metaphor of fluidity for both feminine sexuality and women's writing, the investment in proximity and intersubjectivity, the opposition to criticism that assails female production in the name of intellectual elitism, and a stubborn resistance to categorization. While her work is sometimes disingenuous, it is also slippery, ultimately unpredictable, a characteristic that certainly plays a large part in the interest she has exerted on readers of the past two centuries.

In order to respond to accusations that she is guilty of negligence or sloppy composition, I turn now to Desbordes-Valmore's manipulation of the formal aspects of poetry. In her outpouring does she stop to take stock of the constraints of form? Are her style and her poetic choices the arbitrary result of a hurried and spontaneous writing practice, or do they answer to a specific aesthetic agenda?

## Gender and Form

Of all the various aspects that poetry offers for contemplation—rhetorical, thematic, imagistic, subjective—there is no drier or seemingly more disinterested facet than versification. And yet behind each rhyme, meter, and fixed form, as behind all poetic conventions distinguishing poetry from prose, there lies a history of individual poets and readers whose cumulative activity conspires to codify such technical elements. These histories render formal features no more gender neutral than any other aspect of the lyric. If Desbordes-Valmore's relationship to the métier of poet was conditioned by her gender, it is reasonable to assume that her use of the tools of her trade was as well. A study of the formal level of her poetry shows that its shape was quite literally determined by questions of sexual difference.

Desbordes-Valmore's poetry varies widely in meter and stanzaic divisions. She experimented with unusual rhyme schemes, heterometric combinations, and uneven meters.[19] In her final collection, *Poésies inédites,* she collected poems in meters ranging from the two-syllable line to the alexandrine, and everything in between. She is perhaps best known for her use of the hendecasyllable, or eleven-syllable meter, in the poems "Rêve intermittent d'une nuit triste" and "La fileuse et l'enfant." The peculiarity of this unusual meter lies above all in its proximity to the alexandrine. The hendecasyllable, one syllable shorter, disturbs all the possibilities of symmetry and regularity promised by the twelve syllables of the alexandrine (Mallarmé's "cadence nationale").

"Rêve intermittent" (*Poésies inédites, OP* 2: 531–33) is a poem of 112 lines whose length prohibits a thorough analysis here (see appendix), although a few remarks are in order. The poem celebrates Desbordes-Valmore's birthplace near Flanders.

Addressing the landscape directly, the speaking subject describes a lush countryside in nostalgic terms and then claims it as the final resting place for her daughter. In a note to the 1886 Lemerre edition the poet's son, Hippolyte Valmore, provided a rather mythical account of its composition, contending that Desbordes-Valmore wrote the poem in 1846 while her daughter Inès lay on her deathbed. Desbordes-Valmore, supposedly overcome herself by fever and fatigue after many sleepless nights of attending to Inès, threw herself on a sofa and spontaneously composed the poem. Hippolyte writes:

> Des vers d'une mesure insolite se forment comme d'eux-mêmes en cet esprit qui veille dans le corps endormi, et reproduisent, en la précisant, la création du rêve. La volonté n'est certes là pour rien. Si le poète avait eu conscience de ce qui se passait autour de lui, sous l'empire des tortures éprouvées, il n'eût pas écrit ou bien, sans être beaucoup plus maître de lui, il eût cherché à donner la mesure et la rime aux tristes pensées, aux effrois qui secouaient si brutalement son cœur. [. . .] Mais n'est-il pas à croire que dans ce moment de prostration complète, la pauvre femme ne s'appartenait pas et n'était plus là qu'un instrument. (*OP* 2: 745)

This account offers a poor explanation for why Ondine, Desbordes-Valmore's first daughter (who lived until 1853) appears in the poem rather than Inès. More startling still is how closely Hippolyte's scenario concurs with his mother's pretense of having no responsibility for her own poetic production (evident in "Une plume de femme"). The obvious care of composition which "Rêve intermittent" exhibits defies the claim of a spontaneous emanation. In response to Hippolyte's account, Planté queries: "Quelle étrange distraction de lecture, ou quelle très idéologique et obstinée volonté de ne voir dans la poésie d'une femme que les forces obscures parlant par la bouche de la sibylle ont-elles pu faire ranger ces vers du côté du spontané, du naturel, du refus de la forme, et y dénier la part de travail du langage?" ("L'art sans art" 167–68).

The poem begins: "Ô champs paternels hérissés de charmilles / Où glissent le soir des flots de jeunes filles!" The first half of "Rêve intermittent" continues with this paternal lexicon, apostrophizing the "patrie absente" and evoking three times a "père" both human and divine. Moreover, it is peopled with authoritative

and masculine characters: "Le bourreau m'étreint: je l'aime!
et l'aime encore, / Car il est mon frère, ô père que j'adore"
(lines 37–38). And even its landscape, if less threatening, is
dominated by imperious figures: "Antiques noyers, vrais maîtres
de ces lieux" (43). But halfway through the poem this field of
reference shifts and with it, the gender of the homeland:

> Je vous enverrai ma vive et blonde enfant
> Qui rit quand elle a ses longs cheveux au vent.
>
> Parmi les enfants nés à votre mamelle,
> Vous n'en avez pas qui soit si charmant qu'elle!
> . . . . . . . . . . . . . . . . . . . . . . . . . . . . . . . . .
> Ce fruit de mon âme, à cultiver si doux,
> S'il faut le céder, ce ne sera qu'à vous!
>
> Du lait qui vous vient d'une source divine
> Gonflez le cœur pur de cette frêle ondine.
>
> Le lait jaillissant d'un sol vierge et fleuri
> Lui paîra le mien qui fut triste et tari.
>
> (lines 51–54, 59–64)

In this section her once-masculine landscape is now endowed
with feminine forms ("votre mamelle"), biological functions
(lactation: "[le] lait qui vous vient") and attributes ("vierge").
It is, moreover, peopled nearly exclusively by feminine figures.
In addition to the female speaking subject and her daughter,
"ma blonde enfant," Albertine (a childhood friend of Desbordes-
Valmore) appears, as well as "la Madone." Gone are the references to fathers and brothers of the poem's first half. The
privileged relationship in this second part is one between mother
and daughter: the *patrie* has become a motherland for whom
both the speaking subject and her daughter are children.[20] The
veiled menaces of the first half disappear, and the birthplace
becomes a metaphor for nurturing: "Quand je la berçais, doux
poids de mes genoux, / Mon chant, mes baisers, tout lui parlait
de vous" (lines 107–08).

Although the poem is written in rhymed couplets, Desbordes-
Valmore breaks up the continuity that they might suggest with
blank lines, thus rendering "Rêve intermittent" a stanzaic poem.
By opting for a series of discrete couplets rather than un-

broken, nonstanzaic *rimes plates* (typical of Romantic poetry), she avoids the association of narrativity that the nonstanzaic poem holds. "Rêve intermittent," like the dream that it names, does not tell a coherent story, but rather offers a series of vivid images. Similarly the meter, which Desbordes-Valmore consistently breaks into uneven measures of five, followed by six, syllables, works against the effect of continuity and regularity produced by the alexandrine's steady rhythm of six. But the airy spacing of the poem and the slight irregularity of its meter, more than simply reinforcing the hazy landscape of a dream, make an important statement about Desbordes-Valmore's poetic viewpoint. The feminine half of "Rêve intermittent" offers reflections about poetic language that summarize many of the qualities of the poems discussed above. For example, this couplet recalls the language and images of "L'eau douce": "Que vos ruisseaux clairs, dont les bruits m'ont parlé, / Humectent sa voix d'un long rythme perlé!" (83–84). The fluid metaphor for poetic language, the privileging of the voice as source of poetry, and the meaning invested in nonhuman natural elements all take part in the poetic practice upon which Desbordes-Valmore relies. The "long rythme perlé" is perhaps the hendecasyllable itself, which, like the pearl, is a gem formed of an irregularity.

The poem further reflects on rhythm and meter:

> Sans piquer son front, vos abeilles là-bas
> L'instruiront, rêveuse, à mesurer ses pas;
>
> Car l'insecte armé d'une sourde cymbale
> Donne à la pensée une césure égale.
>
> (99–102)

Desbordes-Valmore's insistence on (bucolic rather than scholastic) instruction encourages one to read this poem as a kind of *art poétique*. The "vous" in question is still the motherland, and the pronoun "la" refers to "ma blonde enfant" who is the recipient of the instruction. Just as the preceding couplet (83–84) calls on the maternal landscape to prepare the daughter's voice for singing with her stream, here too another element of that landscape, its bees, will teach her to write in verse, "à mesurer ses pas." The following couplet contains another phrase

that, like this one, suggests rhythmic regularity: "une césure
égale." But the regularity Desbordes-Valmore had in mind is
not of the sort championed by the seventeenth-century poet
Nicolas Boileau-Despréaux, who writes: "Ayez pour la cadence
une oreille severe. / Que toûjours dans vos vers, le sens coupant
les mots, / Suspende l'hemistiche, en marque le repos" (*Art
poétique* 159).

The *Art poétique* (1674) of this self-styled "législateur du
Parnasse" became a handbook of classical poetics whose tenets
Desbordes-Valmore was among the first to oppose. The regularity of her hendecasyllables, consistently tailored in measures
of five and six, is tempered by the irregularity of that meter,
and she respects the caesura with more subtlety ("d'une sourde
cymbale") than does the sharply marked military cadence of
Boileau's classical alexandrines. Likewise, while Boileau vaunts
clear and seasoned thought over obscure reasoning ("Selon que
nostre idée est plus ou moins obscure, / L'expression la suit,
ou moins nette, ou plus pure" [160]), Desbordes-Valmore rejects the classical model of clarity in favor of the thoughts of a
child who is characterized as "rêveuse." As if he were writing
so that Desbordes-Valmore could contradict him nearly 175
years later, Boileau includes these lines that seem to be addressed
directly to her:

> J'aime mieux un ruisseau, qui sur la molle arene,
> Dans un pré plein de fleurs lentement se promene,
> Qu'*un torrent débordé* qui d'un cours orageux
> Roule plein de gravier sur un terrain fangeux.
> (161; emphasis mine)

Desbordes-Valmore's poetry, marked by irregularity, flooded
by torrents, exhibits a preference for variety and change over
order. Consequently, she deserves a place among the canonized
Romantics who strove to unhinge the rigid poetics represented
by Boileau's classicism. That she chose the eleven-syllable meter
with which to mark her differences with the rigidity of classical poetics is not surprising, and by associating her *ars poetica*
with a feminine universe and addressing its lessons to a female
heir, she places both her poetic practice and this meter under
the sign of femininity. As we shall see, her reawakening of the
hendecasyllable, which had lain dormant since the Middle Ages,

would later have a significant impact on the poetry of Verlaine, who seized upon it as the meter of sexual alterity in his homo-erotic poetry.

As she preferred to avoid predictable meters, Desbordes-Valmore eschewed fixed forms, in particular the sonnet, which she identified as a masculine genre: "Mon avis est [. . .] que ce genre régulier n'appartient qu'à l'homme, qui se fait une joie de triompher de sa pensée même en l'enfermant dans cette entrave brillante."[21] While Romantic poets (with the obvious exception of Charles Sainte-Beuve) generally ignored the sonnet, let us note that Louise Ackermann did also, setting out her reasons for avoiding it quite explicitly, in language similar to Desbordes-Valmore's:

> Pour des sonnets en fasse qui les aime;
> Chacun son goût, mais ce n'est pas le mien.
> Un bon, dit-on, vaut seul un long poème;
> Heureux qui peut en amener à bien.        4
> Mon vers, hélas! a l'humeur vagabonde;
> Ne lui parlez d'entraves seulement.
> Un peu de rime, encor Dieu sait comment!
> S'il peut souffrir, c'est tout le bout du monde.   8
> Ruisseau furtif, je le laisse courir
> Parmi les prés, le livrant à sa pente;
> Il saute, il fuit, il gazouille, il serpente,
> Chemin faisant il voit ses bords fleurir.      12
> Qu'un voyageur parfois s'y désaltère,
> Et d'un merci le salue en partant,
> Ou ses attraits qu'une jeune bergère
> Vienne y mirer, c'est un ruisseau content.    16
> ("Pensées diverses" V, *Contes et poésies* 226–27)

Like Desbordes-Valmore, Ackermann describes the sonnet as an "entrave," an obstacle or constraint that both poets counter with fluid metaphors. While this metaphor appears more consistent with the entirety of Desbordes-Valmore's oeuvre than with that of Ackermann, both poets clearly identify the sonnet with a classical and masculine poetics.

Baudelaire, on the contrary, found in its very constraints the beauty of the form: "Parce que la forme est contraignante, l'idée jaillit plus intense" (*Correspondance* 1: 676). And similarly associating the form with difficulty born of constraint, one condescending critic wrote of Desbordes-Valmore that "le sonnet pour elle [était] trop difficile" (qtd. in Planté, "L'art sans art" 168). But there is certainly more to her refusal of the form than flight before the intellectual problems posed by the imperative to reconcile quatrains and tercets, or the technical difficulty of constructing a tightly knit rhyme scheme. In the quotation above she makes an association between the gendered sonnet and the masculine propensity to tinker with intricate objects. If we look to the history of the sonnet in France, we find that Desbordes-Valmore had obvious reasons for repudiating a form dominated by a masculine tradition. Introduced from Italy in the first half of the sixteenth century, the sonnet came bearing Petrarchan conventions that, in the image of Laura, locked the female beloved in a specularized and objectified position. No fixed form was more bound by tradition and therefore more antithetical to the quest for feminine subjectivity in poetry. In particular, the conventions of the sonnet run counter to Desbordes-Valmore's approach to the love lyric, wherein she attempts to evoke proximity between lover and beloved and prefers spoken diction to the lofty eloquence of conventional poetic language. That Louise Labé succeeded in writing a unique and highly subjective series of feminine sonnets in spite of the constraints of tradition is an admirable achievement.[22] That Desbordes-Valmore declined to enter the fray, with the following exception, suggests her sensitivity to an exclusive tradition.

Her more than 650 poems include only one sonnet that has been definitively attributed to her, entitled "Au livre des Consolations par M. Sainte-Beuve":

> Quand je touche rêveuse à ces feuilles sonores
> D'où montent les parfums des divines amphores,
> Prise par tout mon corps d'un long tressaillement,
> Je m'incline, et j'écoute avec saisissement.    4
>
> Ô fièvre poétique! ô sainte maladie!
> Ô jeunesse éternelle! ô vaste mélodie!
> Voix limpide et profonde! invisible instrument!
> Nid d'abeille enfermé dans un livre charmant!    8
>
> Trésor tombé des mains du meilleur de mes frères!
> Doux Memnon! chaste ami de mes tendres misères,
> Chantez, nourrissez-moi d'impérissable miel:

Car je suis indigente à me nourrir moi-même;    12
Source fraîche, ouvrez-vous à ma douleur suprême,
Et m'aidez, par ce monde, à retrouver mon ciel![23]
*(Bouquets et prières, OP* 2: 452)

The rhyme scheme of this sonnet, whose quatrains progress by couplets, is hardly usual for the normally more intricate form of repeated *rimes embrassées.* But this irregular and rather prosaic scheme betrays the poem's primitive form, which manuscripts show to be a twelve-line piece of three quatrains (like "La jeune fille et le ramier") in *rimes plates.* Desbordes-Valmore surely chose to rework it into a sonnet as an homage to Sainte-Beuve, one of the first nineteenth-century proponents of the form that had fallen out of favor since the sixteenth century, and whose *Consolations* (1830) contains several examples. Thus while publicly paying her respect to the man and the form he helped renew, Desbordes-Valmore privately questions its validity for a woman writer.

Even without her avowed disinclination for the form, there would be reason to question the sincerity of Desbordes-Valmore's sonnet, given its contradictions with the rest of her poetry. While she offers this poem in praise to a book, we have established that elsewhere she treats books rather lightly, and seems to question whether the printed and published page is indeed the poet's highest aspiration. Needless to say, this is an attitude that the financially vulnerable Desbordes-Valmore would have taken pains to conceal from the literary critic Sainte-Beuve, a man who made his living by pronouncing judgments on books and who helped assure her livelihood through his favorable reviews.[24]

Certain uncharacteristic rhetorical flourishes, such as the string of apostrophes in the second quatrain, would also indicate this to be a poem more conventional than sincere. In a none-too-successful attempt to adopt an exalted tone that was not her own, Desbordes-Valmore made, it would seem, some unintentional gaffes that rather work to condemn than praise the poet and his sonnets. By the principle of equivalence, the second measure of line 5, "ô sainte maladie," casts a dubious shadow on the name Sainte-Beuve, likening it to illness. And the formula in line 9, "trésor tombé des mains," hardly attests to an appreciation for a work allowed to tumble so carelessly to the ground. Indeed, while ostensibly praising *Les consolations,* this poem, like "À celles qui pleurent," describes the book as a place of confinement: "Nid d'abeille *enfermé* dans un livre charmant." Finally, although calling on Sainte-Beuve's work as a source of guidance and inspiration, Desbordes-Valmore never again employed its most privileged form, the sonnet.

Desbordes-Valmore's prosodic choices reveal as much as her preferred metaphors about her relation to the lyric and to the context in which she wrote. While she shaped her poetry in the face of specific cultural obstacles, numerous traces of discontent underlie her apparent conformity to expectations. I end this chapter with a discussion of the sonnet because this form, rejected by Romantics and women Romantics in particular, would become a mainstay for the following generation of poets. The Parnassians exploited the sonnet in the context of a poetics of constraint and objectivity, which they perceived as uniquely masculine. In turning to a critique of Parnassian poetic ideology, I shall also demonstrate that vacillation and floating subject positions are not the specific domain of women poets such as Desbordes-Valmore. Even the "descriptive" verse of the Parnassians reveals uncertainty and contradictions. Could one expect any less complexity from a genre devoted to representing a concept as unsettled and unsettling as the "I"?

# Part 2
# Parnassian Impassivity and Frozen Femininity

*Je hais le mouvement qui déplace les lignes.*
Charles Baudelaire
"La beauté"

*Parfois une Vénus, de notre sol barbare,*
*Jaillit, marbre divin, des siècles respecté,*
*Pur, comme s'il sortait, dans sa jeune beauté,*
*De vos veines de neige, ô Paros! ô Carrare!*
Théophile Gautier
"Parfois une Vénus . . ."

# Introduction

Although Baudelaire is more often considered a precursor of Symbolism than a proponent of neoclassicism, he became Parnassian in name the year before his death by contributing sixteen poems to the 1866 volume of *Le Parnasse contemporain*.[1] And his insistence that "Je hais le mouvement qui déplace les lignes" ("La beauté" [1: 21]) is strikingly Parnassian. This line and the sonnet containing it exemplify classical formalism, an appreciation of symmetry, and the representation of beauty as unyielding and motionless ("comme un rêve de pièrre"). While in chapter 6, I will explore the various and sometimes contradictory strands of Baudelaire's complex poetic corpus, for now I call upon him as commentator of a movement to which he did not actively ascribe.

In the pages to follow, I examine the aesthetic and ideological underpinnings of Parnassianism. This least-studied and most reactive of nineteenth-century poetic tendencies was characterized by rigid formalism and objective description. Théophile Gautier, Charles de Leconte de Lisle, Théodore de Banville, and José-Maria de Heredia number among the more prominent poets associated with this neoclassical movement, although nearly a hundred others published in its journals. Like Baudelaire, Mallarmé and Verlaine contributed to Parnassian publications. While rarely named in the context of this poetic tendency, they engaged, if only for a limited time, with its discourse and style.

A repudiation of movement, or poetic fluidity, in favor of a rigid model lies at the heart of Parnassianism, as does a repudiation of the "movement" called Romanticism. Associated with such unseemly manipulations as the disappearance of the caesura in trimeter alexandrines, hardy enjambments, and other trespasses of classical prosody, Romanticism would become the foil against which Parnassians defined their own poetic stance.

While opinions to this day are divided between a view of the Parnasse as a continuation of Romanticism and as a reaction against it,[2] I interpret Parnassianism as a rejection of Romanticism's perceived femininity and an attempt to reclaim poetry as a masculine domain. Consequently, I shall demonstrate that criteria for the new aesthetic such as objectivity, compositional and intellectual rigor, antiutilitarianism, and concision were championed, tacitly, as masculine values. My analysis will point to a direct link between, on the one hand, Parnassian poetics of immobility and permanence and, on the other, a conservative ideology striving to contain femininity.

Spanning the century's third quarter, Parnassianism interrupted the liberatory aesthetics that defined so much of French poetry from the Romantics to the Symbolists and Decadents. It is not by chance that this intellectually elite poetic tendency followed shortly after the tumultuous and disillusioning revolution of 1848, which, according to Richard Terdiman, "[rigidified] the separation of elite and popular culture" ("Class" 707). It also coincided with the Second Empire (1852–70), an era of censorship and repression. This regime was particularly unfriendly to literary daring, as exemplified by the 1857 trials of *Madame Bovary* and *Les fleurs du Mal*.[3] While not actively supportive of Napoléon III, Parnassian poets were certainly guilty of passive acceptance and retreat. Accordingly, they culled both their political and poetical values from the past and disdained provocative, visionary, or innovative poetry. Although the Parnassians cloaked their political agenda in the mantle of apolitical indifference, in fact they stood in consistent and conscious opposition to the poetry of social commitment championed most energetically by Desbordes-Valmore and Hugo.[4] They similarly refused to engage in politics, unlike their Romantic predecessors Chateaubriand, Lamartine, and, once again, Hugo. While the ramifications of this apolitical stance are vast, I will consider in particular the implications for sexual politics that lie embedded in Parnassian aesthetics. This will entail an analysis of the textual representation of femininity, of the gendered conception of form, and of the place of women—largely overlooked—in the movement.

If the Romantics admitted symbolic femininity in an oblique or recuperative manner and accepted female poets within limits, the values projecting the Parnassian clan forward constituted quite a different matter. The muscular conception of the poetic act, coupled with the banishment of affect that characterized their writings, was particularly uninviting to women poets. Heretofore, women's only lyrical outlet appeared in the sentimental and subjective guise of Romanticism. Indeed, more so than surrounding poetic movements of the nineteenth century, Parnassian representations relegated woman to the role of frozen object, a passive and impassive incarnation of idealized beauty, forbidding her subjective expression more stringently than before.

Let us recall that although the Parnassians named themselves after the poetry review *Le Parnasse contemporain: Recueil de vers nouveaux* (1866–76), traces of Parnassian aesthetics emerged well before the appearance of this review. The poetic principles associated with Parnassianism date back, in fact, to the tumultuous midcentury. The year 1852 was a key one for those who would come to be central players among the nearly one hundred poets represented in the *Parnasse contemporain*. During this first year of the Second Empire, Gautier published his collection *Émaux et camées,* whose poems stand as manifestos and exemplars of the Parnassian cult of formal perfection. This date also marked the appearance of Leconte de Lisle's *Poèmes antiques,* which attest to the author's fascination with ancient history and poetics.

The poets who would later call themselves Parnassians were initially derided as "Formistes," "Stylistes," and "Impassibles," labels they considered recuperating as their own. Poetry journals prior to the *Parnasse contemporain,* including *L'artiste* (edited by Gautier from 1857 to 1858 and by Arsène Houssaye thereafter), *La revue fantaisiste* (1861, edited by Catulle Mendès), and Louis-Xavier de Ricard's two publications, *Revue du progrès* (1863–64) and *L'art* (1865–66), championed the cult of beauty and the return to classicism, publishing works by those poets who would later appear in the *Parnasse contemporain.*[5] While only three volumes were published, between 1866 and 1876,[6] they effectively named and capped the poetic movement that dominated the nineteenth century's third quarter.

The review's publisher, Alphonse Lemerre (1838–1912), deserves as much credit as its poets for the consolidation of Parnassianism. In his *Petits mémoires d'un parnassien,* Ricard reveals that Lemerre "rêvait une gloire [. . .] personnelle," which was to affix "son nom à une édition, si possible définitive, des poètes de la Pléiade" (50). The young Lemerre created not only a forum for objective poetry, but also a meeting place for its poets. His bookstore in the passage Choiseul became known as the "Entresol du Parnasse," thanks to a poem bearing this title by Gabriel Marc, which enumerates the "chercheurs d'astres et d'infinis" who congregated there.[7] Those named by Marc constituted an entirely masculine coterie, as did the three editorial committees responsible for choosing the participants for each issue.[8]

Nor must the importance of salons and public gatherings in the development of the group be under-emphasized, since social relations among poets clearly helped determine literary affinities. Women were often excluded from this predominantly male poetic community. Leconte de Lisle presided as a patriarch over his Saturday evenings and Sunday mornings, which were called the "salon mâle" in their early days. While women eventually infiltrated these and other reunions ("avec le succès arrivèrent les dames, avec les dames la déchéance" [Calmettes 307]), their role was largely circumscribed to that of frivolous parasite: "les femmes riches qui s'ennuient ont besoin d'un joli jouet. [. . .] elles s'abattent sur le génie. Proie facile" (Calmettes 307).

Thanks to Mendès, there existed as well a "salon femelle" attended by women including, undoubtedly, the writer Judith Gautier, his spouse and the daughter of Théophile. Women also fulfilled the function of hostess. Ricard's mother, la Marquise de Ricard, invited poets from 1865 to 1868, and Nina de Villard's salon flourished as a Parnassian meeting place for young poets interested in this new poetic stance from 1868 until her exile following the Commune. But apart from the involvement of these women as hosts, the Parnassian community remained largely homosocial.[9]

A review of the poetry and critical writing of Parnassian adherents points to a strict relationship between the defense of masculinity, on one hand, and the cult of beauty, anti-utilitarianism, formal immobility, and objectivity, on the other. In the following two chapters, I consider Leconte de Lisle as a case study and then broaden the scope of my analysis to follow the avenues of Parnassian thought in poetry by his contemporaries. In keeping with my desire to listen to the voices of women poets, I devote chapter 5 to the *Parnassiennes,* surveying their poetic attempts at both assimilation to and critique of Parnassian doctrine.

# Chapter Three

# Leconte de Lisle's Hardening Arteries

Charles de Leconte de Lisle (1818–94), the Parnassians' most distinguished and impassible elder, was a Creole (one of European descent born in the colonies) from the Île Bourbon (now de la Réunion). In his article on Leconte de Lisle, Baudelaire calls the Creoles "des âmes de femmes" who have nothing original to contribute to French poetry.[1] Attributing to them the characteristics of fragility, physical delicacy, languor, kindness, and a natural faculty of imitation, Baudelaire appears to suggest that Creoles, regardless of their sex, make wonderful women but bad poets. In a rhetorical move characteristic of Baudelaire's love for antithesis, he then calls Leconte de Lisle "la première et l'unique exception" (2: 176) and describes him in this way: "Un front puissant, une tête ample et large, des yeux clairs et froids, fournissent tout d'abord l'image de la force" (2: 176). Baudelaire's interest in physiognomy was not peculiar to him; indeed, several of his contemporaries described Leconte de Lisle's physical features using a vocabulary also descriptive of his aesthetics of power, clarity, and coldness. Here is Mendès's portrait of Leconte de Lisle: "[Sa] tête est un rêve de statuaire; la face, au large front, domine; les yeux percent au loin; la lèvre, un peu mince, se plisse avec le dédain bienveillant qu'explique et qu'autorise la conscience de la force" (*Figurines* 24). Like Mendès, Adolphe Racot likens Leconte de Lisle to a statue, writing that "L'homme est de marbre" (*Portraits-cartes* 49).

This imposing and manly figure, "le chef du Parnasse" (according to Maurice Souriau), would preside over a poetic tendency whose privileged metaphor was statuary. His first collections—*Poèmes antiques* (1852), *Poèmes et poésies* (1855),[2] and *Poèmes barbares* (1862)—prepared the terrain for younger poets who would emulate the impeccable composition

and detachment of Leconte de Lisle's poetry. No less important for the elaboration of his aesthetic stance were the prefaces to his first two collections and a series of articles published
in *Le nain jaune* entitled *Les poètes contemporains* (1864).
These prefaces and articles consolidated his role as Parnassian
leader and announced a poetic agenda that was later associated with the Parnassians as a group.

## Crystallized Criticism

In the preface to the *Poèmes antiques,* Leconte de Lisle set forth,
with characteristic pessimism and defensiveness, poetic values countering all that had come to be associated with Romanticism. With equally characteristic precision and rigidity, he
chisels an aesthetic program that includes the following fac-
ets: the importance of intellectual and formal rigor, the privileging of the past (its tradition, its poetic forms) over the present
(the ephemerality of current events, politics, passions, and poetic
fads), and the cultivation of an impersonal and neutral subject
position. Leconte de Lisle elaborates upon his preference for
"neutral" poetry and defends his "retour réfléchi à des formes
négligées ou peu connues" (*Articles* 108). The adjective "réfléchi" signals a critique of Romantic effusion and sentimentality, for here Leconte de Lisle explains his return to ancient forms
and standards by opposing them to qualities that define Romantic
poetry. Thus, "l'impersonnalité et la neutralité de [s]es études"
(109) counter the "émotions personnelles" (108) and "les passions politiques" (109) of the "modern" (Romantic) poetry that
he so abhors. Leconte de Lisle betrays his erudite bias with the
word "étude," which suggests poetry is an intellectual and not
evocative practice. His call for reasoned reflection and formal
perfection ("de[s] formes plus nettes et plus précises" [110])
implies the thoughtless inspiration with which he characterizes
Romanticism. He writes against "la vie instinctive, spontanée,
aveuglément féconde de la jeunesse" and against the association of poetry with "les vertus sociales" (110). For Leconte de
Lisle, Romantic poetry is the expression of "de mesquines
impressions personnelles, envahie par les néologismes arbi-
traires, morcelée et profanée, esclave des caprices et des goûts
individuels" (110). He proposes instead a learned, authoritative

approach to poetic production, looking toward a "génération savante" (110) that will raise poetic art to the realm of a science.

When Leconte de Lisle published his *Poèmes antiques,* he offered the poetry-reading public a collection clearly in opposition to the prevailing current. But then his relation to this population was consistently combative, given his outspoken contempt for the common reader and facile poetry. Leconte de Lisle's intellectual arrogance was one of his trademarks, and his unpopularity and proud disdain provide a leitmotif in his prose writings as in criticism of him, both positive and negative. This passage exemplifies Leconte de Lisle's antidemocratic intellectualism:

> L'Art, dont la Poésie est l'expression éclatante, intense et complète, est un luxe intellectuel accessible à de très rares esprits.
> Toute multitude, inculte ou lettrée, professe, on le sait, une passion sans frein pour la chimère inepte et envieuse de l'égalité absolue. Elle nie volontiers ou elle insulte ce qu'elle ne saurait posséder. De ce vice naturel de compréhensivité découle l'horreur instinctive qu'elle éprouve pour l'Art. (*Articles* 156–57)

Baudelaire concurred with such elitism, and his essay on Leconte de Lisle indicates an equal contempt for the French reading public. Moreover, it points to their shared belief in the incompatibility of popularity and poetic greatness.

> Le caractère distinctif de sa poésie est un sentiment d'aristocratie intellectuelle, qui suffirait, à lui seul, pour expliquer l'impopularité de l'auteur, si, d'un autre côté, nous ne savions pas que l'impopularité, en France, s'attache à tout ce qui tend vers n'importe quel genre de perfection. [. . .] [*Leconte de Lisle*] *s'élève bien au-dessus de ces mélancoliques de salon, de ces fabricants d'albums et de keepsakes où tout, philosophie et poésie, est ajusté au sentiment des demoiselles.*[3]

With this reference to those writing for "les demoiselles," Baudelaire implicitly attributes popular acclaim to a female audience. Like Leconte de Lisle, he repudiated women readers, assuming that heedfulness of feminine tastes necessarily en-feebled poetry: "Ce n'est pas pour mes femmes, mes filles ou mes sœurs que ce livre [*Les fleurs du Mal*] a été écrit" (*Œuvres complètes* 1: 181). We can conclude that both poets aimed not only to overturn poetic values, but also to reserve poetry as a genre addressed to an elite, male audience. Leconte de Lisle's poetry was as *mâle* as his salon, and his intended readers re-sembled his habitués, intellectual male poets such as himself. This, of course, represented an about-face from Lamartine's cultivation of a female readership and encouragement of women poets. In the context of his study on poetry in the industrial age, Walter Benjamin makes a case for the superfluity of the poet beginning with Baudelaire, stating that "les circonstances sont devenues plus défavorables au succès de la poésie lyrique" (*Baudelaire* 150). One might also say, conversely, that the cli-mate for an inclusive audience had become increasingly inhos-pitable, and that the alienation of the modern Poet was in many senses a self-sought isolation.

In his preface to *Poèmes et poésies*, Leconte de Lisle de-fends himself against criticism of the earlier *Poèmes antiques*. This preface, like the earlier one, is notable for its beleaguered tone and the author's stubborn pride in standing firm against criticism, which he describes as the lot of a poet devoted to artistic perfection and the cult of beauty. Claiming that "je hais mon temps" (*Articles* 127), Leconte de Lisle rails against in-dustrial progress, bourgeois capitalism, and the mass market, which, he contends, lower the value and therefore the quality of poetry. Benjamin's critique of "the inhospitable, blinding age of big-scale industrialism" (*Illuminations* 157) echoes Leconte de Lisle's lament of the incompatibility of poetry and progress: "[l']alliance monstrueuse de la poésie et de l'industrie" (127).

Here he elaborates upon his preference for the past and the value that antiquity holds for the arts. Calling for a renewal of the epic, which he believes has lost its currency with the dete-rioration of modern poetry, he touches once again on contem-porary weakness and intellectual inferiority. Epics, "nobles récits qui se déroulaient à travers la vie d'un peuple, qui exprimaient son génie, sa destinée humaine et son idéal religieux" (134), are to be cultivated. And although Leconte de Lisle himself exploits this genre in the *Poèmes antiques,* he is pessimistic that it will regain its prominence during his day. The conditions necessary for the revitalization of the epic are telling: he believes that it is possible "que l'épopée renaisse un jour de la reconstitution et du choc héroïque des nationalités oppressives et opprimées" (135). This is an uncharacteristic statement, inconsistent for suggesting that good, true poetry can spring from social movements or the movement of societies. At the same time it is highly characteristic in its association of quality poetry with traditionally masculine values, such as armed combat and heroism.

A common theme links together the various strands of Leconte de Lisle's preface, associating all that is durable, time-tested, difficult, tempered, and aristocratic. Permanence and restraint counter the frivolity of the new and the passions of the day. This poetic confrontation pits objective erudition against spontaneity, restraint against effusion, exterior description against subjective feeling, the conservation of traditional poetic forms against the prosodic rule-bending that began with Romanticism. In his prefatory remarks, Leconte de Lisle implicitly conceives of the former as masculine values, the latter as feminine and constitutive of weak poetry.

We can draw some important conclusions regarding the status of lyric poetry at the midcentury from these prefaces. One involves the identity of the Poet, under Romanticism a benevolent and heroic intercessor between the reader and a higher insight. The construction of the Poet as Romantic hero underwent modification with the proto-Parnassians. While maintaining his prodigiousness, this figure appeared now as the austere and aristocratic predecessor to the Poet of *poésie pure.* Because of his intolerance for a mass readership, Leconte de Lisle (like Baudelaire and Mallarmé) disdained the humanitarianism and didacticism evident in some Romantic works. The belief in imagination, divine insight, or inspiration attributable to a Muse was replaced by a work ethic that elevated erudition and science above the human emotions. Verlaine points to Baudelaire as the one who first freed the Poet from his dependency on the trope of inspiration: "le poète [a été] trop longtemps réduit, par d'absurdes préjugés, à ce rôle humiliant d'un instrument au service de la *Muse*" (*Œuvres en prose* 606). Baudelaire himself writes of the necessity of regular work as a means of overcoming passivity and depression: "Pour guérir de tout, de la misère, de la maladie et de la mélancolie, il ne manque absolument que le *Goût du Travail*" (*Œuvres complètes* 1: 669).

This reconsideration of the Poet's role nonetheless left intact his solitary stance. Before isolated as a priest or seer, now the Poet's exceptionality sprang from his elite intellect. Formerly the Poet of election, the Parnassian Poet was now cursed, misunderstood, unappreciated by the vulgar and uneducated. The aesthetics of the Parnasse were consequently more pessimistic than even the melancholic strain of Romanticism. An actively bitter defensiveness had replaced the passive depression of a Lamartine, just as the ivory tower of elitism had become the Poet's refuge when once he wandered, like Hugo, among the people.

A second and more profound consequence of Leconte de Lisle's shift involves the abandonment of subjective for objective poetry, in essence the abandonment of lyricism itself. This went beyond a simple critique of "le moi haïssable" and excessive "émotions personnelles," in fact replacing the exploration of interiority with the descriptive study of exteriors. Baudelaire and Gautier, among other allies of the Parnassian clan, also endorsed this impersonal stance, although none to the degree of Leconte de Lisle. Baudelaire, for example, admired Gautier's "regard sur le *non-moi*" (*Œuvres complètes* 2: 107). And Leconte de Lisle states that "seul est *un vrai poète* qui donne à ses créations la diversité multiple de la vie, et *devient,* selon qu'il le veut, *une Force impersonnelle*" (*Articles* 182; emphasis mine). While Leconte de Lisle claims not to condemn "l'art individuel [et] la poésie intime et cordiale," his insistence on neutrality underlines his distaste for Romantic self-absorption: "Le romantisme [. . .] était surtout *égotiste*" (Huret 284). The quest for impersonality thus presents a dramatic first step toward the separation of the Poet and the speaking subject. The self-conscious opacity of the lyric "I" is often taken as the hallmark of modern poetry. And yet this stance, in descriptive poetry, shares the same illusions of realist fiction; that is, a pretense of neutrality and the repression of the self.

How then does gender come to play in these modulations? Above all in the perception that the Romantics cultivated an effusive, feminine subjectivity, thus demeaning the nobility of a restrained and masculine poetic voice. While Leconte de Lisle's defense of masculinity is only implied in his prefaces, his essays on the Romantic poets in *Les poètes contemporains* announce with resounding clarity his desire to protect poetry from the incursion of femininity (*Articles* 149–88). Leconte de Lisle studies five poets in this series of portraits, as follows: Pierre-Jean de Béranger, Lamartine, Hugo, Vigny, and Auguste Barbier. The essays on the three figures central to the Romantic poetic tradition convey clearly the gender bias that founds Leconte de Lisle's literary program.

Once again, Lamartine stands as a ready scapegoat for those imputing feminine effusiveness to Romanticism. Of Lamartine's "Jocelyn," for example, Leconte de Lisle writes: "il y a dans ce gémissement continu une telle *absence de virilité* et d'ardeur réelle, cette langue est tellement molle, efféminée et incorrecte, le vers manque à ce point de muscles, de sang et de nerfs [. . .]" (*Articles* 170; emphasis mine). Leconte de Lisle's gender-laden vocabulary amplifies his already categorical condemnation. He assails not only the self-involvement of Lamartine's speaking subject ("ce gémissement continu"), but also casts doubt upon the poet's ability to forge a worthwhile poem and, indeed, upon his virility. Leconte de Lisle associates imprecise word choice at once with femininity and bad poetry ("cette langue [. . .] molle, efféminée et incorrecte"). Sloppy composition, too, renders the poem soft and shapeless ("le vers manque à ce point de muscles"). Leconte de Lisle finally leaves Lamartine awash in aspersions of unmanliness.

This condemnation takes aim at poetic evils of which "Jocelyn" is only one manifestation. Lamartine represents a tendency whose weakness threatens not simply the state of poetry but, seemingly, of masculinity itself. Leconte de Lisle describes *Les méditations* as follows:

> [L]a mélopée lyrique en elle-même n'est plus qu'une longue lamentation musicale non rhythmée qui se noie finalement dans les larmes. On sait que les larmes sont d'un usage constant et obligé dans l'école Lamartinienne. Mais [. . .] l'héroïque bataillon des élégiaques verse moins de pleurs réels que de rimes insuffisantes. (*Articles* 170)

The association of Lamartine with an elegiac school implicitly evokes and rejects a network of women poets, including

93

the elegiacs Desbordes-Valmore and Tastu. The profusion of tears suggests feminine sentimentality that, for Leconte de Lisle, demeans the restrained grandeur of masculine poetry. Similarly, his ironic reference to the elegy implies that this form, characteristically plaintive and, in its Romantic guise, highly subjective, holds no merit. Leconte de Lisle's hierarchy of values begins to emerge for us, at the top of which lies the historic masculine epic, and at the bottom, the subjective feminine elegy. He again accuses the rank and file of encouraging such poetry: "Le goût public encourage [les élégiaques] dans l'exercice de cette profession immorale dont le premier mérite est d'être à la portée de tous" (*Articles* 170). This does not surprise us, given our familiarity with the author's antidemocratic sentiment. And yet at one interesting moment, he places himself in the position of the reader, lamenting that Lamartine's poetry has the power to sicken those who read it: "il est impossible d'en poursuivre la lecture et l'étude sans un intolérable malaise" (170–71). What prompts this display of solicitude for the reading public, elsewhere worthy of the poet's greatest contempt? Here he appears to step out of his role as elite poet, discovering himself to be a man threatened by the corrupting force of femininity. Effeminate poetry not only lacks vigor, but also threatens the health of the populace with an "intolérable malaise." Leconte de Lisle reasons in a cyclical fashion on this point, regularly accusing a vapid public of sustaining vaporous and feminine poetic production, but here implying that it is the poetry itself that weakens or emasculates its reader.[4] If exposure to feminine poetry provokes discomfort or sickness, then with it comes the danger of contagion.

The vocabulary of disease that pervades Leconte de Lisle's descriptions of Romantic poetry suggests such infectiousness. This thoroughgoing physiological lexicon is one of the most remarkable aspects of his invective against feminine Romanticism. With this language, Leconte de Lisle not only condemns weak poetry, but also presents us with the image of a physical body in decay and a decomposing social body associated with a corrupt morality ("cette profession immorale"):

> [L]es premières paroles [de Lamartine] ont ému les âmes attentives et bienveillantes [. . .] à l'heure précise où il leur

> a plu de s'attendrir sur elles-mêmes, où la phtisie intellec-
> tuelle, les vagues langueurs et le goût dépravé d'une sorte
> de mysticisme mondain attendaient leur poète. [. . .] Les
> germes épidémiques de mélancolie bâtarde [. . .] se repre-
> naient à la vie [. . .]. (*Articles* 168)

The metaphor is physical ("phtisie," "germes épidémiques"),
and yet the real danger appears to be moral ("le goût dépravé")
and emotional ("[la] mélancolie"). Above all, Leconte de Lisle
associates the Romantic era with depressive self-pity: "à l'heure
précise où il leur a plu de *s'attendrir sur elles-mêmes.*" In the
mirror of his horror of self-involvement we can glimpse Leconte
de Lisle's own repression, and in his fierce refusal of self-
contemplation perhaps the denial of his own femininity.

Moreover, he exhibits an anxiety of legitimacy that is not
limited to this passage. Why "mélancolie *bâtarde*"? Could it
be that Leconte de Lisle perceives his own melancholy to be
more authentic than the Romantic *mal du siècle?* His preoccupation with legitimacy undoubtedly relates to two issues, one
sociopolitical and the other poetic, which find their nexus in
the person of Lamartine. Leconte de Lisle began his writing
career in journalism as a young follower of Fourier;[5] disillu-
sioned after the violence of 1848, he abandoned his socialist
engagement and distanced himself from his earlier writings.
This repudiation helps to explain the virulence of Leconte de
Lisle's disdain for the angst and idealism of high French Romanticism. It sheds light as well on the mature persona of
Leconte de Lisle as an alienated intellectual clinging to the
straws of a mythically stable past.

Poetically alienated as well, Leconte de Lisle far surpassed
the Bloomian model of the anxiety of influence. While rejecting nearly the entire tradition of French poetry and seeking
legitimacy in the ancient past, he saved his harshest invective
for his immediate predecessors. Lamartine, political loser to
Louis-Napoléon in the 1848 presidential elections, suffered an
equally humiliating disavowal, as we have seen, in the poetic
arena. Not simply an effeminate poet or an impotent liberal
humanitarian, Lamartine was a failure as a father, as a leader
of any kind: "M. de Lamartine laissera derrière lui, comme une
expiation, cette multitude d'esprits avortés, loquaces et stériles,

qu'il a engendrés et conçus, pleureurs selon la formule, cervelles liquéfiées et cœurs de pierre, misérable famille d'un père illustre" (*Articles* 172). The unnatural father of a degenerate and sterile family, Lamartine presided over a panoply of elegiac poets, thus debasing the poetic patrimony of France. Leconte de Lisle posits, contrary to this "misérable famille" of sentimental Romantics, another, intellectually rich family nonetheless deprived of recognition. In the *avant-propos* to his series of portraits, Leconte de Lisle writes that "Les grands poètes [. . .] appartiennent à *une famille spirituelle que [le peuple] n'a jamais reconnue et qu'il a sans cesse maudite et persécutée*" (157; emphasis mine). Although consistently suspicious of affiliation and affirmation, Leconte de Lisle here evokes a family to which he would give all to belong and in which he would position himself as leader (father) rather than admirer (son).

In his portraits of Vigny and Hugo, Leconte de Lisle abandons his hostile tone and consequently provides a more reasoned critique of a Romanticism that strikes him as more virile. These literary appraisals are consistently hierarchical. Edgard Pich has suggested that "Leconte de Lisle distingue le grand public qui se plaît aux chansons à boire de Béranger, le public cultivé qui goûte 'Jocelyn' et l'élite restreinte qui apprécie les poètes comme Vigny" (*Articles* 170n12). Corresponding to this hierarchy of taste, ranging from low culture to high, is Leconte de Lisle's hierarchy of poets ranging from effeminate to manly.

Thus Vigny belongs to "le monde des vrais poètes" (*Articles* 178) whose "La mort du loup" is "un cri de douleur autrement fier et viril que les lamentations élégiaques acclamées par la foule contemporaine" (182). His poetic voice escapes self-indulgence; his poems are epic rather than elegiac: "toujours élevés, graves et polis comme l'homme lui-même" (179). If Vigny's virility emerges from his noble reserve, as from his refusal to pander to the masses, Leconte de Lisle nonetheless finds signs of weakness ("faiblesse") in his work. Too inspirational, Vigny's poems do not exhibit "la certitude constante de la langue, la solidité de vers et la précision vigoureuse de l'image" (179). Moreover, he fails to adopt the neutral stance so valued by Leconte de Lisle: Vigny does not "dégager nettement l'artiste de l'homme" (182).

Leconte de Lisle concludes that "il est visible que la timidité de l'expression ne rend pas, très fréquemment, la virilité de la pensée" (*Articles* 181), finding fault above all in Vigny's excessive delicacy. Of "Éloa," for example, he writes: "Cette conception est très indécise; l'exécution en est d'une élégance un peu molle et onctueuse. [. . .] Une sorte de vapeur rose et lactée enveloppe, du premier vers au dernier, les péripéties gracieuses du poème [. . .]" (180–81). Leconte de Lisle's adjectives ("indécise," "molle," "onctueuse," "rose," "lactée," "gracieuses"), grammatically feminine, evoke a world of feminine languor and inactivity. Although vaporousness appears in some of Baudelaire's most daring representations of undecidable subjectivity, and indecision would become the hallmark of Verlaine's contribution to Symbolism, for Leconte de Lisle these are negative characteristics of flawed poetry. What is more, they threaten the constitution of a solid subject, for they lack "une armature de vigueur et de passion contenues" (181). We seem to have come upon the secret of Leconte de Lisle's unyielding position against the vagaries of vaporous femininity, be that in the voice or composition of the poem: that which is floating rather than fixed and solid risks evaporation. The danger of uncertainty or impermanence is perhaps most real for the alienated subject clinging defensively to a fortified identity.

The vigor, solidity, and certainty that Leconte de Lisle finds lacking in Vigny's work attract his praise in Hugo's, which "nous offre le spectacle d'un esprit très mâle et très individuel" (*Articles* 174). Leconte de Lisle seems ready to overlook the democratic stance of Hugo's engaged poetry for the vision of healthy masculinity that it projects. Indeed, the vocabulary of robustness, which Leconte de Lisle draws upon to describe Hugo and his work, appears in stark contrast to the sickliness evoked to describe Lamartine's poetry. Hugo's oeuvre is "immense [. . .] et sans cesse en voie d'accroissement, [. . .] embrassant d'année en année une plus large sphère par le débordement magnifique de ses qualités natives [. . .]." Leconte de Lisle fairly gushes at the size of Hugo's oeuvre, whose scope pays tribute to the author's voraciousness and omnipotence. While our critic alludes to certain faults, which in Hugo are "défauts" and never "faiblesses," these too are "extraordinaires [. . . et] commandent encore une sorte de vénération" (174).

Although Hugo's work lacks the objectivity, neutrality, and perhaps even the erudition constitutive of Leconte de Lisle's poetic values, the latter nonetheless defends him ardently against all attackers. Strikingly, the poet of constraint praises the excessiveness (never effusion or verbosity) of Hugo: "C'est un esprit excessif, qui le nie?" (*Articles* 175). Hugo's forcefulness, likened to "éruptions volcaniques," is perhaps incompatible with Leconte de Lisle's formalist requirements: "J'avoue volontiers que les saines doctrines académiques s'en accommodent peu" (175). But what matter, concludes Leconte de Lisle, since "hélas! la poésie est un excès dont nous ne nous rendrons jamais coupables" (175). The guilty pleasure that Leconte de Lisle takes from Hugo's enormous eruptions is one of the only manifestations of unbridled sexuality present in his work.

Let us note, moreover, that this article is less specific and analytic than the others, and that here Leconte de Lisle's voice is more impassioned than critical. His vociferousness subsides before Hugo's vitality and robustness. Leconte de Lisle even explains away Hugo's sentimentality and delicacy, elsewhere subject to ridicule as the mark of effeminate poetry: "Les sentiments tendres, les délicatesses même subtiles, acquièrent en passant par une âme forte une expression souveraine, parce qu'elle est plus juste. C'est pour cela que *la sensibilité des poètes virils est la seule vraie*" (*Articles* 176; emphasis mine). Thus even a subjective and impassioned "I" is redeemed by the perceived virility of the poetry of Hugo, "un génie mâle" (206).

## Poesis perfecta

One would expect to find in Leconte de Lisle's finely wrought poetry the extension and illustration of his objectivist aesthetics. But does his verse confirm the values and biases of his prose? In his oeuvre, as in the work of other poets, the poetic text inevitably exhibits greater complexity than the critical essay, often displaying perplexing contradictions. Leconte de Lisle offers a particularly posed critical discourse, possessed of a fairly consistent voice, which is often polemical, sometimes provocatively oppositional. Although such provocation is not absent from his poetry, the voice of his poetic texts differs in its intensity and subjectivity. While Leconte de Lisle remains firmly opposed to emotive lyricism in his critical works, traces of affect come to light in his poetry. His two pre-Parnassian collections, *Poèmes antiques* and *Poèmes barbares,* betray curious fissures in his poetic dogma. They play out struggles with femininity that are masked by the dismissive gestures of his masculinist criticism. In particular, the author works through issues of self and otherness by placing a male speaking subject in proximity with a variety of female figures. Leconte de Lisle's poetry is no more popular today than during his lifetime, perhaps appearing pedantic and at times arcane in its historical references.[6] The *Poèmes antiques* contain several cycles, beginning with a set of Hindu poems and followed by a more substantial group devoted to ancient Greece and Rome. These poems reflect the antiquarian tendency of Parnassian poetry, representing historic and mythic figures from ancient cultures. Leconte de Lisle, an avid orthographist, gave many of his poems phonetically and semantically cryptic titles, such as "Sûryâ," "Çunacépa," and "Kybèle." The erudite vocabulary accompanying these and other unfamiliar proper nouns most likely won the author no new readers among the French masses he disdained as uncultivated. The collection ends incongruously with six "Chansons écossaises," inspired by the poetry of Robert Burns, which have feminine voices ("Jane," "Nanny," "Nell," etc.). These light, lyrical songs contrast sharply with the rest of the collection in voice, subject matter, and composition.

If the "Chansons écossaises" unmistakably mark an intrusion of the lyrical and personal in Leconte de Lisle's manifesto collection of impersonal verse, one wonders whether the antique poems stand up under scrutiny to the detached objectivity promised by their preface. Many of these are long narrative or dialogue poems, often with epic qualities. But the epic is not the only classical form exploited by Leconte de Lisle in this collection whose preface, let us recall, labels it "un retour réfléchi à des formes négligées ou peu connues." Its "studies" include as well the ode ("Odes anacréontiques"), hymn ("Sûryâ, hymne védique"), eclogue ("Églogue"), the bucolic genre ("Les bucoliastes"), and several dramatic dialogues, some complete with antique chorus ("Hélène," among others). While Leconte de Lisle's poetic genres vary widely, his prosody is more stable; with few exceptions he limits himself to the tragic alexandrine.

Such long narrative poems, Leconte de Lisle's preferred venue in the *Poèmes antiques,* permit the author to pursue his interest in character description and development. Indeed, he elaborates on poetic character representation in several critical texts,[7] where he establishes a distinction between real (or individualized) and ideal (general, typical, or symbolic) figures. Not surprisingly, Leconte de Lisle privileges the universal over the particular, and pursues an abstract ideal in his poetry. He follows the model of the Greeks, believing that they had the unsurpassed ability to capture something essential and eternal, and to distill it into a character. In the modern era, he finds only a few examples of successful epic characterization ("à la fois si vivante et si idéale" [*Articles* 132]). He names Hamlet, expresses an interest in Byron's female characters, and praises "la création des types plutôt que l'analyse des caractères individuels" (213) in Hugo's novels.

Leconte de Lisle betrays a particular interest in the articulation of female figures, as his article on Byron ("Les femmes de Byron") indicates. Moreover, his discussion of feminine character types often revolves around the inadequacy of existing models. Claiming that "le monde moderne ne réussit à concevoir des types féminins, qu'à la condition d'altérer leur essence même [. . .]" (*Articles* 132), he goes on to name two ways that modern writers fail to capture the feminine "essence" of their characters. Their first error consists "en leur attribuant un caractère viril, comme à lady Macbeth ou à Julie," and their second "en les reléguant dans une sphère nébuleuse et fantastique, comme pour Béatrice" (132). It is difficult to know what for Leconte de Lisle would constitute "le symbole spécial [. . .] des forces féminines" (132), for he rejects not only those too manly or too imaginary, but occasionally some quite traditionally feminine ones as well, such as the Virgin Mary. Although she is a "symbole de pureté, de grâce et surtout de bonté," she nonetheless leaves Leconte de Lisle unsatisfied: "mais cette protestation du sentiment féminin ne tient plus à la terre, et fait maintenant partie du dogme" (131). He aspires to a realistic (tangible) and yet idealized character, a fully rounded one exhibiting the qualities of a people or a type. Leconte de Lisle's studies in female characters both pose the riddle of femininity and seem to promise us his answer to it.

While many male heros and warriors people the antique poems, Leconte de Lisle also uses the collection as a workshop in the representation of femininity, foregrounding female characters in numerous pieces, including "Hypatie," "Thyoné," "Glaucé," "Hélène," "Kybèle," "Klytie," "Vénus de Milo," and "Niobé." The latter two poems focus on female statues, and are therefore thoroughly consistent with the Parnassian trope of the immobile woman, and with the Parnassian recuperation of Hellenist statuary as a model for ideal beauty. Théodore de Banville was among the first to exploit this figure in his collection *Les cariatides* (1842), named for architectural supporting columns sculpted in the form of a woman. Gautier, as we shall see, brought the study of the feminine statue to its culmination in *Émaux et camées*. The mythical Niobe, upon the slaughter of her seven sons and seven daughters by the gods she defied, wept until she turned to stone. In the conclusion to his lengthy poem (of nearly 500 lines), Leconte de Lisle describes the petrifaction of the queen ("Niobé," *Poèmes antiques* 156–70).

> Comme un grand corps taillé par une main habile,
> Le marbre te saisit d'une étreinte immobile:
> Des pleurs marmoréens ruissellent de tes yeux;
> La neige du Paros ceint ton front soucieux [. . .].
> (lines 434–37)

Although immobilized as a statue, her motherly attributes remain intact:

> *Tes larges flancs,* si beaux dans leur splendeur royale
> Qu'ils brillaient à travers la pourpre orientale,
> Et *tes seins jaillissants,* ces futurs nourriciers
> Des vengeurs de leur mère et des Dieux justiciers,
> Tout est marbre! [. . .].
> (442–46; emphasis mine)

In fact, her pathos and beauty, even her vitality, appear enhanced by her frozen attitude:

> Que ta douleur est belle, ô marbre sans pareil!
> . . . . . . . . . . . . . . . . . . . . . . . . . . . . . .
> On dirait, à te voir, ô marbre désolé,
> Que du ciseau sculpteur des larmes ont coulé.
> Tu vis, tu vis encor! [. . .]
> (448, 460–62)

Frozen by the excess of her emotions, Niobe offers a fitting and idealized image of both maternal devotion and the incapacitation of femininity.

"Vénus de Milo," an apostrophe to the ancient statue, presents another curious admixture of immobility and femininity. Ostensibly representing the goddess of love, this statue and Leconte de Lisle's verse description of it embody all the hard and cold attributes of marble. This poem's relative concision allows us to read it in its entirety and to follow the narrative movement from its descriptive beginnings to the subject's emergence in its concluding stanzas. In doing so, we cannot fail to notice that the author couples his pursuit of feminine characterization with an unannounced inquiry into lyric subjectivity.

> Marbre sacré, vêtu de force et de génie,
> Déesse irrésistible au port victorieux,
> Pure comme un éclair et comme une harmonie,
> Ô Vénus, ô beauté, blanche mère des Dieux!    4
>
> Tu n'es pas Aphrodite, au bercement de l'onde,
> Sur ta conque d'azur posant un pied neigeux,
> Tandis qu'autour de toi, vision rose et blonde,
> Volent les Rires d'or avec l'essaim des Jeux.    8
>
> Tu n'es pas Kythérée, en ta pose assouplie,
> Parfumant de baisers l'Adônis bienheureux,
> Et n'ayant pour témoins sur le rameau qui plie
> Que colombes d'albâtre et ramiers amoureux.    12
>
> Et tu n'es pas la Muse aux lèvres éloquentes,
> La pudique Vénus, ni la molle Astarté
> Qui, le front couronné de roses et d'acanthes,
> Sur un lit de lotus se meurt de volupté.    16
>
> Non! les Rires, les Jeux, les Grâces enlacées,
> Rougissantes d'amour, ne t'accompagnent pas.
> Ton cortège est formé d'étoiles cadencées,
> Et les globes en chœur s'enchaînent sur tes pas.    20
>
> Du bonheur impassible ô symbole adorable,
> Calme comme la Mer en sa sérénité,
> Nul sanglot n'a brisé ton sein inaltérable,
> Jamais les pleurs humains n'ont terni ta beauté.    24

Salut! À ton aspect le cœur se précipite.
Un flot marmoréen inonde tes pieds blancs;
Tu marches, fière et nue, et le monde palpite,
Et le monde est à toi, Déesse aux larges flancs!    28

Îles, séjour des Dieux! Hellas, mère sacrée!
Oh! que ne suis-je né dans le saint Archipel,
Aux siècles glorieux où la Terre inspirée
Voyait le Ciel descendre à son premier appel!    32

Si mon berceau, flottant sur la Thétis antique,
Ne fut point caressé de son tiède cristal;
Si je n'ai point prié sous le fronton attique,
Beauté victorieuse, à ton autel natal;    36

Allume dans mon sein la sublime étincelle,
N'enferme point ma gloire au tombeau soucieux;
Et fais que ma pensée en rythmes d'or ruisselle,
Comme un divin métal au moule harmonieux.    40
(*Poèmes antiques* 151–52)

Leconte de Lisle proposes the Greek statue to his reader as an ideal poetic symbol: she exudes her Hellenist origins, is pure, white, and impassible. Her impassivity suggests physical inalterability, thanks to the hardness of the marble from which she is fashioned. But it evokes as well an interior passionlessness characterized by her calm serenity. These attributes are all in keeping with Leconte de Lisle's aesthetic agenda represented in his prose writings. Additionally let us observe that, as in his prose, here his language is largely negative. "Vénus de Milo" might be called a program piece, which focuses on the "symbole adorable" that is the statue it describes, and yet its author holds fast to an oppositional stance from which to expose his views. Once again we find reaction to lie at the heart of Leconte de Lisle's poetic agenda.

The poem's first half (in particular the second through fifth quatrains) lists several female figures to whom the poet compares his Venus de Milo: she is neither the light-hearted Aphrodite, nor the supple Kythérée smothering Adonis with kisses, nor the soft Astarte, the Phoenician goddess of love and fertility. Venus, the goddess of love and beauty, is clearly not herself: Leconte de Lisle has stripped her of all accoutrements of love and sexuality. Indeed, this Venus de Milo is concerned neither with her sexual fulfillment nor her modesty: "tu n'es pas [. . .] la pudique Vénus." Rather than pliant and ready for love, she is fitted out for war ("Marbre sacré, vêtu de force et de génie") and triumphs over others: "Tu marches, fière et nue, [. . .] et le monde est à toi [. . .] Beauté victorieuse." Here, as elsewhere, Leconte de Lisle englobes with opposites: his Venus is neither voluptuous nor chaste, both clothed and nude. She retains her identity as the goddess of beauty, for even in her impassive permanence, Venus remains an "irresistible" love object who provokes the emotion of her admirers: "À ton aspect le cœur se précipite [. . .] et le monde palpite." And yet her armor renders her inappropriate for love, as her masculine characteristics (heroism, unyieldingness, force) negate the docility and elasticity of her sex.

If not given to the comportment of a lover, Venus de Milo appears as a mother ("mère des Dieux") whose body, like Niobe's, emphasizes maternal attributes: "Déesse *aux larges flancs.*" Indeed, maternal figures and a concern for generation pervade this poem, reminding us of the poetic families evoked in Leconte de Lisle's essays. But although his critical discourse focuses on paternity and avoids matrilineage entirely, in this poem he does not shrink from such representations. In addition to the maternal Venus, we encounter the personified "Hellas, mère sacrée" and Thetis, protecting mother of Achilles. The reader will perhaps even discover a Romantic pun in the comparison of stanza 6: Venus is "calme comme la Mer [la mère] en sa sérénité."

Just as indicative of Leconte de Lisle's obsession with origins is the emergence of the speaking subject in the poem's second half. The "je" appears explicitly in the final three stanzas to bemoan his unworthy birth ("que ne suis-je né dans le saint Archipel"). This evocation of ancient Greece as the birthplace of beauty ("[l']autel natal [de la] beauté victorieuse") and the origin of poetic glory recalls Leconte de Lisle's repudiation of the French poetic tradition. It also points to the speaking subject as a double for the poet in search of affiliation. While admitting his poetic illegitimacy ("si mon berceau [. . .] ne fut point caressé" by the waters of the Grecian islands), the "je" implores the statue, as representative of ancient beauty, to touch him with her eminence and animate within him the poetic gifts of the past. If the statuesque and silent Venus de Milo "n'es[t] pas la Muse aux lèvres éloquentes," she nonetheless has the ability to inspire poetic eloquence in the speaking subject, as witnessed in the final stanza: "Allume dans mon sein la sublime étincelle, [. . .] Et fais que ma pensée en rythmes d'or ruisselle."

At the heart of "Vénus de Milo" lie several contradictions. First of all, the poem is not so antilyrical as the inscrutability that it praises might suggest. The speaking subject pleads to a symbol of impassivity ("nul sanglot n'a brisé *ton sein inaltérable*") for the passion he condemns: "*Allume dans mon sein* la sublime étincelle." Read in the context of the author's prose, whose obsessions it confirms, this poem nonetheless carries some of the subjective markers of the Romantic texts he abhors. Its own speaking subject, at first veiled by his invocation of the other (Venus de Milo, "tu"), reveals himself finally as an imploring creature whose passionate entreaties betray ambition as much as despair ("N'enferme point ma gloire au tombeau soucieux"). Although aiming for an objective, chiseled poem that would double for the statue it describes, Leconte de Lisle leaves his readers with one that climaxes with the drama of the subject.

Secondly, this poem offers a vision of sexual difference strikingly inconsistent with the stark oppositions of Leconte de Lisle's prose essays. His Venus is all-powerful and robust, a far cry from the soft and vapid femininity he associates with feeble Romantic poetry. Her exceptional characteristics, such as strength and genius, are elsewhere associated with masculinity by Leconte de Lisle. While in his essays he repudiates poetic fathers, here he eagerly beseeches a phallic mother, thus erring according to his own stipulations for characterization by attributing a "caractère viril" to Venus. Rather than following the rigid lines of his criticism and solving the riddle of femininity, Leconte de Lisle betrays an ambivalence in this poem that takes two directions in his oeuvre as a whole. He first questions paternal authority and secondly feminine weakness, leaving only the uncertain position of dependence on virile maternity for his lyric subject.

While not about fathers, this poem is ultimately less concerned with mothers even than it is with its emerging poetic subject who does battle with the same contradiction exhibited in the article on Hugo. That is, how can virility (or impassivity) and affect coexist? Let us recall Leconte de Lisle's refrain, which might also serve as his motto: "La sensibilité du poète viril est la seule vraie." It sheds light on the author's conundrum by suggesting that his desire for impassivity coincides with the rejection of only those passions that are deemed frivolous ("les Rires, les Jeux") and soft ("molle"). Femininity is ultimately aligned with love. Thus Leconte de Lisle's speaking subject repudiates an association with the lover Adonis, but aligns himself with the warrior Achilles, son of Thetis. Love is therefore denied, and glory coveted. So if Leconte de Lisle's poetry does not live up to his own strict ideal of impassivity, his speaking subject nonetheless clings to a virile sensitivity associated with the epic values of excellence and triumph (the Latin *vir* gives us both virtue and virility).

At question, finally, is the acclaim sought by the speaking subject for these qualities. Would Leconte de Lisle have a greater interest in the reading public than he admits? Ultimately, this poem is as much about its subject's poetic aspirations as it is the projection of masculine values onto a female figure or the petrifaction of traits perceived as feminine. These concerns coalesce in the author's ambivalence about the gender of recognition. Whether it be the confirmation of insipid talent by a feminized readership or the crowning moment of poetic achievement for the virile poet, Leconte de Lisle remains uncertain. A consideration of his *Poèmes barbares* further illustrates this hesitation between the desire for renown and the cultivation of obscurity.

*Poèmes barbares* (1862) brings us closer to the Parnassian moment and contains a good deal of metapoetic commentary that helps clarify Leconte de Lisle's battle with affect. As do the *Poèmes antiques,* the *Poèmes barbares* contain many pieces of epic quality. But here Leconte de Lisle draws from non-Greek and non-Roman ("barbaric") sources, employing his titular adjective in its most specific etymological sense of foreignness. The sources alien to ancient culture include the Bible ("Qaïn," "L'ecclésiaste"), Norse mythology ("La légende des Nornes," "L'épée d'Angantyr") and Celtic legends ("Le barde de Temrah," "Le jugement de Komor"). While such legends dominate the collection's first half, it then wanders far from its Germanic and Celtic beginnings to include poems colonial and contemporary in setting. Leconte de Lisle's birthplace, the Île Bourbon, provides the backdrop for a number of those exuding a foreign exoticism ("La fontaine aux lianes," "La ravine Saint-Gilles"), while others travel as far as South America. Numerous animal poems ("Les éléphants," "La panthère noire," "Le jaguar," "Le colibri") contribute to the volume's exploration of alterity and savagery.

By teasing out some associations to Leconte de Lisle's program in each collection we encounter a striking confirmation of the author's alienation, both literary and generalized. With the *Poèmes antiques,* Leconte de Lisle yearned for a Greek poetic heritage that was not his own, while much that is "foreign" or "uncivilized" in the *Poèmes barbares* was, for the poet, very close to home, his native Île Bourbon. In fact, he reserved much of his animosity for that which was closest to him, and this becomes evident in the contemporary pieces. Thanks to the currency of these poems, the *Poèmes barbares* is more accessible in its language and its subjects. This collection also contains more short lyric forms and therefore greater concision, a Parnassian trait that countered Romantic excess. Leconte de Lisle embraces the sonnet with a dozen pieces, most of which depart from the form's Petrarchan antecedent as a poetic structure devoted to the subject of love. Instead, the sonnet often provides Leconte de Lisle with a self-reflexive frame in which to ruminate upon poetic values and renown.

With "Les montreurs," Leconte de Lisle takes aim at the proponents of subjective poetry:

Tel qu'un morne animal, meurtri, plein de poussière,
La chaîne au cou, hurlant au chaud soleil d'été,
Promène qui voudra son cœur ensanglanté
Sur ton pavé cynique, ô plèbe carnassière!　　4

Pour mettre un feu stérile en ton œil hébété,
Pour mendier ton rire ou ta pitié grossière,
Déchire qui voudra la robe de lumière
De la pudeur divine et de la volupté.　　8

Dans mon orgueil muet, dans ma tombe sans gloire,
Dussé-je m'engloutir pour l'éternité noire,
Je ne vendrai pas mon ivresse ou mon mal,

> Je ne livrerai pas ma vie à tes huées,                12
> Je ne danserai pas sur ton tréteau banal
> Avec tes histrions et tes prostituées.
>
> (*Poèmes barbares* 192)

We can read this sonnet as a complement to "Vénus de Milo," indeed as its modern, disdainful face whose voice is equal in its passion. While the former conjures up a family romance by appealing fervently to an ancient figure as model and guide, "Les montreurs" addresses a contemporary public with the greatest of contempt ("plèbe carnassière"). Rather than extolling the virtues of the Greek precedent, here Leconte de Lisle catalogues the trespasses of modern poetry, cheapened by its excessive emotion and its pandering to a thrill-seeking public. In the quatrains, Leconte de Lisle alludes to the Romantic Poet, who wears his heart on his sleeve ("Promène qui voudra son cœur ensanglanté") for public acclaim ("Pour mendier ton rire ou ta pitié grossière"). The first-person subject appears in the tercets to distance himself from the frothy sentiment and facile confession of those criticized in the quatrains. Opposing the exhibitionist roars with his own "orgueil muet," the "je" disdains a cheap public forum ("ton pavé cynique," "ton tréteau banal"). He would rather retire into nothingness ("Dussé-je m'engloutir pour l'éternité noire") than model himself after his contemporaries.

Although this poem differs from "Vénus" in form, tone, and setting, the two poems share certain stylistic and semantic consistencies. Like "Vénus," "Les montreurs" is overwhelmingly negative, here signaled both grammatically ("Je ne vendrai pas [. . .] Je ne livrerai pas [. . .] Je ne danserai pas") and through condemning epithets ("tes histrions et tes prostituées"). The poem's worldview is once again oppositional, but its subject seizes upon his solitude born of difference with contemptuous pride. Leconte de Lisle repeats some of the vocabulary of "Vénus," as well as the use of antithesis to roundly reject the object of the speaking subject's contempt. Once again, the repudiation of "pudeur" and "volupté" go hand in hand. And the oppositional clauses, "ton rire ou ta pitié" and "mon ivresse ou mon mal," likewise are coupled to the same effect of denouncing conspicuous affect, regardless of its form.

Although Leconte de Lisle never names the poetic enterprise explicitly in this sonnet, its two primary lexical groupings, evoking first the street ("ton pavé") and secondly the theater ("ton tréteau"), suggest metaphorically the author's contempt for self-exposure and populism in verse. We are clearly not on the Champs-Elysées or in the Comédie française ("Avec tes histrions et tes prostituées"), but rather among the unwashed masses in search of a cheap thrill. This negative view of public display is opposed by the silent and forgotten grave, "ma tombe sans gloire," to which the speaking subject threatens to retreat. The verb *s'engloutir*, one appearing throughout this collection, opposes public, outward-reaching expression to interiority and submersion. Better to bury oneself than show oneself, to sublimate than to dramatize, to write epics than elegies.

Let us recall that, contrary to the voice of "Les montreurs," the speaking subject in "Vénus de Milo" invoked the goddess to assure his glory beyond the grave: "N'enferme point ma gloire au tombeau soucieux." Although contradictory, the preoccupation with acclaim in these poems indicates an investment in the reading public greater than what Leconte de Lisle admitted. While the poetic aspirations present in "Vénus" are expressed openly, in this sonnet both the author and the speaking subject aspire covertly for recognition while threatening to retreat from it. Leconte de Lisle courts the sonnet tradition and meditates on poetic values, and his speaking subject solicits reaction through provocation. In both poems, the call for affectlessness is set forth in a highly subjective language with forceful images.

While one might expect such prevarication from the ambiguous discourse that is poetry, in Leconte de Lisle's case it points to the subtle contradictions of his self-fashioned poetic identity. As if to confirm his circumlocution, Leconte de Lisle makes a spectacle of his restraint: "Je ne vendrai pas mon ivresse ou mon mal." The speaking subject offers a classic example of preterition by performing exactly what he claims not to do. Such coy indirection perhaps counters the tenets of Leconte de Lisle's objective poetics, and yet this contradiction (like the author's oppositional rhetoric more generally) is surely due to ambivalence rather than insincerity. We can ascribe Leconte de Lisle's dance between reticence and vehemence (whether condemning or laudatory), like the fissures in his poetics of containment, to an all-too subjective irresolution in the face of acclaim, which he defines in consistently gendered terms.

Let us not forget that women and Romantics are condemned, like Leconte de Lisle's "Montreurs," when they show too much of themselves. The speaking subject hangs onto his masculinity by refusing to parade himself in the public arena, "avec [. . .] tes prostituées." Etymologically, prostitution signifies no more than to "place oneself forward" (*pro-statuere*), although for Leconte de Lisle as for Baudelaire any movement toward the other signals weakness and femininity.[8] Thus rather than sharing the fate of his emasculated contemporaries, whom Leconte de Lisle describes in "Les modernes" as "châtrés dès le berceau par le siècle assassin" (*Poèmes barbares* 290), he retreats into antiquity or veils himself modestly in "la robe de lumière." His austerity is no more than a cover for contained desire, and his poetics of immobility are perhaps no more than a reaction, like Niobe's, to excessive emotion.

# Parnassian Obsessions

*Obsession* (*obsidere:* to sit down before, besiege): "Compulsive preoccupation with a fixed idea or unwanted feeling or emotion, often with symptoms of anxiety."[1] "Obsessional ideas are invariably transformed self-reproaches which have re-emerged from repression and which always relate to some sexual act that was performed with pleasure in childhood."[2]

Leconte de Lisle's work exhibits numerous obsessive elements. His criticism, a conscious discourse governed by the language of reason, returns incessantly to the ideas of hardness, embattled isolation, and the reassuring repetition of confronting obstacles. Such obstacles are both external, as the stubborn incomprehension of an unenlightened readership, and self-imposed, as the demands of a rigorous poetics. Leconte de Lisle's representation of his lyric subject, a creative undertaking open to the multiform language of poetry and the unconscious, reveals more clearly the significant role played by repression in his writing. What would this hardness be whose challenge assures the writing subject's virility? Poetry, perfection fashioned from impossibility, represents the mastery of language. Successful domination assures wholeness and the mark of accomplishment. Leconte de Lisle's poetic obsessions were, however, not unique to him, but instead governed the poetic production of an entire generation that wrote as a group besieged. Like Leconte de Lisle, other Parnassian poets fashioned images of hardness with which to master poetic language and capture femininity. Poetic language, at once an interior voice and an ungraspable alterity, has always been represented as a woman. Until the Parnassian poets, it had not so relentlessly been characterized as impenetrable and petrified. Moreover many Parnassian poets followed Leconte de Lisle in looking to flawless sculpture as a metaphor for the all-consuming poetic, feminine object. Like his, their chiseled, unyielding verse and perfected, static forms stood as monuments of security and longevity. And like his work, theirs exhibits a denial of repression through the insistence on neutrality, a sublime indifference that pretends not to care.

My intent here is therefore to show how Leconte de Lisle's poetry translates into the thought and practice of a movement. It is true that many deny the coherence of a Parnassian school: "Le groupement parnassien ne s'est fait sur aucune théorie, sur aucune esthétique particulière; jamais l'un de nous n'a entendu imposer à un autre son optique d'art" (Mendès, interviewed by Huret 289). I would, however, take issue with this appraisal. Leconte de Lisle's hard-line poetic stance in fact lends unity to the group's production, and the containment of femininity plays an integral role in Parnassian theory.

## Théophile Gautier

Leconte de Lisle began his poetic career as a Parnassian, but Théophile Gautier's Parnassianism represented the final phase of his poetic production. Although of the same generation as Leconte de Lisle, Gautier (1811–72) began his literary activities at an early age and wrote his first poetry under the prevailing Romantic style. So while they both came to occupy the position of Parnassian elder, each cut his teeth on projects and associations far removed from its aesthetic and ideological programs (Leconte de Lisle, let us recall, began as a Fourierist journalist). Their literary and ideological evolutions illustrate the instability and malleability of historical subjects and in so doing counter the rigid dogmatism of the movement.

Gautier's poetic career began with his long Byronic poem, *Albertus* (1832). While Romantic in tone and inspiration, it nonetheless conserves traces in its preface of the artistic (*artiste*) stance with which Gautier was associated throughout the various periods and styles of his lengthy career as a writer of poetry, prose, and criticism. In his preface to *Albertus* we read that "L'auteur du présent livre [. . .] n'a vu du monde que ce que l'on en voit par la fenêtre, et il n'a pas envie d'en voir davantage. Il n'a aucune couleur politique; il n'est ni rouge, ni blanc, ni même tricolore; il n'est rien, il ne s'aperçoit des révolutions que lorsque les balles cassent les vitres" (*Albertus* 81). Among the first to take up the battle cry of *l'art pour l'art,* Gautier elaborated upon this notion in the oft-cited preface to his novel *Mlle de Maupin* (1835), where he writes that "il n'y a de vraiment beau que ce qui ne peut servir à rien; tout ce qui est utile est laid, car c'est l'expression de quelque besoin" (57).[3] In the domain of poetry, his claim that utility was inimical to the quest for beauty resulted not only in the abandonment of *la poésie pour le progrès,* but also of the visionary lyricism that motivated so much of Romantic and, later, Symbolist production.

Gautier is remembered as the historian of Romanticism and, indeed, his *Histoire du romantisme* (1874) has helped literary historians define the movement. His essay entitled "Les progrès de la poésie française depuis 1830" (1867), while less studied, describes the *nouvelle école* of the Parnassians with the analogous authority of a participant and literary elder. Careful to refute the suggestion of political motivation, in this essay Gautier insists that "la révolution de Février ne fut pas une révolution littéraire" (in *Histoire* 323), thus echoing his preface to *Albertus* where he claims that revolution and poetry have nothing to do with each other. And yet this poetic movement is unavoidably linked to the generation of 1848. Gautier himself continually returns to this date as a dividing line between the old (Romantic) and the new (Parnassian). He views the events of 1848 as a turning point for poetry, defining the subject of his essay as "[l]es poètes surgis après la révolution de Février" (294). Naming Leconte de Lisle "le soleil central de ce système poétique," he describes *Le Parnasse contemporain* as representative of "l'état actuel de la poésie" in the 1860s (359).

Although Gautier and Leconte de Lisle share the antiutilitarianism, erudition, and formalism of the Parnassian aesthetic, and even though they stand together as two Parnassian patriarchs, the work of each poet must be granted its individuality. Whereas Leconte de Lisle never strays from his elitist view of the poetic endeavor, Gautier is not afraid to expose his poetry to daily life. And if both pose challenges with their sometimes arcane allusions to places and people, Gautier alone peppers his work with references to contemporary events and settings

("L'obalisque de Paris," "Après le feuilleton"). Leconte de Lisle's focus on the past is fixed, as his notion of a virile poetics is unchanging; he strikes the reader as pristine and arid next to Gautier's pulpy love for the fantastic and the macabre.[4] We might characterize Leconte de Lisle by his consistency, even predictability, whereas Gautier's poetry retains an appeal for today's reader thanks in part to its variety and unpredictability.

Gautier's last published poetic collection, *Émaux et camées* (1852)[5] brings its author's defense of *l'art pour l'art* to a culminating point and aligns it with the aesthetic that would come to be known as Parnassian. Like "Les progrès de la poésie," this collection illustrates Parnassian formalism and antiutilitarianism; its poetic agenda is to "traiter sous forme restreinte de petits sujets" (*Histoire* 322). The insistence on limits and concision is important here, for it goes to the heart of the Parnassian aesthetic of hardness and its privileging of rigor over innovation. The collection's poems are written entirely in octosyllabic verse (with the occasional exception of short meters in heterometric poems). It is thus not notable for any kind of poetic innovation, but rather for a tendency toward the miniature that subsequently gets played out in the sonnet, Parnasse's preferred form. Gone is the long-winded elegy, nor do we find in this collection examples of the Parnassian epic dear to Banville and Leconte de Lisle, among others. Gautier gravitates toward shortness as he does to small objects: "Les poèmes de longue haleine sont assez rares dans l'école nouvelle" (*Histoire* 315). The very title *Émaux et camées* provides its reader with a jewel metaphor: the poem is to be small and hard and precious.

This collection exemplifies Parnassian indifference, which links the notion of pure poetry to a neutral stance. Of course Gautier's pretended neutrality already signaled a political choice: the refusal to engage in political struggle was a tacit acceptance of the power of the Second Empire. As the poet will not be moved by the change and tumult of his surrounding environment, so too will his ideal of beauty be characterized by impassive hardness. Gautier's poetic "Préface" to his collection unites the antiutilitarian aesthetic with an allusion to the revolution of 1848, placing *Émaux et camées* under the sign of both the new and the apolitical.[6] It reiterates, in sonnet form,

Leconte de Lisle's abdication of involvement in the world and subsequent retreat into his poetry of erudition. While Leconte de Lisle stated plainly that "je hais mon temps" and railed against "je ne sais quelle alliance monstrueuse de la poésie et de l'industrie" (*Articles* 127), Gautier merely closed his windows to the tumultuous events of 1848 and applied himself to the composition of his collection:

> Pendant les guerres de l'empire,
> Gœthe, au bruit du canon brutal,
> Fit *le Divan occidental,*
> Fraîche oasis où l'art respire.                    4
>
> Pour Nisami quittant Shakspeare,
> Il se parfuma de çantal,
> Et sur un mètre oriental
> Nota le chant qu'Hudhud[7] soupire.        8
>
> Comme Gœthe sur son divan
> À Weimar s'isolait des choses
> Et d'Hafiz effeuillait les roses,
>
> Sans prendre garde à l'ouragan            12
> Qui fouettait mes vitres fermées,
> Moi, j'ai fait *Émaux et Camées.*
> (*Émaux et camées* 25)

Goethe's *Westöstlicher Divan* (1819),[8] composed in spite of tumultuous political events, serves as a model for Gautier. He suggests that Goethe ignored the turmoil at Weimar that was contemporary to the collection's composition by leaving the west ("quittant Shakspeare") for eastern inspiration (the Persian poets Nisami and Hafiz). Like Goethe (whose name resonates in his own), Gautier distances himself from the political "ouragan" and retreats into art, into the past, and, occasionally, to the Orient. His "new" poetry thus represents a refuge from contemporary events and the brutality of war, whether those of the Empire or of the 1848 revolution. Let us not forget, however, Gautier's willing engagement in other, poetic, battles. Present at the battle of *Hernani,* with *Émaux et camées* he enlists in a campaign against engaged poetry. The dissent implicit in this "neutral" poem is betrayed by the oppositional

115

semantic content of many of its rhymes: "empire" / "respire"; "canon brutal" / "*le Divan occidental*"; "Shakspeare" / "le chant qu'Hudhud soupire"; "divan" / "ouragan." While his battle cry is less vitriolic than that of Leconte de Lisle, it is at least equally as persistent. He repeats the image of the closed window found in his preface to *Albertus,* but leaves it even more tightly shuttered here. In 1832 the author "voit par la fenêtre" and admits the possibility of intrusion when "les balles cassent les vitres." Twenty years later he allows no such interruption, taking no notice of the revolution that "fouettait mes vitres fermées."

The final poem of the collection, Gautier's Parnassian *ars poetica,* entitled simply "L'art," states most clearly the poet's embrace of solidity and motionlessness as the *sine qua non* of artistic perfection (*Émaux et camées* 148–50). It calls for a poetics of hardness and constraint, once again echoing Leconte de Lisle's poetic doctrine:

> Oui, l'œuvre sort plus belle
> D'une forme au travail
> Rebelle,
> Vers, marbre, onyx, émail.
>
> (stanza 1)

"L'art" contains several references to the collection's title, for in it Gautier praises inelastic or resistant materials, "marbre, onyx, émail." By placing "vers" in the company of these tangible and solid objects, Gautier counters the Romantic model of facile expression with the demands of exacting prosodic standards. The challenge offered by the manipulation of marble, as by the rigorous pursuit of classical poetic values (syntactic symmetry, chiseled alexandrines, perfectly wrought sonnets) provides the resistance necessary for the muscular thrust toward petrified perfection. The poem addresses poets in the broad sense of the term; "makers" of verse, of statues, and of paintings. Statuary, Parnasse's privileged metaphor, provides Gautier's first model for poetic production:

> Statuaire, repousse
> L'argile que pétrit
> Le pouce,
> Quand flotte ailleurs l'esprit;

> Lutte avec le carrare,
> Avec le paros dur
>     Et rare,
> Gardiens du contour pur.

(4–5)

Marble wins out over clay thanks to its resistance and rarity. It guarantees not only formal purity ("contour pur"), but also intellectual concentration, which goes a-wandering in the face of the malleable, undemanding clay. Once again, a battle ("lutte") precedes and defines poetic success.

Gautier's next reference is to painting:

> Peintre, fuis l'aquarelle,
> Et fixe la couleur
>     Trop frêle
> Au four de l'émailleur.

(8)

Like clay, watercolor is weak ("frêle"); like marble, enamel assures permanence. Gautier leads us to the predictable conclusion that art lasts longer than life:

> Tout passe. —L'art robuste
> Seul a l'éternité.
>     Le buste
> Survit à la cité.

(11)

Less predictable is his marriage of the concrete (marble endures because it is a resistant matter) with the intangible, which language necessarily is. His literalistic metaphor for what constitutes enduring art relies on the physical qualities of marble and enamel, which assure their longevity. Language, the matter of poetry, necessarily depends on its manipulation rather than its makeup, on how it is used rather than what it is composed of. By pretending that this is not the case, Gautier insists on the transparency of language, a stance to be overturned by the following generation of Symbolists.

The poem concludes with this stanza, which instructs the poet how to mold language in order to perfect it, thus rendering it hard and enduring:

Sculpte, lime, cisèle;
Que ton rêve flottant
    Se scelle
Dans le bloc résistant!

(14)

Gautier's pure ideal, like the luxurious Italian marble from Carrera and the marble named after the Greek island of Paros, is colored white, and invariably delineated like the contours of a statue of a woman. His desire to capture in stone what is fluid or ungraspable ("ton rêve"), as well as his equation of whiteness with poetic purity, point to the role that both race and sexual difference play in the elaboration of his aesthetic agenda, regardless of his pretended neutrality.[9]

Between the initial "Préface" and the concluding "L'art," the poems of *Émaux et camées* provide further examples of and elaborate upon the interrelated qualities of hardness, whiteness, and femininity. His "Symphonie en blanc majeur," a highly descriptive piece, juxtaposes numerous white objects called upon as similes to describe a feminine figure.[10] Her breast is as white as "neige moulée en globe," and her shoulders resemble white fur. Her whiteness is draped in white satin, and this image of a white-on-white swan-woman ("femme-cygne") offers a precursor to Mallarmé's "Le vierge, le vivace et le bel aujourd'hui," which features a white swan frozen in snow-covered ice.[11] Gautier also evokes coldness, likening white marble to the "chair froide et pâle" of a snowy-cold woman. Other materials, both hard and soft, conspire to color her white, including ivory, ermine, lace, flowers, and duvet. Ultimately, while these softer materials admit movement ("le col blanc courbant les lignes"), the woman is frozen like Mallarmé's swan and petrified in snow, frost, wintery ice, and glaciers. In the end she is desired for her cold rigidity, for her "implacable blancheur" that is her purity. All, however, is not stillness, for Gautier describes the shock of whiteness in military terms: "des combats insolents," "ces grandes batailles blanches."

Associations of femininity with virginal white frigidity run throughout many poems of *Émaux et camées,* suggesting that the poetic values of immobility and permanence depend upon the immobilization and petrifaction of feminine sexuality. "Le poème de la femme" offers a curious example. This narrative poem traces the metamorphoses of a female figure whose subject positions are as multiple and ambiguous as its title. Is this a poem by a woman or about one? In what way can it be said to belong to her? Here is Gautier's "Le poème de la femme: Marbre de Paros" in its entirety:

Un jour, au doux rêveur qui l'aime,     1
En train de montrer ses trésors,
Elle voulut lire un poème,
Le poème de son beau corps.

D'abord, superbe et triomphante     2
Elle vint en grand apparat,
Traînant avec des airs d'infante
Un flot de velours nacarat:

Telle qu'au rebord de sa loge     3
Elle brille aux Italiens,
Écoutant passer son éloge
Dans les chants des musiciens.

Ensuite, en sa verve d'artiste,     4
Laissant tomber l'épais velours,
Dans un nuage de batiste
Elle ébaucha ses fiers contours.

Glissant de l'épaule à la hanche,     5
La chemise aux plis nonchalants,
Comme une tourterelle blanche
Vint s'abattre sur ses pieds blancs.

Pour Apelle ou pour Cléomène,     6
Elle semblait, marbre de chair,
En Vénus Anadyomène
Poser nue au bord de la mer.

De grosses perles de Venise     7
Roulaient au lieu de gouttes d'eau,
Grains laiteux qu'un rayon irise,
Sur le frais satin de sa peau.

Oh! quelles ravissantes choses,     8
Dans sa divine nudité,
Avec les strophes de ses poses,
Chantait cet hymne de beauté!

Comme les flots baisant le sable          9
Sous la lune aux tremblants rayons,
Sa grâce était intarissable
En molles ondulations.

Mais bientôt, lasse d'art antique,          10
De Phidias et de Vénus,
Dans une autre stance plastique
Elle groupe ses charmes nus.

Sur un tapis de Cachemire,          11
C'est la sultane du sérail,
Riant au miroir qui l'admire
Avec un rire de corail;

La Géorgienne indolente,          12
Avec son souple narguilhé,
Étalant sa hanche opulente,
Un pied sous l'autre replié.

Et comme l'odalisque d'Ingres,          13
De ses reins cambrant les rondeurs,
En dépit des vertus malingres,
En dépit des maigres pudeurs!

Paresseuse odalisque, arrière!          14
Voici le tableau dans son jour,
Le diamant dans sa lumière;
Voici la beauté dans l'amour!

Sa tête penche et se renverse;          15
Haletante, dressant les seins,
Aux bras du rêve qui la berce,
Elle tombe sur ses coussins.

Ses paupières battent des ailes          16
Sur leurs globes d'argent bruni,
Et l'on voit monter ses prunelles
Dans la nacre de l'infini.

D'un linceul de point d'Angleterre          17
Que l'on recouvre sa beauté:
L'extase l'a prise à la terre;
Elle est morte de volupté!

Que les violettes de Parme,                    18
Au lieu des tristes fleurs des morts
Où chaque perle est une larme,
Pleurent en bouquets sur son corps!

Et que mollement on la pose                    19
Sur son lit, tombeau blanc et doux,
Où le poète, à la nuit close,
Ira prier à deux genoux.

(*Émaux et camées* 29–31)

The poem's first quatrain introduces its two main characters. The woman appears as both reading subject and object of the poem, while a poorly defined male character, "le doux rêveur qui l'aime," occupies the position of listener. Insofar as she is a poet herself, she is an exhibitionist, one who unveils herself ("*montrer* ses trésors") while reading. Three poses follow, all introduced by temporal adverbs ("d'abord," "ensuite," "bientôt"), which structure the poem's narrative. The poem's first moment, described in stanzas 2 and 3, elaborates on the appearance of the female figure, and here the ambiguity of her position remains constant. Gautier first places her in a contemporary setting ("sa loge aux Italiens"), familiar to the reader. At once performer and spectator, these two roles are conflated in the image of the flamboyantly dressed woman who goes to the theater as much to be seen decoratively framed in her box as to view a show. In this mirroring, where she watches herself being performed or praised ("Écoutant passer son éloge / Dans les chants des musiciens"), she has slipped away from the position of subject to that of object. She also recuperates the place of the spectator, for the "doux rêveur" has disappeared, not to return until the end of the poem.

In the second moment (stanzas 4–9), "la femme" leaves nineteenth-century Paris and moves to an antique setting. She begins with a striptease: "Laissant tomber l'épais velours, [. . .] Glissant de l'épaule à la hanche, / La chemise aux plis nonchalants." This dance reminds us once again of the Romantic association of feminine poetry with exhibitionism, although Gautier does not decry the indecency of the woman who reveals herself. Instead he offers his reader, identified with the "doux rêveur," the pleasurably titillating spectacle of a woman who bares herself. Her unveiling ends when her clothing falls about her "pieds blancs," a stance reminiscent of ancient sculpture. Indeed, the following stanza offers a direct comparison to the work of two ancient Greek sculptors and an invocation of Venus of the seas. The poem's subtitle, "Marbre de Paros," reinforces this comparison. "La femme" continues her movements, described as moments in a poem ("les strophes de ses poses"), thus uniting once again the essential elements of the ideal Parnassian object: femininity, poetry, and stasis.

In its third moment (stanzas 10–16), the poem leaves antiquity behind ("Lasse d'art antique") and travels in space to the East, Parnasse's preferred setting for escape after ancient Greece. With references to Ingres's painting, Gautier evokes the exoticism and sensuality of the harem. His immodest odalisque displays her body ("Étalant sa hanche opulente [. . .] / De ses reins cambrant les rondeurs") for her own pleasure: "Riant au miroir qui l'admire." This third tableau provokes a shift to the present tense and provides a greater sense of immediacy through the direct address and deictics ("voici") of stanza 14. We must also notice the suppleness of this third figure, who differs in her pleasure and her movement from the immobility of the statue. Indeed, stanza 15 appears to represent masturbatory pleasure ("le rêve qui la berce") under which the odalisque pants ("haletante") and writhes ("sa tête penche et se renverse"). She continues to perform for herself, now with no audience other than the poem's readers.

But Gautier does not allow her solitary pleasure to remain unpunished, nor does he leave his "femme" within the closed circle of self-admiration. In the poem's dénouement (stanzas 17–19), her orgasm coincides with her death ("Elle est morte de volupté!"), and a masculine figure reappears. After these forays into the past and the Orient, the poem finally returns to familiar European territory (England, Parma), at the same time returning the female figure to the position of static object, draped in white and lying on a soft, white bed. Let us take a final look at the masculine figure of the poem's end who recaptures the position of subject. Is he, now called "poète," the "doux rêveur" of the poem's first stanza? Although seemingly absent in the body of the poem, there is a hint of his agency in stanza 15: "Aux bras du rêve qui la berce." This recalls the dreamer, at the same time pointing to an author directing the woman's movements (her fantasy rocks her, but the author's fantasy first provokes her actions). Both male and female figures thus undergo a transformation in the poem, the woman from mistress of her own movement to immobile object and the man from passive spectator to subject of writing (poet). We can conclude from this poem that the stasis and objectification of the female figure (be she dead, frozen in marble, or fixed in a painting) is a necessary requirement for the arrival of the poet.

"Le poème de la femme" offers many consistencies with other poems by Gautier, from its comparisons to the plastic arts (painting, sculpture, enamel) to its obsessions with whiteness and immobility. Ultimately, its equivocation between movement and petrifaction is as short-lived as the freedom of expression it grants its female character. This poem shows perhaps more clearly than any other that "woman" and "poem" function as synonyms, and that Parnassian ideology strives to control both.

Like Leconte de Lisle's pre-1866 collections, *Émaux et camées* stands as a precursor to the movement that would be crowned by *Le Parnasse contemporain*. While nearly all of Leconte de Lisle's contributions to the 1866 and 1871 *Parnasse contemporain* eventually made their way into *Poèmes barbares* (1872), none of Gautier's contributions hails from prior or subsequent editions of his *Émaux et camées*. Let us now turn to the *Parnasse contemporain* and notice with what consistency the poems studied above translate into Gautier's Parnassianism. All the preoccupations of *Émaux et camées* appear in his contributions to the first volume: Orientalism ("Le Bédouin et la mer"), Greek mythology ("Le lion d'Atlas," "Parfois une Vénus . . ."), solid materials ("Le banc de pierre"), and femininity ("La Marguerite"). The three latter themes come together once again in "L'impassible," Gautier's program piece from the second *Parnasse contemporain*.

> La Satiété dort au fond de vos grands yeux;
> En eux plus de désirs, plus d'amour, plus d'envie;
> Ils ont bu la lumière, ils ont tari la vie,
> Comme une mer profonde où s'absorbent les cieux.     4
>
> Sous leur bleu sombre, on lit le vaste ennui des Dieux,
> Pour qui toute chimère est d'avance assouvie,

Et qui, sachant l'effet dont la cause est suivie,
Mélangent au présent l'avenir déjà vieux.                    8

L'infini s'est fondu dans vos larges prunelles,
Et, devant ce miroir qui ne réfléchit rien,
L'Amour découragé s'assoit, fermant ses ailes.

Vous, cependant, avec un calme olympien,                    12
Comme la Mnémosyne, à son socle accoudée,
Vous poursuivez, rêveuse, une impossible idée!

                                                    (2: 261)

This female figure, identified only as "vous," shares the impassivity of Leconte de Lisle's serene Venus and Baudelaire's implacable "Beauté." Gautier conveys an aesthetics of hardness less through the metaphor of statuary than through one of subjective impenetrability. Although her pose, "à son socle accoudée," alludes to a statue at its pedestal, here Gautier elaborates petrified femininity mostly through her characterization as an unmoving creature before whom even love holds no power ("L'Amour découragé").

The most striking physical characteristic of this unfeeling creature is her eyes, whose description occupies the majority of the sonnet. Vast and blue like the sea, they become a symbol for infinity. The ocean simile ("comme une mer") favors images of liquidity rather than solidity, and indeed is accompanied by a vocabulary of absorption ("les cieux s'absorbent"). These eyes have the power to extract liquid: "Ils ont bu la lumière, ils ont tari la vie." They draw it in or dry it out, but give nothing in return: "L'infini s'est fondu dans vos larges prunelles." If this feminine figure succeeds in drinking eternity through her eyes, it melts into hardness rather than emotion or tears. Her eyes become a mirror, like ice or a solidified liquid, that attracts images but does not return them: "ce miroir qui ne réfléchit rien."

These ocular descriptions allow no specific indication of the gender or the identity of "vous" before the final tercet. Here Gautier compares her to Mnemosyne, the goddess of memory and mother of the muses, and reveals her femininity with the adjective "rêveuse." Relying on the oft-exploited homophony in his comparison, "comme une mer," Gautier presents us with the image of an ungiving and unyielding maternal figure who would suck the life from those around her rather than suckle and nurture her children. This clearly symbolic "woman" suggests at once the perfected poem and the self-involvement of the poet. She has consumed light, life, and infinity to the point of complete satiation; she has achieved perfection and admits no more changes. And yet a dreamer like the poet of "Le poème de la femme," she avidly pursues "une impossible idée," as if satisfaction were unattainable. Does Gautier question the viability of his poetic ideal in leading us from the title, "L'impassible," to the impossibility of his last image?

With this sonnet, Gautier creates yet another image of hardened femininity, but this time a menacing one. Unlike "Le poème de la femme," where petrifaction serves to control feminine sexuality, "L'impassible" offers the portrait of a petrified female figure who controls and appropriates all that surrounds her. Similar to Leconte de Lisle's equivocation, Gautier vacillates between representing solidification as a controlling gesture and as a threatening posture. Such consistent, almost obsessive references to statuary allow the Parnassians to explore the nuances of femininity within the confines of poetic language. Although they pursue a poetics of mastery, one wonders finally who is the controller and who the controlled.

## Sculpted Femininity

A reading of the *Parnasse contemporain* confirms the centrality of petrified femininity to the entire group's aesthetic program. As many historians of the Parnasse have noted, the three volumes follow an itinerary that begins with coherence and tends toward the dissolution of specificity. It is not surprising to find that the first volume abounds with statuesque female figures, also a prominent but less concentrated feature of the second volume. The third volume, which I will consider in greater detail in the following chapter, takes a firm step away from such conventions.

A survey of the female characters who people the first two volumes reveals numerous borrowed types consistent with Leconte de Lisle's studies: the Parnassians called upon mythology, history, literature, and the Bible to people their poems.

Following Leconte de Lisle's lead, other poets relied on ancient mythology for a host of female figures, including the huntress Diana, Cybele (the Great Mother), Helen of Troy, the sweet-voiced yet dangerous Sirens, the Danaides (all fifty of whom murdered their husbands), and the sorceress Circe. Literary models include Dante's Beatrice, Petrarch's Laura, Tasso's Clorinda, and Shakespeare's Ophelia. The mythical women tend to fall into the category of victimizers, while the literary ones appear largely as victims.

By relying so heavily on pre-existing fictions for their female characters, the Parnassians largely followed Leconte de Lisle's lead in limiting their exploration of femininity to a study of archetypes rather than to the creation of new representations. While some nontypical female figures appear in Parnassian poems, these remain consistently unnamed and consequently ill-defined. Not molded on the pattern of mythical or literary figures, they remain nonetheless archetypal through their identification with a category. They are classified by age (Henri Cazalis's "Enfant blonde," Antoni Deschamps's "Jeune femme"), sexual or marital status (Louis-Xavier de Ricard's and Emmanuel Des Essarts's virgins, Armand Renaud's "Fiancées," André Lemoyne's "Veuve"), social status (Philoxène Boyer's "Patricienne"), activity (Lemoyne's "Baigneuse"), or nationality (Baudelaire's Malabaraise, Louis Salles's Javanaise). Not afforded the individual identity that a proper name confers, they remain two-dimensional and objectified figures.

The Parnassians described their female characters, whether archetypal, generic, or simply vague, in similar terms. They lauded feminine beauty with a strikingly consistent vocabulary of statuary. The following examples all hail from the first volume and speak for themselves. Ricard's speaking subject admires a virgin, saying: "J'aime *son front de marbre impassible,* et son œil / Où rayonne le froid soleil de son orgueil" ("Une vierge" [1: 117]). Deschamps describes his "Jeune femme" in living detail, only to surprise his reader with this punch line: "elle . . . *était de pierre!*" (1: 136). Arsène Houssaye's "La maîtresse du Titien" is equally stonelike: "Sur *le marbre un peu blond de ton épaule* altière, / Que j'aime tes cheveux à longs flots répandus!" (1: 149). And Mallarmé: "*ton sein de pierre* est habité / Par un cœur que la dent d'aucun crime ne

blesse" ("À celle qui est tranquille" [1: 164]). And Des Essarts:
"Elle est rhythmique par ses hanches / Et *sculpturale par ses
seins*" ("Les vierges" [1: 191]). Charles Coran: "Non, ton corps
est trop beau . . . *viens poser pour le marbre*" ("Sonnet" [1: 240]).
Eugène Villemin: "*Au marbre elle donnait des poses* de créole"
("Le drame de Rachel" [1: 246]). And so on.[12]

While the immobilization of female figures is a mainstay of
Parnassian poetry, this process is at work in a very particular
setting. That is, with great consistency, Parnassian poets turn
to the goddess Venus. Leconte de Lisle's "Vénus de Milo" is
in fact only one of numerous petrified Venuses to spring fully
formed from Parnassian pens. The statue *Venus de Milo* (c. 150
BC), rediscovered in 1820, provided the historical object that
gave rise to this flurry of interest. Installed in the Louvre for
all Parisian poets to contemplate, it become a tangible and forceful, if armless, figure of beauty, albeit one divorced from her
own sexuality. Touched and manipulated by the Parnassians,
she was herself neither touching nor able to touch.

A review of antique lore points to the multiplicity of associations that this figure provokes. Venus was modeled after and
conflated with Aphrodite, the Greek goddess born of the foam
(*aphros*). Thus Aphrodite becomes associated with the sea and,
although the goddess of love, she is invoked as well in war. A
symbol of fertility, she also appears as the patron of prostitutes.
Like her, Venus embodies these sometimes conflicting attributes.
Venus Anadyomene, represented in Botticelli's *Birth of Venus,*
figures the goddess rising from the sea on a shell. As we have
seen, Gautier's "Le poème de la femme" transforms the goddess of foam into one of stone. Other Parnassians invoke this
same image, including Lemoyne: "Voyant mes cheveux d'or
ondoyer sur mes reins, / La Vénus à la conque aurait pâli
d'envie" ("Baigneuse" [1: 107]). And Houssaye: "Tu sortis de
la mer comme une autre Vénus" ("La maîtresse du Titien"
[1: 150]).

For the Parnassians, Venus remains a symbol of beauty and
appears frequently as a point of comparison or an ideal model:
"Tu m'as fait voir Vénus, Zoraïde et Diane, / Corps de déesse
grec à tête de sultane" (Gautier, "Parfois une Vénus . . ." [1: 273]).
However her patronage of love remains doubtful, for she consistently appears as a combative rather than a giving model. Rather

than goddess of love, in Parnassian poems Venus more frequently plays the role of a goddess of war: "Elle avait dix-sept ans; elle était blonde & belle, / Comme Vénus *Victrix* ou la grande Cybèle" (Deschamps, "Annonciade" [2: 65]). Deschamps's Venus Victrix recalls Leconte de Lisle's "Vénus victorieuse," and we also find her aligned with Astarte, Phoenician goddess of war and love.[13] And yet the loving Venus remains consistently overshadowed by the warring one. Not once do the Parnassians represent the maternal Venus Genetrix, Venus Verticordia (the protector of chastity), or Venus Erucina (protector of prostitutes).

The Parnassians thus exhibit a clear preference for the stone figure and warring Venus (or the hard Diana[14]) over softer Venuses who patronize love and sexuality. Hardened Venus becomes harder still in statue form, a figure of unyielding and cold femininity. Coran sums up the Parnassian imperative toward feminine sexuality: "Sois Vénus dans un parc" ("Sonnet" [1: 240]). Venus thus ceases to exist as a representation of an ancient mythological figure and, as a statue, becomes instead a material symbol for pure Beauty.[15] Parnassian love of permanence is thus transferred from the immortality of the gods to the permanence of the hardest and most enduring of plastic arts. As Gautier suggested in "L'art," "les dieux eux-mêmes meurent."

A less characteristic rendering of the Venus statue appears in Alexis Martin's "À Vénus de Milo (Statuette)." Appearing in the 1866 *Parnasse contemporain* (1: 268–72), it offers an interesting response to Leconte de Lisle's "Vénus de Milo" (first published in 1846). One of the more obscure Parnassians, Martin contributed this sole poem to the Parnassian effort. His position in the hierarchical table of contents mirrors his status among the Parnassian poets: while Gautier, Banville, Heredia, and Leconte de Lisle open this first volume, Martin appears last. Without passing judgment on his merits as a poet, Parnassian or otherwise, let us read Martin's piece in light of Leconte de Lisle's.

As in Leconte de Lisle's "Vénus de Milo," here a poet apostrophizes the Greek statue. Martin's speaking subject, who defines himself as a "poète sans maîtresse," addresses a diminutive replica of the famous statue, lamenting the betrayal and loss of his lover. While the poem's subtitle ostensibly labels it miniature, the poem, if not its Venus, is in fact substantial (thirty-two quatrains). It begins thus:

> Ô Vénus de Milo! ma chère statuette,
> Seul reste d'un amour comme toi mutilé,
> Mon cœur, mon pauvre cœur, qui souffre et qui regrette,
> En ces strophes t'adresse un soupir désolé;
>
> Je crois que tu dois bien comprendre ma tristesse,
> Ô chef-d'œuvre incomplet! —comme tout ici-bas. —
> Où puis-je mieux pleurer, poète sans maîtresse,
> Que sur le sein meurtri de la Vénus sans bras?
>
> (lines 1–8)

Although the object of this poem may appear Parnassian, its style, tone, and form are markedly Romantic. It is both narrative (telling the story of a betrayal) and conversational (thanks to its meandering direct address to the statuette, the poet's "chère confidente"). It is, moreover, highly personal, replete with confessions, exclamations ("Hélas!"), outbursts ("Ce n'est pas vrai!"), judgments ("C'était lâche"), among other stylistic markers of subjectivity. Every fourth quatrain, Martin employs the *strophe-à-queue* (in this instance, the final line is a hemistich rather than a full alexandrine) to punctuate his poem's alexandrine quatrains and, perhaps, to offer a poetic version of the statue's incompleteness ("chef-d'œuvre incomplet"). He not only borrows this form from Lamartine's "Le lac," but also mentions this piece by name when remembering the voice of his lover: "Chut! —Elle va chanter *le Lac,* de Lamartine" (line 38).

So here there is Romantic affect and elegiac tears in abundance ("où puis-je mieux pleurer"), whereas Leconte de Lisle's poem offers the pretense of impassivity. These two Venuses, while both serving as interlocutors to poets, could not be more different. Martin's is miniature, mutilated, and as fragile as the spurned lover. Leconte de Lisle's is sturdy, unmoving, and triumphant. Martin's armless Venus has "le sein meurtri," while Leconte de Lisle's boasts "[un] sein inaltérable." The latter poet transforms the famous statue into an idea: Venus constitutes one of his feminine "types" or special symbols. On the contrary, Martin never loses sight of the physical object, forgotten by the departed lover and rediscovered in an obscure corner of the mourning lover's room. Moreover, the statue's metaphoric import is confined to that of remnant of the speaking subject's very personal loss.

Martin's intimate poem appears to contradict the Parnassian aesthetics of impassivity and concision on many points. Opposing Leconte de Lisle's model, which appeals to coldness for warmth, Martin's poet speaks to a symbol of fragility in order to confront the coldness of his lover. Throughout most of the poem the speaking subject identifies with the broken feminine object: both suffer from the heart. And yet he also clings to her as the last remnant of his departed lover, and his final stanza leaves the reader with an image that is ultimately Parnassian:

> Souvent, je t'entretiens pendant une heure entière,
> Et tu restes muette! —En ce monde moqueur
> Parlerai-je toujours à des Vénus de pierre,
>     À des femmes sans cœur?
>
> (lines 125–28)

Even Martin's delicate Venus is rendered immobile, mute, and impassive, like Leconte de Lisle's and Gautier's stony women.

This final image also reveals another reversal: the movement from woman to statue illustrated in so many Parnassian poems is occasionally answered by an inverse alchemy that strives to breathe life into a statue. While Martin's enslaved and wounded poet fails, his peers created more virile models of the artist who, like Pygmalion, succeeded in changing stone to flesh. Pygmalion, the mythological sculptor who opted for statuesque beauty instead of human companionship, only to call later on Venus to breathe life into his beloved statue, remains curiously unnamed by the Parnassian poets. Nonetheless, the Pygmalion myth lurks behind many Parnassian representations of the Poet and his work.

Arsène Houssaye introduces the figure of the sculptor alongside that of Venus in "La beauté":

> Armé du ciseau d'or, le divin Praxitèle
> Cherchait dans le paros la Vénus Astarté;
> Mais il ne trouvait pas. "Ô Vénus immortelle!
> Descends du ciel et parle à mon marbre lacté."     4

Du nuage d'argent Vénus descendra-t-elle?
"Qu'importe!" s'écria Praxitèle irrité:
"Daphné, Léa, Délie, Hélène, Héro, Myrtelle
Me donnent par fragments l'idéale beauté."          8

L'artiste ainsi créa Vénus victorieuse.
S'il vous eût rencontrée, ô beauté radieuse,
Femme et déesse, amour des hommes et des dieux,

Il eût fait sa Vénus sans détourner les yeux;          12
Ou plutôt, embrasé des feux de L'Empyrée,
Il eût brisé son marbre et vous eût adorée.

                                        (1: 152)

Praxiteles, Greek sculptor of the fourth century BC, represents
the archetypal maker in Houssaye's poem. He is also the sculptor
of the archetype, since his statue of Aphrodite became a model
for the *Venus de Milo* that, in turn, became the model for many
Roman copies. In this sonnet, Venus plays two roles, first as
the Venus Astarte, which Praxiteles attempts with some frus-
tration to capture in marble. He then invokes a second Venus,
the immortal goddess, to serve as muse and to help him create
a sculpted image of beauty. But the impatient Praxiteles finally
refuses Venus's intervention, opting instead for a whole list of
female inspirers. This rather anachronistic grouping includes
mythical, literary, and biblical figures of great beauty who, as
united fragments, will offer the sculptor "l'idéale beauté." Let
us not overlook the adjective "divin" affixed to the sculptor's
name. While he refuses the intervention of the goddess Venus,
he perhaps does not need it, since the maker already possesses
divine attributes.

Indeed, "l'artiste" successfully creates his warring Venus.
The tercets move from the specific (Praxiteles) to the general
(the artist), as well as from the third person to direct address.
The speaking subject addresses not the sculptor, but rather the
spurned Venus. Here Houssaye's poem begins to resemble a
variation on the Pygmalion myth. Had Praxiteles given Venus
the time of day, he would have adored her and cast aside his
chisel. But like Houssaye's Parnassian colleagues, he presents
us with a Venus who is unattainable, uncaring, and unrespon-
sive. In short, an obstacle rather than a helpmate. It is not surprising to find the figure of Pygmalion stalking so many Parnassian
poems, since the poet is so often figured as a sculptor who creates

beauty from hard objects and presides over a transformation
from soft to hard and, occasionally, back again. While the Parnassians went wild over mythological female figures, they
clearly preferred historical male figures to mythological ones
and thus left Pygmalion nameless. Hence in addition to ancient
sculptors and painters (Praxiteles, Phidias, Apelles, Cleomenes),
historical poets, and musicians people their poems to reflect
on the artistic endeavor.[16]

Pygmalion remains nonetheless a prominent, if anonymous,
presence. Houssaye's Praxiteles stands for the first Pygmalion,
focused on his art, insensitive to human warmth and disdainful of female companionship. Here is how Ovid described him:

> One man, Pygmalion, who had seen these women
> Leading their shameful lives, shocked at the vices
> Nature has given the female disposition
> Only too often, chose to live alone,
> To have no woman in his bed. But meanwhile
> He made, with marvelous art, an ivory statue,
> As white as snow, and gave it greater beauty
> Than any girl could have, and fell in love
> With his own workmanship.
>
> (10. 243–51)

But then Pygmalion, having fallen in love with his own creation, appeals to Venus to give it life, and she grants his wish.

This second, softened Pygmalion also serves as an unat-
tributed model for Gautier's "Sonnet," from the second *Parnasse
contemporain:*

> J'aimais autrefois la forme païenne;
> Je m'étais créé, fou d'antiquité,
> Un blanc idéal de marbre sculpté
> D'hétaïre grecque ou milésienne.          4
>
> Maintenant j'adore une Italienne,
> Un type accompli de modernité,
> Qui met des gilets, fume & prend du thé,
> Et qu'on croit Anglaise ou Parisienne.          8
>
> L'amour de mon marbre a fait un pastel,
> Les yeux blancs ont pris des tons de turquoise,
> La lèvre a rougi comme une framboise,

Et mon rêve grec dans l'or d'un cartel      12
Ressemble aux portraits de rose & de plâtre
Où la Rosalba met sa fleur bleuâtre.

(2: 262)

Gautier's sonnet describes a reverse movement that appears to be anti-Parnassian; indeed, in many respects it contradicts such poems as "Le poème de la femme" and "L'art." Here the female object is transformed from ideal to human, stone to flesh, marble to pastel, white to living color, antique to modern, from frozen object to responsive lover.

And yet while appearing to belie Gautier's other poems, "Sonnet" in fact provides a key to understanding the unstable representation of the Parnassian feminine object. We can attribute his Venus's floating role (like that of Houssaye's Venus and Gautier's "la femme") to her double association, proffered first as a model of ideal beauty but at the same time identified with the role of maker. For here the speaking subject occupies the conflated positions of both Pygmalion, the sculptor, and Venus, the goddess who holds the power to transform a statue into a woman. In "L'impassible," the stony female figure strangely resembles Leconte de Lisle's virile Poet and Gautier's indifferent one. In these instances, statuesque female figures are stripped of their sexuality to become doubles for the artist (whether poet or sculptor). In the opposite case, Parnassian poets contain living, breathing feminine sexuality by freezing it in ice, casting it in bronze, or capturing it in stone. Rather than countering Parnassian ideology, Gautier's sonnet might be said instead to provide the confirming exception. More forceful than Pygmalion, Gautier's sculptor-poet and Houssaye's Praxiteles wield transformative powers that function in both directions, powers recuperated from the all-powerful (and sometimes notoriously vengeful) female goddess. Thus in all senses the male maker contains femininity and renders it powerless.

## Frigid Form

Despite their ferocious neoclassicism, in one aspect the Parnassians were resolutely more modern than the Romantics: they spent quite a lot of time contemplating their own métier and writing about writing. While the figure of the Poet provided ample material for the Romantic lyric, Parnassian self-reflexivity differed insofar as it focused on the creation of the poetic text rather than the personality of the Poet-persona. As we have seen, the poetry of both Leconte de Lisle and Gautier offers metapoetic commentary, be that criticism of sentimentality, meandering forms, and carelessly composed verse; or exhortations to cultivate a poetics of obstacles; or simply metaphoric representations of the creator working his poem-statue-woman into a state of unmoving perfection.

As I suggested in chapter 2, the hierarchy of poetic genres follows clearly gendered divisions. The emotiveness, expansion, and lyricism of the feminine elegy opposes the perfection, exactness, concentration, and description of the masculine sonnet. The sonnet came to France from Italy around 1538, introduced by Clément Marot to his contemporaries, including Du Bellay and Pierre de Ronsard. Their sonnet series were heavily influenced by the Petrarchan tradition. Indeed, Petrarch's *Canzoniere* did a great deal to codify both the form and content of love poetry. Following the model of the Petrarchan sonnet, French men of the sixteenth century addressed their sonnets to beloved women, often absent or unattainable, sometimes dead. After enjoying a vogue, the sonnet fell into disfavor in the seventeenth century, not to be resuscitated until the nineteenth. Gautier attributed the renewal of this form to Sainte-Beuve: "L'école romantique a remis en honneur le sonnet, depuis si longtemps délaissé. La gloire de cette réhabilitation appartient à Sainte-Beuve, qui, dans les poésies de *Joseph Delorme*, s'écria le premier: 'Ne ris pas des sonnets, ô critique moqueur!'" (*Histoire* 344). While it is true that Sainte-Beuve was among the first nineteenth-century poets to revive the sonnet, Gautier would have more accurately attributed its restitution to the Parnassian, rather than the Romantic, school. Gautier himself notes that Hugo, "le grand forgeur de mètres, l'homme à qui toutes les formes [. . .] sont familièr[e]s, n'a jamais fait de sonnet."[17] Nor were other major Romantics known for their exploitation of this form, and indeed, Sainte-Beuve's 1829 collection (*Vie, poésies et pensées de Joseph Delorme*) did not meet with success from his contemporaries.

The renaissance of the sonnet can therefore be connected to the Parnassian cult of form. Gautier suggests as much:

"[Sainte-Beuve] en a fait lui-même qui valent de longs poèmes, car ils sont sans défauts, et depuis lors cette forme charmante, taillée à facettes comme un flacon de cristal, et si merveilleusement propre à contenir une goutte de lumière ou d'essence, a été essayée par un grand nombre de jeunes poètes" (*Histoire* 344). The concentration of the sonnet ("une goutte [. . .] d'essence"), its preference over long forms, its perfectability ("sans défauts"), its intricacy ("taillée à facettes"), and its hardness ("comme un flacon de cristal"), all these qualities become aligned with the Parnassian, not the Romantic, aesthetic. So it is up to Gautier's "jeunes poètes," the proto-Parnassian generation of 1848, to return the sonnet to its previous glory. In doing so they followed the lead not of Sainte-Beuve, but rather of Baudelaire, who, let us recall, appreciated and exploited the sonnet's constraints. The letter in which Baudelaire admires this form ("parce que la forme est contraignante") also praises one of the more obscure Parnassians, Joséphin Soulary, the author of *Sonnets humouristiques* (1859): "Que M. Soulary soit un grand poète, cela est évident aujourd'hui pour tout le monde, et cela a été évident pour moi dès les premiers vers que j'ai pu lire de lui. Quel est donc l'imbécile [. . .] qui traite si légèrement le Sonnet et n'en voit pas la beauté pythagorique?" (*Correspondance* 1: 676).

In fact, the sonnet often serves as a vehicle with which to criticize Romantic effusion. In a lighter vein than Leconte de Lisle's "Les montreurs," but like him, in sonnet form, Soulary condemns the elegiac excesses of the Romantics in his "À un poète élégiaque":

Dans les notes en deuil d'une plainte touchante
C'est trop psalmodier ton romantique émoi.
L'être qui souffre est seul & doit souffrir pour soi:
Fauvette il nous attriste, aigle il nous désenchante.     4

Hé! qui n'a pas son faix de peine desséchante?
C'est par l'épine au front que le Génie est roi.
Meure enfin l'élégie! Enfant, redresse-toi!
Ce n'est pas en pleurant que le poète chante.     8

L'harmonie est un vin qui met la vie au cœur.
Si tu n'eus que le luth pour outil de labeur,
Sois cher aux fronts courbés sous la tâche inégale.

> Fais-toi l'écho du Dieu qui rit à l'ouvrier,     12
> Soleil dans la campagne, amour dans le foyer;
> Sois la voix du travail, ô céleste cigale!
>
> (109)

Like Leconte de Lisle, Soulary presents the sonnet as the counterpoint or antidote to Romantic excess. The sonnet represents not only formal perfection, but also the work ethic of the poet confronted by its structural demands. Gautier, the poet of enamels and cameos, employs a jewel metaphor to describe Soulary as "le plus fin joaillier, le plus habile ciseleur de ce bijou rhythmique" (*Histoire* 345). The relationship between constraint and quality of product attracted many other Parnassian poets to the form. While not all Parnassians share Leconte de Lisle's austerity and negativity, or Gautier's often didactic formalism, a significant number turned to the sonnet as the ultimate poetic challenge.

Numerous individual sonnets and sonnet series appear in the three collections.[18] Moreover, the editors grouped seventeen sonnets by as many poets at the end of the first *Parnasse contemporain* to indicate the importance of the form. This final grouping begins with Gautier's "Parfois une Vénus . . ." and includes other bellicose mythological women, such as Artemis (José-Maria de Heredia, "La chasse") and "Les Danaïdes" (Sully-Prudhomme). Deschamps's "Après la mort de Laure"[19] harkens back to the Petrarchan source and fixes his Laura in death, while Mendès's "L'absente" simply erases female presence. Others associate feminine figures with stone ("La Mélencolia se tient sur une pierre," Cazalis [1: 283]) or jewels: "La reine Nicosis, portant des pierreries [. . .] / Son vêtement tremblant chargé d'orfévreries" (Banville, "La reine de Saba" [1: 274]). Others still have become familiar in different settings.[20]

While the preponderance of sonnets has much to say about the Parnassians' formal preferences, just as clearly it serves as an instrument with which to construct and comment upon femininity. Let us follow Gautier's direction and return to his "plus fin joaillier," Joséphin Soulary:

Au commencement des [*Sonnets humouristiques*, Soulary]
compare sa Muse à une belle fille enfermant son corps souple
dans un corset juste et un vêtement qui serre les formes en

les faisant valoir. L'idée entrant dans le sonnet qui la contient, l'amincit et en assure le contour, ressemble en effet à cette beauté qu'un peu de contrainte rend plus svelte, plus élégante et plus légère. (*Histoire* 345)

The sonnet in question does not number among those Soulary contributed to the *Parnasse contemporain.* Moreover, Gautier fails to quote the poem, allowing his paraphrase to suffice as commentary on the sonnet-corset metaphor. Although obscure and admittedly minor, Soulary's "Le sonnet" is too delightfully transparent to pass over so quickly. Here it is:

> "Je n'entrerai pas là," dit la folle en riant,
> "Je vais faire éclater cette robe trop juste."
> Puis, elle enfle son sein, tord sa hanche robuste,
> Et prête à contre-sens un bras luxuriant.                4
>
> J'aime ces doux combats, & je suis patient.
> Dans l'étroit vêtement qu'à son beau corps j'ajuste,
> Là, serrant un atour, ici, le déliant,
> J'ai fait passer enfin tête, épaules & buste.            8
>
> Avec art maintenant dessinons sous ces plis
> La forme bondissante & les contours polis.
> Voyez! la robe flotte, & la beauté s'accuse.
>
> Est-elle bien ou mal en ces simples dehors?             12
> Rien de moins dans le cœur, rien de plus sur le corps,
> Ainsi j'aime la femme, ainsi j'aime la Muse.
>
> (5)

This irregular sonnet confirms rather blatantly the analogy between poetic language and femininity proffered in Gautier's "Le poème de la femme." It appears elsewhere in the *Parnasse contemporain,* as in this comparison: "Ô belle, dont le corps semble un vivant poème" (Louis Ratisbonne, "La volupté et l'amour" [3: 327]). Dominated by a vocabulary of constraint ("trop juste," "étroit," "serrant"), it also leads to the inevitable conclusion that behind the Parnassian quest for formal control, there lies an ideological program that aims to restrict femininity and women's access to subjective positions. The speaking subject describes sonnet-writing and corseting as "doux combats," repeating a war metaphor we have already encountered numerous times. Indeed, the frivolous female of Soulary's sonnet offers a certain resistance: "Je n'entrerai pas là." But if the poem doubles for the female body, then it is a body over which woman ultimately has no empire. Instead, she is obliged to assume various contorsions: "Puis, elle enfle son sein, tord sa hanche robuste, / Et prête à contre-sens un bras luxuriant." Although initially robust of body, when corseted in sonnet form ("l'étroit vêtement"), she lacks both agency and freedom of movement, for it is the poetic persona who clothes her: "J'ai fait passer enfin tête, épaules & buste."

While Romantic mores strove to keep women poets clothed, which is to say silent, they were at least allowed a certain freedom of movement in the ample confines of the elegy. Parnassians apparently found that even such limited liberty exceeded acceptable boundaries: not content to criticize the feminine sentiment and effusion of the Romantics (thereby condemning women poets), they succeeded also in restricting symbolic femininity (the poem itself) within narrow and carefully delineated margins. The corset functions to constrain the female body and, in Soulary's poem, it immobilizes femininity just as surely as do stone, bronze, or ice.

Gautier's "L'art" supplies another image of constrictive clothing:

> Point de contraintes fausses!
> Mais que pour marcher droit
>       Tu chausses,
> Muse, un cothurne étroit.
>
> Fi du rhythme commode
> Comme un soulier trop grand,
>       Du mode
> Que tout pied quitte et prend!
>       (*Émaux et camées* 148, stanzas 2–3)

I will have more to say about Parnassian "feet" in the next chapter; suffice it for now to note that Gautier, like Soulary, subjects his Muse to highly uncomfortable apparel. Behind the Parnassian quest for formal stasis, then, lies a desperate attempt to reclaim the poetic act for masculinity and to render poetry, as a metaphor for femininity, unchanging and fixed beyond time.

The notoriously misogynist critic Barbey d'Aurevilly once asked: "est-ce donc si malheureux d'être, en art ou en littérature, quelque chose comme la Vénus de Milo?" (*Les bas-bleus* xxii). Are corsets so frightfully dreadful, if they make woman "plus svelte, plus élégante et plus légère," to return to Gautier's assessment? Although wildly anti-Parnassian, Barbey rivals Parnassian antifeminism and concurs with this commonplace of nineteenth-century masculinist criticism: women should content themselves to be poetry (an object of beauty) rather than to write it. In the next chapter I will ask Barbey's question of midcentury women poets. How did they react to these lyrical corsets, these statuesque poses, this poetic imprisonment?

# Moving Statues

*Les Parnassiennes*

The Parnassian vision of femininity as sterile, contained, and impassive functioned on a symbolic level to petrify it by controlling its representation. And yet the critical and poetic texts of the overwhelmingly masculine school of the Parnasse also reveal this inherent contradiction: that the predominating image of women in Parnassian poetry as cold, statuesque, and immobile lies in stark contrast with the formless and effusive femininity projected by the Parnassians onto the Romantics. Parnassians clearly equated Romantic and women's poetry since, as I have shown, the qualities they repudiated not only target Romanticism, but also recall critical appraisals of "feminine" poetry. As a corollary, then, the Parnassian school dismissed what its own women poets had to say about poetry and sexual difference and, unlike the Romantics, tolerated no discussion of gender. Although contradictory, these two strategies nonetheless served the same function of incapacitating femininity. On one hand, the Parnasse symbolically characterized femininity as imprisoned in marble and coldness. On the other hand, they sidelined both "feminine" poetic doctrine and women from their community of poets. We can conclude from this that anti-Romanticism covers for antifeminism, and that behind neoclassicism lies an ideology of exclusion.

If the Parnassians succeeded in consolidating the view that Romantic and women's poetry are synonymous, later critics also adhered to this conclusion. For example Jean Larnac, the early-twentieth-century historian of women's literature, conflated Romanticism and women's poetry because he was unable to conceive of a female Parnassian: "Le Romantisme libéra le cœur éperdu de [. . .] Marceline Desbordes-Valmore. Mais [. . .] on ne peut [. . .] citer aucune femme dans la grande famille

Parnassienne. [. . .] Les femmes ne sont à l'aise que dans la liberté. Dès qu'elles ne laissent plus libre cours à leur inspiration, elles perdent leurs ailes" (224–25).[1] Because women's poetry and Romantic poetry have come to be synonymous for so many critics, perhaps Larnac is not alone in his ignorance of the women Parnassians.

## Cherchez la femme

While in general, Parnassian poetry garners a far smaller audience today than Romantic or Symbolist pieces, literary critics have not completely overlooked this body of work.[2] Within a limited frame of study, many historians of the Parnasse have chosen to pass superficially over the contributions of the *Parnassiennes* or to overlook them entirely.[3] Others have given them more developed coverage, but never the serious attention that would allow for an analysis of their work and its relation to the movement as a whole. Nearly all literary historians of the Parnasse have reduced female participation to two roles: either that of hostess to literary salons or outmoded Romantic.

The most prominent *salonnières* of the period included Nina de Villard and Ursule Gaillard (Nina's mother), Louise Colet, and Mme de Ricard (Xavier's mother). Parnassian historians have amply documented the social meetings hosted by these women in the 1860s and 1870s, salons whose habitués and literary allegiances varied tremendously. Although Colet is largely associated with the Romantic old guard, Souriau explains that she "a ouvert son salon aux Parnassiens" (319). The younger inner circle of Parnassian poets peopled Mme de Ricard's gatherings, which Pierre Martino credits as being "plus littéraire que la revue [*Revue du progrès moral, littéraire, scientifique et artistique*] fondée par son fils" (58). Villard and her mother presided over one of the least staid and most bohemian of the Parisian literary salons for nearly twenty years: "De 1863 à 1882, Nina a tenu le salon le plus vivant et le plus intellectuel de Paris" (Raynaud 72). Both participants in and historians of the Parnasse have written liberally on these women and their salons. The poetic exchange and literary contacts provided by these gatherings, as by male-hosted salons, were extremely important for the formation of the group and its poetic doctrine. Consequently, memoirs from and histories of this poetic period abound with anecdotes about the "female" salons, and in a language largely free from the condescension and disapproval evident in their discussion of female-authored poetry.

Studies by Schaffer, Badesco, and Somoff and Marfée provide the most abundant information on the work of the *Parnassiennes*. During the first half of the twentieth century, Aaron Schaffer wrote two books on Parnassian poetry, *Parnassus in France* (1929) and *The Genres of Parnassian Poetry* (1944). He offered one of the early historical perspectives on the movement, following first-hand memoirs by such Parnassians as Mendès, Ricard, and others.[4] In *The Genres of Parnassian Poetry,* Schaffer discusses the "feminine touch" added to the second and third volumes and groups the majority of female-authored works together in his chapter "The Sentimental Genre."[5] He identifies Colet and Léocadie Penquer as "member[s] of the clan of Lamartine" (374), Malvina Blanchecotte as a "Romantique attardée" (377), and Louisa Siefert as a "thoroughly personal poet" (380). Schaffer accords Mélanie Bourotte only a footnote containing this appraisal: "[she was the] author of a volume of worse than mediocre lyric poetry" (377n26).

Luc Badesco's more recent two-volume work, *La génération poétique de 1860* (1971), is admirably researched, offering a broader scope than that of Schaffer. Like Schaffer, he both attends to female participation in the poetry of the midcentury and associates most women Parnassians with the Romantic school. Badesco confines his discussion of their works to an appendix that catalogues satellite poets clustered around "les noms prestigieux" of Romanticism and, in particular, that of Lamartine. Among this "phalange des muses du Second empire" (1326), women belonging to the "misérable famille d'un père illustre" (Leconte de Lisle), Badesco names Bourotte, Blanchecotte, and Penquer. Lamartine's prestige, Badesco affirms, "n'eut aucune influence sur le renouveau poétique" surrounding Leconte de Lisle (139). However Lamartine's reign over women's poetry persists: "[Son influence] s'exerce surtout sur les femmes poètes," including Ackermann ("Elle prolonge donc une agonie" [139]).

As recently as 1979, in their volume dedicated to *Les muses du Parnasse,* the authors J.-P. Somoff and A. Marfée write that the *Parnassiennes* "sont toutes [. . .] immergées dans ce romantisme [dolent dont le chantre privilégié est Lamartine], elles miroitent toutes des reflets du Lac" (7). This review clearly fails to meet the scholarly standards of other histories of the Parnasse, and indeed carries a glib tone and a penchant for generalities that surpass the (occasionally) more subtle condescension of Parnassian scholars toward the female members of the school. Regardless of their academic pedigree, historians of the Parnasse, like the Parnassians themselves, have consistently sidelined its female contributors, dismissing them as Romantic incursions and failing to take their poetry seriously.

Criticism of the *Parnassiennes* resembles the criticism leveled at women Romantics by their contemporaries: they are imitators, not innovators, and have nothing crucial to say about poetry. The Parnassian condemnation carried the extra force of suggesting that, not only did these women lack originality, but they failed even to adopt the style of the poetic movement to which they would belong. In short, the *Parnassiennes* were really not part of the Parnasse.

Whether through distortion or neglect, critics have worked in complicity with the Parnassian patriarchy to silence femininity, a task the male poets accomplished admirably in the first volume of the *Parnasse contemporain.* This exclusively masculine issue includes a piece by Mendès, entitled "L'absente." In retrospect, this sonnet of entirely feminine rhymes provides an ironic commentary on the place of women in the movement:

C'est une chambre où tout languit et s'efférmine;
L'or blême et chaud du soir, qu'émousse la persienne,
D'un ton de vieil ivoire ou de guipure ancienne
Apaise l'éclat dur d'un blanc tapis d'hermine.     4

Plein de la voix mêlée autrefois à la sienne,
Et triste, un clavecin d'ébène que domine
Une coupe où se meurt, tendre, une balsamine,
Pleure les doigts défunts de la musicienne.     8

Sous des rideaux imbus d'odeurs fades et moites,
De pesants bracelets hors du satin des boîtes
Se répandent le long d'un chevet sans haleine.

Devant la glace, auprès d'une veilleuse éteinte,     12
Bat le pouls d'une blanche horloge en porcelaine,
Et le clavecin noir gémit, quand l'heure tinte.

(1: 277)

We might consider this sonnet as a Parnassian variation on a feminine theme. That is to say, it is highly descriptive and impersonal if not entirely objective, since sentience and sensation are transferred onto the room's inanimate, mechanical objects: the harpsichord and clock. It also abides by Parnassian tenets of composition, notably with its rich rhymes and intricate, Mallarméan syntax. Indeed, Mendès's proliferation of imbedded clauses and suspended verbs, along with his precise, miniature images, bring to mind "la délicate phalange / Du doigt" of Mallarmé's "musicienne du silence" ("Sainte," in *Œuvres complètes* 54). And yet while engaging in this masculine poetic play, Mendès strives to penetrate femininity with his vision of a feminine interior and use of feminine rhymes.

Let us consider this "woman's space" a bit more closely, and the eye that is turned to it. Mendès creates a room (Donne called the sonnet "a pretty room") whose female inhabitant is absent, dead one gathers from the vocabulary of passage ("autrefois," "défunt," "éteinte," "sans haleine"). The room nonetheless retains echoes of her presence, thanks to the anthropomorphized harpsichord, which cries and moans. Her voice, her fingers, and her breath are named only to illustrate her absence. While the quiet and precise description of the room abandoned by its owner suggests a still life, the process of decay forms a narrative. The present-progressive verbs point to an attenuation, one which blurs the edges of the carpet's "éclat dur," of the dying flower, of the dank smells. The verbs "languit," "apaise," "se meurt," and "se répandent" all evoke a decline or dispersal. Most interesting, the verb "s'effémine" refers not just to the room's feminine decor (draped in fabric, decorated with flowers and jewelry, colored in muted tones), but to a progression toward femininity: the room, by virtue of its tepid, languorous decay, is *rendered* feminine. The black harpsichord, standing out in contrast against the white ermine rug, is reduced to pathetic silence, now dominated by a dying flower. Like the historians of the Parnasse, "L'absente" silences a feminine voice, stills female hands, and erases woman from the passage of time. The poem not only remarks on the absence of women in the collection, but also helps to create that absence.

Critics, then, have largely followed the Parnassians in silencing female participants. This is, indeed, virgin territory: there is an enormous amount to learn about the women of the Parnasse, and an enormous amount that they have to tell us about their movement.

## Les Parnassiennes par elles-mêmes

While no women poets appeared in the first issue of the *Parnasse contemporain,* by the second volume a token but variegated group integrated the club, such that the inclusion of women coincided with the journal's gradual loss of its rigid identity as a forum for objective poetry. Critics tend to consider the first volume the most coherently "Parnassian" of issues, while suggesting that the third and final volume had lost its specificity. Curiously, this last is the only one to present its poets alphabetically rather than hierarchically. While the first two began with the Parnassian "masters" (1: Gautier, Banville, Heredia, Leconte de Lisle; 2: Leconte de Lisle, Banville), the third volume's alphabetical arrangement placed Louise Ackermann at its head. Oddly enough, her poem "Une femme," which addresses a female readership, stands as its liminal piece. Clearly "less Parnassian" means as well more female and more democratic.

But what of the few women who did manage to break rank and appear in Parnassian publications? For there were in fact eight women among the hundred *Parnassiens:* Louise Colet (1810–76), Louise Ackermann (1813–90), Léocadie Penquer (1817–89), Malvina Blanchecotte (1830–97), Mélanie Bourotte (1832–?), Isabelle Guyon (1833–1911), Nina de Villard (1843–84), and Louisa Siefert (1845–77).[6] What were the reactions of these women to the movement and its poetry? How did Parnassian obsessions get played out in their poems? What was their approach to form, style, and theme? What figures peopled their work? Does their relation to the dominant movement parallel the sly resistance of such women Romantics as Desbordes-Valmore, or did the more hostile environment of Parnassianism provoke a different reaction?

This is an eclectic group of women, including the well-established Ackermann and Colet, both having made their first marks on literary history under Romanticism, alongside the much younger Siefert and Villard. Only these latter two belong to the generation Gautier refers to as "les jeunes poètes." Like them, Coppée, Cros, France, Heredia, Mallarmé, Mendès, Ricard, and Verlaine were born in the early 1840s. While Colet and Villard participated prominently in Parisian literary circles, others such as Guyon, Bourotte, and Penquer led retired lives or masked their identities. We can add economic diversity to these social and generational differences: Blanchecotte, the *poète-ouvrière,* rubs elbows with the aristocratic Guyon in the third volume. While their poems are often dismissed as Romantic and sentimental—decidedly un-Parnassian—in fact their poetry is as diversified as are their personal histories. It is misleading to lump them together as Romantics since many female contributors explored various aspects of the Parnassian poetic doctrine, including the sonnet form, the impersonal voice, or the ancient and orientalist themes favored by the movement.

Because the *Parnassiennes* form such a small and circumscribed group, let us look at them in some detail.[7] Who were these women and how did they come to be admitted to the Parnassian band? In most cases, it appears that their inclusion was due to affinities with individual but influential members of the group, rather than through direct participation with the inner circle, the "entresol du Parnasse" in Lemerre's bookshop.[8] Sainte-Beuve had brought Blanchecotte to public attention with an article in his 1855 *Causeries du lundi;* Bourotte was Gautier's protégée; Colet, long a patron of Leconte de Lisle; Siefert, a protégée of Soulary and member of Anatole France's circle; and Villard, the flamboyant hostess of an important Parnassian salon. Ackermann, Blanchecotte, Guyon, Penquer, and Siefert had been or would be published by Alphonse Lemerre.[9]

I would like to begin my reading of these poets with a consideration of the most characteristically Parnassian among them: Colet and Villard, bookends of the female Parnassians. Although separated by a generation, these two women contributed pieces most in keeping with the school's formal and thematic obsessions. Because they both held salons frequented by Parnassian poets, they enjoyed the most developed social contact with the group. Ironically, they were also engaged in political struggles of the day that their colleagues did their best to ignore.

## Louise Colet

Louise Colet has long been a favorite target of dismissive and *ad feminam* criticism. In *Les bas-bleus,* Barbey d'Aurevilly identifies her as *"le* bas-bleu même" (237). He goes on to detail "le talent qu'elle n'avait pas" (238), "[sa] vanité monstrueuse" (238), "son pédantisme [. . .] échevelé, enflammé, [et] sibyllin" (239), "sa débordante personnalité" (247), among other dubious qualities. As usual, Barbey bars no holds and sets new standards for misogynist invective. His condemnation of Colet's writing is tantamount to character assassination: "L'hypocrisie du *moi* n'a d'égale, en son livre [*Italie des Italiens*], que son impertinence. Elle s'y gonfle comme la grenouille, et quelle déception, elle n'en crève pas!" (250). Barbey's language suggests that his vehement hatred has its roots in identification or projection, since in the following description of Colet he offers a portrait worthy of himself: "pour tout le monde elle resta toujours une plébéienne de son port, une espèce de poissonnière ou d'écaillère superbe, qu'on se représente les poings aux hanches, l'œil allumé, *la bouche ouverte à l'invective: vomitoire jaillissant* [. . .]!" (241; emphasis mine).

While critics since Barbey have not succeeded in equaling his vituperation, their analyses often lead to similar conclusions. Colet is a self-serving, self-promoting "queen of the *arrivistes"* (Schaffer, *Genres* 372) whose success is due to the manipulation of others rather than to any real talent of her own. And Fernand Calmettes, among others, goes to great pains to prove that not one of the four poetry prizes granted her by the Académie française between 1839 and 1854 was merited (69–76). Let us recall that Somoff and Marfée prefer to focus on Colet's physical person: "Il nous a paru utile de montrer à nos oublieux contemporains le beau décolleté de Mme Colet" (95). We are frequently told that she exploited her beauty shamelessly: "Using her physical charms to good advantage, she was the mistress, or at least the *protégée,* of one Academician after another" (Schaffer, *Genres* 372).

Colet was indeed a visible figure throughout her literary career. She wrote prolifically in all genres: poetry, novels, plays, and journalism.[10] She reigned over literary Paris for many years, and counted among her habitués and correspondents numerous Romantics (including Desbordes-Valmore, Béranger, Vigny, Musset, and Hugo). But she was also an early supporter of Leconte de Lisle, investing both literary and personal interest in him from the time he was a young and sometimes financially strapped poet. She helped find him publishers and introduced him to numerous literary figures at her salon. In turn, Leconte de Lisle introduced Colet to the new, antisentimental poetry, for which she and Flaubert expressed their admiration in their correspondence. Known for her tempestuousness, flamboyance, in short, for her "Romantic" personality, Colet began, in the 1860s, to cultivate the detached, objective style of the Parnassians.

Her poetry of this period, while overshadowed by her copious Romantic production, is exemplified by publications in the *Revue fantaisiste* as well as by her contributions to the second and third *Parnasse contemporain,* the latter publications including two sonnet series. These sonnets show an about-face from the Romantic poetry on which she cut her teeth, rather than an allegiance to it as so many critics have suggested. They indicate a conscious attempt on her part to adopt the impersonal style, preferred forms, and central themes of Parnassian poetry. The two sonnets appearing in volume 2 explore the ruins of "Pœstum" (Pæstum) and its relation to ancient Rome. To volume 3, she contributed three sonnets on Arab themes and a short Roman poem. While both subjects reflect her travels, first to Italy and then to Egypt, they are also markedly Parnassian.

Colet's three Roman poems invite an exploration of her relationship to the Parnasse's fascination with antiquity. Unlike Leconte de Lisle's bookish interest in ancient Greece and Rome, Colet's attraction to Italy sprang from family contact (her father was raised in southern Italy), political investment, and personal experience. This is not to say that her poems are less erudite than Leconte de Lisle's, for indeed they illustrate an intimate knowledge of Roman history, geography, and mythology. Both Italophile and Italophone, Colet was drawn by the political events leading up to the reunification of Italy. Ironically, her most conservative poetry sprang from her involvement in leftist political causes. She traveled to Italy in 1859 and stayed several years, during which time she expressed her antipapism in satirical prose, supported the Risorgimento movement for Italian unification, followed its military leader Garibaldi to Naples, and lived in the southern Campagna region.[11] These travels and activities nourished her poems, which are set in ancient cities of southern Italy: Pæstum, Rome, Capua, and Pompeii. Although stripped of Colet's Romantic volubility, these poems do not entirely lack her spirit of rebellion. Here is "Pœstum," the first of Colet's two sonnets from the second *Parnasse contemporain:*

> La lascive Pœstum n'a pas laissé d'annales;
> L'oubli la châtia de son inanité;
> À peine si Tibulle en un vers a chanté
> Les roses qui jonchaient ses molles saturnales.          4
>
> Dans une plaine morne, où grincent les rafales,
> Où la Mal'aria verse un souffle empesté,
> Le néant la coucha de ses mains sépulcrales,
> Et le passant se dit: "Elle n'a pas été."          8
>
> Mais voilà que, vibrant comme trois grandes lyres,
> Surgissent lumineux d'un marécage noir
> Ses trois temples, debout sur la pourpre du soir.
>
> Clairs parvis, pleins jadis d'olympiens délires,          12
> Les spectres de vos dieux errants sur les chemins
> Sont-ils ces pâtres nus aux fiers profils romains?
>
> (2: 135)

Pæstum, situated along the Gulf of Taranto some twenty miles south of modern Salerno, is today known as the site of three splendid Doric temples. First called Poseidonia, it was founded c. 600 BC by Greek colonists from Sybaris. The Sybarites, of course, would eventually bequeath their name along with their reputation for hedonism to this common noun suggestive of excess. The city flourished through the Roman Empire, but was eventually overrun by malarial swampland, thus adding physical decay to its legacy of moral corruption. Sacked by Muslims and deserted in the ninth century, its remains were not rediscovered until the eighteenth century. Such archeological discoveries and concomitant technical advances did much to intensify nineteenth-century French interest for antiquity.

The quatrains of "Pœstum" describe the desertion of this decayed and sickly city, a disarray echoed in their unusually unbalanced rhyme scheme: ABBA ABAB. Swallowed by diseased

149

swamps ("Où la Mal'aria verse un souffle empesté") and overcome by moral corruption ("ses molles saturnales"), Pæstum
sinks into obscurity: "Elle n'a pas été." This obscurity, suggests Colet, is above all due to a lack of written traces, be they
administrative or poetic, which might have preserved its
memory: "Pœstum n'a pas laissé d'annales [. . .] / À peine si
Tibulle en un vers a chanté [. . .]." The tercets then recount
Pæstum's regeneration and the tardy recognition of its mag-
nificent architecture. The sickness and excess of the Roman
city ("olympiens délires") give way to the vibrant and lumi-
nous temples, once the city's center and now open grazing land
for humble shepherds.

This astounding transformation reappropriates ancient grandeur while replacing figures of decay ("vos dieux errants") with
nobler and more innocent ones ("ces pâtres nus aux fiers profils
romains"). It also exchanges the silence of neglect for the sounds
of poetry, thanks to Colet's simile in which the three temples
"vibr[ent] comme trois grandes lyres." Consistent with the Parnassian tendency to represent poetry through enduring visual
objects, "Pœstum" stands, like so much of Leconte de Lisle's
work, as an example of the ancient reclaimed for the glory of
the contemporary.

Indeed, the fate of Pæstum resembles that of the *Venus de
Milo,* both ancient and forgotten gems unearthed in modern
times. Pæstum's temples and the statue are both metaphoric
figures for antique treasures lost and rediscovered, archeological
remnants similar to Leconte de Lisle's revitalized "formes
négligées ou peu connues" (*Articles* 108). And like the *Venus
de Milo* or poetic form, Pæstum is coded as feminine. Colet
not only identifies the city grammatically with feminine pronouns ("elle") and adjectives ("lascive"), but also personifies
Pæstum in a feminized narrative. We can read the city as an
extended metaphor for a guilty woman who is punished and
forgotten, but then rehabilitated and cleansed by the work of
redemption. Her crimes are soft and yet excessive sensuality,
inanity (vanity, emptiness, uselessness), and exultation ("délire"); these traits are more in keeping with the Parnassian view
of Romantic "faults" than with its view of a sober, stoic
antiquity.

So while restoring to the city of Pæstum *her* voice and *her*
purity, Colet leaves the reader with two messages. First, that

she has learned the lessons of Leconte de Lisle by writing an impersonal and descriptive sonnet, one that looks to the stone remains of the classical era for models of purity and beauty. But Colet differs from Leconte de Lisle in the attention she pays to feminine decay, for she recounts the story of a neglected and punished woman who finds a voice and redemption. With this second message, Colet remains indebted to the humanistic feminism of Romanticism and, moreover, refuses to mimic the Parnassian conflation of classicism with misogynist "neutrality." Colet herself had been condemned for her beauty and accused of using her sexuality for personal gain.[12] Her chaste condemnation of Pæstum's sensual excesses in fact belies this reputation of promiscuous self-promotion.

In "La ville des esclaves," the partner sonnet of "Pœstum," we find the same moralistic tone, along with a more highly developed political commentary. While the narrative of "Pœstum" is structured by historical linearity, tracing the decline and regeneration of the city over a period of nearly 2,500 years, "La ville des esclaves" focuses on the event of Spartacus's rebellion (in the first century BC) and delineates a vertical hierarchy.

> Du grand roc Alburno les bergers aux traits hâves
> Ont surnommé Pœstum l'*antre des vals pourris,*
> Stigmatisant ainsi, taciturnes & graves,
> La luxure où sombra cette autre Sybaris.          4
>
> Mais ceux de Campanie honorent les débris
> Qu'incrusta sur leurs monts *la ville des esclaves;*
> La légende a toujours appelé *lieu des braves*
> Ces murs cyclopéens, hantés par des esprits.          8
>
> Indomptable lion qui de ses fers se joue,
> Spartacus, échappé du cirque de Capoue,
> Traversa le Volturne & gravit les hauteurs.
>
> Rome vit fuir vers lui tous ses gladiateurs;          12
> Et sur ces pics neigeux, où libres ils planèrent,
> S'éleva la cité que les pâtres vénèrent.
>
> (2: 136)

Hierarchy functions both geographically and morally in this sonnet. Shepherds reappear as modern witnesses of ancient

151

decay, stigmatizing the city Pæstum, heir to Sybaris, but honoring and then venerating the region of Campania, site of the slave revolt. Opposed to the "antre des vals pourris" that is Pæstum, the mountains of Campania are called "la ville des esclaves" and "lieu des braves." This region is associated with rebellion thanks to the gladiator Spartacus, who fled Capua to form an army of slaves and to become a legendary leader against the tyrannical authority of Rome. Spartacus, like the shepherds, hails from the people and becomes a symbol of moral righteousness.

Here we begin to see modern parallels to Colet's retelling of ancient history. Does not Spartacus suggest the liberator and unifier Garibaldi, whose campaigns Colet followed in the south of Italy? There lie clear parallels as well in the corruption of ancient Rome and that of the nineteenth-century papacy, which ruled over separate states. Colet had been quite vocal in her opposition to the papacy and in particular to the clergy's hypocritical licentiousness. In another work from her Parnassian period, *Les derniers abbés* (1868), she lambastes the clergy as "les exploiteurs d'un culte [. . .] endurcis par la débauche occulte" (qtd. in Gray 323).

But Rome does not supply the only modern referent in these poems. During the same year Colet published a verse pamphlet (*Paris matière*), in which "the materialism and moral pollution of the French capital are compared to the Roman Empire just before its downfall" (Gray 341). Colet's almost prudish condemnation of sexual excess once again contradicts her own reputation for promiscuity. More importantly perhaps, these poems also comment vividly on the current state of political and social life in western Europe. Behind Colet's Parnassian style there lies an unabashedly political agenda.

"Les débris incrust[és] sur leurs monts" evoke the volcanic ashes of Mount Vesuvius, where Spartacus took refuge with other slaves. During part of her sojourn in Italy, Colet lived on the island of Ischia with a view overlooking the volcano. "Absorption dans l'amour," her final Roman poem, recounts the eruption of Vesuvius in AD 79. More Romantic and less political than the two sonnets, this poem nonetheless proceeds like them from the southern Italian landscape and archeological remains uncovered in the eighteenth century. It also returns us obliquely to the figure of Venus, the patron deity of Pompeii.

Comme si ses flancs renfermaient une âme,
Le Vésuve au loin gronde sourdement;
Le ciel est zébré de langues de flamme,
La cendre jaillit du sommet fumant.                4

Au pied du volcan la mer fulgurante
Mugit sur ses bords et sur ses récifs;
Dans les frais ravins où s'endort Sorrente,
Sous les orangers ils restent assis.               8

C'est le premier jour que la femme aimante
A revu celui qu'elle a tant pleuré;
Qu'importe à son cœur la sombre tourmente,
Le gouffre béant, le ciel déchiré?                 12

Ivre de le voir, ivre de l'entendre,
Elle reste sourde aux bruits d'alentour;
La mort serait douce à cette âme tendre
En la foudroyant aux bras de l'amour.              16
                                          (3: 78)

This poem captures a moment preceding the city's destruction and burial by volcanic ash, setting the reunion of two lovers against the backdrop of the exploding mountain. Uninterested in history and objective description, "Absorption dans l'amour" relates a story of love and a state of interiority that is projected onto the surrounding landscape. The contrast is striking between the fuming, roaring volcano and the seated couple, soon to be immobilized for centuries.

Although Barbey once called Colet "la *Vésuvienne* en éruption,"[13] in this hybrid poem, Colet maintains control both of Parnassian imagery and Romantic sentiment. As in the two sonnets, here she presents ancient history and modern culture in tandem, refusing to divorce Parnassian formalism from ruminations on sexual politics. Together, these three poems offer two seemingly contradictory visions of sexuality: first as corrupt and, here, as captivating. Like many other female-authored Parnassian poems, "Absorption dans l'amour" rebuts the petrifaction of sexuality and the silencing of feminine desire.

To conclude this study of Colet's Parnassian poems, we might say that she used a strategy of recuperation, in which she emulated Parnassian styles and themes, but differed fundamentally in her ideology. Both liberal and engaged, Colet questioned Leconte de Lisle's valuation of the past over the present by using history as a metaphor rather than as a descriptive end in and of itself.

## Nina de Villard

Born in 1843 as Anne-Marie Gaillard, Nina de Villard went for a brief time by her married name, Nina de Callias, which is how she appears in the *Parnasse contemporain*. She subsequently called herself Nina de Villard, having taken the name of her mother (née Ursule-Emilie Villard) after abandoning her short-lived marriage. Known during her lifetime as an accomplished concert pianist, with Ursule Gaillard by her side she also opened her salon to the literati, musicians (she was an early and ardent supporter of Wagner's music), and artists (she posed for Manet as *La dame aux éventails* in 1873). The poets who frequented her gatherings included François Coppée, Charles Cros, Anatole France, Mendès, and Verlaine, many of whom wrote of Villard in their poetry, fiction, and memoirs. Verlaine, for one, describes her salon as "ces nuits toutes retentissantes de poésie et de musique" (*Œuvres en prose* 519). During the late 1860s, her salon was closely associated with the Parnassian movement: "[Villard] fut intimement liée [. . .] au développement du Parnasse" (Dufay 324). Curiously, she would subsequently be linked with the "Cercle zutique," a group of young poets (including Verlaine, Rimbaud, and Cros) whose early Parnassian aspirations did not prevent them from penning unruly, obscene poetry, nor from participating in the dawning of Symbolism.

Villard's salon also provided a safe haven for several political radicals during the final years of the Second Empire. She herself was forced into a brief exile because of her association with a number of Republicans, among them Edmond Bazire, who is responsible for the posthumous edition of her only collection of poetry, *Feuillets parisiens* (1885). Ironically, then, although her salon was central to the development of Parnassianism, it was a milieu that countered the movement's professed tenets of noninvolvement. Like Colet, Villard's opinions regarding the relation between poetry and politics would seem to differ sharply from those recorded by the theoreticians of Parnassianism.

As I have already suggested, Villard is more often than not recalled primarily as a hostess to literary bohemia and the colorful participant in various Parisian happenings rather than as a contributing member of a major poetic movement.[14] In the rare instances where her writing is discussed, she has been dismissed from her own day to the present as a poor poet.[15] Here is one example: "J'ai lu ses vers qu'il ne faut considérer que comme une sorte de délassement [. . .] d'une facture trop souvent inexperte" (Raynaud 125). And another: "Il nous reste à parler de Nina poète. Elle ne l'est pas. Elle taquine la rime pour s'amuser, elle ne se prend pas au sérieux [. . .]" (Somoff and Marfée 79). Some critics, who seem more intent on discrediting Villard than on reading her poetry, go so far as to accuse her of relying on others to polish her work: "Il apparaît avec une telle évidence que Nina s'est fait aider dans la rédaction de ses œuvres."[16] France and Cros, both her collaborators and the latter her companion for nearly ten years, frequently enjoy the attribution of her works.

Several of her poems, in fact, provide fascinating and original commentaries on the literary movement that reluctantly included her. "La jalousie du jeune Dieu," one of her two contributions to the second *Parnasse contemporain,* offers both a successful sonnet and a biting critique of Parnassianism:

Un savant visitait l'Égypte; ayant osé
Pénétrer dans l'horreur des chambres violettes
Où les vieux rois thébains, en de saintes toilettes,
Se couchaient sous le roc profondément creusé,     4

Il vit un petit pied de femme, mais brisé
Par des Bédouins voleurs de riches amulettes.
Le baume avait saigné le long des bandelettes,
Le henné ravivait les doigts d'un ton rosé.     8

Pur, ce pied conservait dans ses nuits infernales
Le charme doux & froid des choses virginales:
L'amour d'un jeune dieu l'avait pris enfantin.

Ayant baisé ce pied posé dans l'autre monde,     12
Le savant fut saisi d'une terreur profonde
Et mourut furieux le lendemain matin.

(2: 95)

Many critics contend that Villard did not pen this poem.[17] And yet by denying its female authorship, such analyses elide a pro-vocative interpretation that I would like to sketch out here. At first glance, "La jalousie du jeune Dieu" exemplifies the Parnas-sian style, thanks to its conventional prosody, Oriental setting, impersonality, and descriptiveness. If we grant Villard the rights to this poem, it would appear to belie Somoff and Marfée's claim that "nul n'est moins parnassienne que Nina" (78). The sonnet's fragmentary representation of woman is nothing new, and in fact feminine immobility could be said to reach new extremes with Villard's image of a severed and mummified, yet ever-so-dainty foot, which conserves "Le charme doux & froid des choses virginales."[18] Villard's sonnet is then both predictably and exaggeratedly Parnassian: are these characteristics not part and parcel of satire? Let us examine this foot, its admirers, and its final resting place more carefully.

Male characters abound here, with the "savant" playing the starring role. He encounters the remains and traces of old Theban kings, who are affronted by both Bedouin thieves ("voleurs") and the young god, a "violeur," who long ago carried away the foot's youthful owner. This unidentified female character is therefore represented only synecdochically by her foot. But femininity is evoked a second time, again in a fragmentary manner, in the description of the crypt. Line 2, which sees our "savant" penetrating into the "horreur des chambres violettes," is surely laden with sexual imagery. It recalls the "chambre ou tout [. . .] s'effémine" of Mendès's sonnet "L'absente" and pro-vides a second image of forced entry (echoed in "viol-ettes").

This "petit pied de femme," which drives the "savant" to madness and death, could signal a reproach to the fetishism rampant in Gautier's *Émaux et camées:* fetish in the sense of both "amulette" (line 6)[19] and object of sexual perversion.[20] Gautier's prose works offer another striking intertext for us to consider. His short story "Le pied de momie" (1840) tells the fantastic tale of a man of letters who comes across the mummi-fied foot of a Theban princess in a Parisian curiosity shop.[21] This story offers many points of comparison to the poem, not the least of which is the narrator's description of the foot: "J'aperçus un pied charmant [. . .] pol[i] par les baisers amoureux [. . .] un pied embaumé, un pied de momie" (437). Additionally, the princess's tomb is described as an impenetrable fortress, dug deep in the granite ground by her father in order to "conserver intacte" her remains (447). As in "La jalousie du jeune Dieu," in this story the inviolable chamber ultimately succumbs to pillagers who desecrate its pure feminine remains and make off with the foot, "spoils" evocative of lost innocence.

In the context of a formalist poetic movement such as Parnassianism, a secondary definition of *pied* or foot as a rhythmic unit cannot be overlooked. Who is Villard's "savant" who falls for a virginal yet cold foot, if not the erudite Parnassian poet in love with impassive formal perfection? This foot, once virginal, becomes a ghoulish figure, severed and bloody red. Returned to life ("Le henné ravivait les doigts d'un ton rosé"), it is capable of driving the intruder to madness and death. Might not Villard, then, be avenging the absent and forgotten female owner of the foot (the woman poet), violated by scholar, Bedouins, and young god alike? Like Villard's scholar, Leconte de Lisle's archeological poet, who turns his talents to the unearthing of past forms and reactive poetic values, appears destined to extinction.

There is much more to be said both about this sonnet and the contradictory antifeminism of the Parnassian school. We might linger on the poem's masculine figures—the clash of old kings and young god, as of that between the enthroned and the intruders—and consider their figurative import for this contentious moment in literary history. But I prefer to retain my focus on the small, forgotten female fragment consistently overlooked by that history, a compelling reminder of the effacement of Villard's poetic production. Villard foreshadowed her own erasure at the hands of fellow Parnassians and subsequent critics when she wrote in the *Feuillets parisiens,* "J'ai fait beaucoup de vers dont on se souvient peu."[22]

There exists another poem of Villard, contained neither in the *Parnasse contemporain* nor her *Feuillets parisiens,* in which she once again explores the remains of ancient Egypt and their effects on modern travelers. Like "La jalousie du jeune Dieu," "Le baiser de pierre" relies heavily on Gautier and, indeed, is dedicated to him. I read it as a pastiche that replies to his engrossing interest in both statuary and ancient Egypt. At the same time, it offers a curious counterpart to Villard's own Parnassian sonnet.

C'était dans la tranquille salle
Où l'Égypte enferme ses dieux.
Une femme brune et très-pâle
Marchait d'un pas harmonieux                    4

C'était une nature rare
Passant du cloître au bacchanal,
Une doña Juana bizarre,
Une chercheuse d'idéal.                          8

Une idole de granit sombre
Jeune et très-belle, sous le jeu
D'une lumière blanche et d'ombre
Semblait s'animer peu à peu.                    12

La femme, d'abord amusée,
S'approcha de ce beau corps nu,
Curieuse et magnétisée
Par quelque chose d'inconnu                     16

Très-tranquillement la statue
Descendit de son piedestal
Et l'embrassa—baiser qui tue
Baiser puissant, doux et fatal.                 20

Elle s'enfuit épouvantée
Sentant vibrer éperdûment
Son cœur de dompteuse domptée,
Pâmée aux lèvres de l'amant.                    24

Et puis la pauvre, au pied d'un arbre,
Tomba morte de volupté.
Alors le jeune dieu de marbre
Rentra dans l'immobilité.[23]                   28

(Cros, opposite p. 16)

This poem repeats the sonnet's narrative: in a closed mortuary chamber, curiosity attracts an observer to a relic from the past, which appears to come to life. The archeologist kisses the mummified foot, the woman is kissed by the statue, both are struck with terror and die. While Villard repeats the scenario of "La jalousie du jeune Dieu" in "Le baiser de pierre," the poems also contain contradictory elements. Most notably, gender positions are switched, so that it is a woman who falls victim to the fatal kiss. An intact and lovely male statue replaces the bloody, fragmentary female foot.

Consequently, this poem responds in a different manner to Gautier. Here Villard abandons the sonnet for Gautier's preferred free form: octosyllabic quatrains. Villard's "doña Juana bizarre" suffers the same fate as the woman of Gautier's "Le poème de la femme," where we read: "Elle est morte de volupté." Villard's striking innovation, of course, is to represent the "beau corps nu" with a male statue, to bring it to life as Gautier does his marble woman, and then to will it back to motionlessness. So while Villard appears to mimic Gautier's capital punishment of feminine sensuality, at the same time she parodies his petrifaction of femininity by confining her alluring and dangerous masculine creation in stone: "Alors le jeune dieu de marbre / Rentra dans l'immobilité."

This female character is not typical of Parnassian representations of women, since Villard develops her fairly well, giving her individual features ("brune et très-pâle") and yet refusing to dwell on her physical attractiveness. She possesses a unique and complex personality ("une nature rare"). Although she dies an erotic death, sexuality alone does not define her; instead, she is double, "passant du cloître au bacchanal." With Baudelaire in mind ("chercheuses d'infini" is how he names his "Femmes damnées"), we might see Villard's woman, a "chercheuse d'idéal," as a figure for a poet, one who "marchait d'un pas harmonieux."[24] At once retiring and excessive, cloistered yet dandified, in love with beauty both ideal and material, drawn by the unknown, Villard's woman seems to incarnate Baudelaire's rapprochement of "les amoureux fervants et les savants austères" (*Œuvres complètes* 1: 66) or his "dociles amants [qui] consumeront leurs jours en d'austères études" (*Œuvres complètes* 1:21).

While playing unapologetically with Parnassian conventions, Villard succeeds once again in turning the tables on Gautier by objectifying masculine beauty while offering a non-objectifying representation of the woman poet. The enigmatic and complex quality of Villard's subject remains constant, exemplified by her dense rhyme scheme (the twenty-eight-line poem is based on variations of only seven rhymes) and ambiguous movement from carefree sentiment ("la tranquille salle," "la femme d'abord amusée") to sinister description ("elle s'enfuit épouvantée").

While Colet's central strategy is one of assimilation and recuperation, Villard clearly prefers parody subtle enough to slip by critics who never doubt her sincerity. In addition to these two poems, Villard's participation in a collective volume, *Dixains réalistes* (1876), betrays her predilection for irony and her caustic relationship to another prominent Parnassian.[25] After having their submissions rejected by the jury of the third *Parnasse contemporain,* Villard and "la bande à Nina" (Cros, Germain Nouveau, et al.) collaborated on this collection in which they parodied François Coppée. Coppée was both an influential member of the jury that refused them and the popularizer of the form of the *dizain réaliste,* a descriptive ten-line vignette of scenes from common lives.[26]

Closer to the heart of the movement than any other *Parnassienne,* Villard was perhaps in the best position to lampoon her confreres. Her "Intérieur" exemplifies both her contempt for·Coppée's flaccidity and her repugnance for self-abnegating representations of femininity:

> Quand la lampe Carcel sur la table s'allume,
> Le bouilli brun paraît, escorté du légume,
> Blanc navet, céleri, carotte à la rougeur
> D'aurore, et doucement, moi je deviens songeur;    4
> Ce plat fade me plaît, me ravit; il m'enchante:
> C'est son jus qui nous fait la soupe succulente;
> En la mangeant, je pense, avec recueillement,
> À l'épouse qui, pour nourrir son rose enfant,    8
> Perd sa beauté, mais gagne à ce labeur austère
> Un saint rayonnement trop pur pour notre terre.
> *(Feuillets parisiens* n. pag.)

Villard creates a masculine voice (as in most of her dizains) to be the object of her mockery, and with which to target Coppée's bourgeois self-satisfaction, insipid sentimentality, literalism, and hackneyed description.

Other short poems from her *Feuillets parisiens* critique the idealization of femininity in a more direct fashion. In "Impromptu," for example, she leaves behind the faded beauty of domesticated womanhood and returns to the figure of Venus. But Villard's Venus adamantly refuses to remain petrified in stone:

Vénus aujourd'hui met un bas d'azur
Et chez Marcelin conte des histoires;
Elle garde au fond, dans le vert si pur
De ses grands yeux clairs sous leurs franges noires  4
Le reflet du flot son pays natal.
Quand au Boulevard on la voit qui passe
Déesse fuyant de son piédestal,
Et venant chez nous promener sa grâce,        8
On lui voudrait bien dresser des autels,
Mais elle répond que cela l'ennuie
Et qu'elle permet aux pauvres mortels
De parler argot en sa compagnie.        12

*(Feuillets parisiens* n. pag.)

This Venus not only talks ("conte des histoires," "parler argot")
and walks, but retains her human features ("ses grands yeux
clairs sous leurs franges noires"). While maintaining aspects
of and ties to her ancient Roman roots ("Le reflet de son pays
natal"), she is equally at home on the modern boulevards of
Paris. Not content with the stifling Parnassian portrait of femininity, Villard re-creates a bicultural and bitemporal Venus who
is free in her movements and her speech. She repudiates the
Parnasse by fleeing the objectifying pedestal, embracing contemporary culture, and using antipoetic argot.[27]

While Colet and Villard clearly grapple with Parnassian style
and respond to Parnassian ideology, we cannot readily draw
the same conclusion for some of the other women poets represented in the journal. Ackermann's contribution, "Une femme"
(see appendix), dates from 1835 and shows no traces of the
rebellion present in some of her later poems from *Poésies
philosophiques,* which she composed much nearer to the Parnassian moment. "Une femme" calls upon women to envy the
wife who devotes "sa foi, son but et son labeur" to the husband who depends upon her, condemning the "vie inutile [qui]
en vains plaisirs s'écoule." It could be considered a sincere
version of Villard's critique of the self-sacrificing woman.
Despite Souriau's suggestion that "Une femme" is a feminist
piece (409), the poem remains rather disappointing to feminists, more reminiscent of Tastu's "Ange gardien" than of
Ackermann's own rebellious "Mon livre" or cynical "L'amour
et la mort" (see appendix). Are she and the others, Siefert,

Blanchecotte, Bourotte,[28] and Penquer, simply a group of "Romantiques attardées," as Schaffer would have it?

## Léocadie Penquer

If Colet is the Parnasse's loose woman, Léocadie Penquer stands as one of its most virtuous.[29] Many critics agree that this self-effacing Breton, a dutiful disciple of Lamartine, poured her life's occupations into her poetry: religion, husband, family.[30] They see in Penquer's sole contribution to the *Parnasse contemporain,* a long poem entitled "Le Paradis retrouvé" (2: 285–88; see appendix), the confirmation of its author's conjugal and religious values and a clear echo of the conformist sentiment of Ackermann's "Une femme." Albeit a far cry from the Parnassian style, Penquer's poem finds praise among historians of the Parnasse for its noble sentiment and able imitation of the Romantic masters (particularly Lamartine and Hugo). Like Desbordes-Valmore, Penquer appears to remain within the boundaries of appropriate feminine language and activity, and for this she wins critical approval.

Her subject matter is clearly more Romantic than Parnassian, since biblical sources played such a prominent role at the beginning of the century, while the Parnassians nearly universally shunned the Bible in favor of ancient references. Chateaubriand set the scene for Christian Romanticism with, among other texts, *Le génie du christianisme* and his translation of John Milton's *Paradise Lost.* After him several prominent Romantic poets returned to the stories of Genesis, including Byron ("Cain"), Vigny (numerous pieces from *Poèmes antiques* and *Les destinées*), Lamartine ("Chute d'un ange"), and Hugo ("Le sacre de la femme").[31] These poems run the gamut from Vigny's obsession with treacherous and faulty women to Hugo's accent on pardon and the idealization of femininity.

Penquer's laudatory critics must have read her "Miltonic rhapsody" (Schaffer, *Genres* 374n16) with a particularly blind eye. A Miltonian epic does indeed provide Penquer's most important intertext, but it is not his *Paradise Regained* that resonates in her poem, as one would expect from her title. Instead, her "Paradis retrouvé" begins where Milton left off in *Paradise Lost,* at the moment when Adam and Eve are expelled from Eden. Her subtitle, "Poème de la première heure," identifies this as a moment of beginning rather than one of loss. Penquer embroiders on this short passage from Genesis:

> Therefore the Lord God sent [Adam] forth from the garden of Eden, to till the ground from which he was taken. He drove out the man; and at the east of the garden of Eden he placed the cherubim, and a flaming sword which turned every way, to guard the way to the tree of life. Now Adam knew Eve his wife [. . .]. (3.23–4.1)

Her poem is remarkable not as a translation or repetition of its sources, but as a rebuttal to Milton's misogynist interpretation of Genesis and, occasionally, to the Bible itself. The Bible includes these instructions to Eve: "your desire shall be for your husband, and he shall rule over you" (Genesis 3.16). Milton also condemns Eve to a life of wifely obedience, including as he does such images of bondage as this: "With thee goes / Thy Husband, him to follow thou art bound; / Where he abides, think there thy native soil" (11.290–92).

Penquer, however, turns the tables and has Eve lead the way. This is how her "Paradis retrouvé" begins:

> L'Éden était fermé. La terre ouvrait ses routes:
> Adam, d'un seul regard, les interrogea toutes,
> Et, ne pouvant choisir parmi tant de chemins,
> Il se tourna vers Ève & dit: "Étends les mains:
> Je te laisse le choix entre tous nos domaines."
>
> (lines 1–5)

Throughout Penquer's poem Adam remains a passive follower to Eve. He tells her:

> "Je te suis. Conduis-moi. Dans l'ombre ou la lumière,
> Où tu seras, j'irai. Va, marche la première!
> Regarde ton chemin; moi, je regarderai
> La trace de tes pas. Marche. Je te suivrai."
>
> (49–52)

This reversal of positions turns Adam into a kind of foil for Eve, his leader, and she reveals herself boldly capable of the task. She guides Adam not to the East of Eden, but defiantly to the West:

> Ève se dirigea vers l'occident, légère,
> Non comme une exilée & comme une étrangère,
> Mais comme une habitante à qui tout est connu.
> À peine elle foulait le sol de son pied nu;
> À peine elle hésitait dans sa route. [. . .]
>
> (53–57)

Eve's knowledge precedes her, since she steps into her new world already as its inhabitant. Penquer portrays her as Adam's guide not only in the new and unknown world, but also in desire. Eve refuses the shameful role of the banished woman and exults in the ardent happiness of their present union over the cold ignorance of their life together in Eden:

> Je vivais sans désir, j'ignorais l'espérance;
> Mon bonheur était froid comme mon ignorance:
> L'amour n'était pas né.
> . . . . . . . . . . . . . . . . .
> Mais à présent que Dieu n'est plus là, l'homme est dieu
> Pour mon âme, & beauté pour mon regard de feu.
>
> (29–31, 35–36)

Adam too delights in his newfound sensuality: "ce mot suprême, / Aimer, j'en ignorais hier la volupté" (38–39). Although self-possessed and rebellious, Penquer's Eve still suffers shame, leading Adam "vers l'ombre" since "Pour t'aimer, j'ai besoin, Adam, de me cacher" (20).

Milton, of course, was harsher than the Bible on Eve, characterizing her as weak, guilty, and salacious: "O much deceiv'd, much failing, hapless *Eve*" (9.404; Milton's italics); "Greedily she ingorg'd without restraint" (9.791); "What misery th' inabstinence of *Eve* / Shall bring on men" (11.476–77; Milton's italics); "All by [Eve's wilful crime] is lost" (12.619, 621). Sexuality provokes not only shame, but an entire Pandora's box of bad emotions in his epic poem: "Love was not in thir looks, either to God / Or to each other, but apparent guilt, / And shame, and perturbation, and despair, / Anger, and obstinacy, and hate, and guile" (10.111–14). But Penquer does not punish the first couple. In her dialogue poem Adam and Eve find their second paradise, rather than their punishment, in physical love. While they head toward the shadows, instead of obscurity they find a sexualized landscape. Eve leads Adam toward the setting sun, where "l'ombre était plus obscure" (line 58). They find mountains with enormous caves:

Un peu dans le sud-ouest, des lignes montagneuses
S'étendaient & formaient des voûtes caverneuses.
C'est vers ces antres noirs qu'Ève se dirigea.
Palpitante, éperdue, elle y touchait déjà,
Quand Adam, l'étreignant & l'enlevant de terre,
La porta, frémissant d'amour, dans ce mystère.

(65–70)

Rather than evoking a beckoning and pitiless Hell, these "antres noirs" heighten the sexual excitement of the couple. The dark place of mystery comes to light with stars ("Les astres rayonnaient, l'un par l'autre éblouis" [72]) as Adam and Eve unite "dans un premier secret" (76).

The secret revealed, the sun rises over Eden as if to confer a blessing: "L'aube éclairait déjà l'azur de l'orient" (83). Eve has proven God wrong, or at least replaced him with her new knowledge:

L'Éternel s'est trompé dans sa double sentence;
Sa justice n'a pas atteint notre existence
. . . . . . . . . . . . . . . . . . . . . . . . . . . . . .
L'enfantement divin germa dans la nature:
L'amour, égal à Dieu, créa la créature.

(13–14, 81–82)

Penquer therefore celebrates the departure from Eden and its attendant paternalism, a departure that promises the awakening of human sexuality and female activity. Her model is necessarily more materialistic than the ideal of innocence and feminine virtue that Eden represents for so many male poets. Baudelaire, for one, wrote that "Tout poète lyrique, en vertu de sa nature, opère fatalement un retour vers l'Éden perdu" (*Œuvres complètes* 2: 165). By departing from rather than returning to Eden, Penquer and many other women poets repudiated the values that defined contemporary poetic practice.

In rewriting Milton, Penquer takes a stand against his punitive and rigid interpretation of the Bible, as against his condemnation of female initiative and sexuality. For him, "Man's woe" has two sources, the first being "Woman" (11.632–33)

165

and the second "Man's effeminate slackness" (634). In Milton's text, Adam's woes are not so different from Leconte de Lisle's, whose poetry does battle with both female sexuality and the "effeminate slackness" of Romantic poetry. Penquer preserves certain Romantic topoi (such as the redemptive woman), combining them with her own biblical exegesis (one arguably closer to the original text than Milton's interpretation), which focuses on the negative aspects of Eden, on masculine passivity, and on female initiative. In so doing she counters Leconte de Lisle's vision of poetic hardness with a new model, wherein femininity is not an obstacle, but rather a self-assured guiding force. She replaces Venus with Eve, a newer image of naked womanhood and feminine beauty,[32] at once human, moving, and desiring. She rebuffs the paternalism, rigidity, and punitive stance of both Milton and Leconte de Lisle.

Like Colet's "Pœstum," in "Le Paradis retrouvé" Penquer explores original sin and guilt, which are traditionally attributed to feminine sexuality. Their contributions to the *Parnasse contemporain* appear to contradict their divergent reputations: Colet's poems reveal more *pudeur* than promiscuity, and Penquer's describes a lustiness that is not in keeping with the saintly chastity attributed to her. With divergent approaches, both women rewrote traditional scenarios of feminine fault and redemption.

These readings of Parnassian women point to their attempts to inscribe feminine desire, to question the authoritative stance of the Parnasse, and to return to a poetics of engagement. The feminist content of their poems is sometimes explicit, as in the case of Penquer's celebration of Eve's sexual awakening in "Le Paradis retrouvé." She returns to Desbordes-Valmore's critique of hardness and evocative sensuality in this more fluid, "Romantic" poem. At other times poets employ subtle irony (Villard) or a recuperative strategy (Colet) to question Parnassian doctrine and infuse its poetry with subjective expressions of femininity. Each poet pursued her own relation to the movement and voiced her sense of adherence or divergence in different ways. They were individual women and a diverse collection of poets whose ambitions sometimes coincided with those of their male contemporaries, but whose existence necessarily contradicted the prevailing poetic doctrine. Consequently their poetry can and must be read in context and read with an eye to both conformity and nonconformity. The work of the *Parnassiennes* can be interpreted as a series of varying responses to the dominant poetic milieu.

I have attempted to dig, archeologically, below the exclusion of women from the Parnassian movement and its recorded history, and to unearth some contributions by several of its most colorful and critical female associates. The work of Parnassian women is a rich treasure indeed, and the bulk of it remains to be brought to light. The small fragments studied here in the context of canonical texts have aided us in analyzing symbolic renderings of sexual difference by the Parnassian movement. They have led us to question the Parnassian investment not only in petrifying femininity, but also in feminizing Romanticism. The continued study of the *Parnassiennes* and re-examination of Parnassian poetic discourse can only instruct us further about the sources of these associations and provide us with a rich variety of models to serve as alternatives.

# Part 3
# Symbolist Fluidity

*Après tout, nous sommes si éphémères!*
Jules Laforgue
"Sur la femme"

# Introduction

Parnassianism did not enjoy a long-lived success and, indeed, was soon overwhelmed by the diverse and fragmented poetic moment now known globally as Symbolism. As the events of 1848, which presaged the Second Empire, fueled the then-young Parnassians, so did the end and tumultuous aftermath of Napoléon III's regime coincide with the activity of a new generation of poets and a re-examination of poetic ideology and practice. In a restrained sense, "Symbolism" refers to the movement covering the last two decades of the nineteenth century, which took its name from Jean Moréas's 1886 "Manifeste du symbolisme" and splintered into numerous groups. More broadly, it embraces the poetic production of the century's second half, including the work of Symbolist "fathers" (Baudelaire, Mallarmé, Rimbaud, and sometimes Verlaine, the semivowel of Symbolist literary history) and a diverse range of poetic cliques and schools stretching to the beginning of the twentieth century.[1]

Although several die-hard neoclassicists (including Leconte de Lisle and Heredia) continued to write in the Parnassian vein, the reaction against it was pronounced. Cros, Mallarmé, Verlaine, and Villard, among other Parnassian defectors, participated in the beginnings of the new poetic tendency, creating a bridge of sorts between the traditional and the unabashedly new.[2] Following the *Dixains réalistes* and another, earlier parody, *Le Parnassiculet contemporain* (1872), poets and critics aiming to revitalize French verse took the conservative Parnassians to task, exhibiting an ironic sense of humor absent among the dour formalists. Jules Laforgue's playful "Derniers soupirs d'un Parnassien" (1880), for example, mocked the rhythmic regularity of classical prosody:

> Klop, klip, klop, klop, klip, klop.
> Goutte à goutte égrenant son rythmique sanglot
> Aux vasques du bassin où l'eau dort immobile
> Un jet d'eau trouble seul la nuit calme et tranquille.
>
> *(Les complaintes* 202)

Ironically, Laforgue satirized the Parnassian elders with images borrowed from a young Mallarmé, who later became one of Symbolism's most distinguished proponents: "Derniers soupirs" parodies "Soupir," published in the first *Parnasse contemporain:* "Fidèle, un blanc jet d'eau soupire vers l'Azur! / Vers l'Azur attendri d'octobre pâle et pur / Qui mire aux grands bassins sa langueur infinie / Et laisse, sur l'eau morte [. . .]" (1: 168). Although Laforgue and his peers were no less interested in form than were their Parnassian predecessors (indeed, none remained more formalist than Mallarmé), they focused their efforts on innovation rather than conservation. A new, inclusive ideology governed their approach to both prosody and representation. Above all, the desire to invent different modes of poetic expression motivated Symbolist production and created a fresh vocabulary of values dominated by words such as "l'imprévu," "l'inattendu," "le nouveau," "l'innovation." After the Parnassian era of restricted poetic inquiry, Symbolists worked to surmount boundaries in poetry and, in ways previously unimagined, placed subjectivity and the exploration of difference at the heart of their work on the lyric.

Mallarmé identified Symbolism as a split from Parnassian practice and ideology. In both "Crise de vers" and an interview conducted by Jules Huret in 1891, he described the fall of neoclassicism and poetic impersonality, and the advent of a supple, variegated aesthetic stance.[3] He employed musical metaphors throughout these two pieces, pointing to an entirely different poetic approach from the one suggested by the Parnassian metaphor of statuary: "la Musique rejoint le Vers pour former, depuis Wagner, la Poésie" (365).[4] The importance of music as a referent in and a metaphor for the poetry of this period cannot be underestimated, as the following chapters will show. The intangible fluidity of the medium countered the visual definition of the plastic arts, providing a forceful analogy for the new aesthetics of mobility. Indeed, Mallarmé characterized Symbolist poetry as unpredictably mobile, in contrast to the uniformity and *raidissement* of the Parnassians: "si, d'un côté, les Parnassiens ont été, en effet, les absolus serviteurs du vers, y sacrifiant jusqu'à leur personnalité, les jeunes gens ont tiré directement leur instinct des musiques, comme s'il n'y avait rien eu auparavant" (868).

Poetic values seem to have flip-flopped once again, with classical forms being replaced by innovative rhythms (*vers libéré*) and by a re-evaluation of syllabism (*vers libre*), impersonality by subjective perspectives, constraint by freedom. However rather than being another about-face in the history of poetic movements, the inclusive nature of late nineteenth-century poetry permitted greater liberty of expression, instead of functioning as a simple rejection of the old for the new. Mallarmé himself described the current generation's poetics of renewal as a comprehensive endeavor in both form and representation. While the Parnassians, "amoureux du vers très stricte" (867), engaged in a practice of discipline and repudiation, Mallarmé showed that the Symbolists relied on a non-exclusionary openness in their approach to composition: "les essais des derniers venus ne tendent pas à supprimer le grand vers; ils tendent à mettre plus d'air dans le poème, à créer une sorte de fluidité, de mobilité entre les vers de grand jet, qui leur manquait un peu jusqu'ici" (868).[5]

While re-evaluating traditional approaches to composition, Symbolist poets replaced object-oriented description with a poetics of relativity that favored abstraction. Mallarmé suggested that music, unpredictability, and fluidity of form accompanied allusion, mystery, and obscurity in representation: "les Parnassiens [. . .] prennent la chose entièrement et la montrent: par là ils manquent de mystère; ils retirent aux esprits cette joie délicieuse de croire qu'ils créent. *Nommer* un objet, c'est supprimer les trois-quarts de la jouissance du poème qui est faite de deviner peu à peu: le *suggérer,* voilà le rêve" (869). Numerous poems by Mallarmé illustrate his technique of poetic suggestion. For example, "Sainte" evokes rather than describes a stained-glass representation of Cecilia, the patron saint of music. Mallarmé notes subtle gestures (of the saint's "délicate phalange du doigt") and suggests presence through absence ("sans le vieux santal / Ni le vieux livre, [. . .] / Musicienne du silence" [54]), rather than naming the object of his study or presenting it as a readily identifiable whole. The heightened use of figurative language employed to evoke, rather than to name, produced poetry that was often dense (as in the case of Mallarmé himself and his disciple, Valéry) and sometimes obscure (Rimbaud), nearly always profoundly subjective. If the difficulty of Parnassian poetry lies in its erudite references, Symbolism's difficulty arises from the intangibility of its point of view.

Although Rimbaud called for objectivity in poetry ("Un jour, j'espère [. . .], je verrai dans votre principe la poésie objective" [248]), it would in fact be wrong to elide this with Parnassian impassivity. Instead, Rimbaud sought to distance himself from the transparent subjectivity of Romantic poetry, in which the lyric "I" was assumed to refer back to a fixed self or autobiographical subject. As Michel Collot has admirably demonstrated, "cette impersonnalisation n'est pas une pure et simple disparition du sujet" (42). While trading in the subject of personal poetry for a more playful and opaque relationship to language and poetic identity, Rimbaud cannot be said to renounce subjective poetry: "C'est faux de dire: Je pense: on devrait dire on me pense" (Rimbaud 249). On the contrary, by refuting the false notion of a transcendental "I," he broadens subjective possibilities: "Rimbaud réserve une place au sujet lyrique, défini non plus en termes d'identité et d'intériorité, mais par son ouverture à l'extérieur et à l'altérité" (Collot 41).

The assault on poetic convention thus coincided with the reevaluation of the lyric "I." The Symbolist value of uncertainty would have sweeping import for the representation of "different" subjectivities; by surpassing the oppositional stance of Parnassianism, Symbolists were able to refresh existing approaches to subjective expression. For the first time, poets questioned the transparency of language, which limited the identification of the speaking subject to the figure of a male Poet. Rimbaud's aphorism, "je est un autre," would eventually transform the notion of subjectivity in poetry, marking, as Hugo Friedrich has written, the "divorce of the poetic 'I' from the empirical self," which "forbid[s] any interpretation of modern poetry as biographical statement" (48). Mallarmé too demanded "la disparition élocutoire du poète" (366).

While social and political forces continued to marginalize women poets, new representations of the poetic subject redefined the lyric endeavor and experience by virtue of their multiplicity. Rimbaud was perhaps the first explicitly to link the search for a distinct language to the expression of new forms of love ("Départ dans l'affection et le bruit neufs!" [129]), but he was not alone in reimagining the parameters of gender and sexuality through the renewal of poetic language. Heretofore unexplored subjectivities emerged during this period of poetic anarchism, alongside new forays into liberated and free verse. Female innovators and subjective representations of male and female homosexuality are among the most evident legacies of the period's contributions to diversity, as I aim to demonstrate in my final chapter.

Rimbaud suggested that women's poetry would be on the vanguard of poetic production because of, rather than in spite of, its difference. In his second "lettre du voyant" he wrote:

> Quand sera brisé l'infini servage de la femme, quand elle vivra pour elle et par elle, [. . .] elle sera poète, elle aussi. La femme trouvera de l'inconnu! Ses mondes d'idées différeront-ils des nôtres? —Elle trouvera des choses étranges, insondables, repoussantes, délicieuses; nous les prendrons, nous les comprendrons. (252)

Similar to Rimbaud's acknowledgment of historic oppression ("l'infini servage de la femme"), Laforgue called for women's liberation: "Ô jeunes filles, quand serez-vous nos frères, nos frères intimes sans arrière-pensée d'exploitation!" (*Mélanges* 48). And like Rimbaud, Laforgue saw a link between femininity and modernity: "Ô féminiculture, pôle moderne!" (50). Although Rimbaud's language admittedly retains the suggestion of a colonizing desire ("nous les prendrons"), his interest in feminine subjectivities was only one manifestation of a commitment to the exploration of alterity. Various strains of Symbolism broadened poetic horizons to include new realms of inquiry, new perceptions, new influences, and indeed a new ethic of literature. The Symbolist counterpoint to Parnassian constraint was, in sum, *inclusion,* rather than the effusion of the Romantics.

Laforgue also broke away from Parnassian elitism by proclaiming the legitimacy of all voices: "Chaque homme est selon son moment dans le temps, son milieu de race et de condition sociale, son moment d'évolution individuelle, un certain clavier sur lequel le monde extérieur joue d'une certaine façon. [. . .] Tous les claviers sont légitimes" (*Mélanges* 141). This forward-looking statement of poetic relativism sounds like a precursor to late twentieth-century multiculturalism. Laforgue raised the issue of access to poetic production by proclaiming the validity of diverse subjectivities, and his reference to race and social condition points to an active reinvestment of poetry in politics. Contrary to the apolitical Gautier or to the elitism of Leconte de Lisle, many Symbolist poets returned to the engagement of the Romantics, albeit in a less idealistic fashion (consider, for instance, the strong ties between Symbolism and the anarchist movement). Kahn insisted that "l'art devait être social" (32).[6] Echoing Rimbaud's "nous comprendrons [les femmes]," he suggested in a reciprocal fashion that "le peuple comprendra. [. . .] La preuve fut faite dans les réunions populaires [. . .] où les poèmes symbolistes, et les poèmes des vers libristes reçurent un bel accueil [. . .]" (70). This desire for a dialogue between poet and audience entailed a redefinition of the reading public. Borrowings from popular culture including colloquialisms, spoken diction, and songlike structures (such as refrain) invaded the formerly "elevated" language of poetry during the Symbolist era.

A note of caution: I do not mean to overstate the case for Symbolism being exclusively an accessible poetry-of-the-people. Often the vocabulary of inclusion and expansion represented an ethic, rather than a reality in which all had access to poetic production. The shift I describe was in fact more rhetorical than concrete. Moreover, the elitist stance associated with the tradition of hermetic or "pure" poetry survived after the Parnasse, most notably in Mallarmé's own work. Despite his encouragement of the diverse production of the "young generation," Mallarmé (like Baudelaire) betrayed an aversion for the uneducated reader and more than a hint of arrogance: "si un être d'une intelligence moyenne, et d'une préparation littéraire insuffisante, ouvre par hasard un livre ainsi fait et prétend en jouir, il y a un malentendu" (869). Granting this, I focus in this section on the openings made possible by Symbolist poetry.

I do not propose to recount here the history of this long and intense period of poetic production, which has been accomplished admirably and in great detail elsewhere, at least as far as its male participants are concerned.[7] Instead, I concentrate on Charles Baudelaire, Paul Verlaine, and Marie Krysinska, three very different poets who contributed to the *remise-en-question* of the gendered lyric with originality and foresight. By giving Krysinska the final word, I mean to suggest that she and other women poets had important things to say about poetry and its incarnations. I mean as well to press one promise of the Symbolist aesthetic that remains unfulfilled: that the repudiation of fixed and unitary meaning translates into a meaningful appreciation for polyphony and multivalence.

# Chapter Six

# Baudelaire's Frontiers

As the voluminous body of criticism devoted to him suggests, Baudelaire is one of the most intriguing and endlessly revisitable poets of the Western tradition. And yet his work has not attracted the kind of sustained and rigorous attention that feminist critics have devoted to other major authors from Balzac to Zola, leaving an extraordinarily rich terrain open for investigation.[1] Tamara Bassim's *La femme dans l'œuvre de Baudelaire* (1974) represents one of the only comprehensive studies devoted to the question, although its biographical analysis and thematic focus strike today's reader as outdated. In the intervening twenty-five years, Baudelaire's outspoken misogyny has provoked an unproductive contredanse of condemnation and recuperation. On one side line up those who berate the poet for his hatred of women (for example, Anderson, "Baudelaire Misogyne"), and on the other, critics who suggest, on the contrary, "that Baudelaire felt very close to women" (Shaw, "Baudelaire's 'Femmes damnées'" 57). This latter strikes me as one of the more obvious examples of the practice Gayatri Spivak describes as "recovering some concealed radical message from ostensibly reactionary writing" (231), although more subtle varieties exist. To my mind any criticism that contents itself with proving either subversive intent or complicity with dominant structures has its limitations.[2]

In my own analysis, I am interested less in Baudelaire's representation of woman than in what his compositional practice implies about gender. While undoubtedly a slave to masculinist convention in his prose and the author of numerous unflattering female figures in his poetry, he set the scene for a reconsideration of poetic gender ideologies by refusing to align himself exclusively with either a "hard" or a "soft" aesthetic practice. It is in Baudelaire's manipulation of poetic movement and rhythm that I locate his (largely unconscious and highly meta-phoric) articulation of difference. I will argue that Baudelaire's gendered lyric comes to light most clearly when considered in the context of and as a departure from the Romantic and Parnassian aesthetics detailed above.

I therefore depart from the trend in recent criticism that sees Baudelaire as a solitary figure in an urban setting largely unconnected to preceding poetic tendencies. Indeed, current criticism rarely mentions the Parnasse, and depends on Baudelaire's refutation of Romanticism rather than on his position vis-à-vis its ideology of gender. Baudelaire has become such an icon of modernity for contemporary readers and, perhaps, a focus for masculine identification, that many strive to cleanse him of Romantic associations, even while decrying his misogyny.

One of the more prominent strains of Baudelaire criticism attributes to the poet a new modern sensibility that derives from an urban inspiration. Taking Walter Benjamin's analysis of the urban experience of shock as point of departure, these studies tend to focus on Baudelaire's representation of the changing Parisian landscape and his inscription of industrial city life.[3] Without detracting from the importance of this body of criticism, I would like to suggest that its focus on urban representations tends to divert its gaze from both femininity and the lyric.[4] The study of Baudelaire's urban, public landscape, a masculine domain, often obscures his manipulations of gendered categories and, in so doing, fails to account for his investment in masculinist poetic ideology, or to recognize moments in his work that undermine it. Moreover, because of its interest in referential reality (the city and its inhabitants), much of this work privileges Baudelaire's prose writings, be they poetic (*Le spleen de Paris*) or critical,[5] and relegates the specifically lyric context to the margins. (One obvious exception is the "Tableaux parisiens" section of *Les fleurs du Mal*, whose poems illustrate Baudelaire's relation to the changing face of Paris ["Le cygne"] or the experience of the crowd ["À une passante"], but whose lyricism is often overlooked or taken for granted.)

As Benjamin and his inheritors have suggested, Baudelaire's poetic exploration of the urban experience marks both the closure of one poetic era and the first foray into a new, modern one. But rather than define his innovation in terms of his engagement with the urban experience, I would like instead to consider the inaugurative import of his poetry in light of its reaffirmation of the lyric stance. He grappled with both Romantic and Parnassian doctrine in order to overturn oppositions that had defined the poetic endeavor for the first half of the nineteenth century, paving the way for the variegated representations of gender in subsequent Symbolist poetry. Rather than seeing him as a solitary icon of urban modernity divorced from all preceding poetic tendencies, I reread his work as one that ultimately opens doors to representations of alterity.

This chapter will therefore show how Baudelaire's work encompasses and moves beyond several nineteenth-century poetic positions and, in so doing, offers some of the most fascinating and, at times, contradictory, commentary on lyric subjectivity and sexuality. I begin with an overview of his ambiguous relationship both to Romanticism and to "la nouvelle école poétique" that would become Parnassianism. While competing aesthetics are juxtaposed in the poems of *Les fleurs du Mal*, Baudelaire's work recuperates and surpasses dogmatic cleavage. I examine a constellation of texts that re-imagine the lyric subject and offer new representations of subjectivity in poetry. It is in his heterometric poetry that Baudelaire reaches for a new conception of the poetic act and tests out new formulations of lyric subjectivity; these texts would become stepping-stones for future investigations of gender difference in Symbolist poetry.

## Poetic Affiliations

While Baudelaire's work dominates current perceptions of modern poetry's evolution and can be linked to each of France's major poetic movements, it belongs properly to none. At the very least, his disdain for affiliation renders labels such as "Romantic," "Parnassian," or "pre-Symbolist" inadequate. Notoriously antifamily, Baudelaire once wrote that "Je n'aime rien tant que d'être seul."[6] But rather than granting him his wish for isolation, I propose to consider Baudelaire within his specific poetic context in order to re-evaluate the gendered ideology implicit in his work. While his conception of the Poet had its roots in the figure of the Romantic hero, and his treatment of female figures conformed to conventional gender biases exhibited by Parnassian poetry, in a much less tangible fashion he moved beyond the inalterable opposition of masculine and feminine.

Baudelaire is quite familiar to us in the role of craftsman, and in this guise he appears fundamentally opposed to the spirit of Romanticism. His rigorous attention to style and form, his intellectual elitism, and his disdain for didactic, humanitarian, or effusively sentimental poetry all point to a shared agenda with Leconte de Lisle. When we add to these observations Baudelaire's mistrust of femininity and repudiation of nature for an inquiry into artifice, he seems to be right in step with Parnassian sensibilities and ideology. Further indications in his work, however, suggest otherwise. These include his commitment to the "modern" (which he aligns with Romanticism), and above all his valorization of subjective poetry.

Baudelaire's early art criticism and transcendental poems reveal him to be a defender of Romanticism and an heir to its ideology. *Les fleurs du Mal* is, of course, a supremely lyrical collection, one that spurns epic forms and modes, preferring short, highly subjective poems.[7] These latter include the pieces placed at the beginning of the "Spleen et idéal" section of *Les fleurs du Mal*, which represent the Poet in both his melancholic (spleenful) and exalted (idealized) guises. Leo Bersani considers these to be "some of Baudelaire's most famous, and least interesting, poems," because of their transparency: "it is here that Baudelaire expresses most unambiguously an idealistic view of the poet which, on the whole, *Les fleurs du Mal* simply dismisses" (23). While I would agree with Bersani that "Bénédiction," "L'albatros," "Élévation," and "Les phares" offer "the most familiar romantic version of that [idealistic] view," I wonder whether Bersani's dismissiveness aims to disassociate Baudelaire from the negligibility and femininity of Romanticism.

"Élévation" describes the buoyant, creative élan of the Poet who masters "Le langage des fleurs et des choses muettes." This is a boldly masculine stance: "Mon esprit, tu te meus avec agilité, / [. . .] / Avec une indicible et *mâle volupté*" (1: 10). But next to the vigorous Poet of "Élévation," elsewhere Baudelaire develops the figure of the misunderstood Poet-in-exile. Indeed, more frequent in *Les fleurs du Mal* are representations of the Poet overcome by self-doubt and the disdain of his contemporaries, as in "Bénédiction" and "L'albatros." John Jackson refers to "Bénédiction" when he suggests that "à l'origine des *Fleurs du Mal* [il y a] la conscience d'une rupture qui transforme l'éléction du poète en malédiction" (16). In contrast to the confident, uninhibited Poet of "Élévation," "Bénédiction" describes him as a downtrodden outcast: "Le Poète apparaît en ce monde ennuyé, / Sa mère épouvantée et pleine de blasphèmes" (1: 7). And "L'albatros" offers the simile of a grounded and ungainly bird to counter the free-flying Poet of "Élévation": "Le Poète est semblable au prince des nuées / [. . .] / Exilé sur le sol au milieu des huées" (1: 10).

For Benjamin, the notion of exile or alienation is central to Baudelaire's poetic stance. He has suggested that "La signification tout à fait exceptionelle de Baudelaire tient en ceci que, le premier [. . .], il a appréhendé [. . .] la force productive de l'homme aliéné: il l'a reconnue et, par la réification, lui a donné plus de force."[8] While Baudelaire's alienated Poet confirms the Romantic association of virility with solitude and superiority, the masculinity represented in his work is a fundamentally threatened one. In contrast to the exploratory, expansive maleness of Romanticism, Baudelaire often represented his Poet as an emasculated creature in unfamiliar or hostile surroundings. Again, "L'albatros" provides an example of the impotent Poet: "Ses ailes de géant l'empêchent de marcher" (1: 10).

Baudelaire's work would seem to have initiated, as both Benjamin and Jackson have suggested, the transition of the Poet from Romantic hero to alienated hero. Just as Romantic criticism participated in the consecration of the Romantic hero through its transparent reading practices, a good deal of contemporary criticism is complicitous, albeit in a much more subtle fashion, in the crowning of the Poet as the symbol for a disaffected masculine modernity.

Baudelaire's early art criticism idealizes Romanticism. In his *Salon de 1846*, written at a time when the anti-Romantic "new poetic school" began to manifest itself, Baudelaire associates Romanticism with newness and innovation: "S'appeler romantique et regarder systématiquement le passé, c'est se contredire. [. . .] Pour moi, le romantisme est l'expression la plus récente, la plus actuelle du beau. [. . .] Qui dit romantisme dit art moderne, —c'est-à-dire intimité, spiritualité, couleur, aspiration vers l'infini [. . .]. Le romantisme est fils du Nord" (2: 420, 421). In this passage, Baudelaire occupies a position directly opposed to the one Leconte de Lisle would take in his prefatory essays. Baudelaire devalues "le passé" in favor of "l'expression la plus récente, la plus actuelle [et] moderne." He associates poetic aspiration toward infinity with newness, while suggesting that a preoccupation with the past contradicts such aspirations. Moreover, his last sentence reveals the influence of Staël's theories in *De l'Allemagne*, in which she associates northern climes with Romantic sentiment and criticizes the classical pretensions of French poetry.[9]

Notwithstanding Baudelaire's admiration for Gautier, his laudatory article on Leconte de Lisle, and his own formalist tendencies, of which I will have more to say below, his critical works reveal a strong streak of anticlassicism. This becomes clear in "L'école païenne," an article first published in 1852,[10] just before the appearance of Leconte de Lisle's *Poèmes antiques* and Gautier's *Émaux et camées*. Despite his indebtedness to and respect for these poets, this article nonetheless reaffirms Romantic poetic values by denouncing pre-Parnassian tendencies. Without naming names, Baudelaire attacks the new literary program that supplanted Romantic Christianity with renewed interest in "pagan" (Greek and Roman) deities. He criticizes its lack of innovation and its obsession with the past: "ce n'est pas autre chose qu'un pastiche inutile et dégoûtant" (2: 47). Does his sardonic essay take aim at Leconte de Lisle or at Banville, whose *Cariatides* (1842) and *Stalactites* (1846) both drew from Hellenistic sources and predated Baudelaire's article? In either event, he condemns Parnassianism *avant la lettre*, ridiculing what would become one of its dearest-held points of reference, classical antiquity, as a regression from the beauties of modern life. He addresses the "malheureux néopaïens" (2: 47) as follows: "Vous avez sans doute perdu votre âme quelque part, [. . .] pour que vous couriez ainsi à travers le passé comme des corps vides pour en ramasser une de rencontre dans les détritus anciens?" (2: 47).

Baudelaire goes on to elaborate upon "les détritus anciens," leftover forms and objects, and offers a perceptive analysis of the "pagan school's" fascination with female statues. In the following passage he seems to suggest that the "neopagan" exploration of femininity involves a defensive projection of injured masculinity: "Est-ce Vénus Aphrodite ou Vénus Mercenaire qui soulagera les maux qu'elle vous aura causés? Toutes ces statues de marbre seront-elles des femmes dévouées au jour de l'agonie, au jour du remords, au jour de l'impuissance?" (2: 47). While Baudelaire ultimately is as defensive as the Parnassian poets, his own poetry betrays signs of engagement with femininity, rather than clinging to denial or avoidance.

Baudelaire associates the fascination for the past with a loss of subjective expression ("perdu votre âme"), which constitutes a weakening of the lyric endeavor. In the "goût immodéré de la forme" (2: 48) and "spécialisation excessive [qui] aboutit au néant" (2: 49) of the "pagan school," Baudelaire perceives a loss of affect: "la dureté du cœur et une immensité d'orgueil" (2: 49). He accuses the proto-Parnassians of a repressed and soulless literary practice. What Baudelaire laments above all in his condemnation of objective and neoclassical poetry is the loss of subjective inquiry, which is to say the abandonment of the lyric endeavor ("il faut être absolument lyrique" [2: 166]). His admiration for Gautier suggests that it is not formalism *per se* that he criticizes, but a detached formalism that loses sight of the subject.[11] Christianity, rather than antiquity, supplies Baudelaire with his dualistic framework, that of good and evil, with which he explores the limits and contradictions of the subject. In neoclassicism, then, he sees the repudiation of this work, in particular a refusal of his counterintuitive aesthetics of evil, which relies on sordid images to illustrate sublimity (several striking examples include "Une charogne" and "Les épaves").

These poetic and critical texts point to Baudelaire's association with Romanticism's transcendentalism, one of its privileged ideological frames of reference (Catholicism), its poetics of openness, and commitment to the subjective voice of lyricism. And yet he would eventually attach his name to Parnassianism, thanks to the publication of fifteen "Nouvelles fleurs du Mal" in the 1866 *Parnasse contemporain*. Mendès solicited these poems, which had appeared in neither the 1857 nor 1861 editions of *Les fleurs du Mal*. It is quite possible that Baudelaire's interest in the poetry review was more financial than aesthetic, since his letters to Mendès reveal an urgent need for reimbursement: "mettez-moi à la poste, le plus tôt possible, LES ÉPREUVES, et même les 100 francs, j'ai honte de le dire" (*Corr.* 2: 575). These are later poems for the most part, and curiously not the most Parnassian of Baudelaire's work. Highly subjective and often introspective ("Recueillement"), they include several love poems, both idyllic ("Hymne") and ironically pessimistic ("Madrigal triste"). Dark Christian images and austere doctrine color "Épigraphe pour un livre condamné," "L'examen de minuit," "Le rebelle," and "Le gouffre." In contrast, references to antiquity are minimal. The "Nouvelles fleurs" include as well an earlier poem, "À une Malabaraise" (first published in 1846), which counters the Parnassian preoccupation with white femininity: "Tes pieds sont aussi fins que tes mains, et ta hanche / Est large à faire envie à la plus belle blanche" (1: 173). Finally, some of the sonnets of the "Nouvelles fleurs" represent Baudelaire's most liberal treatment of the form, which the Parnassians themselves approached with greater reverence: "Bien loin d'ici" is an inverted sonnet and "L'avertisseur" a fourteen-line poem whose tercets are framed by quatrains.

While the "Nouvelles fleurs" do not strike the reader as particularly "Parnassian," other poems from *Les fleurs du Mal* include representations of immobilized femininity typical of the movement. In Baudelaire's work, which abounds with sundry and dangerous female figures (including prostitutes, vampires, and lesbians), the threat posed by the "hard" woman is all the more evident. "Spleen et idéal" includes a group of poems in which a male speaking subject addresses a highly aestheticized woman who is defined in terms of her sterility, cruel hardness, and cold, cutting eyes. Her interest for Baudelaire might be summarized by the line "La froide majesté de la femme stérile," from poem XXVII. She appears in a number of other poems, including XXIV: "Et je chéris, ô bête implacable et cruelle! / Jusqu'à cette froideur par où tu m'es plus belle!"[12] The aesthetic and ideological value of this figure resembles that of feminine statuary for the neoclassical Parnassian poets; as a representation of ideal beauty, it kept woman objectified and unmoving.

I presented a line from "La beauté" as an epigraph for my Parnassian chapters because it relies on the stone metaphor and strikes me as one of Baudelaire's most Parnassian of poems. Let us now consider this sonnet in greater detail:

> Je suis belle, ô mortels! comme un rêve de pierre,
> Et mon sein, où chacun s'est meurtri tour à tour,
> Est fait pour inspirer au poète un amour
> Éternel et muet ainsi que la matière.                          4
>
> Je trône dans l'azur comme un sphinx incompris;
> J'unis un cœur de neige à la blancheur des cygnes;
> Je hais le mouvement qui déplace les lignes,
> Et jamais je ne pleure et jamais je ne ris.                    8
>
> Les poètes, devant mes grandes attitudes,
> Que j'ai l'air d'emprunter aux plus fiers monuments,
> Consumeront leurs jours en d'austères études;
>
> Car j'ai, pour fasciner ces dociles amants,                   12
> De purs miroirs qui font toutes choses plus belles:
> Mes yeux, mes larges yeux aux clartés éternelles!
>
> (1: 21)

In contrast to some of the texts reviewed above, "La beauté" appears to issue directly from Gautier's doctrine of art for art's sake. It is also exemplary of the Parnassian aesthetic of objective description, impassivity, and formal harmony. The personified beauty of this poem is typical of the Parnassian incarnation (or incarceration) of woman, portrayed as a severe and immobile creature in verses whose chiseled perfection mirrors her own statuesque, unyielding beauty. The hardness of the feminine speaking subject ("comme un rêve de pierre," "j'[emprunte] aux plus fiers monuments"),[13] her cold whiteness ("J'unis un cœur de neige à la blancheur des cygnes"), and her impenetrability ("comme un sphinx incompris") are accompanied by a poetic message that is clearly Parnassian: "Je hais le mouvement qui déplace les lignes." Beauty's preference for stasis is illustrated by the classical balance of the line that follows: "Et jamais je ne pleure et jamais je ne ris." This mirrored symmetry constitutes poetic perfection: "De purs miroirs qui font toutes choses plus belles."

The influence of such poems by Gautier as "Symphonie en blanc" and "Le poème de la femme" is evident here. And yet the self-ironic tone of Baudelaire's sonnet, one of the few in *Les fleurs du Mal* to present a female speaking subject, must not be overlooked. Irony, which played a negligible role both in the Romantic poetics of sincerity and in the Parnassian poetics of solemnity, is essential to Baudelaire's work. The Poet of "La beauté" represents an object of disdain in the eyes of all-powerful femininity. Rather than controlling femininity by freezing it in stone images as did the Parnassians, Baudelaire's sonnet finds the helpless Poet himself manipulated and controlled by that image. Because Baudelaire's feminine figures occasionally spring into movement, they are ultimately much more dangerous than their Parnassian equivalents.

As evident in "La beauté" and other poems, Baudelaire's poetic sensibility relies a good deal on classicism. He is a supreme craftsman, ever attentive to form and having a pronounced predilection for binarisms, exemplified by his "double postulation," and his fondness for antithesis and oxymoron. Several passages from his *Journaux intimes* reveal aesthetic ruminations that are illustrative of this penchant, but which at the same time indicate an unresolved tension between the paired terms. Baudelaire is rarely exclusive, or when he is it is largely rhetorical; indeed, his enduring interest for contemporary readers is largely due to the complex cohabitation of contradictory elements. He cannot be located in the clear-cut debate between the Classics and the Romantics or that between the Romantics and the Parnassians. Instead, his work reflects upon these oppositions and articulates a definition of the lyric that springs from the heart of such contradictions. Such unresolved debates reveal Baudelaire's engagement with the gendered subject and point the way to the multiform poetic projects of the final quarter of the nineteenth century.

A binary world therefore structures *Les fleurs du Mal,* from its thematic content ("Spleen et idéal"), its representation of femininity (sterile or fecund), and its moral outlook (good and evil), to its rhetorical figures and its prosody. To illustrate how fundamental gender is to this dualist structure and to indicate where Baudelaire's binarisms eventually dissolve, I turn now to a key passage from his *Journaux intimes*.

## Vaporization and Centralization

This opening statement from Baudelaire's *Mon cœur mis à nu*
provides a forceful example of the relationship between constraint and diffusion in his work:

> De la vaporisation et de la centralisation du *Moi*. Tout est
> là. (1: 676)

I would suggest that the couple "la vaporisation et la centralisation" represents a code for sexual difference that traverses
all levels of Baudelaire's thinking and writing. The tag "tout
est là" points to the multiplicity of meanings imbedded in this
pithy aphorism. It provides a key for understanding Baudelaire's
positions on a broad range of poetic issues, including the elaboration of both the writing subject and the lyric subject, formal
composition and aesthetic theory, as well as the import of sexual
difference for the poetic text and textual subjectivity. Femininity
and masculinity govern a variety of relationships, including
those shared by dispersal and concentration, irregularity and
regularity, body and mind, pleasure and work, dependence and
autonomy, merger and identity.

On one level, this polarity summarizes the debate between
Romanticism and the Parnasse, in which the effusive and at
times intangible subject of the Romantic lyric counters the objectifying and fixed point of view of the Parnassians. As we
have seen, images of watery or vaporous landscapes played a
significant role during the Romantic era, from misty seascapes
(Chateaubriand's "horizons de mer légèrement vaporeux") to
hazy landscapes at the turn of day, which Parnassian poets later
opposed with hardened, concentrated metaphors. The opposition also governs formal concerns, wherein the Romantics favored an expansive, centrifugal practice and the Parnassians a
concentrated, centripetal one.

With his aphorism, Baudelaire suggests as well that there is
a fundamental duality in the makeup of the subject, a duality
upon which he relies in the elaboration of his poetic theory.
The polarity of vaporization and centralization is in many ways
definitive of Baudelaire's thought on subjectivity and of his
representation of sexual difference. Although his critical prose
often contradicts his poetry, and his poetry itself sometimes

reveals incongruities, much of his work can be seen to exist on a continuum between the poles of vaporization and centralization, indeed to be fascinated by this opposition.

Concentration, centralization, and *recueillement* represent the posture of the working Poet, the writing subject. In passages from Baudelaire's intimate journals where he muses on poetic production, he appears to concur with a rather Parnassian-sounding credo: "The one prudence in life is concentration; the one evil is dissipation."[14] These journals[15] sometimes read like self-help guides for the Poet who struggles with his work against the forces of dissipation, striving for control and concentration. He relies on repetition and regularity, rather than inspiration, in his work habits: "Un peu de travail, répété trois cent soixante-cinq fois [. . .]" (1: 662).

As Claude Pichois points out, Baudelaire often associates vaporization with "la perte de la substance intellectuelle et de la volonté" (1: 1063). "Au lecteur," for example, describes the loss of consciousness in terms of vaporization, under the unhealthy influence of Satan Trismégiste: "Et le riche métal de notre volonté / Est tout *vaporisé* par ce savant chimiste" (1: 5). Vaporization is clearly threatening to the Poet seeking self-mastery through the consciously acquired control of language. Similarly, "L'amour et le crâne" describes an engraving by Hendrick Goltzius of a cupid blowing bubbles from his mouth while seated on a skull. In this battle between love and intellect, between vaporization and centralization, the skull addresses the cupid in the following manner:

> [. . .] ce que ta bouche cruelle
> Eparpille en l'air,
> Monstre assassin, c'est ma cervelle,
> Mon sang et ma chair!
>
> (1: 120)

Baudelaire does two things with this vision of lyric production. First, he reconfigures the image of the Romantic Poet, passively dependent on a muse, proposing instead the conscious, self-possessed model of a diligent worker.[16] He recasts the Romantic Poet in an active, more masculine mold. This masculinity, while threatened, plays a more central role and permits fewer forays into the pathos of femininity evident in the poetry of Lamartine or even Hugo. Secondly, he slips into a puritanical stance in his condemnation of sexuality: "Le Plaisir nous use. Le Travail nous fortifie" (*Hygiène* [1: 669]). Sexual pleasure leads to dissipation: ultimately, vaporization represents the fearful specter of feminine sexuality. Baudelaire's professed aversion to sexuality labels it as a disruptive force, one that unsettles or vaporizes the unified subject. Without the concentration of intellectual forces, the contours of the self are blurred and the writing subject risks vaporization. Loss of intellectual capacity leads to physical dispersal, and finally to the loss of the psychological boundaries of the self. Sexual activity, moreover, is responsible for such dispersal and loss of definition: the dissipation of bodily fluid, such as ejaculated sperm, becomes a metaphor for the loss of identity and concomitant intellectual concentration (in stark contrast to the productive outpouring of Valmorian tears).[17] Consequently, abstinence is a requirement of poetic production: "Plus l'homme cultive les arts, moins il bande. Il se fait un divorce de plus en plus sensible entre l'esprit et la brute. La brute seule bande bien, et la fouterie est le lyrisme du peuple. Foutre, c'est aspirer à entrer dans un autre, et l'artiste ne sort jamais de lui-même" (1: 702).

The work habits of the Poet represent a safeguard against dissipation and the loss of the self in the other. Solitude signals introspection and is associated with an isolating, self-protective stance as much as it is with intellectual exile. In a sense, and whether consciously or not, Baudelaire's writings reveal much more directly than Leconte de Lisle's the fear of the feminine other. In both their works, sexuality and love represent the greatest danger to the masculine poetic subject. But Baudelaire addresses this danger head-on with his synonymous treatment of love and prostitution. He associates prostitution with dispersal or vaporization, since sexuality in any form represents the desire to "sortir de soi" (1: 650): "Goût invincible de la prostitution dans le cœur de l'homme, d'où naît son horreur de la solitude. Il veut être *deux*. [. . .] C'est cette horreur de la solitude, le besoin d'oublier son *moi* dans la chair extérieure, que l'homme appelle noblement *besoin d'aimer*" (*Mon cœur* [1: 700]). The singularity and solitary stance of genius opposes this dispersal of the self: "L'homme de génie veut être *un*, donc solitaire" (1: 700). The Poet, then, bent before his conscious task, opposes multiplicity and femininity.

For Barbey d'Aurevilly, let us recall, genius is predicated on "[une] immense virilité" (*Les bas-bleus* xvii), and poetic identity relies on the fear and repudiation of (female) sexuality. Vapors travel even farther away than liquidity from the solid and cold Parnassian metaphors: Littré defines "vapeur" as "[une] fumée qui s'élève des corps par l'effet de la chaleur" (3: 2422). Nineteenth-century associations between vapors and the corruption of feminine sexuality were quite clear: "vapeur de fille" was a synonym for hysteria ("maladie provenant de la matrice" [3: 2422]), a "dérèglement cérébral," or a dispersal of the self due to debilitating physical causes.[18] To be a Poet is to stand apart, to live in solitude, to flee the other, to create a separate and distinct identity, and to be free of the urges and vagaries of the body.[19]

Baudelaire's defense of masculinity and attendant misogyny is therefore necessary to his task. His disgust for feminine corporeality and fecundity, as well as his fearful admiration for hard women and sterile lesbians, are corollaries to his desire for autonomy. There is, moreover, the proto-Freudian suggestion in his work that separation from the (m)other constitutes maturity: "Le goût de la concentration productive doit remplacer, chez un homme mûr, le goût de la déperdition" (*Fusées* [1: 649]). Ironically, however, the work (daily writing habits) of the Poet is at cross-purposes with the Poet's work (the content of the poems he produces). That is, while Baudelaire's personal writings announce a desire for autonomy and differentiation, some of his most intriguing poems deal with merger and lack of differentiation.

Philippe Hamon has suggested that Baudelaire's aphorism defines not only the writing subject, but the genre of the lyric itself: "genre que [. . .] Baudelaire [définit] comme une hésitation entre un mouvement de 'vaporisation' et un mouvement de 'centralisation' du moi" ("Texte" 17). Although the more personal passages from his journals suggest ambivalence about the conflicting desires that assail the writing subject, Baudelaire's aesthetic ruminations insist, on the contrary, that centralization and vaporization are interdependent. In *Fusées* he writes, on the one hand, that "la régularité et la symétrie [. . .] sont un des besoins primordiaux de l'esprit humain [. . .]" (1: 663). As we have seen, the need for regularity motivates Parnassian production and such Baudelairian poems as "La beauté." But on the other hand, and in the same text, he defines irregularity as an essential component of the successful work of art: "Ce qui n'est pas légèrement difforme a l'air insensible; d'où il suit que l'irrégularité, c'est-à-dire l'inattendu, la surprise, l'étonnement sont une partie essentielle et la caractéristique de la beauté" (1: 656).

Several images in Baudelaire's prose and verse poetry offer visual metaphors for a cooperative collaboration between regularity and irregularity, centralization and vaporization. The prose poem "Le thyrse," for example, presents a tangible image of this duality and embroiders upon its gendered associations:

> *Qu'est-ce qu'un thyrse? Selon le sens moral et poétique,* c'est un emblème sacerdotal *dans la main des prêtres ou des prêtresses célébrant la divinité dont ils sont les interprètes et les serviteurs. Mais physiquement ce n'est qu'un bâton, un pur bâton, perche à houblon, tuteur de vigne, sec, dur et droit. Autour de ce bâton, dans des méandres capricieux, se jouent et folâtrent des tiges et des fleurs,* celles-ci sinueuses et fuyardes, celles-là penchées comme des cloches ou des coupes renversées. Et une gloire étonnante jaillit de cette complexité de lignes et de couleurs, tendres ou éclatantes. Ne dirait-on pas que la ligne courbe et la spirale font leur cour à la ligne droite et dansent autour dans une muette adoration? Ne dirait-on pas que toutes ces corolles délicates, tous ces calices, explosions de senteurs et de couleurs, exécutent un mystique fandango autour du bâton hiératique? Et quel est, cependant, le mortel imprudent qui osera décider si les fleurs et les pampres ont été faits pour le bâton, ou si le bâton n'est que le prétexte pour montrer la beauté des pampres et des fleurs? *Le thyrse est la représentation de votre étonnante dualité* [. . .]. —*Le bâton, c'est votre volonté, droite, ferme et inébranlable; les fleurs, c'est la promenade de votre fantaisie autour de votre volonté; c'est l'élément féminin exécutant autour du mâle ses prestigieuses pirouettes. Ligne droite et ligne arabesque, intention et expression, roideur de la volonté, sinuosité du verbe, unité du but, variété des moyens, amalgame tout-puissant et indivisible du génie,* quel analyste aura le détestable courage de vous diviser et de vous séparer?[20]

Baudelaire addressed this prose poem to Franz Liszt, suggesting music as a metaphor for both poetic composition and intersubjectivity.[21] The thyrsus offers one of Baudelaire's most concrete descriptions of sexual and aesthetic cooperation in a corpus rife with images of conflict between analogous elements. Here Baudelaire's duality is "étonnante" and interacts in "muette adoration." The emblem of the thyrsus relies equally on centralization ("volonté," "intention") and vaporization ("fantaisie," "expression"). Together, the straight line and the arabesque line unite in a heterosexual dance: "c'est l'élément féminin exécutant autour du mâle ses prestigieuses pirouettes." So although femininity and its dissipative effects represent a danger for the Poet at work, the poem itself, according to Baudelaire, depends upon a "feminine element," which he defines in terms of sinuosity, capriciousness, and delicacy. By embracing femininity in his poetic doctrine, no matter how conventionally defined, Baudelaire differs markedly from Parnassians who do their best to evacuate it entirely.

A similar metaphor appears in Baudelaire's verse poetry, that of the *jongleur* who manipulates a snake around a staff. In "Le serpent qui danse," Baudelaire compares this image to a woman in motion:

> À te voir marcher en cadence,
> Belle d'abandon,
> On dirait un serpent qui danse
> Au bout d'un bâton.
>
> (1: 30)

And poem xxvii begins with the same metaphor: "Même quand elle marche on croirait qu'elle danse, / Comme ces longs serpents que les jongleurs sacrés / Au bout de leurs bâtons agitent en cadence" (1: 29). Elsewhere, he compares the Poet explicitly to a "psylle," which Littré defines as "un charletan qui apprivoise les serpents et joue avec eux" (3: 1376). Baudelaire asks: "Pourquoi le poète ne serait-il [. . .] un éleveur de serpents pour miracles et spectacles, un psylle amoureux de ses reptiles?" (2: 238). As *jongleur* or *psylle*, the Poet-priest retains his position of masculine mastery, since he is the central controlling figure of this dance of opposites, be that the baton and flowers of the thyrsus, the staff and snake, meter and rhythm, regularity and irregularity.

The straight line and arabesque clearly fascinate Baudelaire as a metaphor for the poetic line, which depends upon the interaction of regularity (meter) and the unregulated or spontaneous (rhythm). This metaphor is sexualized, not only by virtue of Baudelaire's attribution of male and female parts in this interaction, but also thanks to the insistence with which the image returns to describe the female body. Baudelaire recognizes the meeting of the straight and the sinuous in the undulating line of a woman's hem,[22] as in the synesthetic image of perfume encircling a woman's body in "Le chat" (XXXIV): "Et, des pieds jusques à la tête, / Un air subtil, un dangereux parfum / Nagent autour de son corps brun" (1: 35). This tercet illustrates the tension that complicates the strict binarism I have been discussing up to this point, pointing to the instability of the opposition in Baudelaire's work. First, the danger of the perfume threatens the body around which it floats, and threatens the unity of the two elements. Secondly, one can read a reversal of sexual positions in this poem (the female body takes the place of the thyrsus's masculine baton), as in the image of phallic snakes entwined around the agitated staff.

These subtleties become particularly interesting when we return to the less tangible realm of subjectivity, which Baudelaire defines as the interaction between "la vaporisation et la centralisation du *Moi*." For the thyrsus not only serves as a metaphor for the poetic line, but also refers to subjective states, a privileged moment on a continuum of conscious control (coded masculine) and unconscious dissipation (aligned with femininity). Although Baudelaire represents the writing subject clinging to the pole of concentration, elsewhere he meditates upon the boundaries of subjectivity, where the speaking subject flirts with the dangers of dissipation and femininity. There are several places in his lyric oeuvre where he explores this formal and subjective duality, which he calls alternately vaporization/centralization, irregularity/regularity, dispersal/concentration, or femininity/masculinity. Baudelaire grapples with this opposition, and in so doing works toward a new definition of the subject, in a specific prosodic context. Not surprisingly perhaps, a number of poems engaged in this program are heterometric, combining long and short meters that graphically represent a thyrsuslike image on the page. In addition to "Le chat," "Une charogne," "Le serpent qui danse," and "L'amour et le crâne," Baudelaire exploits this formal technique in "La musique" to assist in his representation of difference.

## "La musique"

The complexities of Baudelaire's poetic world spring to the fore when we contrast his "Parnassian" poems with his heterometric pieces. While the former exhibit a neoclassical appreciation for symmetry and metaphors of hardness, and seem to hover around the pole of centralization, the latter show a rather contradictory penchant for sinuosity, employ quite openly images of dispersal, and betray a kind of "vaporized" approach to form. In such poems, Baudelaire travels farthest on the limb away from the certainty of centralization, toward a precarious position of undecidability, a place where both poetic subject and poetic form strive to escape definition. Baudelaire is at his most daring in these poems in which his reflections on gender difference, be they conscious or not, stray from the strict confines of polarized identities, which are so evident in his rigid, masculinist construction of the Poet and his antifeminist diatribes.

I propose here a leisurely reading of "La musique" to illustrate how Baudelaire manipulates poetic structures to plot the emergence of an ill-defined subject, one that conforms neither to Romantic transparency nor to the hypermasculinity of Parnassianism. The elusive subject of "La musique" is not explicitly aligned with either gender and, indeed, suggests a shift in the lyric tradition toward a much more complex, polyvocal representation of subjectivity. Although, like the Parnassians, Baudelaire was attracted to the constraints of the sonnet, "La musique" exhibits his ability to use formal restrictions as point of departure for openness. This sonnet confronts the opposition of vaporization and centralization on the levels of rhythm, subjectivity, and thematic structure, and in so doing illustrates Baudelaire's manipulation of gender in the poetic text. While offering a fascinating commentary on the double motivation of Baudelaire's poetic practice, it also represents an investigation into the boundaries of subjectivity and intersubjective relations. As such it seems to suggest psychic sources for its author's poetic speculations, revealing his obsession with the work

of separation and distancing, and his uncertainty before the terror
and security of merger. I begin my analysis with a consideration of the sonnet's prosodic structures in order to illustrate
how rhythm frames Baudelaire's articulation of his lyric subject.

> La musique souvent me prend comme une mer!
>   Vers ma pâle étoile,
> Sous un plafond de brume ou dans un vaste éther
>   Je mets à la voile;                                4
>
> La poitrine en avant et les poumons gonflés
>   Comme de la toile,
> J'escalade le dos des flots amoncelés
>   Que la nuit me voile;                              8
>
> Je sens vibrer en moi toutes les passions
>   D'un vaisseau qui souffre;
> Le bon vent, la tempête et ses convulsions
>
>   Sur l'immense gouffre                             12
> Me bercent. D'autres fois, calme plat, grand miroir
>   De mon désespoir!
>                                                (1: 68)

Heterometricity, the principle of alternation between two
meters, coincides with the vaporization/centralization duality
and in so doing functions as a prosodic feature that is gender
coded. This link becomes clear when we consider the specific
meters that constitute the alternation in "La musique": alexandrines and pentasyllabic lines. While this is the only such
occurrence in Baudelaire's poetry, it is not fortuitous; this
heterometric scheme contrasts a notoriously "regular" meter
with an oddly irregular one. Indeed, there is no meter more
central to French prosody than the alexandrine, which offers a
poetic norm based on symmetry and convention. The twelve
syllables of the alexandrine serve as a ruler against which to
measure all meters. This "foot," divisible into two even parts
of six, evokes the "ligne droite" of the baton of the thyrsus and
seems to satisfy "la régularité et la symétrie qui sont un des besoins
primordiaux de l'esprit humain" (1: 663). Insofar as the abstraction of meter can carry meaning, the alexandrine signifies tradition and order in French poetry. The contrasting pentasyllable

serves an entirely different function and has no specific tradition in the history of French verse. Since it misses repeating the six beats of the hemistich by a single syllable, alternating with alexandrines in "La musique," the pentasyllable gives the effect of deforming the hemistich, of upsetting a regular beat. It provides for Baudelaire "l'inattendu, la surprise, l'étonnement [qui] sont une partie essentielle et la caractéristique de la beauté" (1: 656) and resembles the frivolous play of the thyrsus's flowers. And it is certainly not coincidental that the irregularly metered short lines are all (save for the last) feminine, ending in the mute *e*.

Baudelaire rarely exploited uneven meters, but when he did it was with a particular object in mind. He penned only two other heterometric poems that rely on the five-syllable meter, both ones we have already encountered. "Le serpent qui danse" and "L'amour et le crâne" both alternate octosyllabic and pentasyllabic lines in a series of quatrains, thus presenting visually, like all heterometric poems, the image of a sinuous or arabesque line, rather than the straight edge of a justified margin. As does "La musique," these poems comment on the interaction of vaporization and centralization so that, by coincidence or by design, Baudelaire's pentasyllabic poems echo the poetic elements of his emblematic thyrsus.

"La musique" plays with the dialectics of regularity and irregularity, of sameness and difference, of masculine and feminine, in other ways, not the least by opposing symmetric quatrains to asymmetric tercets. On the level of the stanza an analogous rule of symmetry governs the quatrains while one of disymmetry operates in the tercets. This is immediately visible in the superposition of the two vertical organizing principles of the sonnet, on one hand the alternation of long and short lines, and on the other hand the two quatrain / two tercet distribution. Musically this can be represented by two measures in 4/4 time followed by two measures in 3/4 time, where the even alternation of the lines coincides with the even beat of the quatrains but clashes with the odd beat of the tercets. When the one-two of the alternating meter meets the tercets, the resulting effect is poetic syncopation in line 12, beginning the final tercet on the "up-beat." This effect is typographically visible, since the "up-beat" of line 12 is the only short line to begin a stanza.

The final tercet creates several other irregularities in the structural economy of the poem, irregularities that depend on the
relative regularity of the quatrains. The rhyme scheme coincides with the heterogeneous meter in the latter (ABAB CBCB:
12-5-12-5 12-5-12-5), whereas the tercets cannot frame the
third unit of *rimes croisées*; consequently, they end with a
couplet that produces a mismatched counter-rhyme (DED *EFF:*
12-5-12 *5-12-5*).

In contrast with the irregularity of the tercets, the quatrains
are governed by symmetry and regularity. Syntactically, the quatrains provide end-stopped lines and alexandrines that are balanced in various ways with clearly defined caesuras. The first
and last measures of line 1 mirror the two terms of the poem's
inaugural comparison: "La musique souvent / me prend comme
une mer!" Line 3 is balanced by two grammatically identical
prepositional phrases: "Sous un plafond de brume / ou dans
un vaste éther." Likewise, two equivalent units—semantically
related, alliterative nouns (both related to breath, the origin of
voice) and their modifiers—divide line 5: "La poitrine en avant /
et les poumons gonflés." Finally line 7, like line 1, is shared
by the two elements of a poetic figure, here of the metaphor
"dos" for "flots": "J'escalade le dos / des flots amoncelés." While
the symmetrical presentation of the comparison in line 1 is
effected syntactically (the placement of the terms in the first
and last measures of the line) and by alliteration in [m], the
metaphor in line 7 obtains this symmetrical aspect above all
through the rhyme gravitating around the caesura ("le dos / des
flots"), which mirrors in turn an internal rhyme of identical
position in line 1: "souvent / me prend."

In contrast, the tercets, whose principal rhythmic effect is
enjambment, unfold a progressive discordance of meter and
syntax. Hence the stanzaic enjambment in line 11 precedes two
subsequent enjambments and the rather surprising *rejet* of line
13 that concludes the long sentence making up most of the poem.
Because the poem's sentences straddle its lines and blur their
boundaries, the horizontal balance of the quatrains' alexandrines
is lost to an effect of continuity in the tercets, whereby the caesuras serve as momentary pauses in a forward progression, no
longer as fulcrums dividing two equivalent parts. Syntactically,
the sentences wind their way through the tercets in a sinuous

manner, thus forming the "ligne arabesque" of the *thyrse*. Roman Jakobson might say that the principle of equivalence governs the quatrains, the principle of contiguity, the tercets. Hence in line 11 there is an accumulation of elements mismatched by the caesura, which distributes them unevenly, two to one ("Le bon vent, la tempête / et ses convulsions"), and separates the tempest from "ses convulsions." The diereses of the rhyme pair "passions/convulsions" similarly heighten the contiguous aspect of the first tercet by lengthening and slackening this rhyme. The vertical logic of this sonnet's formal and grammatical features seems, in sum, to begin with classical balance, coded masculine, and to progress to feminine waywardness.

Through its extended metaphor, "La musique" recounts a story of emerging subjectivity. But on the level of representation, it is at first notable for its lack of concrete referents, since all of its sea images unfurl from an extended metaphor for music, announced in the first line. Its principal referents differ dramatically from stock Parnassian images of statuary by favoring a metaphor for an unrepresentable art form (music) and a constantly moving substance (the ocean). Rhythm is clearly the basis for a comparison of music and poetry, but Baudelaire believed, moreover, music to be capable (like poetry) of transmitting meaning: "la véritable musique suggère des idées analogues dans des cerveaux différents" (2: 784). The "ligne droite et ligne arabesque" of poetic rhythm signify, as does music, by correspondences. Sound evokes images by analogy, and music too can translate another medium. Elsewhere, Baudelaire exhibited an interest in the spatialization of music: "La musique donne l'idée de l'espace [. . .]. La musique creuse le ciel" (1: 702, 653).

In so many of Baudelaire's verse poems, one finds a geometrical, multidimensional universe constructed with points ("C'est un phare allumé sur mille citadelles" [1: 14]), lines ("la pluie étalant ses immenses traînées" [1: 75]), planes (cf. the many images of desert and sea), and volume (spaces such as "le ciel profond" or "le gouffre noir" [1: 24]).[23] The figures evocative of Baudelaire's poetics of space tend to function geometrically and are seemingly impelled toward volume. Hence the "ligne droite et ligne arabesque" of the thyrsus represent not so much, as this description might at first suggest, the encounter of two lines (which would form a plane), as they do the interaction of a straight line (one dimension) with a spiral (already constitutive of a volume). Similarly, centralization captures a fixed point, by definition nondimensional, whereas vaporization images an ever-expanding volume.

What these spatial transformations serve to capture is lyricism's nostalgia for physical and vocal presence. They suggest the translation of the volume of a voice into lines of poetry (or the plane of the page) as well as the desire to reanimate the poem and its speaking subject with spatial expansion and by the restitution of a voice. Perhaps music too can be thought of as phonic volume composed of its own "ligne droite" (a fixed meter) and "ligne arabesque" (a changeable rhythm). Rhythm thus forms the bridge between poetry and music, poetry's voluminous equivalent.

The spatialization of music is effected on many levels in the poem. The poem's typography renders its rhythm visible on the page. On a figurative level, a transposition between the corresponding modes of time and space is also effected. In *The Sonnet over Time*, Sandra Bermann has noticed "Baudelaire's fascination with the pictorial allegorization of the temporal" (107). "La musique" illustrates this fascination in its two central comparisons, where the spatial relationship between a ship and the sea is substituted for the temporal and aural relationship between a "listening subject" and a piece of music. The poetic tropes that develop these comparisons eclipse the music thematic with a marine vocabulary ("voile," "toile," "vaisseau," "vent," "tempête") and turbulent images. Although the speaking subject is seemingly depersonalized by being compared to a ship, the ship in turn is personified ("un vaisseau qui souffre"), as is the sea ("le dos des flots"). Through this personification, the ostensibly inanimate comparison (of the subject to a ship at sea) is finally more interactively human than the initial tableau suggests (the solitary, intellectual experience of listening to music). It is this translation to physical movement through space that reveals the link between rhythm and the lyric subject.

To state this more clearly, I propose a brief detour by way of an analogy between Baudelaire's design in "La musique" and Benveniste's program in his article "La notion de 'rythme' dans son expression linguistique" (1: 327–35). Benveniste demonstrates that the modern definition of rhythm, having to do with temporal periodicity, is in fact a modern rendering of the Greek *rhuthmos,* which, at its origin, referred to movement in space. Benveniste quotes this passage from Socrates: "il se produit d'autres qualités analogues, inhérentes cette fois aux mouvements du corps, lesquelles sont soumises aux nombres et qu'il faut appeler *rythmes* et *mesures*" (334; Benveniste's italics). Benveniste concludes that movement in space is at the origin of the word that has come to be known as rhythm. Similarly, the work of "La musique," where spatial movement is also retrieved, is one of origins: those of the speaking subject. The shift in the poem from "musique" to "mer," from sound to movement, is a shift to the most primitive of the senses: touch. The eighth line ("Que la nuit me voile") shadows the images of the poem in darkness, depriving the speaking subject of sight—the most distant and intellectual of the senses—leaving her to feel her way on the poem's strange and amniotic landscape, located between the winds and waves of the sea where boundaries are fluid and distances vast.

In "La musique," Baudelaire does the work of an archeologist, digging through time to locate the emergence of a speaking subject born of the hesitation between vaporization and centralization. If one level of meaning operative in this poem refers to the acquisition of subjectivity, the establishment of uniqueness or physical distinction, it is in terms of attachment to and separation from the maternal body that we must consider the lyric subject's emergence. This register is signaled most directly by the image in lines 11–13 of the elements that rock ("bercent") the subject, as well as by the homophony of "une mer" and "une mère." I have pointed to the importance of this metaphor for Romantic poetry, and to Bachelard's and Irigaray's theorization of the association between femininity and fluidity. Even outside of the French language where this homophony does not hold, a metaphoric link between water and maternity has long been established in the psychoanalytic arena.[24]

Bersani has written of "the movement of rocking or cradling [. . .] at the heart of [. . .] 'La chevelure,'" reading in the poem a nostalgia for infancy, the era of caresses and luxurious languor. In the through-going water imagery of "La chevelure,"

Bersani finds the basis for this association with the maternal body: "The emphasis on the sea even suggests the memory of a prenatal life in the liquid environment of the womb." And further: "Perhaps the purest pleasure Baudelaire can imagine is to be rocked as boats are rocked on a gentle sea" (42). Although Bersani does not mention the poem, "La musique" depends on this association as well. In fact, of all those that form a cycle of utopic poems evocative of an exotic or watery terrain (such as "La géante," "La chevelure," "Parfum exotique," "L'invitation au voyage"), its images and rhythms link it most clearly with an anterior ocean scene.[25] The rhythmic pleasure of a rocking boat equals the primitive pleasure of an infant lulled to sleep. Indeed, the poem gives several indications of the passive, silent (*infans*) nature of the speaking subject.

On one level, "La musique" betrays a nostalgia for what Mallarmé called "l'ancien souffle lyrique" (366). The reader encounters images of inspirational respiration in "le bon vent" and the singing bard, with his "poitrine en avant et les poumons gonflés." But although the sonnet appears to conjure up a primitive version of the subject, the "je," instead of a producer of music, exists in a passive relation to it: "la musique souvent *me* prend." If the Poet is shaped by and finds his identity in the production of verse, his lyric subject, on the contrary, is described in terms of the effect that music has upon her: she will be produced by music.

Since nothing in this poem identifies the sex of the speaking subject, I reach somewhat arbitrarily for the generic "she," all the better to distinguish her from the generically masculine Poet—but not to be confused with Woman, the quintessential poetic object. More appropriate still would be a nongendered, yet human pronoun, something more animate than "it." But the inadequacies of both the English and the French language only point to Baudelaire's avoidance of explicit gender distinctions for his speaking subject. Sexual difference is not yet meaningful for his pre-oedipal subject, who is neither male nor female. We have come a far cry indeed from the Poet whose existence depends on that distinction. The first line reveals by its structure that of central concern here is not music as agent, but the speaking subject as receptor. Music and sea, as we have seen, reflect each other from the first and last measure of line 1. At the heart of these corresponding elements, following the hemistich, is the first-person object pronoun, the first indication of the speaking subject. Framed between "la musique" and "une mer / mère," the subject is nestled between the [ã] rhyme of the phrase "souvent me prend." Literally central to the line, of central concern to the poem, the speaking subject will nonetheless move toward a certain psychic vaporization illustrated by her passive position and the elements that surround her. This ultimate locus is at once a place of centralization (union, oneness, being at the heart of) and dispersal in which psychic and physical boundaries are indistinguishable from those of mother, sea, or universe. The poem appears to identify a moment of dependence and security that precedes movement toward separation and independence.

On the level of enunciation, "La musique" tends to follow a different principle of organization from that which we have seen on strictly formal and syntactic levels. Instead of a duality, a process of framing is at work that, as a general principle, serves to privilege the emotive function, thus centralizing the speaking subject. As in line 1, the poem's frames serve literally to center the subject pronoun as if to spotlight her drama of emergence. The poem itself is framed by two short exclamatory sentences falling before and after a long central sentence: the initial "La musique souvent me prend comme une mer!" and the final "D'autres fois, calme plat, grand miroir / De mon desespoir!" form the frame. These shorter sentences express polar sentiments (jubilation and despair), and in so doing set off the central sentence as a kind of emotional playground in which the lyric subject experiences a variety of sensations.

Thus the three syntactically equivalent prepositional phrases of lines 2 and 3 offer three different possible experiences, as if the lyric subject were a blank slate, waiting for some external element (music, sea, mother) to guide or push her: "Vers ma pâle étoile, / Sous un plafond de brume ou dans un vaste éther." Line 3 in particular brings together in syntactic and prosodic equivalence two emotive states generally found in opposition in Baudelaire's work. "Sous un plafond de brume" recalls this first line of "Spleen" (LXXVIII) and, by association, his other splenetic poems: "Quand le ciel bas et lourd pèse comme un couvercle" (1: 74). Conversely, "dans un vaste éther" evokes the euphoric landscape of "Élévation": "Par-delà le soleil, par-delà les éthers [. . .]" (1: 10). This poem also echoes Baudelaire's letter to Wagner where he writes that the experience of listening to music "ressemble à celle de monter dans l'air ou de rouler sur la mer" (2: 1452).

Although seemingly in opposition, both these states are characterized by a certain passivity. That slowness and inactivity are associated with melancholy or spleen goes almost without saying. But even the jubilant sensation is described by Baudelaire in passive terms: "c'est [. . .] la jouissance [. . .] de me laisser pénétrer, envahir, volupté vraiment sensuelle [. . .]" (2: 1452). All these are sensations expressly rejected by the conscious Poet. In a poem where movement is foremost, the prepositions "sous" and "dans" ("Sous un plafond de brume ou dans un vaste éther") betray a particular lack of movement, marking placement alone.

On the contrary, the preposition "vers" of the preceding line indicates action and specific direction. The phrase "vers ma pâle étoile" finds the principle of centralization, of fixed subjectivity, inscribed in several other ways. Of the three prepositional phrases it is the only one to indicate the speaking subject grammatically with the possessive "ma," possession forming one aspect of mastery. Likewise, to the vaporous "brume" and "éther" is contrasted the singular "étoile," which stands as a model of consciousness. Finally, "vers ma pâle étoile" suggests an autonomous subject by recalling such expressions as "une bonne étoile" and above all "l'étoile polaire," the North Star that guides the navigator toward a fixed point.

These clauses thus suggest a variety of subjective stances, from melancholy to jubilation, activity to passivity, but a variety having more internal logic than is at first apparent. For what they trace is an inverted chronology leading from a state of independence, summarized by "vers ma pâle étoile," back to an era of intimacy and well-being productive of Freud's oceanic feeling ("an all-embracing feeling which correspond[s] to a more intimate bond between the ego and the world around it" [*Civilization* 15]): "dans un vaste éther." If melancholy is to be associated with loss,[26] then the passage from euphoria to despair, to "sous un plafond de brume," witnesses a parting of bodies, the separation from the maternal ocean.

Another framing device operates on the level of pronouns and, in turn, registers levels of subjectivity and activity. The speaking subject utters the pronoun "je" three times, these occurrences falling roughly in the center of the poem and framed in lines 1–2 and 13–14 by object pronouns and possessive adjectives as oblique indicators of subjectivity. At the very center of the poem (lines 7–8) arrives a climax of movement and a literal centralization of the speaking subject: this second and therefore centrally framed utterance of "je" is coupled with a verb indicating the most intense activity of all the poem's verbs: "j'escalade le dos."

Here the passive stance of the subject gives way to turbulent activity, an activity that involves the meeting of bodies, movement at once evocative of a sexual encounter ("Je sens vibrer en moi toutes les passions") and playfully affectionate caresses. This association of playfulness is derived, above all, intertextually, for the line "J'escalade le dos des flots amoncelés" clearly corresponds to some images of "La géante," in which a naive speaking subject expresses the desire to cavort upon a mythic, maternal giant as if a child on a hilly landscape: "J'eusse aimé [. . .] / Parcourir à loisir ses magnifiques formes; / Ramper sur le versant de ses genoux énormes [. . .]" (1: 22–23).[27] The youthful frolicking of Baudelaire's poetic subject also recalls Byron's watery precedent in *Childe Harold's Pilgrimage:*

> And I have loved thee, Ocean! and my joy
> Of youthful sports was on thy breast to be
> Borne, like thy bubbles, onward: from a boy
> I wantoned with thy breakers—they to me
> Were a delight; and if the freshening sea
> Made them a terror— 'twas a pleasing fear,
> For I was as it were a child of thee,
> And trusted to thy billows far and near,
> And laid my hand upon thy mane—as I do here.
> (Byron 201)

This moment of extreme pleasure, of movement without vision ("Que la nuit me voile"), of interaction with a huge maternal body (whether imaged as sea, mountains, or giant), locates and surpasses the too-simple opposition of centralization and vaporization. The subject of "La musique" says "I"—is subject—and yet exists in a state of continuity with another, the first other, body. Rather than the debasement of love expressed in the *Journaux intimes*, where it is elided with prostitution, this poem traces an archetypal love, established at a moment of hesitation between continuity and difference.

Lines 9–13, which describe the emotion of this moment, are governed by the poetic figure of the oxymoron. "Le bon vent" is associated with the tempest; in turn, the violent elements of this tempest cradle ("bercent") the speaking subject. All is sound and fury: what matters is the continual movement of the ship, the wind in the sails, the movement of the poetic line, the continual caress.

And then—"d'autres fois"—the poem ends on a note of incongruity and loss when the movement of ship and line stops abruptly, after the *rejet* of line 13. No verb in the short and unbalanced final sentence, no movement on the sea, no action. Without a verb, even the speaking subject disappears into nothingness, and the single reference to time and mode is lost. Not only does the final couplet witness a sudden atemporality, but space too is altered, the voluminous universe deflated to a plane such that the final *rime plate* mirrors the melancholic stillness of the sea ("calme plat") and of the speaking subject. The sonnet's last oxymoron links the calm of the sea to the despair of the speaking subject, already united, drowned, vaporized in the sea ("grand miroir / De mon désespoir"). This final union is not a happy one, for it effaces the difference maintained by the comparison of the lyric subject to a ship at sea. This moment of mirroring, of identity, brings in fact a loss of identity, nothingness, despair. It undoes poetic figures, displaces the line, stops movement.[28]

We have arrived at a clear contradiction of "La beauté," which expresses a mistrust of poetic movement, and have come a far cry from the representation of an isolated masculine subject. Indeed, "La musique" appears to confirm the necessity of movement and intersubjectivity in the constitution of the lyric subject, for their loss is her own. Between complete dispersal and a fixed identity lies the subject in formation; likewise between vaporization and centralization the poem is set in motion. Visually perceptible movement fascinated Baudelaire insofar as it was able to capture the rhythms of a poem and assure the presence of a body. In this quotation from *Fusées* he describes a being born of poetic movement and animated by human breath, the lyric subject *par excellence:* "L'idée poétique qui se dégage de cette opération du mouvement dans les lignes est l'hypothèse d'un être vaste, immense, compliqué, mais eurythmique, d'un animal plein de génie, souffrant et soupirant tous les soupirs et toutes les ambitions humaines" (1: 663–64).

With this reading, I have endeavored to show how Baudelaire's poetic ruminations on dispersal and constraint surpass fixed dichotomies and create a space for difference. By reaching back to an unlocatable subject, Baudelaire elides sexual categories and creates the possibility of a lyric practice free of confining oppositions, a possibility pursued by subsequent Symbolist poets. Heterometricity became one tool for Baudelaire in his investigation of gender and lyric alternatives, although later poets pursued more daring prosodic options with which to question poetic ideologies. Rimbaud, for one, tempered his admiration for Baudelaire by suggesting that "Baudelaire est le premier voyant, roi des poètes, *un vrai Dieu.* [. . . Mais] la forme si vantée en lui est mesquine: les inventions d'inconnu réclament des formes nouvelles" (253–54). In my final chapter I explore how, in their own musical and watery works, Verlaine and Krysinska pursued Baudelaire's lead and followed Rimbaud's urgings by seeking new forms with which to represent the unimaginable and to invent the unknown.

# Chapter Seven

# Loose Ends

In an article on Rimbaud, Anne Berger asks this question:

> qu'est-ce qui fait [. . .] d'une certaine poésie, sinon un genre
> féminin, du moins un genre littéraire plus féminin que
> d'autres, tel que le sujet de l'écriture—mais aussi celui de
> la lecture—puisse s'y concevoir comme femme, et ce, que
> le poète, voire son lecteur, soit de sexe masculin ou de sexe
> féminin? ("Le sexe du cœur" 125)

In this chapter, I attempt to answer Berger's question by considering the broadening possibilities for lyric expression in the
late nineteenth century and their relationship to a new poetics
of fluidity in the works of Paul Verlaine (1844–96) and Marie
Krysinska (1864?–1908). These two poets exemplify, in very
different ways, innovations in verse that defied the masculinist
ideology of the Parnassians and permitted the softening of conventionally fixed gender assignments. By rejecting assumptions
about sexuality and gender imbedded in the lyric tradition, both
complicate the poetic representation of sexual difference.

Verlaine's poetic practice intersects with the beginnings of an
openly gay male poetic tradition. Although generations of critics
have consequently feminized him, his experimentation with the
French verse line (in particular his attempts to "loosen" line
endings and blur boundaries) continued and expanded the work
of the virile Baudelaire and was, in fact, a conscious and rigorous practice employed specifically to accompany forays into
the representation of sexual alterity. Krysinska's free verse
subsequently attempted to liberate not only poetic rhythm from
syllabic constraint, but also the representation of femininity from the confines of poetic tradition.

A word about my pairing of a gay male poet and a presumably heterosexual woman poet in a study on gender. As Eve Sedgwick has pointed out, since gender and sexuality are structured differently, analyses of them are not necessarily coextensive. In particular, invisibility has historically determined gay oppression, while femininity remains a largely visible target. And yet she suggests that diverse forms of oppression can intertwine in unpredictable ways (27, 32). While avoiding a generalizing analogy, I would like to suggest that within the specific context of lyric conventions and Symbolist experiments, femininity and homosexuality functioned in similar fashions by repudiating the solitary masculine poetic persona. Verlaine posited a masculine "tu" and Krysinska a feminine "je" to resist poetic discourses of exclusion, which locked male and female into an objectifying heterosexual relationship. Moreover, each pursued an aesthetics of fluidity to counter masculinist poetic doctrine. As I show, an analysis of gender is central to Verlaine's representation of male homosexuality, which he inscribes rhetorically and formally by deploying femininity.

## Verlaine's Sexualities

Mallarmé unfailingly acknowledged Verlaine's importance for Symbolism, telling Huret that "le vrai père des jeunes, c'est Verlaine" (870). Moreover in "Crise de vers" he credits Verlaine ("si fluide") with preparing the terrain for the poetic crisis of free verse (361). Despite Mallarmé's recognition of his centrality in the elaboration of modern poetry, literary history has tended to relegate Verlaine to the position of a melodic, melancholic songster. Indeed, Verlaine provides a clear example of how critics rely on gender constructions to determine canonicity of male as well as female authors, even as his work confronts and challenges fixed dichotomies imposed by such critical discourses. His reception by twentieth-century critics can be characterized as fluctuating and ambivalent, rather than by a sustained and unequivocal appreciation. General criticism tends to underestimate his work or treat it as secondary to Baudelaire, Mallarmé, and Rimbaud. Verlaine specialists have on numerous occasions tried to rectify his equivocal status by demonstrating the originality of his poetic vision and the complexity of his technique.[1] And yet, despite excellent new scholarship in Verlaine studies, most agree that his work remains underappreciated. The unresolved history of his reception indicates no notable sign of change.[2]

How can we explain such indecision in the face of a work that many find compelling, complex, and broadly influential? I propose that the fundamental problem resides in the perception of Verlaine's femininity. Until the often implicit prejudices of this perception are exposed and accepted, Verlaine will remain the younger brother (or sister) of his contemporaries.

Ever since Verlaine himself announced that "je suis vraiment un féminin" (qtd. in Zimmermann, "Variété" 6), it has become commonplace to invoke his femininity without considering what that might mean for the reception of his poetry. With few exceptions, critics from his day to ours form a united front when the sexual identity of his work is in question. In an article written in 1896, on the occasion of Verlaine's death, Zola concluded that "il n'était [. . .] qu'une de ces âmes femmes" ("Le solitaire" 75). In 1904, Maurras wrote predictably of "le féminin Verlaine" ("Le romantisme féminin" 193), and Jean-Pierre Richard similarly evoked "la féminité verlainienne" in his esteemed 1955 essay *Poésie et profondeur* (172). More recently, the authors of "Symboles de la féminité dans l'œuvre de Verlaine" describe "la tendance nettement féminisante de son imagination poétique" (Cornea and Titieni 42). And in his 1995 biography, *Verlaine: Histoire d'un corps,* Alain Buisine wonders if "une certaine féminité de Verlaine a été programmée par l'attente et le désir de ses parents" (25).

The enduring perception of Verlaine's femininity has contributed to the trivialization, rather than to an appreciation of the complexity of his poetry. Qualities considered feminine include his predilection for diminutive words, his intimist subject matter (such as *La bonne chanson* or the miniature poems of *Fêtes galantes*), what Richard calls his "fadeur" and "attitude de passivité" (166), and the lightness of tone in many of his songlike poems. Dominant criticism's marked preference for hermetic poetry and the theoretical gesture (often paired, as in Mallarmé and Valéry) tends to devalue poets whose work does not conform to traditional definitions of exceptional poetry. The difficulty of Mallarmé or Rimbaud enhances their status, while the apparent transparency of Verlaine's poetry contributes to the lowering of his. The most reductive variety of this kind of analysis feminizes the poet by associating his poetry with an anti-intellectual Romanticism. Though they evaluate Verlaine in a laudatory tone, critics from the end of the nineteenth century to the middle of the twentieth rendered judgments that often depreciate his poetry. According to these writers and literary historians, Verlaine's poetry is characterized by his spontaneity (Zola, "Le solitaire"), by its naïveté, sincerity, and refinement (Lanson), or by his sentimental and intimate lyricism (Raymond). These attributes recall negative criticism of Lamartine, a poet derided for his softness and lack of virility since the fall of sentimental poetry. This perspective tends to characterize Verlaine's work by his early collections, such as *Fêtes galantes, La bonne chanson,* and *Romances sans paroles,* rather than by his more audacious *Parallèlement, Jadis et naguère,* or *Hombres.* The early poems are delicate, elegant, miniature, and do nothing to shock; in short, they are feminine. Thus is Verlaine associated with a feminized and feminizing poetic school, one that literary history condemns for its self-indulgence and lack of rigor.

In an analogous fashion, the notion that Verlaine, in contrast to other Symbolist poets known for their metapoetic production, lacked a cogently theorized poetic program implicitly contributes to his feminization. The same critics mentioned above claim that "Nul ne fut moins théoricien que lui" (Raymond 29), that he had "aucune curiosité intellectuelle" (Lanson 1121), and that "Jamais il n'a rien voulu, jamais il n'a rien discuté, combiné, exécuté, dans le plein exercice de son intelligence" (Zola, "Le solitaire" 74). Though dated, these sources contribute to the poet's image, against which Verlainians struggle to this day. They contrast the appreciative tone of Verlaine's literary essays (such as *Les poètes maudits*) with the more explicitly analytic approach evident in Baudelaire's criticism, Mallarmé's essays, or Rimbaud's correspondence. In response we might recall Mallarmé's definition of Symbolism as a work of *suggestion* rather than one of *naming,* and consider that Verlaine similarly preferred to elaborate upon his poetic stance indirectly through his poetry, rather than by means of concrete exposition.

Although considered an important poet, Verlaine's refusal of virile poetic activity thus maintains him in a position secondary to the poetic luminaries of his time. Like so many women poets, Verlaine—whether imaged as a debauched, alcoholic homosexual or a delicate and weak-willed songster[3]—never quite lived up to the vision of the Poet well enough to merit an unambivalent place among other canonized male poets. Affirmations of Verlaine's femininity are sometimes based on the poet's life (his "passivity," his homosexuality) and other times on a reading of his poetry (as sentimental, naive, spontaneous), but they rarely, if ever, delve into the ambiguity suggested by the poet's self-stated femininity.

Verlaine's sexuality is undoubtedly a significant source of critical ambivalence. Indeed, the homosexuality of canonical writers has always posed a problem for traditionalist criticism: should it be confronted or ignored? In Verlaine's case, those who address his sexuality have tended to do so within the context of his relationship with Rimbaud and to differentiate between the passive homosexuality of the former and the active homosexuality of the latter. If it had not been for Rimbaud, literary criticism would certainly have glossed over Verlaine's sexuality more than it has. But given the centrality of each to the study of the other, literary inquest often ends up feminizing the oeuvre of the "vierge folle" in relation to that of Rimbaud. Their physical relationship has offered up to literary historians a comparison between the two men that is extrapolated to their poetry. Literary history tells the tale of a strapping young Rimbaud who seduces and leads astray an ungainly, uncertain, and passive Verlaine. This scenario masculinizes Rimbaud both in terms of his poetry (which is more audacious, pushing beyond syllabic verse to prose poetry and free verse) and his sexual proclivities (ostensibly the active partner).[4] The obscurity of Rimbaud's work is thus opposed to the melodic simplicity of Verlaine. Consequently Rimbaud, although homosexual himself, was permitted to transcend his deviance and attain canonical ("universal") status, while Verlaine continues to be marginalized by his sexual specificity.

Even when we put aside dated homophobic criticism, we find persistent traces of this tendency in more analytical and more recent studies. Why, long after the fall of Sainte-Beuve's "l'homme et l'œuvre" criticism, do some insist upon reading Verlaine's poetry as the mirror of his life? For it is indisputable that his poetry is read in a much more autobiographic fashion than is that of Baudelaire, Mallarmé, or even Rimbaud. Indeed, he is read as if he were a woman, which is to say that traditional critics read him literally or autobiographically. Homosexual poets would therefore belong in a category with women poets, "feminine" elegiacs, and sentimentalists, who similarly attract literal readings.

Given, on one hand, critical insistence on a biographical approach to Verlaine and, on the other, the necessity of biography to define minority literatures, I would like to pause to consider some biographical writings on Verlaine. As I suggested in my introduction, fields such as Women's Studies and Gay and Lesbian Studies depend on knowledge of the author's sexual and gender identity. We cannot and should not adhere blindly to Foucault's assertion that it does not matter who is speaking. And yet reductive biographizing of the sort indicated above, which seeks to explain a work or categorize an author strictly on the basis of his or her sexual identity, can be catastrophic whether its intent be to marginalize or to lionize. My own interest in Verlaine's homosexuality, as in the gender of women poets, is to consider how their historical identities translate into rhetorical differences in poetry.

In Verlaine's case, the debate over the relationship between "l'homme et l'œuvre" tends to focus on this question: are his life and literary work indivisible or diametrically opposed? In "Villon et Verlaine" (1937; 1: 427–43), Paul Valéry meditated upon the parallel between the life and the work of these two poets, "mauvais garçons [qui] mêl[aient] dans leurs ouvrages l'expression des sentiments les plus pieux [. . .] aux propos les plus libres" (1: 427). Pursuing this comparison, Valéry (a "masculine" poet if ever there was one) concluded that "la connaissance de la biographie des poètes est une connaissance inutile" and, furthermore, that "la curiosité biographique peut être nuisible" (1: 428). Regardless of his suspicion of biographical criticism, Valéry insisted that Verlaine's case was exceptional: "mais, cette fois, le problème biographique est inévitable. Il s'impose et je dois faire ce que je viens d'incriminer" (1: 429). What prompts this contradiction?

In this article, Valéry approached in writing what he avoided confronting in the day-to-day: Verlaine's life. "Que de fois je l'ai vu passer devant ma porte, furieux, riant, jurant, frappant le sol d'un gros bâton d'infirme ou de vagabond menaçant," he remembered (1: 440). But elsewhere, in "Passage de Verlaine" (1926), he had already admitted that "quelque chose d'invincible m'a toujours retenu d'aller faire [s]a connaissance" (1: 710). Although Valéry preferred to maintain public silence on the subject of the sexuality of this "invert[i] [. . .] convert[i]," I am led to believe that Verlaine's homosexuality contributed to the "obscure résistance à [s]oi-même et [. . .] une espèce d'horreur sacrée" that Valéry felt in his presence (1: 1781, 710).

Buisine's *Histoire d'un corps* (1995) offers another, more recent example of biographical approaches to Verlaine's work. Challenging contemporary disdain for biographical readings, Buisine's study places the historical man at the center of his literary analysis. He insists like Valéry, although without the latter's equivocation, that "l'histoire de sa poésie [se confond] avec l'histoire de son corps" (14). Buisine goes even further: "Le corps en représentation fait ici partie du corpus poétique" (15). While Valéry suggested that a "sordid" life and the most delicate poetry were not incompatible (1: 440), Buisine attempts to reverse the "entreprise dissociative" that seeks to "sauver le corpus poétique du corps de l'écrivain, à mettre la sublime quintessence de l'œuvre à l'abri des trivialités et des infamies de la vie" (15).

Although Valéry and Buisine seem to occupy opposing positions with respect to biographical criticism, they are equally disingenuous in speaking of the man while pretending to do something different. Valéry forces himself to confront Verlaine despite the repugnance that his personality and "lifestyle" inspire. Conversely, Buisine proposes a deconstructed biography that seeks to destabilize the poetry (soul) / life (body) duality, and in so doing to avoid facile conclusions. But this task is full of traps, and Buisine is led to ironic contortions, such as this: "À force de s'intéresser à tout ce que [Verlaine et Rimbaud] font ensemble, il devient grand temps de poser la question— grossière, triviale, déplacée—qu'il ne faudrait surtout pas poser dans ce livre: quand commencèrent-ils à coucher ensemble?" (175). Buisine and Valéry are finally confined by the same dualism of a refined poetry against a decadent life, one choosing to ignore it and the other seeking to expose it.

In her article "Variété de Verlaine," Éléonore Zimmermann attempts to explode certain myths that Verlaine studies have had trouble shaking: that Verlaine was weak, that his poetry relies on *fadeur,* that his compositional approach was governed by spontaneity. The masculine/feminine duality can easily be seen behind such characterizations, which Zimmermann tries to replace with an appreciation for Verlaine's *variety.* The exploration of sexuality in Verlaine's work recalls further oppositions that have so often defined his person as well as his poetry for both general and specialized readers. The pious and penitent Verlaine of *Sagesse, Bonheur,* and *Amour* contrasts with the hedonistic drunk of the *Album zutique.* Verlaine, the *fils de bonne famille,* seems to contradict his random wanderings with Rimbaud echoed in *Romances sans paroles.* Verlaine, the man of letters, his young wife at his side in the comfortable home of his in-laws (*La bonne chanson*), clashes with his brutality toward Mathilde, his renunciation of bourgeois self-importance, and his homosexuality (*Parallèlement, Hombres*). The platonic admirer of young men (*Amour*) belies the fallen has-been who took aging prostitutes for lovers (*Chansons pour elle, Odes en son honneur*). Is he a refined lyric poet (*Fêtes galantes*) or a pornographer whose language is as shocking as his subject matter (*Hombres*)? And so on.

As Zimmermann suggested over thirty years ago, psychological and biographical criticism found the contradictions of "l'homo duplex" too enticing to ignore (*Magies* 9). Indeed, the vision of a dualistic Verlaine renders his gender-bending less threatening by confining it to an oppositional frame that maintains the hierarchical opposition of masculine and feminine. If we want to refuse the reductive notion of a "homo duplex" today, it is therefore imperative to recognize and study the variability of sexuality in Verlaine's work. In order to do so, I propose to revisit the question of the poet's femininity while aiming toward a more precise conclusion of its function in Verlaine's poetry and its criticism. What value has been placed on his "femininity" in the past? How can we today, in light of gender and sexuality studies, understand the complex relationship between Verlaine's sexuality and his poetry?

Verlaine, more than all of his contemporaries (with the exception, perhaps, of Rimbaud), formulated his poetic practice from a conscious exploration and re-evaluation of sexual identity and difference. His intent was to remove the pall of neutrality from poetic gender and to render it visible. Verlaine's complication of the relationship between sexuality and gender extends the Symbolist project of fluidity to a new field of inquiry in which gender difference breaks out of fixed oppositions and can no longer be pinned down by invariable readings. I therefore consider his corpus to be a multigendered work, rather than a strictly feminine or even masculine one. Above all, it would be a mistake to view his poetry as neutral. But let us return to Verlaine's literary beginnings to trace the development of his aesthetic project.

Verlaine's poetic trajectory was somewhat erratic, but then inconsistency characterized all aspects of his life, work, and critical reception. His evolution as a poet began in relative conformity with the publication of his first collection, *Poèmes saturniens* (1866). As the title and section titles (including "Melancholia" and "Paysages tristes") indicate, he was strongly affected by Baudelaire's spleen poems, like so many young poets in the 1860s. But the Parnassian aesthetic also exerted an influence on his early writings, and it is perhaps no coincidence that *Poèmes saturniens* appeared the same year as the inaugural *Parnasse contemporain*. For example, "Vers dorés," one of his contributions to the first *Parnasse contemporain*, mimics the stoicism of Leconte de Lisle and the political apathy of Gautier:

> L'art ne veut point de pleurs et ne transige pas,
> Voilà ma poétique en deux mots: elle est faite
> De beaucoup de mépris pour l'homme et de combats
> Contre l'amour criard et contre l'ennui bête.        4
>
> Je sais qu'il faut souffrir pour monter à ce faîte
> Et que la côte est rude à regarder d'en bas.
> Je le sais, et je sais aussi que maint poète
> A trop étroits les reins ou les poumons trop gras.    8
>
> Aussi ceux-là sont grands, en dépit de l'envie,
> Qui, dans l'âpre bataille ayant vaincu la vie
> Et s'étant affranchis du joug des passions,

Tandis que le rêveur végète comme un arbre    12
Et que s'agitent, —tas plaintif, —les nations,
Se recueillent dans un égoïsme de marbre.[5]

Verlaine seems to be trying to convince himself as much as his elders of his allegiance to a poetics of disinterest and self-abnegation, which would soon become antithetical to this highly subjective poet's plaintive persona. Despite its call for impassivity, "Vers dorés" already contains un-Parnassian prosodic traits specific to Verlaine's work on softening the alexandrine (such as the enjambment in the first quatrain and the trimetric line 13). But this was only the beginning of the liberties Verlaine would take.

After his early alliance with the Parnasse, Verlaine's subsequent work revealed poetic aims in direct contradiction with the inflexible formalism of the movement. In the company of Rimbaud, he headed off in an entirely different direction; the collections *Romances sans paroles* (1874) and *Cellulairement* (1875) represent the poetry written during the time of their collaboration. The former collection reflects an era of expansion for Verlaine and his first re-evaluation of the constraints of traditional prosody. Like *La bonne chanson* (1870), *Romances sans paroles* evokes music in its title, marking a departure from impenetrable Parnassian metaphors and heralding the melodic approach to poetic freedom that would characterize Symbolist production. Moreover, the music metaphor indicates Verlaine's refusal of concrete images and descriptive realism, and marks a turn toward the representation of uncertainty and intangibility that accompanied his softening of metric forms.

In many of the poems of *Romances sans paroles,* he does away with the alternation of rhyme gender, showing a marked preference for feminine rhymes, characterized by an unpronounced final mute *e.* Such rhymes present a kind of visible surplus or loose ending to the poetic line. He also takes a wide-ranging approach to meter, experimenting with all lines ranging from four to twelve syllables, in addition to employing a wide range of stanzaic forms. By breaking the hegemony of the alexandrine and privileging uneven meters, he forged new tools for expressing the fluidity of perception. The second of the "Ariettes oubliées" provides one of many possible examples from *Romances sans paroles*. Written in an unusual nine-syllable meter, it begins with this evocation of impressionistic subjectivity: "Je devine, à travers un murmure, / Le contour subtil des voix anciennes" (*OP* 191).

*Cellulairement* continued the work Verlaine had begun in *Romances sans paroles*. Unable to find a publisher for this collection, which was written in a Belgian prison after his final, violent separation from Rimbaud, Verlaine dispersed its poems in later collections, most notably in *Sagesse* (1881), *Jadis et naguère* (1884), and *Parallèlement* (1889). While *Cellulairement* remained unpublished until 1992, its reconstitution is informative for the study of his poetic practice in the mid-1870s. This prison collection includes some of his most daring poems, including "Art poétique," his manifesto for a poetics of fluidity. Relying on metaphors of painting and music, it overturned the inflexible aesthetic of Gautier's "L'art," and called for subtlety instead of definition in the lyric:

> De la musique avant toute chose,
> Et pour cela préfère l'Impair
> Plus vague et plus soluble dans l'air,
> Sans rien en lui qui pèse ou qui pose.          4
>
> Il faut aussi que tu n'ailles point
> Choisir tes mots sans quelque méprise:
> Rien de plus cher que la chanson grise
> Où l'Indécis au Précis se joint.          8
>
> C'est des beaux yeux derrière des voiles,
> C'est le grand jour tremblant de midi,
> C'est, par un ciel d'automne attiédi,
> Le bleu fouillis des claires étoiles!          12
>
> Car nous voulons la Nuance encor,
> Pas la Couleur, rien que la nuance!
> Oh! la nuance seule fiance
> Le rêve au rêve et la flûte au cor! [. . .]          16
> (*OP* 326–27)

His predilection for intangibility distanced Verlaine from classical Parnassian doctrine, while his new approach to the French verse line furthered Baudelaire's tentative deconstruction of binarisms. Verlaine purposely shunned a virile poetics: herein lies the strength, not the weakness, of his poetry. Behind his cultivation of elusive lines, settings, and subjects lies a concerted poetic practice. Verlaine produced impressionistic poetry often devoid of referentiality, symmetry, and sometimes even of subjective presence,[6] relying on a precise compositional practice to achieve this effect of imprecision.

The use of the "impair," or uneven meters, such as the nine-syllable line of "Art poétique," became an important element of Verlaine's poetics of imprecision. His hendecasyllabic (eleven-syllable) poems are particularly interesting, since they signal his debt to Desbordes-Valmore in his exploration of the rhythmic and subjective possibilities of poetic language. Verlaine credited Desbordes-Valmore's precedent in the essay on her included in his *Poètes maudits:* "[elle] a, le premier d'entre les poètes de ce temps, employé avec le plus grand bonheur des rythmes inusités, celui de onze pieds entre autres [. . .]" (*Œuvres en prose* 674).[7] Verlaine's interest in this meter was narrowly implicated in his poetic and affective bonds with Rimbaud. He tells us that it was Rimbaud who encouraged him to reread and reconsider Desbordes-Valmore: "Arthur Rimbaud [. . .] nous força presque de lire *tout* ce que nous pensions être un fatras avec des beautés dedans" (666). The eleven-syllable line, inherited from a poetic mother and shared with his lover and poetic companion, had a particular significance for Verlaine: he used it to write about homosexuality.

They both began in 1872 to use the eleven-syllable line in their compositions. Rimbaud's hendecasyllabic poems ("Larme," "La rivière de cassis," "Michel et Christine," "Est-elle almée?") show the primacy of an eroticized water metaphor and a desire to speak differently about love, elements of a poetic project that he shared with both Desbordes-Valmore and Verlaine. As in Rimbaud's case, Verlaine's affinity for Desbordes-Valmore's poetry surpassed simple borrowing. Traces of her poetry in his own serve as material evidence not simply of her influence in formal matters, but also as intertextual signs of her legacy of a fluid poetics that played an important role in the undoing of the Parnasse. First adopting her eleven-syllable meter, Verlaine eventually introduced rhythms and rhymes more daring than her own.[8]

Prosodic studies have brought to light an innovative and complex Verlaine who is completely conscious of his manipulation of versification. Metricians have long noted Verlaine's contributions to the undoing of conventional French prosody. Indeed, Cornulier has remarked that "Quand il faut donner un exemple d'alexandrin 'anarchique,' [. . .] on cite Verlaine" (211).[9] He privileged imprecision over decisiveness and cultivated fluid rhythms that underscored the often vague and intangible content of his poems, achieving these effects by exploiting techniques of what is now known as *vers libéré.* Verlaine's liberated verse freed syllabic poetry from the constraints of long-standing prosodic rules, including the alternation of rhyme gender and the blurring of the boundaries of the verse line. Verlaine's loose alexandrine rode roughshod over the median caesura and, through enjambment, threw its syntactic conclusion into the following line. His new alexandrine had lost its symmetry, and so was related to the uneven meters with which he experimented; he employed both odd and even meters to produce irregularity within the confines of syllabic regularity.

I would therefore agree with prosodic analyses that demonstrate that Verlaine's poetic practice relies on a concerted reexamination of French versification. However, meticulous formalist studies sometimes fail sufficiently to articulate the manipulation of the gender categories that are an essential part of Verlaine's work in verse. Such studies could go further in examining his treatment of sexed categories, since feminizing his work and ignoring his poetic manipulations of gender end with the same result, which is to overlook his commitment to a poetics of sexual ambiguity. Furthermore, one must resist the temptation to establish his virility; it would be better to change dominant conceptions of poetic creation in order to give Verlaine his due.

As for poststructuralist criticism, it has almost completely ignored Verlaine, preferring to locate poetic modernity in the works of Baudelaire, Rimbaud, and Mallarmé. This is as much a shame as it is ironic, given Verlaine's contribution to the deconstruction of traditional French verse. While committed to and often successful in exposing blind spots, deconstructive criticism would do well to reflect upon its valorization of "difficult" literature. My hunch is that Verlaine's work, perceived as transparent or not sufficiently challenging, lacks the hardness or muscularity of texts that attract the attention of deconstructionists. My contention is that there is nothing transparent about Verlaine's oeuvre. Indeed, the consideration of the "feminine" elements of Verlaine's poetic practice (his handling of verse and rhyme, his evocation of equivocal subjectivities, his images that lose themselves in fog) confirms a conscious, rather than spontaneous, method in his poetry. An analysis attentive to the lessons of both metricians and deconstruction, which I propose to undertake, demonstrates his attempt to expose the sexual hierarchy that implicitly governs poetry. It makes it clear that Verlaine's accomplishment resides in his very refusal to reproduce the categories and to conform to the demands of what traditionalists call "great poetry."

Verlaine's homoerotic poetry endures as a prominent example of this refusal, which relied on his dismantling of the classical French line. It is to the legacy of this poetry that I would now like to turn. He began with a lesbian sonnet series, *Les amies* (1867), which took part in a literary obsession inaugurated by Baudelaire's lesbian cycle (including the two "Femmes damnées" poems and "Lesbos"). Contemporary poetic representations of lesbianism included Banville's chaste "Erinna" (1861), Mallarmé's characteristically obscure allusion to the embrace of the nymphs in "L'après-midi d'un faune" (1875), and Pierre Louÿs's *Chansons de Bilitis* (1894). It was not until the turn of the century that subjective representations of lesbians came to light, as with the poetry of the group that came to be known as Sapho 1900 (including Natalie Clifford Barney and Renée Vivien).[10]

While Verlaine's engagement with this literary fad does not partake of what Sedgwick has called the "epistemology of the closet," his male homosexual poetry clearly involves self-revelation. The poem from *Parallèlement* beginning "Ces passions qu'eux seuls nomment encore amours" describes the ignorance of a "monde inattentif aux choses délicates" (*OP* 521–22). Like Lord Alfred Douglas's "love which dare not speak its name" ("Two Loves" [1894]), Verlaine's verse points to obstacles that hinder the declaration of homosexuality and to the compulsion to silence and secrecy. Until the end of the nineteenth century, lyric poetry dealing with male homoeroticism was practically unheard of. How could it be named and expressed within such a tradition?

We might read the chronology of Verlaine's corpus as a process of coming out, in which his first evocations of male homosexuality were tentative and veiled, but then became increasingly explicit. Verlaine included elusive representations of homosexuality, many belonging to a Rimbaud cycle, in *Romances sans paroles* (1874, "Ariettes oubliées" IV), *Sagesse* (1881, "L'espoir luit . . ."), and *Jadis et naguère* (1884, "Vers pour être calomnié," "Crimen amoris"). *Amour* (1888) then presented a platonic picture of the love for a young man. But with *Parallèlement* (1889), Verlaine finally began to grapple more openly with the implications of his "secret" ("Explications," "Ces passions . . ."), to write appreciatively of masculine bodies ("Sur une statue de Ganymède," "Pierrot gamin") and joyously of homosexual relationships ("Læti et errabundi"). Verlaine's final outing came posthumously in 1903, with the publication of his explicitly homoerotic collection *Hombres,* for which there was no precedent in his work or that of any other.

Verlaine's progressive self-revelation meant forging new subject positions in the face of lyric conventions that proscribed homosexuality. The earlier poems of the Rimbaud cycle necessitate a return to the question of Verlaine's interest in the eleven-syllable line. In the past, critics have seen Verlaine's borrowing from Desbordes-Valmore as his investment in the heritage of sentimental lyricism,[11] but I contend that his experimentation must be considered as an extension of poetic aims that were rooted in her experience as a woman poet working in a hostile environment. Like Desbordes-Valmore's refusal of the sonnet and adoption of the asymmetric eleven-syllable meter, Verlaine's rhyme play and fresh rhythms worked to disrupt not only the formal, but also the ideological conventions embedded in the tradition of lyric poetry. And like Desbordes-Valmore, Verlaine strove to overturn the rigid and conventional roles that confined woman to the position of love object and excluded the possibility of homoerotic verse. His dislocation of time-honored meters not only paved the way for the *vers libre* of Symbolism and beyond, but also created new possibilities for the enunciation of subjectivity in the lyric. Verlaine's borrowing from Desbordes-Valmore marked an implicit attempt to inscribe homoeroticism in his early and tentative poetic forays into the subject. Indeed, the majority of Verlaine's hendecasyllabic poems from this period evoke same-sex relations.[12] This unusual meter functioned both as a personal sign of his poetic and affective ties with Rimbaud, and as an ideological sign of resistance. Taken together, these poems point to a strict parallel between the departure from official prosodic practice and the refusal of normative sexuality.

Verlaine's sonnet "À la louange de Laure et de Pétrarque," written in the eleven-syllable meter, helps to locate his position relative to the tradition of received forms. Let us recall that the tradition of the love lyric dating back to Petrarch's sonnets invariably represented a male speaking subject in contemplation of a female object. This configuration left little room for either a female lyric subject or the representation of other intersubjective relationships. Like Desbordes-Valmore, Verlaine was sensitive to the constraints of a form held for so long in lofty esteem by an exclusive brotherhood of poets. But while she rejected sonnet-writing, Verlaine worked from within the form to render it more supple. He ultimately would opt for Shakespeare's homosexual model rather than Petrarch's heterosexual one.

Chose italienne où Shakspeare a passé
Mais que Ronsard fit superbement française,
Fine basilique au large diocèse,
Saint-Pierre-des-Vers, immense et condensé,           4

Elle, ta marraine, et Lui qui t'a pensé,
Dogme entier toujours debout sous l'exégèse
Même edmondschéresque ou francisquesarceyse,
Sonnet, force acquise et trésor amassé,               8

Ceux-là sont très bons et toujours vénérables,
Ayant procuré leur luxe aux misérables
Et l'or fou qui sied aux pauvres glorieux,

Aux poètes fiers comme les gueux d'Espagne,           12
Aux vierges qu'exalte un rhythme exact, aux yeux
Épris d'ordre, aux cœurs qu'un vœu chaste accompagne.
                                        (*OP* 320)

Published in *Jadis et naguère,* "À la louange de Laure et de
Pétrarque" comments retrospectively, if satirically, on the form
valued most by the Parnassians. While ostensibly praising
the tradition of the love sonnet in France, it undermines that very
tradition with its own iconoclastic poetic technique. It begins
by lauding the Ronsardian tradition of the sonnet: "Chose
italienne où Shakspeare a passé / Mais que Ronsard fit superbement française." Here lies the sonnet's first irony, for its eleven-
syllable lines are an affront to the alexandrine that Ronsard
popularized in the sixteenth century and that the Parnassians
later engaged in their cult of form. When the sonnet regained
favor in the nineteenth century, the alexandrine was the line
*de rigueur* used for its composition.

As did the Parnassians, who took their preferred metaphor
for compositional perfection from the art of statuary and stone-
work, Verlaine compares the sonnet to the massive architecture of a "basilique," equating the poetic line and unmoving
stone, "Saint-Pierre-des-Vers." Although this metaphoric language is highly Parnassian, Verlaine's use of the least stonelike,
most fluid of meters suggests his ironic distance. As "À la
louange de Laure et de Pétrarque" progresses, its satire becomes
more evident and its sarcasm more biting. In addition to the
hendecasyllable, Verlaine's use of neologisms, such as the adjectives in line 7, "edmondschéresque ou francisquesarceyse"
(derisively derived from the names of two contemporary critics), defies the lofty tradition of the sonnet. By introducing a
lexicon that is anything but elegant, Verlaine aims to trouble
the revered position of the sonnet on its pedestal.[13]

Like Parnassian alexandrines and fixed forms, women represented in Parnassian poetry were chiseled into frozen, perfect statues. Banville, writing of "les formes féminines plus
belles que les corps," suggests that such formalism depends
on and disposes of the female body. Petrarch's objectified Laura
and the feminine statuary of the Parnassian poets are satirized
in Verlaine's "vierges qu'exalte un rhythme exact" and the
"cœurs qu'un vœu chaste accompagne." Here the sterility of
objectified love and the symmetry of pristinely balanced verses
are inextricably associated. In this final tercet all semblance
of classical balance breaks down with the enjambment "aux
yeux / Épris d'ordre," whose message ironically continues to

praise formal perfection, belying borrowed images carved in stone.

By escaping the constraints of the Parnasse, Verlaine sought to find a language to speak of loves forbidden by such traditions. It is above all in his hendecasyllabic poems, which depart from conventional poetic models and represent the bond, both passionate and literary, shared by the two poets, that Verlaine took up Rimbaud's project to "reinvent" love ("L'amour est à réinventer, on le sait" [103]). The sex of the two subjects in these poems either goes unrevealed or is feminized. At the same time, rhyme gender provides a formal terrain for the poet to manipulate conventional gender configurations. Of the five hendecasyllabic poems from this period, three break conventional rules of rhyming, specifically the traditional alternation of so-called masculine and feminine rhymes codified by Ronsard.

The fourth of the "Ariettes oubliées" (*Romances sans paroles*) represents Verlaine's first essay of the meter he borrowed from Desbordes-Valmore. Written from the point of view of a feminine speaking subject and her female companion, it has exclusively feminine *rimes embrassées* and includes this rhyme borrowed from the first couplet of Desbordes-Valmore's "Rêve intermittent": "Soyons deux enfants, soyons deux jeunes filles / [. . .] / Qui s'en vont pâlir sous les chastes charmilles." In terms of the speaking subject's identity and the prosodic procedures of poetry, this poem is among the most "feminine" of Verlaine's corpus:

Il faut, voyez-vous, nous pardonner les choses:
De cette façon nous serons bien heureuses
Et si notre vie a des instants moroses,
Du moins nous serons, n'est-ce pas? deux pleureuses.　4

Ô que nous mêlions, âmes sœurs que nous sommes,
À nos vœux confus la douceur puérile
De cheminer loin des femmes et des hommes,
Dans le frais oubli de ce qui nous exile!　8

Soyons deux enfants, soyons deux jeunes filles
Éprises de rien et de tout étonnées
Qui s'en vont pâlir sous les chastes charmilles
Sans même savoir qu'elles sont pardonnées.　12
(*OP* 193)

This poem plays with sexual difference on several levels and creates a feminine world within its twelve lines. In addition to its feminine rhymes and characters, the grammatical gender of the majority of its nouns is feminine. Even masculinity is neutralized by the feminine rhyme of the seventh line ("hommes"). Indeed, this poem represents the questioning of gender roles that is an inevitable aspect of homosexual coupling. Through the feminization of "je" and "tu," Verlaine lets us see a relationship of solidarity and of resemblance that opposes a long poetic tradition in which a male speaking subject and his female interlocutor exist in a relationship of otherness. By presenting a female couple, Verlaine creates a doubly "inverted" world (inversion, of course, was a word used by nineteenth-century sexologists to designate same-sex eroticism), in terms of both gender and physiological identity. Here Verlaine seems to approach Wesling and Slawek's "intersubjective account that makes much of the role of alterity, the equal-to-self role of others in the constitution of subjectivity" (60).

It should be noted, however, that this process of inversion reveals a certain timidity before its subject matter, perhaps meant to render it less threatening. On one hand, Verlaine confronts the homosexual couple by transposing its sex, thereby masking male homosexuality under the cover of lesbianism, an acceptable (or at least fashionable) topos in French poetry after 1850. On another hand, the relationship is infantilized, and thus rendered chaste and ingenuous, with two young girls seeking bliss and anonymity. The poem's tone is demure, framed by the search for forgiveness for a transgression or unspecified secret ("Il faut [. . .] nous pardonner les choses" " Sans même savoir qu'elles sont pardonnées"). The anonymity of exile suggests a desire to silence transgression and to flee from a critical world. As with the poem's content, Verlaine's approach toward the hendecasyllable in this, his first attempt with the meter, betrays a certain precaution. Rhythmically, it depends on a regular caesura after the fifth syllable, following Desbordes-Valmore's model but not yet hinting at the more daring *vers libérés* that would follow in poems such as "Vers pour être calomnié."[14]

This hendecasyllabic sonnet presents another same-sex couple. In "Vers pour être calomnié" the speaking subject peers at a frail and sleeping body. The sonnet alternates rhyme gender stanza by stanza rather than line by line. As in the poetry of Desbordes-Valmore, affinity and resemblance, instead of the distancing and specular relationship of the Petrarchan and Parnassian models, are established between subject and object by the direct address that draws them into proximity:

> Ce soir je m'étais penché sur ton sommeil.
> Tout ton corps dormait chaste sur l'humble lit,
> Et j'ai vu, comme un qui s'applique et qui lit,
> Ah! j'ai vu que tout est vain sous le soleil!            4
>
> Qu'on vive, ô quelle délicate merveille,
> Tant notre appareil est une fleur qui plie!
> Ô pensée aboutissant à la folie!
> Va, pauvre, dors! moi, l'effroi pour toi m'éveille.       8
>
> Ah! misère de t'aimer, mon frêle amour
> Qui vas respirant comme on expire un jour!
> Ô regard fermé que la mort fera tel!
>
> Ô bouche qui ris en songe sur ma bouche,                12
> En attendant l'autre rire plus farouche!
> Vite, éveille-toi. Dis, l'âme est immortelle?
>
> (*OP* 330)

The verb tenses progress from objective distance to presence and intimacy. From the studious looking of the first quatrain described in the past tense, to the present tense and direct address of the two central stanzas, the sonnet finally ends with a gesture (awakening the sleeper) and a question, drawing the silent, immobile object into the active position of interlocutor. The body described is mirrored by that of the speaking subject ("Ô bouche qui ris en songe sur ma bouche"), and the two bodies merge in the modulation from "ton corps" to "notre appareil." This similarity alone suggests that the poem's addressee is a man, like its speaking subject whose gender is revealed grammatically by the past participle in the phrase "je m'étais penché." To counter the rigid gender categories that order the relations of the traditional love sonnet, Verlaine often softens such distinctions by attenuating or even eliminating grammatical gender markers.

In many ways this poem is about the blurring of differences—
between sleep and wakefulness, life and death, self and other.
The uncertainty of these distinctions, the tenuousness of the
living, and the frailty of the human body are echoed by the
fragility of the irregular poetic line, as opposed to the unshak-
able granite alexandrine. Verlaine's highly irregular rhythm,
which strays from the regular division in five-six measures, and
the absence of the twelfth syllable attenuate the borders of the
lines, rendering them fluid, "plus vague et plus soluble." The
implicit metaphor of body and poem ("j'ai vu, comme un qui
s'applique et qui lit" and the Baudelairian "tant notre appareil
est *une fleur*") counters the Parnassian model of stonelike verse
with an animate poetics.

By the end of his life, Verlaine had moved from such cautious representations of same-sex relationships to the explicitly homoerotic collection *Hombres*. Written around 1891 but
published posthumously in 1903, this collection represents the
culmination of his homoerotic work. *Hombres* has received little
critical attention to date, even among the few articles that focus
on the study of Verlaine's sexuality.[15] This collection has only
recently appeared in a critical edition by Jean-Paul Corsetti and
Jean-Pierre Giusto (along with the erotic collection, *Femmes*).
*Hombres* was long suppressed for its content, most notably in
the misnamed Dantec-Borel edition of the *Œuvres poétiques
complètes* (however, in 1992 the Pléiade editors finally did complete this volume by adding a *Supplément: Œuvres libres*).

Although many have dismissed these poems for their "pornographic" or crude vocabulary, on several levels they are in
fact instructive for Verlainian criticism. They necessarily refute the statements of Barbey d'Aurevilly and others who see
Verlaine as a "Baudelaire puritain." Their recent availability,
coupled with a more open eye, permit us to study this expressly
homosexual poetry. Their tardy inclusion in Verlaine's corpus
forces a reconsideration of his femininity and of the opposition between a corrupt life and a delicate poetry, upon which
so many readers have insisted. Although the poems in *Hombres*
display none of the refined elegance of the "Ariettes oubliées,"
neither do they merit the dismissal of which they have been
victim. A closer look shows them to be neither prosaic nor
pornographic, nor even "une sorte de saccage de la littérature

et suicide littéraire," as Buisine describes Verlaine's erotic works (448), but instead "carefully constructed, sensually charged, evocative, even provocative, works of art," as Charles Minahen suggests in his ground-breaking article on *Hombres* (121).

*Hombres* represents the culmination of the evolution of Verlaine's homosexual poetry. More than a simple erotic curiosity, the collection completes his lyric examination of homosexuality, begun with Rimbaud twenty years earlier. It demonstrates poetic innovations and subjective representations of active sexuality that refute many critical clichés about Verlaine. Moreover, a consideration of the entire collection highlights its literary aspects, framed as it is by poems referring to literary traditions and styles. Composed of tender as well as crude pieces, it opens with an apology for male homosexuality addressed to Verlaine's poetic colleagues. "Ô ne blasphème pas, poète . . ." establishes the historical and poetic precedents for homosexuality, beginning its overview with the Greeks:

> "C'est mal," a dit l'Amour. Et la voix de l'Histoire,
> "Cul de l'homme, honneur pur de l'Hellade et décor
> Divin de Rome vraie et plus divin encor
> De Sodome morte martyre pour sa gloire."
> *(Femmes; Hombres* 92)

He rapidly traces a homosexual genealogy from the Valois, "fous du mâle," up to his day, represented by Louis de Bavière. Shakespeare's sonnets are invoked as a literary precedent:

> Shakespeare, abandonnant du coup Ophélia,
> Cordélia, Desdémona, tout son beau sexe
> Chantait en vers magnificents qu'un sot s'en vexe
> La forme masculine et son alléluia.
> *(Femmes; Hombres* 92)

Verlaine concludes his poem with the invitation: "Il faut parfois, poète, un peu 'quitter la dame.'"

Let us consider the fourteenth poem in *Hombres* ("Ô mes amants . . ."), which offers not simply a formal representation of male homosexuality, but also its author's attempt to find a new language for that which, in the lyric poetry that preceded him, had not been representable:

Ô mes amants,
Simples natures,
Mais quels tempéraments!
Consolez-moi de ces mésaventures
Reposez-moi de ces littératures                    5
Toi, gosse pantinois, branlons-nous en argot,
Vous, gars des champs, patoisez-moi l'écot,
Des pines au cul et des plumes qu'on taille,
Livrons-nous dans les bois touffus
    La grande bataille                    10
    Des baisers confus.
Vous, rupins, faisons des langues en artistes
    Et merde aux discours tristes,
    Des pédants et des cons.
    (Par cons, j'entends les imbéciles,          15
    Car les autres cons sont de mise
    Même pour nous, les difficiles,
Les spéciaux, les servants de la bonne Église
    Dont le pape serait Platon
    Et Socrate un protonotaire                  20
Une femme par-ci, par-là, c'est le bon ton
Et les concessions n'ont jamais rien perdu.
Puis, comme dit l'autre, à chacun son dû
Et les femmes ont, mon Dieu, droit à notre gloire
    Soyons-leur doux,                          25
    Entre deux coups
    Puis revenons à notre affaire.)
Ô mes enfants bien-aimés, vengez-moi
    Par vos caresses sérieuses
Et vos culs et vos nœuds, régals vraiment de roi,   30
    De toutes ces viandes creuses
Qu'offre la rhétorique aux cervelles breneuses
De ces tristes copains qui ne savent pourquoi.
    Ne métaphorons pas, foutons
    Pelotons-nous bien les roustons              35
    Rinçons nos glands, faisons ripailles
Et de foutre et de merde et de fesses et de cuisses.[16]
           (*Femmes; Hombres* 118–19)

In a tone clearly different from the restrained "Ariette" or the enigmatic "Vers pour être calomnié," this poem nevertheless takes part in the same project of forging a poetic space for homosexual subjectivity, of inscribing a "nous" so rarely articulated in heterosexual poetry. While the fourth "Ariette" creates an ex-

clusively feminine context, "Ô mes amants" represents relationships among men (notwithstanding the "concession" to heterosexuality in parentheses[17]). The refinement of the earlier poems
opposes the crudeness of the other as, according to some, erotic
literature opposes pornography. Although these poems seem
to belong to contradictory discursive frameworks, the following analysis will suggest that they belong to the same project.

In "Ô mes amants," Verlaine pretends to abandon poetry and
literary style: "Reposez-moi de ces littératures," "vengez-moi
[. . . de] la rhétorique," "ne métaphorons pas." The poem's
speaking subject seems to be looking for a way to replace figurative language with another, materialist, one. Poetic formal-
ity and rhetorical figures are abandoned for the immediacy of
the body, represented by a brutal and literal lexical field. The
voice of the poem begs its lovers to eradicate "[les] discours
tristes / Des pédants et des cons" while delivering themselves
to corporeal joys.

But while opposing homosexuality to literature (a contradiction lived by Verlaine and every other homosexual poet
writing within heterosexual poetic conventions), the poem ends
up speaking as much about language as about sexual relations:
"branlons-nous en argot," "patoisez-moi l'écot," "faisons des
langues en artistes." This poem is therefore not about the abandonment of poetry but of conventions; it is in search of a
language that is both "new" and marginal, a language of the
initiated. Like the references to the Greeks in the collection's
first poem, this penultimate poem cites Plato and Socrates, thus
giving a literary frame to the collection. Far from opposing homoeroticism to the poetic act, be it explicitly (in his heterosexual poetry) or implicitly (in poems such as the "Ariette"),
here Verlaine gives a voice and an expression to love between
men, a highly antipoetic subject in nineteenth-century France.

Unlike the "Ariette," "Ô mes amants" seeks no forgiveness
for its sexual or poetic transgressions. On the contrary, its
raw vocabulary and slang replace the euphemisms of the earlier poem ("pardonner *les choses*"). The sexualized "bois touffus" take the place of the young girls' "chastes charmilles,"
whose childish "vœux confus" give way to the "baisers confus"
of grown men. The prosodic straying of "Ô mes amants" accom-
panies and supports the audacity of its content. Its versification

is situated somewhere between the heterometric *vers mêlés* of La Fontaine and the free verse of the Symbolists.[18] The final line, devoid of rhyme, attacks both the moral and literary establishments: "Et de foutre et de merde et de fesses et de cuisses." This explicit list of body parts and their secretions suggests not a departure from poetry, but rather an attempt to renew poetic expression by enlarging its field of reference.

At first timid, often repressed, later more daring and open, the exploration of sexuality in Verlaine's poetry proves to be intimately linked to his questioning of poetry itself. As in any other minority corpus, in Verlaine's work (here sexual) identity occupies an important place. His poetic production points to a path that leads us to the study of homosexuality and sexual difference in Symbolist poetry. To ignore Verlaine's homoerotic production would be to overshadow an important, and even central, field of reference in his work. As Rimbaud said, "ça ne veut pas rien dire."[19]

Verlaine stands at the beginning of a tradition of homoerotic verse that flourished with the Decadent movement, which took its name from Verlaine's sonnet "Langueur": "Je suis l'Empire à la fin de la décadence" (*OP* 370). While I cannot do justice here to the vast and largely unexplored corpus of *fin-de-siècle* gay and lesbian poetry, I would like to suggest with this analysis of Verlaine's homoerotic verse that the study of sexuality is crucial to understanding the gendering of the lyric. By pushing French verse to its limits and refusing to reproduce unquestioningly the preceding generation's gender categories and assumptions about sexuality, gay and lesbian poets joined other women poets to offer a new cast of subjects to the dawning twentieth century.

## Krysinska's Women

During the Symbolist period, a significant number of women poets were composing in a variety of veins, although as we have seen critics such as Maurras grouped them together as neo-Romantics or dismissed them altogether. These largely forgotten women, who wrote poetry from the 1870s through the prewar years, include Judith Gautier (1846–1917), Marie Nizet (1859–1922), Marie Daguet (1860–1942), Rachilde (1860–1953),

Marie Krysinska (1864–1908), Jane Catulle Mendès (1867–1965), Gérard d'Houville (pseud. of Marie de Régnier, 1875–1963), Anna de Noailles (1876–1933), Lucie Delarue-Mardrus (1880–1945), Catherine Pozzi (1882–1934), and Marie Noël (1883–1967). These women clearly had then and still have now more to worry about than Verlaine when it came to professional recognition, since they have been virtually erased from literary history and largely overlooked by contemporary critics.[20] Despite persistent critical resistance, the context of poetic production had nonetheless changed sufficiently to increase the ranks of women poets and tolerate a greater diversity of voices. Notably, several wealthy expatriates, including Natalie Barney and Renée Vivien, formed a lesbian literary salon at the turn of the century.[21]

In the following pages, I focus on the poetry of Marie Krysinska because of her important contribution to Symbolist poetry and her egregious neglect by critics. There are few studies to consult and little is known about her life.[22] Born in Poland, Krysinska was the only female member of the Hydropathes and, like Nina de Villard, a pianist and composer. Krysinska first published her poems in French Symbolist journals (such as *Le chat noir, Mercure de France, Lutèce, La plume*) in the early 1880s. Her collections began to appear in the following decade: *Rythmes pittoresques* (1890), *Joies errantes* (1894), *Intermèdes* (1903). Her claim to fame, derided by most critics, was to have inaugurated free verse in France. It appears clear to me, although not all concur, that Krysinska was the first to publish, if not to compose, free verse (in *Le chat noir,* 1882 and 1883). Since then, numerous critics and poets have employed various strategies to minimize or dismiss her contribution to French poetry. Gustave Kahn set the polemic in motion by suggesting that Krysinska was merely copying him, and that he himself had "created" free verse (68).[23] According to Kahn and others, 1886 marks the emergence of "true" (authenticated and theorized) *vers libre* in France. This was indeed a watershed year, witnessing, in addition to poems by Kahn, the publication of Rimbaud's *Illuminations* (which included several free-verse poems written around 1872), Laforgue's translations of passages from Whitman's *Leaves of Grass,* and several poems by Laforgue himself.[24]

Without belaboring the question of ownership, it is interesting to review the terms of the debate, and to see with what
tenacity misogynist critics continued to undermine the accomplishments of women poets. André Barre wrote in 1911 that:

> Les essais de Marie Krysinska sont des fantaisies à l'origine
> sans prétentions, écrites sur les conseils ironiques de Charles
> Cros. Ils manifestent avant tout l'indolence féminine en
> matière d'art, l'antipathie de la femme pour tout travail fini.
> Ils sont l'expression instinctive et nullement théorique d'une
> double nonchalance, celle d'une femme et celle d'une Slave.
> (335)

In his condemnation of Krysinska's work, Barre relies on accusations that we have come to expect of antifeminist criticism,
whether its object be Romantic, Parnassian, or Symbolist.
Women's poetry is unoriginal (Krysinska depended on Cros's
"conseils"), lacks rigor ("l'antipathie de la femme pour tout
travail fini"), relies on instinct, and has no supporting theoretical
basis. To this list of deficiencies, Barre adds the issue of
Krysinska's nationality, much in the manner of Maurras.[25]

Others since have more or less repeated Barre's appraisal:
"D'origine polonaise, et ignorant tout de la prosodie, elle avait
dû en transgresser les règles d'abord, sans s'en douter. La théorie
n'était venue qu'après" (Saint-Georges de Bouhélier, qtd. in
Cornell 50). More recently, in his otherwise remarkable study
*Vers libre* (1990), Clive Scott dates the emergence of free verse
from 1886, sidelining Krysinska's earlier publications. While
presenting both sides of the debate, in the end he concurs with
the suggestion that her journal publications were not really free
verse, but rather a modified form of prose poetry that lacked a
"developed awareness of what [she was] trying to do" (74).
Scott raises the interesting issue of the ambiguous dividing line
between prose poetry and free verse, a distinction that depends
upon both rhythmicity and disposition on the page. It is true
that some of Krysinska's poems were initially organized "with
each frequently short sentence beginning a new line, but with over-
runs mostly conforming to a 'prose' margin" (68). But then the
same thing can be said of the typography of numerous pieces
that Scott accepts as free verse (including Rimbaud's "Départ"
and Claudel's *Cinq grandes odes*). None of these texts shares

the prosaic features (paragraph form, narrative content) associated with unambiguous prose poetry, such as Baudelaire's *Spleen de Paris* or Mallarmé's *Poèmes en prose*. As for the rhythmicity of Krysinska's poetry, at least two studies exist that demonstrate its "rhythmic integrity," which constitutes French verse poetry.[26]

Krysinska provided her own response to the marginalization of her work. In her introduction to her final collection, *Intermèdes,* she displayed a feminist acumen not exhibited by her predecessors: "Une initiative émanant d'une femme—avait sans doute décrété le groupe—peut être considérée comme ne venant de nulle part, et tombée de droit dans le domaine public" (xxi). For the first time, a woman poet dared to address directly the obstacles faced before a male literary establishment that, in her case, deemed it unimaginable that a woman could write in an innovative rather than imitative fashion.

Krysinska did have defenders, including Verlaine: "Est-ce que Arthur Rimbaud [. . .] n'a pas fait tout cela avant eux? Et même Krysinska!" (*Œuvres en prose* 1135).[27] She defended herself quite ably as well, pointing in the preliminary remarks of her three poetic collections to the role she played in launching free verse. *Rythmes pittoresques* begins with a laudatory preface by one J. H. Rosny, who claimed priority for her efforts. It also includes this excerpt from the *Annales artistiques et littéraires,* intended certainly for Kahn and perhaps for his close friend Laforgue as well:

> Nous désirons rappeler à ceux qui se sont intéressés [. . .] que [Krysinska] est le premier qui ait eu l'initiative de ces innovations prosodiques [. . .]. Il y eut donc—de la part des confrères manifestants et propagateurs de symbolisme en 1885—pas mal de perfidie à ne jamais prononcer le nom de Marie Krysinska [. . .]. (v)

Krysinska wrote her own "Avant-propos" to *Joies errantes,* adopting a much humbler tone than did Kahn in his self-promoting *Symbolistes et décadents*. In this book, Kahn claims that "Il m'a paru nécessaire de reformer l'instrument lyrique. On m'a cru" (68). He concludes that "je faisais école" (29). In contrast Krysinska, while noting that her free verse appeared before any other, writes unpretentiously that "En cette époque où il est fort à la mode d'être *chef* de quelque école [. . .] nous tenons à déclarer notre indépendance littéraire [. . .]. Nous déclarons en outre n'avoir jamais prétendu révolutionner quoi que ce soit" (*Joies errantes* v–vi). Krysinska's "Avant-propos" includes a description of her aims in abandoning syllabism and rhyme:

> Notre proposition d'art est celle-ci: atteindre au plus de Beauté expressive possible, par le moyen lyrique, subordonnant le cadre aux exigences *imprévues* de l'image, et rechercher assidûment la *surprise de style* comme dans la libre prose avec, de plus, le souci d'un rythme particulier qui doit déterminer le caractère poétique déjà établi par le *ton* ou pour mieux dire le *diapason* ÉLEVÉ du langage. (vi)

Here Krysinska emphasizes the expressivity of free verse and its engagement in a poetics of unpredictability ("surprise de style"). She indicates as well that attention to the rhythm of the phrase replaces the metric structure of syllabic verse as an organizing principle. Krysinska contends that rhyme and meter are not crucial aspects of poetry, and she perceives free verse as a gain rather than as a loss of poetic possibilities: "le dispositif inattendu, asservi aux attitudes de l'idée et de l'image—est un moyen d'effet de plus" (vi). She identifies rhythm, not rhyme, as the constitutive feature of poetry: "Seul le caractère rythmique est significatif; mais qui dit rythme est bien éloigné de dire symétrie" (vii). The syntax of free verse is not molded to fit pre-existing prosodic segments (line and hemistich), but rather depends on rhythmic measures imposed by the author's engagement with the subject matter, which is contingent on personal style.

Krysinska suggests, moreover, that free verse agrees with specific subject matters: "Telle pièce traduisant quelque capricieux coin de nature, ou quelque anxieux état de rêve, perdrai[t] toute son intensité à être enfermée dans un cadre régulier—alors que d'autres sujets appellent à eux les rigides architectures du vers, que nous admirons dans les immortels chefs-d'œuvre des Maîtres" (*Joies errantes* vi–vii). Krysinska's poetry and that of other *vers-libristes* confirm the association of particular themes and tones with the genre. Scott points to its expressive, instantaneous, and unpredictable qualities. The capricious nature and anxious dreams identified by Krysinska are present as well in Laforgue's *Complaintes*. Poetic images of water regain their validity in her "Marines" as in Rimbaud's "Marine." Moreover, free verse heightens subjectivity thanks to its intangibility and its focus on wavering states of consciousness. It has been used as a vehicle by Decadent poets to represent the neurotic, somatizing subject and presurrealist dream states. Its ambiguity lends itself to irony and social critique. By focusing on the relativity of its subjects' translations of experience, free verse both produces greater instability in meaning and involves the reader in a more intimate fashion by giving her greater power of interpretation and engaging her own subjectivity.

Free verse can therefore be seen as an extension of Symbolist aims, providing a formal tool that evokes uncertainty and liquidity. It also privileges music both as a referent and as a stylistic device, since refrains and other repetitions are important features of free-verse poetry. In contrast with the mechanisms that traditional versification imposes on poetry (regular meters, caesuras and coupes, end-stop lines, and so forth), the "open frame" suggested by Krysinska favors individual expression and ambiguity. The formal ambiguity born of the refusal of traditional prosodic rules (above all, difficulty in scansions due to the uncertain status of dieresis and the mute *e*) reflects the ambiguity of its subject matter.

As in Verlaine's poetry, music provides a prominent referent for Krysinska's work. *Rythmes pittoresques* includes a series of eight "Danses," two "symphonies" ("Symphonie des parfums" and "Symphonie en gris"), and a "Sonate," which is accompanied by musical directions (*rinforzando, dolce rittard.*). Similarly, *Joies errantes* begins with a series of "Chansons," and includes a second set of "Petites chansons," a "Suite d'orchestre," and a "Sérénade."

"Symphonie en gris" (*Rythmes pittoresques*) provides an excellent example of Krysinska's free-verse aesthetic. Clearly written in response to Gautier's "Symphonie en blanc majeur" and, by extension, to the poetics of definition and rigidity detailed in his manifesto poem "L'art," she chose the uncertainty of gray to represent the variability of perception:

> Plus d'ardentes lueurs sur le ciel alourdi,
> Qui semble tristement rêver.
> Les arbres, sans mouvement,

Mettent dans le loin une dentelle grise.—
Sur le ciel qui semble tristement rêver,               5
Plus d'ardentes lueurs.—

Dans l'air gris flottent les apaisements,
Les résignations et les inquiétudes.
Du sol consterné monte une rumeur étrange, surhumaine.
Cabalistique langage entendu seulement          10
Des âmes attentives.—
Les apaisements, les résignations, et les inquiétudes
Flottent dans l'air gris.—

Les silhouettes vagues ont le geste de la folie.
Les maisons sont assises disgracieusement       15
Comme de vieilles femmes—
Les silhouettes vagues ont le geste de la folie.—

C'est l'heure cruelle et stupéfiante,
Où la chauve-souris déploie ses ailes grises,
Et s'en va rôdant comme un malfaiteur.—         20
Les silhouettes vagues ont le geste de la folie.—

Près de l'étang endormi
Le grillon fredonne d'exquises romances.
Et doucement ressuscitent dans l'air gris
Les choses enfuies.                             25

Près de l'étang endormi
Le grillon fredonne d'exquises romances.
Sous le ciel qui semble tristement rêver.

(16–17)

Although written in the third person, this poem expresses subjective sensations of uncertainty and anxiety. Against the brightness and clarity of Gautier's white images, it calls upon vagueness and avoids objective representation. Light is replaced by obscurity ("plus d'ardentes lueurs"), and visual images of pristine femininity give way to gray doubt. While Gautier's poem presents its readers with white lace and plumage, gray lace suggested by distant tree branches at dusk and the gray wings of a bat accompany Krysinska's vocabulary of insecurity. Gautier's series of explicit comparisons serves to describe the whiteness of a woman's body, relying fairly consistently on unambiguous and tangible objects (swans, snow, satin, marble, ivory, and so on). But the referent of Krysinska's "Symphonie en gris" lacks definition, and her word choice invites hesitation. Indeed, the poem is more interested in impression and mood than representation, and relies on the indirection of metonymy rather than Gautier's expository similes. Krysinska projects abstract sensations onto a dimly lit landscape ("Dans l'air gris flottent les apaisements, / Les résignations et les inquiétudes"), maintaining the dreamy and ethereal tone of her poem with refrainlike recombinations of phrases. Vacillating between absence and presence ("doucement ressuscitent dans l'air gris / Les choses enfuies"), between human (the poem is rife with personification) and inanimate or unearthly qualities ("une rumeur surhumaine"), Krysinska proceeds much in the manner of Verlaine's impersonal but highly subjective impressionism. And like Verlaine, she succeeds in articulating the intangible, countering Gautier's imperative ("Que ton rêve flottant / Se scelle / Dans le bloc résistant!" ["L'art," *Émaux et camées* 150]) with insistent evocations of dreaming and images of floating sensations. Indeed, the poem's references to hidden meanings and symbolic signification ("Cabalistique langage entendu seulement / Des âmes attentives") counter all the certitude of Parnassian doctrine, just as the irregularity of her lines and stanzas disconcert expectations of regularity.

If the songlike quality of Krysinska's refrains and her allusions to music ("Le grillon fredonne d'exquises romances") are not specific to this poem, neither is its intangible subjectivity. Like "Symphonie en gris," the majority of Krysinska's poems avoid the lyric "I" or employ a more general "we." Without the mark of person, the mark of gender is frequently lacking, resulting in the absence of a clearly determinable female lyric subject. And yet Krysinska's body of poetry carries ample evidence of its author's interest in feminine subjectivity through its spheres of reference. *Rythmes pittoresques* contains a section entitled "Femmes," which presents five poems named after biblical and mythical women. *Joies errantes* similarly includes two "feminine" series, "Notes féminines" and "Ombres féminines." Krysinska's intended readers obviously included women as well, since she dedicated numerous poems to women.

In her "women's poems," Krysinska displays particular interest in examining the physical representation of femininity.

We see women from a variety of perspectives, ranging from blatant artistic objectification to highly personal self-examination. Krysinska's studies address a number of crucial issues, including the aesthetics of artificiality and the divided woman who is both subject of and object in poetry. Her poems respond to such texts as Baudelaire's "Éloge du maquillage," which represents the antinatural aesthetic doctrine that flourished in Decadent literature, and to the more general and pervasive poetic tradition of dehumanizing femininity through obsessions with exteriority.

Her "Effigies" present five short portraits of feminine types viewed from masculine perspectives (*Joies errantes* 69–72; see appendix). These poems are mannered and primarily descriptive, enumerating feminine traits praised by great male artists. The first effigy begins with a woman who is "Frêle et blonde, sentimentale et sensuelle" (69). The unnamed artist is not interested in her interiority, but rather in the effect of her fragility and sadness on her physical appearance: "L'artiste, pour cette Fleur de Mélancolie / Souhaite—afin qu'elle soit encor plus jolie— / Le fard d'Insomnie et la parure des Larmes" (69). Art trades in emotion and translates the signs of affect into mere exteriority ("fard," "parure"). The second portrait presents a regal animal, "Chatte brune au beau geste hiératique et hautain" (70). This time Krysinska calls upon a sixteenth-century sculptor, rather than the generic artist, to appraise her: "Jean Goujon eût aimé sa taille longue et fière" (70). The third, aristocratic, model, described succinctly as "factice simplement" (70), appeals to the eighteenth-century painter: "telle l'eût rêvée Greuze" (71). Next "la Française de race" is presented in all her contradictions to the approval of the sixteenth-century miniaturist painter Clouet: "Muse et rapin; les traits mignards et volontaires; / Aussi parfaits que si Jean Clouet les eût peints" (71). The final portrait of ingenuous femininity framed in a bucolic setting echoes Watteau:

> Le cher souci d'Art a mis dans ses yeux gris,
> Rieurs de malice, un rien de graves songers,
> Mais sa bouche demeure le fruit frais des vergers
> Aimés de Watteau et—tout parfumé d'esprit.
>
> (72)

An ambiguity is raised in this stanza: does the concern for art that subtly alters the woman's eyes belong to her or to the artist who paints her? Is she cunning or artless? Is the artist true to life or engaging in projection? The overwhelming objectification of these portraits would suggest the latter. In either event, one wonders about Krysinska, a woman poet observing male artists observing female objects, and her investment in the aestheticization of femininity. Although these poems lack any intrusion from a first-person commentator and, on one level, appear to be exercises in description, a tension persists between these viewpoints. Her "Effigies" betray a subtle irony in their tone, established most forcefully in the opening piece, which describes the artist's insensitivity to feminine suffering.

Her "Ombres féminines" also take great pains to paint feminine finery, and yet each ends in violence that undermines the project of translating female charms into a pleasant visual tableau (*Joies errantes* 43–51; see appendix). The biblical Judith arrives "ceinte de grâce, en ses vêtements joyeux" (44), to behead the leader of an enemy army with a sword held "dans sa main charmante" (45). Oumé, a Japanese princess ("Dont la robe [. . .] est joyeuse" [47]) takes her life when her lover does not return from war: "Des cordes tendues le frémissement cesse" (48). Joan of Arc, with her "beauté de vierge," is reduced to ashes at the stake (49). And finally, "un odieux cauchemar" (51) troubles Du Barry, "toute poudrée de grâces mièvres" (50), who chases away this prophetic and bloody vision: "C'était, au milieu d'une hurlante multitude . . . / Un lourd couteau / Tombait sur son cou délicat" (51). Krysinska's juxtaposition of feminine grace and beauty with brutal scenes is unsettling, and open to a variety of interpretations. Are these women to be evaluated by their appearance or by their actions? Would exteriorization—the chronic focus on feminine adornment—itself do violence to women?

Baudelaire wrote quite forcefully on the aesthetic value of feminine beauty in two short essays, "La femme" and "Éloge du maquillage," included in his *Peintre de la vie moderne* (first published in *L'art romantique* [1868]):

> Tout ce qui orne la femme, tout ce qui sert à illustrer sa
> beauté, fait partie d'elle-même [. . .]. La femme [. . .] est

surtout une harmonie générale, non seulement dans son al-
lure et le mouvement de ses membres, mais aussi dans les
mousselines, les gazes, les vastes et chatoyantes nuées
d'étoffes dont elle s'enveloppe, [. . .] dans le métal et le mi-
néral qui serpentent autour de ses bras et de son cou, qui
ajoutent leurs étincelles au feu de ses regards, ou qui jasent
doucement à ses oreilles. *Quel poète oserait [. . .] séparer
la femme de son costume?* (2: 714; emphasis mine)

Krysinska's poetry suggests that her own aesthetic and ideological values opposed those of Baudelaire. His admiration for
Du Barry, for example, is clearly related to his fascination with
the artificiality of feminine finery, while Krysinska's poetry
attempts to de-aestheticize and criticize it. She must have read
and responded to Baudelaire's sonnet "À Madame Du Barry"
with her own poem, since they forefront identical embellish-
ments (powdering) and dress ("la robe à panier"). And while
Baudelaire relates the anecdote of Du Barry spurning the advances of Louis XV by putting on makeup ("C'était en s'embel-
lissant qu'elle faisait fuir ce royal disciple de la nature" [2: 716]),
Krysinska ironically has the powdered, rouged, and lipsticked
courtesan avoiding not the king's advances, but thoughts of the
guillotine.

A number of pieces significantly more subjective than the
"Effigies" and "Ombres féminines" come down on the side of
naturalness and condemn artificiality. In "Les bijoux faux," for
example, Krysinska contrasts colors found in nature with the
aberrant shades of artificial objects: "Et j'oubliais les roses
vraies, les roses, filles des bleus matins, pour ces roses artificielles" (*Rythmes* 32; see appendix). And in her ironically titled
"Nature morte," she describes a mannered scene in which a
coupled "Elle" and "Lui" illustrate their love through a series
of pretentious poses rather than through meaningful exchange:
"*Elle* est teinte en blonde, car *Il* n'aime que les blondes"
(*Rythmes* 85; see appendix). This poem is not so much a still
life as a portrait of the death of guilelessness, or a critique of
inauthenticity.

However, Krysinska certainly did not seek to return to the
Romantic exultation of nature and sentimentality. Indeed, the
irony ("Roman de la lune"), decadent tone ("Berceuse macabre," in appendix), and unbridled sexuality ("Le poème des
caresses," in appendix) of a number of her pieces are a far cry

from such platonic idealism. Her unspoken aim appears instead to be to question the representation of feminine beauty in love poetry and in so doing open the possibility of non-objectifying intersubjectivity in the lyric.

In several poems, Krysinska explores the status of the female body and its artificial enhancements as definitive of beauty. She reflects on the instability of physical beauty and on the superficiality of feminine embellishment. In "La parure" (in appendix), for example, she begins by enumerating the jewels and materials worn by women, much in the manner of Baudelaire:

> Un peu de l'âme somptueuse et barbare
> De nos primitifs aïeux
> Passe en nous avec les feux des pierres rares
> Et l'éclat du métal précieux.
>
> L'or ciselé en bagues alliantes
> Et en bracelets nous enchaîne
> D'une fidèle tendresse où s'enchante
> La tendresse de nos grand'mères lointaines.
>
> . . . . . . . . . . . . . . . . . . . . . . . . . . . . . .
>
> Les mousselines légères
>     Nous font
> Un cœur de papillon,
> Et les fraîches toiles à fleurettes suggèrent
> Un cœur de bergère.
>
> . . . . . . . . . . . . . . . . . . . . . . . . . . . . . .
>
> Le riche apparat des velours
>     Nous fait un peu reine,
> Un peu châtelaine aux fastueuses amours.
>                     (*Joies errantes* 33–34)

And yet Krysinska describes such apparel not so much in terms of its ability to enhance, but in its ability to transform women into something else ("Le riche apparat des velours / *Nous fait* un peu reine"), in their own eyes and as viewed by others. Her use of the verb "enchaîner" is equivocal and suggests ambivalence toward all this finery, as do the poem's final lines:

> Mais en l'asile discret des sombres laines
> Une âme de nonnain
> Nous vient;
>
> Tant l'Art et le Rêve sont les vrais vainqueurs
> De nos faibles cœurs.
>
> (34)

Away from any scene of spectacle ("en l'asile discret"), dressed in the inconspicuous clothing of a woman far from men, Krysinska's women finally flee from representation, vanquished by the expectations of masculine art and dreams. Her use of the plural *nous* places her feminine subject in league with all women and generalizes the author's critique of specularity.

"Notes féminines" analyzes woman's self-examination more directly still, attributing feminine vanity to the unrealistic precedents created by artistic conventions that aestheticize the female body. Its three poems ("Devant le miroir," "Coquetterie," and "Caprice") are dedicated to Edmond de Goncourt who, with his brother Jules, wrote *La femme au dix-huitième siècle* (1862), among other works that reveal their obsession with femininity (ranging from fictional treatments of prostitutes to nonfictional essays on Marie-Antoinette and other women of the court). The Goncourts were renowned misogynists: Krysinska's dedication to Edmond is surely either ironic or challenging.

"Devant le miroir" begins by describing a woman's anxious interview with her mirror:

> Cette grave entrevue
> Est fertile en émois,
> L'image, pourtant connue,
> Surprend toujours; —est-ce bien soi
> Cette soudaine apparue?                    5
>
> Et les petites mines d'aller
> Pour calmer l'inquiétude qui vient
> De n'être pas—il se peut—aussi bien
> Que l'on voudrait;
>
> Mais, bientôt, une distribution de récompenses    10
> Généreuses, commence.
> Les cheveux? ah! les cheveux, parfait!
> Surtout de profil; on dirait

De telle peinture d'artiste admiré;
Puis on retrouve à des détails menus,                    15
Le souvenir du même visage des jours révolus
Des jours enfantins si vite—en somme—disparus.

Et l'on songe à cet autre miroir enchanté
Si impressionnant pour nos jeunes cœurs:
L'eau de l'étang que l'on croyait                        20
Un morceau de ciel tombé
Où poussaient aussi des herbes et des fleurs.
                              (*Joies errantes* 35–36)

Outside representations intrude upon and mediate this encounter with the self ("l'inquiétude qui vient / De n'être pas—il se peut —aussi bien / Que *l'on* voudrait"), troubling the woman's sense of identity ("est-ce bien soi?"). In the fourth stanza, Krysinska once again names artists as those responsible for creating images so unsettling to feminine identity. She ends by evoking "cet autre miroir enchanté," one associated with nature and youth, not yet tarnished by artistic projections or self-consciousness.

Although Krysinska often calls upon painters to represent the arbiters of feminine beauty, it is certainly not a great step to transpose such scenes into a confrontation between the woman poet and the idealized, circumscribed Muse of lyric poetry. Krysinska reveals in these pieces the ambiguity of one for whom femininity is linked to objectification and stripped of self-determined identity. Her meditations on women who seek a subjective stance amidst the hurly-burly of prescribed and pre-conceived representations often remain on the level of implicit, and sometimes ambivalent, critique. But that very critique would have been inconceivable at the start of the century and, as Krysinska herself suggested, impossible within the "regular frame" of traditional, syllabic verse.

Scott addresses a fascinating question in *Vers libre,* that of the violent reaction against free verse, which a poet as recent as Robert Frost likened to playing tennis without a net (Scott 3). Nineteenth-century critics, closer to its emergence, were predictably more agitated still by this new form, which many characterized as sloppy, impressionistic and, in short, a poor excuse for poetry. Scott's analysis quite plausibly suggests that free verse was viewed as an ideological threat to literary authority (5). By undermining pre-existing standards for aesthetic value, it gives greater liberty to the reader and, perhaps, smacks of a democratization of poetry that conservative poets found appalling.

I would certainly agree with Scott, but would like to end by suggesting that such poets and critics were particularly threatened by the *femininity* of free verse. Free verse encapsulated subjective stances, specific referents, and compositional techniques previously deemed feminine by the literary establishment. The loss of rules and regularity threatened a loss of control for the masculine guardians of poetic tradition, raising the specter of feminine dispersal that so frightened Baudelaire. Krysinska exploited free verse as a vehicle with which to question alienated feminine subjectivity and to liberate women from confining models of representation. The relativity, ambiguity, and fluidity of Krysinska's work helped to transform lyric poetry into a genre in which "le sujet de l'écriture—mais aussi de la lecture—puisse [se] concevoir comme femme."

\* \* \*

The title of this chapter, "Loose Ends," refers not only to Verlaine's playful obscuring of line endings or Krysinska's refusal to count syllables. It points more generally to the impossible task of defining the heterogeneous practice of late-nineteenth-century poetry, which I take to be its very triumph. There is no neat way to tie up the poetic story of an era that strives for multiplicity and refuses rigid oppositions or conventional subject positions. At times joyously anarchistic, at others carefully premeditated, poets of this period took part in a revolution that irrevocably changed the subjective possibilities of French poetry.

# Conclusion

## Poetry Matters

My aim in *The Gendered Lyric* has been to demonstrate that gender is not only implicated in, but *central to* the transformations of poetry. Nineteenth-century France witnessed an important period of poetic renewal, a moment that crystallized the synonymy of "lyric" and "poem," a time when traditional forms were continually under attack. When the century began, conventional and restrictive gender ideology dominated the lyric genre, which by the century's end had gained the potential for multivalent subjectivity.

As with any time of change or any genre in flux, the vagaries of gender signification cannot be expected to have fixed values. It was deployed by traditional critics and poets to preserve poetry as a masculine domain, naïvely evoked by some, and playfully explored by others aiming to unhinge confining binarisms in order to redefine the lyric. By foregrounding rather than erasing gender in the discussion of male-dominated movements, my study highlights the complexity of this body of poetry and permits the recuperation of women poets long forgotten by literary critics.

A feminist retelling of the history of nineteenth-century French poetry implies not only the re-evaluation of movements, poets, and poetic practice, but also the interrogation of gender studies itself, which has, paradoxically, neglected an area of inquiry that illuminates so many questions fundamental to the discipline. I hope to have convinced my readers not only that gender matters to modern French poetry, but also that poetry matters to gender studies.

I began by pointing to work by feminist critics on English-language poetry and would like to evoke them again as I close, for I believe that French Studies has much to learn from them. They show us that poetic issues, such as the history of movements, lyric subjectivity, poetic conventions, rhetorical language, and experimental poetics, *are* feminist issues. They suggest to us as well that central concerns of Women's Studies and Gender Studies (including representation, female literary traditions, canon formation, genre theory, gendered textual practice, cultural studies, sexuality studies) need not be confined to the narrative sphere; that in fact the inclusion of poetry in such disciplines complicates our understanding of these very topics. Ironically, the influx of French feminist theories of female subjectivity has, as Lynn Keller and Christianne Miller show, become "central to many Anglo-American discussions of women's poetry" (6) since the early 1980s, giving such discussions a more theoretical bent and moving them away from earlier tendencies toward thematic and biographical analysis. I would hope that, in turn, Anglo-American discussions of women's poetry inspire more feminists to re-evaluate the French poetic tradition.

As specialists of English-language poetry such as Margaret Homans and Jan Montefiore have shown, female-authored poetry is by no means limited to an intimist tradition and yields fascinating results when subjected to close reading. I have aimed to demonstrate that this holds true in the French context as well. Until now critics of French poetry have considered women's poetry as a translation of female experience, while continuing to read men's poetry as opaque language. We need not associate female poetic production with Romanticism and transparency, and therefore deem it unworthy of rigorous study. We must address the problem of difficulty and oppose assumptions that associate "high" literary qualities (including but not limited to erudition, opacity, density, and abstraction) with a masculine poetics.

My goal in these pages has been to reconcile an uncritical love of poetic language with a rigorous analysis of its pretensions, my tendency to give priority to poetic voices and to listen for their differences. And yet one message I have done my best to ignore is Desbordes-Valmore's and so many other women poets' plea to remain "dans l'ombre et sans me nommer." Although both poets and critics have used fluidity so forcefully as a metaphor for change (in the guise of both femininity and the acceptance of alterity—or rather the repudiation of limits and boundaries), I end with a *caveat* about what I think of as the *Awakening* syndrome. By this I mean the tradition in nineteenth-century women's literature to end by drowning (which is self-abnegation). Kate Chopin did it, as did Colet with her "femme du peuple": "Elle fendit la foule, et, courant au rivage, / S'élança dans le fleuve" (Stanton 144). And even the very masculine Ackermann: "À deux mains j'ai saisi ce livre de mon âme, / Et l'ai lancé par-dessus bord." She writes:

> C'est mon trésor unique, amassé page à page.
> À le laisser au fond d'une mer sans rivage
> Disparaître avec moi je n'ai pu consentir.
> En dépit du courant qui l'emporte ou l'entrave,
> Qu'il se soutienne donc et surnage en épave
> Sur ces flots qui vont m'engloutir!
>
> (*Œuvres* 71)

At the risk of countering nineteenth-century mores that silence female voices, let me insist that the purpose of poetry, whether plaintive or celebratory, intimist or impersonal, is to make noise and be heard.

Although women poets sometimes betrayed their own art with drowning self-doubt, they were free with their admiration for other women artists. So let us listen with Desbordes-Valmore to the multiform, pre-Baudelairian synesthetic qualities of "La voix de Mlle Mars": "Ta voix a des parfums, des formes, des couleurs. / Parles-tu d'une fleur? Dès que tu l'as nommée, / De ta bouche entr'ouverte elle sort embaumée" (*Œuvres poétiques* 634). And follow Ackermann's exhortation, which defies her own pessimism, to an unnamed woman artist:

> Ah! tandis que pour nous, qui tombons de faiblesse
> Et manquons de flambeau dans l'ombre de nos jours,
> Chaque pas a sa ronce où notre pied se blesse,
> Dans votre frais sentier marchez, marchez toujours.
>
> (*Œuvres* 14)

Or admire Villard's portrait of this defiant musician:

> La main blanche, aristocratique,
> Nerveuse, dompte un instrument,

> Et des arômes de musique
> Rôdent dans l'air languissamment.
> . . . . . . . . . . . . . . . . . . . . . . . . .
> Hautaine, l'œil plein de menace,
> Sein de lys et cœur indompté,
> Blagueuse, rouée et tenace,
> Mais pure par férocité.
>
> ("Vers à peindre," *Feuillets parisiens*)

And finally, rather than to Tastu's policing angel, let us listen to the voice of Krysinska's "Ange gardien," whose words spring from the sea not to swallow up, but to accompany and encourage the woman artist:

> Dans la grondante voix de la mer,
> Dans le silence mélancolique des soirs,
> Dans la douleur et dans la joie,
> Au milieu du saint émoi dont nous vibrons quand l'aile
>     prodigieuse de l'Art nous effleure;—
> Et au milieu des hymnes de flamme que chantent nos
>     cœurs à l'Amour victorieux et sublime;
> Notre oreille entend la voix de l'Être blanc
> Qui, consolant et radieux,
> Suit nos pas tout le long de la vie.
>
> (*Rythmes pittoresques* 116)

# Appendix

## Poems

Following are some of the poems by women authors that are studied above but not reproduced in their entirety on those pages. For the most part these works have been long out of print. I reproduce them to accompany my analyses, and in the spirit of disseminating difficult-to-find texts.[1]

# Amable Tastu

## L'ange gardien

*Dieu a ordonné à ses anges de*
*vous garder pendant tout le*
*temps de votre vie.*

Psalm XC

Oh! qu'il est beau, cet esprit immortel,
Gardien sacré de notre destinée!
Des fleurs d'Éden sa tête est couronnée,
Il resplendit de l'éclat éternel.                          4
Dès le berceau sa voix mystérieuse,
Des vœux confus d'une âme ambitieuse,
Sait réprimer l'impétueuse ardeur,
Et d'âge en âge il nous guide au bonheur.                  8

L'ENFANT

Dans cette vie obscure, à mes regards voilée,
Quel destin m'est promis? à quoi suis-je appelée?
Avide d'un espoir qu'à peine j'entrevois,
Mon cœur voudrait franchir plus de jours à la fois!       12
Si la nuit règne aux cieux, une ardente insomnie
À ce cœur inquiet révèle son génie;
Mes compagnes en vain m'appellent, et ma main
De la main qui l'attend s'éloigne avec dédain.            16

L'ANGE

Crains, jeune enfant, la tristesse sauvage
Dont ton orgueil subit la vaine loi.
Loin de les fuir, cours aux jeux de ton âge;
Jouis des biens que le ciel fit pour toi:                  20
Aux doux ébats de l'innocente joie
N'oppose plus un front triste et rêveur;
Sous l'œil de Dieu suis ta riante voie,
Enfant, crois-moi, je conduis au bonheur.                 24

LA JEUNE FILLE

Quel immense horizon devant moi se révèle!
À mes regards ravis que la nature est belle!
Tout ce que sent mon âme ou qu'embrassent mes yeux

S'exhale de ma bouche en sons mélodieux! 28
Où courent ces rivaux armés du luth sonore?
Dans cette arène il est quelques places encore;
Ne puis-je, à leurs côtés me frayant un chemin,
M'élancer seule, libre, et ma lyre à la main? 32

L'ANGE

Seule couronne à ton front destinée,
Déjà blanchit la fleur de l'oranger;
D'un saint devoir doucement enchaînée,
Que ferais-tu d'un espoir mensonger? 36
Loin des sentiers dont ma main te repousse,
Ne pleure pas un dangereux honneur,
Suis une route et plus humble et plus douce.
Vierge, crois-moi, je conduis au bonheur. 40

LA FEMME

Oh! laissez-moi charmer les heures solitaires;
Sur ce luth ignoré laissez errer mes doigts,
Laissez naître et mourir ses notes passagères
Comme les sons plaintifs d'un écho dans les bois. 44
Je ne demande rien aux brillantes demeures,
Des plaisirs fastueux inconstant univers;
Loin du monde et du bruit, laissez couler mes heures
Avec ces doux accords à mon repos si chers. 48

L'ANGE

As-tu réglé, dans ton modeste empire,
Tous les travaux, les repas, les loisirs?
Tu peux alors accorder à ta lyre
Quelques instants ravis à tes plaisirs. 52
Le rossignol élève sa voix pure,
Mais dans le nid du nocturne chanteur
Est le repos, l'abri, la nourriture . . .
Femme, crois-moi, je conduis au bonheur. 56

LA MÈRE

Revenez, revenez, songes de ma jeunesse;
Éclatez nobles chants; lyre, réveillez-vous!
Je puis forcer la gloire à tenir sa promesse;
Recueillis pour mon fils, ses lauriers seront doux. 60
Oui, je veux à ses pas aplanir la carrière,

À son nom, jeune encore, offrir l'appui du mien,
Pour le conduire au but y toucher la première,
Et tenter l'avenir pour assurer le sien.                    64

L'ANGE

Vois ce berceau, ton enfant y repose;
Tes chants hardis vont troubler son sommeil;
T'éloignes-tu? ton absence l'expose
À te chercher en vain à son réveil.                         68
Si tu frémis pour son naissant voyage,
De sa jeune âme exerce la vigueur:
Voilà ton but, ton espoir, ton ouvrage.
Mère, crois-moi, je conduis au bonheur.                     72

LA VIEILLE FEMME

L'hiver sur mes cheveux étend sa main glacée;
Il est donc vrai! mes vœux n'ont pu vous arrêter,
Jours rapides! et vous, pourquoi donc me quitter,
Rêves harmonieux qu'enfantait ma pensée?                    76
Hélas! sans la toucher, j'ai laissé se flétrir
La palme qui m'offrait un verdoyant feuillage,
Et ce feu qu'attendait le phare du rivage,
Dans un foyer obscur je l'ai laissé mourir.                 80

L'ANGE

Ce feu sacré, renfermé dans ton âme,
S'y consumait loin des profanes yeux;
Comme l'encens offert dans les saints lieux,
Quelques parfums ont seuls trahi sa flamme.                 84
D'un art heureux tu connus la douceur,
Sans t'égarer sur les pas de la gloire;
Jouis en paix d'une telle mémoire;
Femme, crois-moi, je conduis au bonheur.                    88

LA MOURANTE

Je sens pâlir mon front, et ma voix presque éteinte
Salue en expirant l'approche du trépas.
D'une innocente vie on peut sortir sans crainte,
Et mon céleste ami ne m'abandonne pas.                      92
Mais quoi! ne rien laisser après moi de moi-même!
Briller, trembler, mourir comme un triste flambeau!
Ne pas léguer du moins mes chants à ceux que j'aime,
Un souvenir au monde, un nom à mon tombeau!                 96

254

Il luit pour toi, le jour de la promesse,
Au port sacré je te dépose enfin,
Et près des cieux ta coupable faiblesse
Pleure un vain nom dans un monde plus vain.          100
La tombe attend tes dépouilles mortelles,
L'oubli tes chants; mais l'âme est au Seigneur.
L'heure est venue, entends frémir mes ailes:
Viens, suis mon vol, je conduis au bonheur!          104

[Amable Tastu, "L'ange gardien," *Poésies complètes* (Paris: Didier, 1858), 54–57; originally published in *Poésies,* 1826.]

# Marceline Desbordes-Valmore

## Une plume de femme

Courez, ma plume, courez: vous savez bien qui vous l'ordonne.

Je prie un génie indulgent de répandre sur votre travail le charme mystérieux de la fiction, afin que nul ne sache la source de vos efforts et de la fièvre qui vous conduit: on se détourne des sources tristes. Que mon âme soit ouverte seulement au regard du Créateur. Laissez-la seule dans ses nuits d'insomnie: elle ne raconte pas la cause de ses débats avec la terre. Dieu sait qu'à cette sainte cause est suspendu l'espoir de rentrer un jour dans son ciel, comme un enfant dans la maison de son père. L'enfant prodigue a souffert avant de voir la porte maternelle se rouvrir devant lui: sans ses larmes amères y serait-il jamais revenu?

Courez donc, ma plume, courez: vous savez bien qui vous l'ordonne.

Je vous livre mes heures, afin qu'elles laissent, par vous, une faible trace de leur passage dans cette vie. Quand elles traverseront la foule, sur les ailes de mon affliction, si l'on crie: "Elles n'ont pas d'haleine," dites que le grillon caché dans les blés forme une musique faible aussi; mais qui n'est pas sans grâce au milieu du tumulte pompeux des merveilles de la nature; répondez pour moi ce que Dieu a répondu pour le grillon:

"Laissez chanter mon grillon; c'est moi qui l'ai mis où il chante. Ne lui contestez pas son imperceptible part de l'immense moisson que mon soleil jaunit et fait mûrir pour tous."

Courez donc, ma plume, courez: vous savez bien qui vous l'ordonne.

L'austère inconstant, le Sort, qui m'a dit: *Assez,* quand je lui demandais ma part des biens de l'existence; le Sort qui m'a dit: *Non!* quand je levais mes yeux pleins de prières pour obtenir encore un de ses sourires, a laissé pourtant tomber dans ma consternation, un bien dont l'apparence était de peu de valeur, mais qui deviendrait une palme de salut, si quelque fil de la Vierge l'enveloppait de divine pudeur: c'est vous, ma plume, détachée du vol d'un pauvre oiseau blessé comme mon âme, peut-être; c'est vous, que personne ne m'apprit à conduire; c'est vous, que sans savoir tailler encore, j'ai fait errer sous ma pensée avec tant d'hésitation et de découragement; c'est vous, tant de fois échappée à mes doigts ignorants, vous, qui par degrés plus rapide, trouvez parfois, à ma propre surprise, quelques paroles moins indignes des maîtres, qui vous ont d'abord regardée en pitié.

Ainsi, courez, ma plume, courez: vous savez bien qui vous l'ordonne.

Vous ne blesserez pas; vous ne bégayerez pas un mot de haine, quand ce serait pour repousser l'injure: il vaudrait mieux tomber en poussière, afin que, quand je serai poussière aussi, je ne tressaille encore que d'amour et jamais de honte; afin que si j'attends au fond du purgatoire décrit si triste, mais si doux, par Dante, qui l'a vu, toutes les âmes heureuses, en passant légères et sauvées devant moi, me disent avec un sourire: au revoir!

À ce prix donc, trempée d'encre ou de larmes, courez, ma plume, courez: vous savez bien qui vous l'ordonne.

## Rêve intermittent d'une nuit triste

Ô champs paternels hérissés de charmilles
Où glissent le soir des flots de jeunes filles!

Ô frais pâturage où de limpides eaux
Font bondir la chèvre et chanter les roseaux!     4

Ô terre natale! à votre nom que j'aime,
Mon âme s'en va toute hors d'elle-même;

Mon âme se prend à chanter sans effort;
À pleurer aussi, tant mon amour est fort!     8

J'ai vécu d'aimer, j'ai donc vécu de larmes;
Et voilà pourquoi mes pleurs eurent leurs charmes;

Voilà, mon pays, n'en ayant pu mourir,
Pourquoi j'aime encore au risque de souffrir;     12

Voilà, mon berceau, ma colline enchantée
Dont j'ai tant foulé la robe veloutée,

Pourquoi je m'envole à vos bleus horizons,
Rasant les flots d'or des pliantes moissons.                    16

La vache mugit sur votre pente douce,
Tant elle a d'herbage et d'odorante mousse,

Et comme au repos appelant le passant,
Le suit d'un regard humide et caressant.                        20

Jamais les bergers pour leurs brebis errantes
N'ont trouvé tant d'eau qu'à vos sources courantes.

J'y rampai débile en mes plus jeunes mois,
Et je devins rose au souffle de vos bois.                       24

Les bruns laboureurs m'asseyaient dans la plaine
Où les blés nouveaux nourrissaient mon haleine.

Albertine aussi, sœur des blancs papillons,
Poursuivait les fleurs dans les mêmes sillons;                  28

Car la liberté toute riante et mûre
Est là, comme aux cieux, sans glaive, sans armure,

Sans peur, sans audace et sans austérité,
Disant: "Aimez-moi, je suis la liberté!                         32

"Je suis le pardon qui dissout la colère,
Et je donne à l'homme une voix juste et claire.

"Je suis le grand souffle exhalé sur la croix
Où j'ai dit: Mon père! on m'immole, et je crois!               36

"Le bourreau m'étreint: je l'aime! et l'aime encore,
Car il est mon frère, ô père que j'adore!

"Mon frère aveuglé qui s'est jeté sur moi,
Et que mon amour ramènera vers toi!"                            40

Ô patrie absente! ô fécondes campagnes,
Où vinrent s'asseoir les ferventes Espagnes!

Antiques noyers, vrais maîtres de ces lieux,
Qui versez tant d'ombre où dorment nos aïeux!                   44

Échos tout vibrants de la voix de mon père
Qui chantait pour tous: "Espère! espère! espère!"

Ce chant apporté par des soldats pieux
Ardents à planter tant de croix sous nos cieux,                48

Tant de hauts clochers remplis d'airain sonore
Dont les carillons les rappellent encore:

Je vous enverrai ma vive et blonde enfant
Qui rit quand elle a ses longs cheveux au vent.               52

Parmi les enfants nés à votre mamelle,
Vous n'en avez pas qui soit si charmant qu'elle!

Un vieillard a dit en regardant ses yeux:
"Il faut que sa mère ait vu ce rêve aux cieux!"               56

En la soulevant par ses blanches aisselles
J'ai cru bien souvent que j'y sentais des ailes!

Ce fruit de mon âme, à cultiver si doux,
S'il faut le céder, ce ne sera qu'à vous!                     60

Du lait qui vous vient d'une source divine
Gonflez le cœur pur de cette frêle ondine.

Le lait jaillissant d'un sol vierge et fleuri
Lui paîra le mien qui fut triste et tari.                     64

Pour voiler son front qu'une flamme environne
Ouvrez vos bluets en signe de couronne:

Des pieds si petits n'écrasent pas les fleurs,
Et son innocence a toutes leurs couleurs.                     68

Un soir, près de l'eau, des femmes l'ont bénie,
Et mon cœur profond soupira d'harmonie.

Dans ce cœur penché vers son jeune avenir
Votre nom tinta, prophète souvenir,                           72

Et j'ai répondu de ma voix toute pleine
Au souffle embaumé de votre errante haleine.

Vers vos nids chanteurs laissez-la donc aller;
L'enfant sait déjà qu'ils naissent pour voler.                     76

Déjà son esprit, prenant goût au silence,
Monte où sans appui l'alouette s'élance,

Et s'isole et nage au fond du lac d'azur
Et puis redescend le gosier plein d'air pur.                       80

Que de l'oiseau gris l'hymne haute et pieuse
Rende à tout jamais son âme harmonieuse! . . .

Que vos ruisseaux clairs, dont les bruits m'ont parlé,
Humectent sa voix d'un long rythme perlé!                          84

Avant de gagner sa couche de fougère,
Laissez-la courir, curieuse et légère,

Au bois où la lune épanche ses lueurs
Dans l'arbre qui tremble inondé de ses pleurs,                     88

Afin qu'en dormant sous vos images vertes
Ses grâces d'enfant en soient toutes couvertes.

Des rideaux mouvants la chaste profondeur
Maintiendra l'air pur alentour de son cœur,                        92

Et, s'il n'est plus là, pour jouer avec elle,
De jeune Albertine à sa trace fidèle,

Vis-à-vis les fleurs qu'un rien fait tressaillir
Elle ira danser, sans jamais les cueillir,                         96

Croyant que les fleurs ont aussi leurs familles
Et savent pleurer comme les jeunes filles.

Sans piquer son front, vos abeilles là-bas
L'instruiront, rêveuse, à mesurer ses pas;                        100

Car l'insecte armé d'une sourde cymbale
Donne à la pensée une césure égale.

Ainsi s'en ira, calme et libre et content,
Ce filet d'eau vive au bonheur qui l'attend;                      104

Et d'un chêne creux la Madone oubliée
La regardera dans l'herbe agenouillée.

Quand je la berçais, doux poids de mes genoux,
Mon chant, mes baisers, tout lui parlait de vous,                    108

Ô champs paternels, hérissés de charmilles
Où glissent le soir des flots de jeunes filles.

Que ma fille monte à vos flancs ronds et verts,
Et soyez béni, doux point de l'Univers!                              112

[Marceline Desbordes-Valmore, "Une plume de femme," *Œuvres poétiques,* ed. Marc Bertrand, vol. 2 (Grenoble: PU de Grenoble, 1973), 689–
90; originally published in *Bouquets et prières,* 1843.

Desbordes-Valmore, "Rêve intermittent d'une nuit triste," *Œuvres poétiques* 2: 531–33; originally published in *Poésies inédites,* 1860.]

# Léocadie Penquer

## Le Paradis retrouvé

*Poème de la première heure*

L'Éden était fermé. La terre ouvrait ses routes:
Adam, d'un seul regard, les interrogea toutes,
Et, ne pouvant choisir parmi tant de chemins,
Il se tourna vers Ève & dit: "Étends les mains:
Je te laisse le choix entre tous nos domaines.                       5
Puisque j'ai quitté Dieu, qu'importe où tu me mènes?
Ma patrie est partout avec Ève; ses yeux
Me tiendront lieu du jour qui me venait des cieux.
Près de toi rien ne manque à mes regards; ma vie,
Condamnée à la mort & maudite, est ravie,                            10
Puisque le Créateur, qui te créa pour moi,
M'ordonne de te suivre & de mourir pour toi.
L'Éternel s'est trompé dans sa double sentence;
Sa justice n'a pas atteint notre existence:
Ève, tous deux unis, maîtres dans ces déserts,                       15
Tu seras reine, & moi, le roi de l'univers.
Je te suis. Où veux-tu que nous allions?"

"Vers l'ombre,"
Reprit-elle, "là-bas, vers cette enceinte sombre,
Où l'œil de l'Éternel ne pourra nous chercher.
Pour t'aimer, j'ai besoin, Adam, de me cacher.                    20
Je ne sais quelle flamme à mon visage monte,
Quand j'arrête sur toi des yeux charmés: j'ai honte.
Je ne t'avais pas vu dans Éden; Dieu couvrait
D'un voile de pudeur tout ce qui m'entourait.
Dans Éden, j'ignorais le charme humain des choses;                25
J'écoutais les oiseaux, je contemplais les roses,
J'aspirais les parfums & j'entendais les sons;
Mais rien ne m'enivrait, ni baumes, ni chansons.
Je vivais sans désir, j'ignorais l'espérance;
Mon bonheur était froid comme mon ignorance:                     30
L'amour n'était pas né. Non, dans Éden, jamais
Je n'aurais pu comprendre à quel point je t'aimais.
J'étais trop près du Dieu, maître de la nature,
Trop près du Créateur, pour voir la créature.
Mais à présent que Dieu n'est plus là, l'homme est dieu          35
Pour mon âme, & beauté pour mon regard de feu."

"Ève," répondit-il, "je l'ignorais moi-même,
Cette loi de l'amour humain; ce mot suprême,
Aimer, j'en ignorais hier la volupté.
Dans Éden je n'ai pas remarqué ta beauté.                        40
Ce que j'aimais hier en toi, c'était ton âme;
En toi ce que j'adore aujourd'hui, c'est la femme.
J'admire les contours élégants de ton col;
J'admire la blancheur de tes pieds sur le sol;
J'admire ton regard où mon regard se noie,                       45
Et le voile onduleux de tes cheveux de soie,
Et ta chair blanche & rose, & ton bras, & ta main,
Et ce beau sein qui doit porter le genre humain.
Je te suis. Conduis-moi. Dans l'ombre ou la lumière,
Où tu seras, j'irai. Va, marche la première!                     50
Regarde ton chemin; moi, je regarderai
La trace de tes pas. Marche. Je te suivrai."

Ève se dirigea vers l'occident, légère,
Non comme une exilée & comme une étrangère,
Mais comme une habitante à qui tout est connu.                   55
À peine elle foulait le sol de son pied nu;
À peine elle hésitait dans sa route. À mesure
Qu'elle avançait vers l'ouest, l'ombre était plus obscure,
Le firmament prenait des tons gris, les vapeurs
Des grandes mers montaient du flot sur les hauteurs.             60

On entendait déjà les bruits sourds du rivage.
La solitude avait un aspect plus sauvage;
L'arome des sapins résineux chargeait l'air
De son effluve au suc nourrissant, mais amer.
Un peu dans le sud-ouest, des lignes montagneuses          65
S'étendaient & formaient des voûtes caverneuses.
C'est vers ces antres noirs qu'Ève se dirigea.
Palpitante, éperdue, elle y touchait déjà,
Quand Adam, l'étreignant & l'enlevant de terre,
La porta, frémissant d'amour, dans ce mystère.          70
. . . . . . . . . . . . . . . . . . . . . . . . . . . . . . . . .
. . . . . . . . . . . . . . . . . . . . . . . . . . . . . . . . .

La nuit parut. Ce fut la plus belle des nuits:
Les astres rayonnaient, l'un par l'autre éblouis;
Le zéphyr & la fleur échangeaient leur caresse;
Les hôtes des forêts se cherchaient, dans l'ivresse;
Les oiseaux, sans savoir d'où leur vint cet attrait,          75
Se rapprochaient, unis dans un premier secret;
Et le ruissellement des eaux autour des mousses
Avait des bruits de luth, de baisers, de voix douces.
On entendit alors, à travers l'infini,
Les palpitations du Verbe humain, béni;          80
L'enfantement divin germa dans la nature:
L'amour, égal à Dieu, créa la créature.
. . . . . . . . . . . . . . . . . . . . . . . . . . . . . . . . .
. . . . . . . . . . . . . . . . . . . . . . . . . . . . . . . . .
L'aube éclairait déjà l'azur de l'orient.
Adam regardait Ève & l'aube en souriant,
Comme un être enivré des douceurs de la vie.          85
Ève ne regardait qu'Adam. Belle & ravie,
Les yeux pleins de langueur, elle attachait sur lui
Un long regard encor plus charmé qu'ébloui.
Il dit: "Voici le jour saluant l'hyménée."
Elle: "Voici l'épouse à tes pieds pardonnée:          90
Dieu bénit notre hymen, Adam. L'Éden perdu,
Nous l'avons retrouvé; l'amour nous l'a rendu."

[Léocadie Penquer, "Le Paradis retrouvé," *Le Parnasse contemporain*, vol. 2 (Paris: Lemerre, 1869/71), 285–88.]

# Louise Ackermann

## Une femme

S'il arrivait un jour, en quelque lieu sur terre,
Qu'une entre vous vraiment comprît sa tâche austère,
Si, dans le sentier rude avançant lentement,
Cette âme s'arrêtait à quelque dévoûment,                4
Si c'était la Bonté sous les cieux descendue,
Vers tous les malheureux la main toujours tendue,
Si l'époux, si l'enfant à ce cœur ont puisé,
Si l'espoir de plusieurs sur Elle est déposé,           8
Femmes, enviez-la. Tandis que dans la foule
Votre vie inutile en vains plaisirs s'écoule,
Et que votre cœur flotte, au hasard entraîné,
Elle a sa foi, son but et son labeur donné.             12
Enviez-la. Qu'il souffre ou combatte, c'est Elle
Que l'homme à son secours incessamment appelle,
Sa joie et son appui, son trésor sous les cieux,
Qu'il pressentait de l'âme et qu'il cherchait des yeux, 16
La colombe au cou blanc qu'un vent du ciel ramène
Vers cette arche en danger de la famille humaine,
Qui, des saintes hauteurs en ce morne séjour,
Pour branche d'olivier a rapporté l'amour.              20

## L'amour et la mort

*À M. Louis de Ronchaud*

### I

Regardez-les passer, ces couples éphémères!
Dans les bras l'un de l'autre enlacés un moment,
Tous, avant de mêler à jamais leurs poussières,
    Font le même serment:                4

Toujours! Un mot hardi que les cieux qui vieillissent
Avec étonnement entendent prononcer,
Et qu'osent répéter des lèvres qui pâlissent
    Et qui vont se glacer.                 8

Vous qui vivrez si peu, pourquoi cette promesse
Qu'un élan d'espérance arrache à votre cœur,

Vain défi qu'au néant vous jetez, dans l'ivresse
    D'un instant de bonheur?                 12

Amants, autour de vous une voix inflexible
Crie à tout ce qui naît: "Aime et meurs ici-bas!"
La mort est implacable et le ciel insensible;
    Vous n'échapperez pas.              16

Eh bien! puisqu'il le faut, sans trouble et sans murmure,
Forts de ce même amour dont vous vous enivrez
Et perdus dans le sein de l'immense Nature,
    Aimez donc, et mourez!             20

## II

Non, non, tout n'est pas dit, vers la beauté fragile
Quand un charme invincible emporte le désir,
Sous le feu d'un baiser quand notre pauvre argile
    A frémi de plaisir.               24

Notre serment sacré part d'une âme immortelle;
C'est elle qui s'émeut quand frissonne le corps;
Nous entendons sa voix et le bruit de son aile
    Jusque dans nos transports.         28

Nous le répétons donc, ce mot qui fait d'envie
Pâlir au firmament les astres radieux,
Ce mot qui joint les cœurs et devient, dès la vie,
    Leur lien pour les cieux.            32

Dans le ravissement d'une éternelle étreinte
Ils passent entraînés, ces couples amoureux,
Et ne s'arrêtent pas pour jeter avec crainte
    Un regard autour d'eux.            36

Ils demeurent sereins quand tout s'écroule et tombe;
Leur espoir est leur joie et leur appui divin;
Ils ne trébuchent point lorsque contre une tombe
    Leur pied heurte en chemin.         40

Toi-même, quand tes bois abritent leur délire,
Quand tu couvres de fleurs et d'ombre leurs sentiers,
Nature, toi leur mère, aurais-tu ce sourire
    S'ils mouraient tout entiers?         44

Sous le voile léger de la beauté mortelle
Trouver l'âme qu'on cherche et qui pour nous éclôt,

Le temps de l'entrevoir, de s'écrier: "C'est Elle!"
Et la perdre aussitôt, 48

Et la perdre à jamais! Cette seule pensée
Change en spectre à nos yeux l'image de l'Amour.
Quoi! ces vœux infinis, cette ardeur insensée
Pour un être d'un jour! 52

Et toi, serais-tu donc à ce point sans entrailles,
Grand Dieu qui dois d'en haut tout entendre et tout voir,
Que tant d'adieux navrants et tant de funérailles
Ne puissent t'émouvoir, 56

Qu'à cette tombe obscure où tu nous fais descendre
Tu dises: "Garde-les, leurs cris sont superflus.
Amèrement en vain l'on pleure sur leur cendre;
Tu ne les rendras plus!" 60

Mais non! Dieu qu'on dit bon, tu permets qu'on espère;
Unir pour séparer, ce n'est point ton dessein.
Tout ce qui s'est aimé, fût-ce un jour, sur la terre,
Va s'aimer dans ton sein. 64

### III

Éternité de l'homme, illusion! chimère!
Mensonge de l'amour et de l'orgueil humain!
Il n'a point eu d'hier, ce fantôme éphémère,
Il lui faut un demain! 68

Pour cet éclair de vie et pour cette étincelle
Qui brûle une minute en vos cœurs étonnés,
Vous oubliez soudain la fange maternelle
Et vos destins bornés. 72

Vous échapperiez donc, ô rêveurs téméraires!
Seuls au pouvoir fatal qui détruit en créant?
Quittez un tel espoir; tous les limons sont frères
En face du néant. 76

Vous dites à la Nuit qui passe dans ses voiles:
"J'aime, et j'espère voir expirer tes flambeaux."
La Nuit ne répond rien, mais demain ses étoiles
Luiront sur vos tombeaux. 80

Vous croyez que l'Amour dont l'âpre feu vous presse
A réservé pour vous sa flamme et ses rayons;

La fleur que vous brisez soupire avec ivresse:
     "Nous aussi nous aimons!"     84

Heureux, vous aspirez la grande âme invisible
Qui remplit tout, les bois, les champs de ses ardeurs;
La Nature sourit, mais elle est insensible:
     Que lui font vos bonheurs?     88

Elle n'a qu'un désir, la marâtre immortelle,
C'est d'enfanter toujours, sans fin, sans trêve, encor.
Mère avide, elle a pris l'éternité pour elle,
     Et vous laisse la mort.     92

Toute sa prévoyance est pour ce qui va naître;
Le reste est confondu dans un suprême oubli.
Vous, vous avez aimé, vous pouvez disparaître:
     Son vœu s'est accompli.     96

Quand un souffle d'amour traverse vos poitrines,
Sur des flots de bonheur vous tenant suspendus,
Aux pieds de la Beauté lorsque des mains divines
     Vous jettent éperdus;     100

Quand, pressant sur ce cœur qui va bientôt s'éteindre
Un autre objet souffrant, forme vaine ici-bas,
Il vous semble, mortels, que vous allez étreindre
     L'Infini dans vos bras;     104

Ces délires sacrés, ces désirs sans mesure
Déchaînés dans vos flancs comme d'ardents essaims,
Ces transports, c'est déjà l'Humanité future
     Qui s'agite en vos seins.     108

Elle se dissoudra, cette argile légère
Qu'ont émue un instant la joie et la douleur;
Les vents vont disperser cette noble poussière
     Qui fut jadis un cœur.     112

Mais d'autres cœurs naîtront qui renoueront la trame
De vos espoirs brisés, de vos amours éteints,
Perpétuant vos pleurs, vos rêves, votre flamme,
     Dans les âges lointains.     116

Tous les êtres, formant une chaîne éternelle,
Se passent, en courant, le flambeau de l'Amour.

Chacun rapidement prend la torche immortelle
    Et la rend à son tour.               120

Aveuglés par l'éclat de sa lumière errante,
Vous jurez, dans la nuit où le sort vous plongea,
De la tenir toujours: à votre main mourante
    Elle échappe déjà.              124

Du moins vous aurez vu luire un éclair sublime;
Il aura sillonné votre vie un moment;
En tombant vous pourrez emporter dans l'abîme
    Votre éblouissement.           128

Et quand il régnerait au fond du ciel paisible
Un être sans pitié qui contemplât souffrir,
Si son œil éternel considère, impassible,
    Le naître et le mourir,         132

Sur le bord de la tombe, et sous ce regard même,
Qu'un mouvement d'amour soit encor votre adieu!
Oui, faites voir combien l'homme est grand lorsqu'il aime,
    Et pardonnez à Dieu!        136

## Mon livre

Je ne vous offre plus pour toutes mélodies
Que des cris de révolte et des rimes hardies.
Oui! Mais en m'écoutant si vous alliez pâlir?
Si, surpris des éclats de ma verve imprudente,    4
Vous maudissiez la voix énergique et stridente
    Qui vous aura fait tressaillir?

Pourtant, quand je m'élève à des notes pareilles,
Je ne prétends blesser les cœurs ni les oreilles.    8
Même les plus craintifs n'ont point à s'alarmer;
L'accent désespéré sans doute ici domine,
Mais je n'ai pas tiré ces sons de ma poitrine
    Pour le plaisir de blasphémer.    12

Comment? la Liberté déchaîne ses colères;
Partout, contre l'effort des erreurs séculaires,
La Vérité combat pour s'ouvrir un chemin;
Et je ne prendrais pas parti dans ce grand drame?    16

Quoi! ce cœur qui bat là, pour être un cœur de femme,
   En est-il moins un cœur humain?

Est-ce ma faute à moi si dans ces jours de fièvre
D'ardentes questions se pressent sur ma lèvre?             20
Si votre Dieu surtout m'inspire des soupçons?
Si la Nature aussi prend des teintes funèbres,
Et si j'ai de mon temps, le long de mes vertèbres,
   Senti courir tous les frissons?                  24

Jouet depuis longtemps des vents et de la houle,
Mon bâtiment fait eau de toutes parts; il coule.
La foudre seule encore à ses signaux répond.
Le voyant en péril et loin de toute escale,           28
Au lieu de m'enfermer tremblante à fond de cale,
   J'ai voulu monter sur le pont.

À l'écart, mais debout, là, dans leur lit immense
J'ai contemplé le jeu des vagues en démence.       32
Puis, prévoyant bientôt le naufrage et la mort,
Au risque d'encourir l'anathème ou le blâme,
À deux mains j'ai saisi ce livre de mon âme,
   Et l'ai lancé par-dessus bord.             36

C'est mon trésor unique, amassé page à page.
À le laisser au fond d'une mer sans rivage
Disparaître avec moi je n'ai pu consentir.
En dépit du courant qui l'emporte ou l'entrave,    40
Qu'il se soutienne donc et surnage en épave
   Sur ces flots qui vont m'engloutir!

[Louise Ackermann, "Une femme," *Le Parnasse contemporain,* vol. 3
(Paris: Lemerre, 1876), 1–2. Written in 1835. Published as "Aux femmes"
in *Premières poésies* (*Œuvres,* 1877).

Ackermann, "L'amour et la mort," "Mon livre," *Œuvres: Ma vie; Premières poésies; Poésies philosophiques* (Paris: Lemerre, 1885), 81–89,
69–71; originally published in *Poésies philosophiques,* 1871.]

## Marie Krysinska

### Les bijoux faux

À *Georges Duval*

Je rêvais que je me promenais en un jardin merveilleux.

Dans la clarté des lampes allumées, s'épanouissaient des roses en satin et des camélias de velours.
Les feuilles étaient en fin papier luisant,
Et les tiges de laiton, soigneusement enveloppées de ouates et de taffetas,—
Étaient d'un vert radieux et s'élançaient avec des poses gracieuses,—

Dans la clarté des lampes allumées;—

Et parmi cette floraison étrange—de roses roses, de roses bleues et de feuilles en fin papier luisant—
Étaient suspendus des colliers de *fausses* pierres précieuses.

Pareils à des gouttes de vin et pareils à du sang, étincelaient de faux rubis—et clignotaient comme des yeux les émeraudes en verre.
Les saphirs bleus comme des flammes de punch flambaient à côté des grains de corail *trop* rouges et semblables aux lèvres teintées de carmin.
La turquoise en porcelaine mettait sa note mate auprès des changeantes opales;

Et dans cette féerie de pacotille, au milieu des étoiles en doublé, et des lunes en papier d'argent mon spleen inquiet s'endormait comme un enfant malade qu'on berce.
Et j'oubliais les roses vraies, les roses, filles des bleus matins, pour ces roses artificielles.
Et pour ces lunes en papier d'argent, j'oubliais la lune amie des rêveurs qui vont par les soirs parfumés, accablés d'une incurable nostalgie.

Des faux rubis étincelants pleuvait une lumière ardente qui étourdissait.
Le pâle reflet des turquoises charmait comme un coin du ciel.
Et les émeraudes en verre faisaient songer aux énigmatiques profondeurs des flots.

*

Souvent, hélas! le cœur où notre cœur s'est réfugié,
Est un jardin merveilleux où s'épanouissent des roses en satin et des camélias de velours,
Où étincellent—pareils à des gouttes de vin et pareils à du sang, —de faux rubis, auprès des turquoises en porcelaine, dont le pâle reflet charme comme un coin du ciel.

Je rêvais que je me promenais en un jardin merveilleux.

30 juin 1883.

## Berceuse macabre

*À Maurice Vaucaire*

—Qu'elles sont cruelles et lentes, les heures!
Et qu'il est lourd—l'ennui de la mort!
Qu'elles sont cruelles et lentes, les heures.
Les heures silencieuses et froides, qui tombent dans l'Éternité, comme des gouttes de pluie dans la mer.
Donne-moi la main, ô ma sœur, et viens sous la Lune calmante, parler de *ceux* que nous avons laissés seuls quand nous sommes descendues dans la tombe.

—Un sommeil très lourd m'engourdit, et je fais un rêve qui durera toujours; —rendors-toi, ma sœur, —nos aimés nous ont oubliées,

—J'ai mis mon cœur dans son cœur et je suis sienne à travers la Mort.

—Ces murs sont hauts, et la terre des vivants est loin; —rendors toi, ma sœur.

—J'ai senti des diamants humides tomber sur ma bouche desséchée, —c'est mon ami qui pleurait.

—Rendors-toi, pauvre sœur; —c'est la pluie qui violait ton cercueil.

—Ô Souvent j'entends des sanglots lointains; —c'est mon aimé qui gémit, hanté par nos chers souvenirs.

—Non, c'est le hibou qui jette un cri dans la nuit profonde; —profonde comme nos tombeaux, et comme l'oubli de ceux qui nous avaient aimées; —rendors-toi, ma sœur.

2 décembre 1882

# Krysinska

## Nature morte

À *Louis Forain*

Un boudoir cossu:
Les meubles, les tentures et les *œuvres d'art,* ont la banalité requise.
Et la lampe—soleil à gage—éclaire les deux amants.

*Elle* est teinte en blonde, car *Il* n'aime que les blondes.

*Lui,* a les cheveux de la même nuance que son complet très à la mode.

\*

Par la fenêtre ouverte on voit un ciel bleu comme une flamme de
    soufre.
Et la lune, radieuse en ses voiles, flotte vers de fulgurants hymens.

\*

Ayant achevé de lire le cours authentique de la Bourse, *Il* allume un
    cigare cher—et songe:
"C'est une heure agréable de la journée, celle où l'on SACRFIE À L'AMOUR."
*Ils* se sont rapprochés et causent
DE L'ÉGOÏSME À DEUX, DES ÂMES SŒURS . . .
*Lui,* bâillant un peu
*Elle* tâchant à éviter la cendre du cigare.

\*

Par la fenêtre ouverte on voit un ciel bleu comme une flamme de
    soufre
Et les arbres bercés de nuptiales caresses.

\*

*Lui,* ayant fini son cigare, se penche pour donner un baiser à celle
Qu'au club il appelle "sa maîtresse."
*Il* se penche pour lui donner un baiser—tout en rêvant:
"Pourvu que la Banque Ottomane ne baisse pas!"
*Elle,* offre ses lèvres pensant à ses fournisseurs

Et leur baiser sonne comme le choc de deux verres vides.

\*

Par la fenêtre ouverte on voit un ciel bleu comme une flamme de
  soufre
Et les oiseaux veilleurs chantent l'immortel Amour
Tandis que de la terre monte une vapeur d'encens
Et des parfums d'Extase.

*

—Si nous fermions—disent-ils—cette fenêtre qui gêne NOTRE EXTASE?


## La parure

*À Antoine Périvier*

Un peu de l'âme somptueuse et barbare
De nos primitifs aïeux
Passe en nous avec les feux des pierres rares
Et l'éclat du métal précieux.

L'or ciselé en bagues alliantes          5
Et en bracelets nous enchaîne
D'une fidèle tendresse où s'enchante
La tendresse de nos grand'mères lointaines.

Les perles rient en colliers
Sur notre cou qu'elles caressent         10
Licencieuses comme au beau temps
      Des mouches, des paniers
Et des galantes paresses.

Les mousselines légères
      Nous font         15
Un cœur de papillon,
Et les fraîches toiles à fleurettes suggèrent
Un cœur de bergère.

Dans la soie murmurante et câline
C'est l'amoureuse qui veut qu'on devine     20
Ses abandons et ses langueurs, toutes.

Les plis souples de la dentelle
Sont d'aimables routes
Fleuries, vers la fantaisie fière qui s'y récèle.

Le riche apparat des velours         25
      Nous fait un peu reine,
Un peu châtelaine aux fastueuses amours.

Mais en l'asile discret des sombres laines
Une âme de nonnain
       Nous vient;                30

Tant l'Art et le Rêve sont les vrais vainqueurs
     De nos faibles cœurs.

* * *

OMBRES FÉMININES

## Judith

*À Marthe Mellot*

    Elle s'est parée comme une épousée
    La fille d'Israël que le chef de l'armée
    Assyrienne auprès de lui appelle.

Jamais Victoire n'offrit à nul héros de couronne plus belle:
    Les pierreries, aux regards sorciers—      5
Qui brillent sur son sein en murmurants colliers—
Ont moins de lueurs que ses noires prunelles;

    Et les fines étoffes, répandues en nobles plis
    Sur son corps pur, frotté d'huiles odorantes—
Semblent les voiles mêmes de l'aube au doux souris.    10
En sa bouche plaisante sont les discours avisés—
    Comme le miel dans une fleur de grenadier.

    La Nuit diaphane, couronnée d'étoiles,
    Va déclore bientôt son lourd portail;
Mais, avant que le Jour ait fait voguer ses claires voiles,    15
    Le Seigneur accomplira ses desseins
Par cette main petite et tendre comme un ramier sauvage.

    Elle a laissé ses habits de veuve à Bethyloua
    Et vient, ceinte de grâce, en ses vêtements joyeux,
    Au susurrement câlin des pendants d'oreilles    20
    Et des bracelets, sur ses chevilles et sur ses bras.

    Son pas harmonieux est guidé
    Par la puissante droite d'Iahvé,
    Qui veut que son peuple gémissant
Lave son opprobre et sa honte—dans le sang.    25
Et, penchée sur le chef endormi, comme une amante,
Elle prend l'épée recourbée qui, dans sa main charmante,
Va devenir le Saint Glaive vengeur.

## Oumé

*À Mademoiselle Thérèse Duroziez*

Oumé—Fleur-de-Prunier—la petite princesse
Japonaise—aux longs yeux,
Au teint de lotus doré,
      Laisse errer
Ses doigts de fin ivoire                    5
Sur les cordes tendues de la *biva;*
Et de ses lèvres exquisement pâles
      Monte une chanson:

      "Le guerrier farouche,
      Le farouche Samouraï,               10
      Pour moi seule s'attendrit;
      Le baiser de sa bouche
      Est gai comme un éveil de nids."

La chanson vole par delà les lattes délicates
De bambous, avec soin ouvragés;          15
Elle vole par delà les étoffes brodées
Où, songeuses, les cigognes se sont arrêtées;
La chanson vole jusque sous le ciel diapré—
      Sous le ciel rouge, violet et gris—
Et berce, comme d'un souffle léger,      20
Les Chrysanthèmes, les Pivoines et les Iris.

      "Il est parti guerroyer,
      Armé du *kalana* recourbé;
      Mais son baiser dans mon cœur est resté . . .
      Et j'attends, palpitante d'espérer      25
      Le retour du Bien-Aimé."

Les Chrysanthèmes disent: "Viens, petite sœur.
Dont la robe comme nos parures est joyeuse,
Viens parmi nous promener ta langueur amoureuse!
Dans le vent frais, qui souffle de la mer, nous baignerons
   ensemble . . .               30
Viens parmi nous, petite sœur qui nous ressemble!"

      "Le charme de vivre, le charme de voir
      Les fleurs, aux chatoyants reflets,
      Qui, telles de petites sœurs,
      Autrefois me parlaient—      35
      Tout s'est éloigné
      Avec le Bien-Aimé."

Les Pivoines disent: "Nos seins sont éclaboussés
Du sang glorieux des guerriers tombés;
La petite princesse ne reverra jamais                                40
    Son Bien-Aimé!"

    "Si son jeune cœur allait succomber!
    Si mon beau guerrier loin de moi tombait!
    Ah! sûrement les hirondelles sauvages me le diraient."

Et les Iris disent: "Viens, petite sœur,                             45
Te pencher sur l'eau à l'insigne douceur!
Dans les roseaux tremblants dort l'opium suprême . . .
Viens parmi nous petite sœur!"

    "Et s'il ne devait
    Revenir jamais,                                             50
    Mon Bien-Aimé,
    Parmi les iris et les roseaux,
    Tremblants dans l'eau,
    Je m'endormirais."

Des cordes tendues le frémissement cesse                            55
Et la chanson a replié son aile,
Oumé—Fleur-de-Prunier—la petite princesse
Japonaise, aux longs yeux,
Rêve parmi les étoffes brodées
Où, songeuses, des cigognes se sont arrêtées.                       60

## Jeanne d'Arc
SONNET EN PROSE

*À Paul Hugonnet*

Le bûcher est dressé, le triomphal bûcher,
Où Jeanne montera, ainsi que l'on s'exhausse
    Sur un trône d'immortalité.
Court-voyants soudards qui appelez                                   4
Supplice—l'apothéose de sa gloire!
Plus cléments, vous eussiez volé
    Sa belle part
Au patrimoine de l'Histoire.                                        8

La voici, tel un joyeux Archange planant haut
Au milieu des flammes vermeilles,
Qui chantent sa beauté de vierge sans pareille.

Et sa cendre sera 12
La semence précieuse qui fera
Lever une moisson de héros.

## La Du Barry

*À Lucienne Dorsy*

La petite fée du joli, toute poudrée de grâces mièvres,
Tourne d'une main distraite, et blanche à merveille,
La cuiller, dans une tasse—qui est assurément
En fine porcelaine de Sèvres—
Où fume le café odorant, don nouveau 5
D'un monde aussi fabuleux
Que les contrées des contes de Perrault.

Les fleurettes de sa robe à panier
Sont moins futiles et folles que sa tête frisée
À menus frisons, blancs comme du sucre. 10

C'est un oiselet voluptueux et insoucieux;
Fait pour le nid royal et les longues paresses,
Sur des tapis—qui coûtent des provinces.
Tout ce qu'elle sait—cette petite courtisane—
C'est que son amoureux est le plus grand 15
Gentilhomme de France,—
Et que le rose tendre lui va divinement.

Mais le carmin mignard,
De ses joues, pâlit soudain;
Car, le souvenir lui vient 20
D'un odieux cauchemar
Qu'elle eût dernièrement:

C'était, au milieu d'une hurlante multitude . . .
Un lourd couteau
Tombait sur son cou délicat . . . 25

"Ah! le vilain rêve!" dit-elle, de ses mignonnes lèvres roses,
Qu'on dirait peintes par Boucher,
"Décidément, je ne boirai plus de café,
C'est lui qui doit en être cause"

Mais déjà, pensant à autre chose, 30
Elle vide sa tasse à petits traits.

\* \* \*

## Le poème des caresses

Inoubliables baisers qui rayonnez
Sur le ciel pâle des souvenirs premiers!
Baisers silencieux sur nos berceaux penchés!

—Caresses enjouées sur la joue;
Tremblantes mains des vieux parents,—      5
Pauvres chères caresses d'antan,

Vous êtes les grandes sœurs sages
Des folles qui nous affolent
Dans les amoureux mirages.

Baisers ingénus en riant dérobés,      10
Moins à cause de leur douceur souhaités,
Que pour s'enivrer de témérité.

Premières caresses, vacillantes—
Comme, dans le vent âpre,
Des lumières aux lampes;      15

Caresses des yeux, caresses de la voix,
Serrements de mains éperdues
Et longs baisers où la raison se noie!

Puis, belles flammes épanouies,
Sacrilèges hosties      20
Où tout le Dieu vainqueur avec nous communie!

Caresses sonores comme des clochettes d'or,
Caresses muettes comme la Mort,
Caresse meurtrière qui brûle et qui mord! . . .

Baisers presque chastes de l'Amour heureux,      25
Caresses frôleuses comme des brises,
Toute-puissance des paroles qui grisent!

Mélancolique volupté des bonheurs précaires,
Pervers aiguillon du mystère,
Éternel leurre! ironique chimère!      30

Puis, enfin, dans la terre—
Lit dernier, où viennent finir nos rêves superbes,—
Sur notre sommeil, la calmante caresse des hautes herbes.

## Effigies

*À Denise Ahmers*

Frêle et blonde, sentimentale et sensuelle;
Le fatidique Orient sculpta ses traits parlants
De chimère inquiète, inquiétamment belle,
Aux pâles yeux, couleur de vagues déferlant,          4
Où l'âme des lointaines races se révèle.

De son geste félin, alenti de langueur,
Émane un très subtil et très multiple charme;
Des grandes Cléopâtres c'est la petite sœur.          8

L'artiste, pour cette Fleur de Mélancolie
Souhaite—afin qu'elle soit encor plus jolie—
Le fard d'Insomnie et la parure des Larmes.

* * *

*À Renée Derigny*

Chatte brune au beau geste hiératique et hautain;
Frémissante de passions nobles et d'autres;
—Mais les passions sont toutes nobles, même les autres,—
L'enthousiasme rayonne en ses doux yeux châtains          4
Et son sourire a le charme clair des matins.

Jean Goujon eût aimé sa taille longue et fière
Aux bras souples, au cou royal de quelque Diane
Chasseresse de Rêve aux lunaires clairières;          8

Elle eût exquisement porté la blanc hennin
Et le brocart, au temps somptueux de reine Anne—
Chatte brune au beau geste hiératique et hautain.

* * *

*À Irma Perrot*

Factice simplement. Par les grâces savantes
Très femme; mais enfant par la joie ingénue
Qui montre, au gré du rire clair, ses dents charmantes,
Enluminant les lèvres dont l'arc fier s'atténue          4
À cette sonnerie de gaîté enchantante.

Noires le soir, le jour d'outremer ses prunelles
Ont la grave beauté des grandes amoureuses,
Brillant parmi l'iris dont la nacre étincelle;                    8

Finement d'or; les cheveux en boucles câlines
Se pâment vers ses yeux: —telle l'eût rêvée Greuze
En ces boucles—comme des paroles—câlines.

\* \* \*

*À Camille Picard*

Muse et rapin; les traits mignards et volontaires;
Aussi parfaits que si Jean Clouet les eût peints.
De l'esprit comme un diable en ses yeux gris et verts
Et du charme très doux, généreux comme un vin,                    4
Dans le sourire—comme une rose—entr'ouvert.

Depuis les ondes folles de la chevelure
Jusqu'aux fins ongles—c'est la Française de race;
Très complexe: fière et simple, perverse et pure.

De la femme elle a toute la futile grâce,                         8
Mais d'un loyal ami la droiture certaine:—
Un camarade exquis, joli comme une reine.

\* \* \*

*À Luce Colas*

De la grâce ingénue, aussi émouvante
Que la grâce des paysages normands
Où, parmi les doux feuillages bruissants
L'eau coquette, miroite, court et chante.                         4

Le cher souci d'Art a mis dans ses yeux gris,
Rieurs de malice, un rien de graves songers,
Mais sa bouche demeure le fruit frais des vergers
Aimés de Watteau et—tout parfumé d'esprit.                       8

Le siècle des fossettes et des bergeries
Des amours, des rubans et des cœurs aux abois,
Semble l'avoir ornée pour le plaisir des yeux;

Et c'est aussi le charme exquis des causeries                    12
Tendres et raisonneuses des Dames d'autrefois
Qui ressuscite en elle par le vouloir des Dieux.


[Marie Krysinska, "Les bijoux faux," "Berceuse macabre," "Nature morte," *Rythmes pittoresques: Mirages, symboles, femmes, contes, résurrections* (Paris: Lemerre, 1890), 31–33, 41–42, 85–87.

Krysinska, "La parure," "Ombres féminines," "Le poème des caresses," "Effigies," *Joies errantes: Nouveaux rythmes pittoresques* (Paris: Lemerre, 1894), 33–34, 43–51, 57–58, 69–72.]

# Notes

## Introduction

**1.** However, feminist scholars of medieval and Renaissance French poetry have recently begun to address questions of gender. See Krueger, *Women Readers and the Ideology of Gender in Old French Verse Romance* (1993); Jones, *The Currency of Eros: Women's Love Lyric in Europe, 1540–1620* (1990). And prominent women poets of the pre-novel era (Marie de France, Christine de Pizan, Louise Labé) have attracted more attention than their modern peers.

**2.** See Schor, *George Sand and Idealism* (1993) and *Breaking the Chain: Women, Theory, and French Realist Fiction* (1985); DeJean, *Tender Geographies: Women and the Origins of the Novel in France* (1991); N. K. Miller, *Subject to Change: Reading Feminist Writing* (1988) and *The Heroine's Text: Readings in the French and English Novel, 1722–1782* (1980). See also: Stewart, *Gynographs: French Novels by Women of the Late Eighteenth Century* (1993); Danahy, *The Feminization of the Novel* (1991); Kamuf, *Fictions of Feminine Desire* (1982).

**3.** In addition to Schor's work, studies focusing specifically on nineteenth-century narrative fiction include most recently: Miller Frank, *The Mechanical Song: Women, Voice, and the Artificial in Nineteenth-Century French Narrative* (1995); Beizer, *Ventriloquized Bodies: Narratives of Hysteria in Nineteenth-Century France* (1994); Waller, *The Male Malady: Fictions of Impotence in the French Romantic Novel* (1993); Waelti-Walters, *Feminist Novels of the Belle Époque* (1990); Kelly, *Fictional Genders: Role and Representation in Nineteenth-Century French Narrative* (1989). This list is by no means exhaustive.

**4.** Between Gilbert and Gubar in 1979 and Prins and Shreiber in 1997, important studies include: Keller and Miller, eds., *Feminist Measures: Soundings in Poetry and Theory* (1994); Montefiore, *Feminism and Poetry* (1987); Ostriker, *Stealing the Language: The Emergence of Women's Poetry in America* (1986); Middlebrook and Yalom, eds., *Coming to Light: American Women Poets of the Twentieth Century* (1985); Juhasz, *Feminist Critics Read Emily Dickinson* (1983); Homans, *Women Writers and Poetic Identity* (1980). For a more complete bibliography, see Prins and Shreiber.

**5.** For example, see articles by Danahy, Greenberg, Johnson, Paliyenko, and Planté.

**6.** Stanton points to Woolf's assertion: "all the older forms of literature were hardened and set by the time she became a writer. The novel alone was young enough to be soft in her hands" (xvi).

**7.** In 1880, the Camille Sée law established girls' schools; the law of June 16, 1881, mandated free education; and the law of March 28, 1882, made primary education obligatory.

**8.** In 1924, education for both sexes finally became equal under the law, permitting girls to prepare for the baccalauréat.

**9.** See Danahy's article "Marceline Desbordes-Valmore et la fraternité des poètes."

**10.** See Sullerot, *Histoire de la presse féminine en France.*

**11.** Montefiore studies such unrecognized Romanticism in her chapter by this name (*Feminism and Poetry* 8–13).

**12.** For an intelligent and detailed study of this question, see Wesling and Slawek, *Literary Voice* (1995). Smith, *Discerning the Subject* (1988), offers a broader overview of theories of subjectivity across the disciplines.

**13.** Benveniste, *Problèmes de linguistique générale;* see in particular the chapters "De la subjectivité dans le langage" (1: 258–66) and "La nature des pronoms" (1: 251–57). See also Kerbrat-Orecchioni, *L'énonciation de la subjectivité dans le langage.*

**14.** Benveniste elaborates on the nonpersonhood of the third-person pronoun, whose qualities include: "1) de se combiner avec n'importe quelle référence d'object; 2) de n'être jamais réflexive de l'instance de discours; 3) de comporter un nombre assez grand de variantes pronominales ou démonstratives; 4) de n'être pas compatible avec le paradigme des termes référentiels tels que *ici, maintenant,* etc." (1: 256–57).

**15.** Genette: *Figures III.* Todorov: *Les genres du discours.* For an excellent example of feminist narratology, see Lanser's book on the female-authored novel in England, France, and the US: *Fictions of Authority: Women Writers and Narrative Voice.*

**16.** Rabaté suggests that such a meeting is overdue: "À la suite des analyses de Genette, les études narratologiques se sont développées et raffinées à partir des distinctions entre auteur, narrateur et personnage. [. . .] D'une façon générale, l'importance accrue des concepts empruntés à la pragmatique et à la linguistique de l'énonciation ne paraît pas avoir touché aussi largement le champ de la poésie" (6). The essays of this fine volume do much to fill gaps in the study of lyric subjectivity.

**17.** See in particular Meschonnic, *Critique du rythme: Anthropologie historique du langage.* Wesling and Slawek as well as Bedetti provide useful presentations and analyses of Meschonnic's extensive work. Walter Ong (*The Presence of the Word,* 1967) and Paul Zumthor (*Introduction à la poésie orale,* 1983) have contributed ground-breaking studies of orality.

**18.** "La notion d'écriture féminine a particulièrement requis une continuité du corps au langage" (Meschonnic, "Qu'entendez-vous?" 20).

**19.** Meschonnic's major point of difference with Kristeva lies in his repudiation of a psychoanalytic model as source of what he calls "orality": "L''investissement pulsionnel,' et dans le langage, est de toute la vie. [. . .] Pas seulement dans les contacts 'entre la mère et les premiers états psychiques du bébé.' [. . .] [T]out le corps est actif dans le discours. Mais c'est un corps social, historique, autant que subjectif" ("Qu'entendez-vous?" 22–23).

**20.** Kristeva, "The System and the Speaking Subject" (*The Kristeva Reader* 28). Originally published in English.

**21.** Here we see Cixous's debt to certain aspects of Lacanian theory. In "L'instance de la lettre dans l'inconscient," Lacan showed how displacement and condensation function like metonymy and metaphor (*Écrits* 1: 249–89).

**22.** On this point see in particular Irigaray's "La 'mécanique' des fluides" (*Ce sexe* 103–16) and "Quand nos lèvres se parlent" (203–17).

**23.** For an overview, see Fuss.

**24.** See Butler's (*Bodies*) and Montefiore's discussions of Irigaray, which point to this limitation of anti-essentialist feminism.

**25.** N. K. Miller, *Subject to Change* 105. For other feminist treatments of naming, authorship, and gender, see DeJean (*Tender Geographies*) and Kamuf (*Signature Pieces*).

**26.** In fact, most recent theory on gender and sexuality privileges narrative and overlooks poetic texts. I must leave for another study the sustained analysis of this voluminous body of work (I am thinking in particular of Butler and the burgeoning field of queer theory) as it applies to poetic genres and canons.

# Part 1
# Romanticism's Genders

## Chapter One
## Femininity and the Renewal of the Lyric

**1.** On Romantic androgyny, for example, see Weil and Monneyron.

**2.** See Bishop, *The Romantic Hero and His Heirs in French Literature.*

**3.** Staël, *De la littérature* 358. Cf. Rimbaud's identification of Romantic prose with poetry: "*Les misérables* sont un vrai *poème*" (253).

**4.** Cf. Vadé: "[. . .] rien ne distingue *a priori* l'énonciation romantique de l'énonciation lyrique (élégiaque en particulier) telle qu'elle s'est constituée depuis la poésie antique" (Rabaté 18).

**5.** *Trésor de la langue française* 13: 634. The orthographic shift from *poëme* to *poème* was widespread by the late nineteenth century. I use the modern spelling henceforth.

**6.** But inclusive of other parameters such as the *poème didactique* and *poème satirique*. See Genette on the history of the tripartite division of poetry, *Introduction à l'architexte*.

**7.** So Maurras refers to Marie-Louise-Antoinette de Heredia (1875–1963), who wrote under the name of Gérard d'Houville. The Parnassian José-Maria was her father and the Symbolist Henri de Régnier (himself the son of a poet), her husband.

**8.** Maurras, *Pages littéraires* 8. For an excellent critique of Maurras, see Carroll, *French Literary Fascism.*

**9.** Wing suggests as much when he writes that "the lyric sentimentality and poetic forms of Alfred de Musset's verse [. . .] represent so completely certain excesses of French Romantic poetry that it is impossible today to read such poetry without a certain ironic distance" ("Dialogues" 666).

**10.** Vincent-Buffault analyzes the anti-Romantic reaction to excessive emotion in her chapter "Contre la maladie du sentiment."

**11.** The inclusion of brevity as a defining characteristic of lyric poetry began with the predecessors of the "pure" poets. French poets in the tradition of Mallarmé and Valéry conceived of the lyric as brief, concise, and hermetic. For more recent criticism positing concision as definitive of lyric poetry, see Frye's essay "Approaching the Lyric."

**12.** While Laurence Porter's work on the restitution of antique forms under Romanticism points to a classical legacy, Romantics were clearly writing against the French ideal of classicism represented by such poeticians as Boileau.

**13.** See, respectively, Hartman (39) and Peyre, *Literature and Sincerity.*

**14.** "[Lucien avait] la blancheur veloutée des femmes [. . .]. À voir ses pieds, un homme aurait été d'autant plus tenté de le prendre pour une jeune fille déguisée, [. . .] il avait les hanches conformées comme celles d'une femme" (Balzac, *Illusions* 81). "Chatterton, caractère: Jeune homme de dix-huit ans, pâle, [. . .] faible de corps, épuisé de veilles et de pensée, simple et élégant, [. . .] timide et tendre" (Vigny, *Chatterton* 27).

**15.** See Wing's fine discussion of the representation of the Poet in "Les nuits" ("Dialogues" 666–71).

**16.** Johnson claims that "Men are read rhetorically; women, literally" ("Gender" 176), a phenomenon that Chase attributes to the materiality of the maternal function: "The identification of women with the literal has to do with the mother's bearing of the child" (28).

**17.** The exceptions I have found are in Lamartine's work, such as "À une jeune fille poète."

**18.** After *Le sacre de l'écrivain, 1750–1830* (1973), Bénichou produced three more studies on Romanticism: *Le temps des prophètes: Doctrines de l'âge romantique* (1977); *Les mages romantiques* (1988); *L'école du désenchantement* (1992).

**19.** It is interesting to note that Molènes, the author of "Les femmes poètes," was a career soldier greatly admired by Baudelaire for his poetics of war: "'*La guerre pour la guerre!*' eût-il dit volontiers, comme d'autres disent: '*L'art pour l'art!*'" (*Œuvres complètes* 2: 215).

**20.** See Bertrand-Jennings and Planté (*Petite sœur*) on specific obstacles faced by Romantic women writers.

**21.** Cf. Planté's article, "Un monstre du XIX$^e$ siècle: Essai sur la femme auteur."

**22.** Molènes, a soldier, apparently believed that men looked better in uniform than women. Baudelaire admired his sense of style: "M. Paul de Molènes a écrit quelques pages aussi charmantes que sensées, sur la coquetterie militaire [. . .]" (*Œuvres complètes* 2: 707).

**23.** See Greenberg, "Elisa Mercœur."

**24.** For recent work on Ackermann, see Jenson ("Gender" and "Ackermann's Monstrous Nature") and Paliyenko ("Is a Woman Poet Born or Made?").

## Chapter Two
## "Women's Poetry":
## The Case of Marceline Desbordes-Valmore

**1.** Éliane Jasenas's *Marceline Desbordes-Valmore devant la critique* describes, in impeccable detail, the vagaries of the poet's career. I am indebted to her study in the pages to follow.

**2.** *Poésies* (1822); *Élégies et poésies nouvelles* (1824); *Poésies*, 3 vols. (1830).

**3.** Johnson, "Gender" 167. To my mind, Johnson offers one of the most probing analyses of Desbordes-Valmore's poetry to date, for which I am indebted in the pages to follow. In addition to "Gender," see "The Lady in the Lake."

**4.** In his 1843 article "Poetæ minores," the unfortunately named Charles Labitte writes of women's "tendance permanente à l'imitation": "Chez les femmes qui font des vers, cette identité continue de sentimens, cette ressemblance de mélodie facile, sont plus manifestes encore" (131).

**5.** For other treatments of Baudelaire's study of Desbordes-Valmore, see Lloyd (*Baudelaire's Literary Criticism* 190–202), Johnson ("Gender"), Danahy ("Desbordes-Valmore et la fraternité des poètes"), and Lloyd's response to Danahy ("Baudelaire, Desbordes-Valmore et la fraternité des poètes").

**6.** Bertrand and Ambrière, in particular, have devoted an enormous amount of work to Desbordes-Valmore's writing and biography. Bertrand has edited not only her complete poetry, but also prose works and children's literature. Ambrière spent thirty years researching and writing his 1,000-page biography of the poet.

**7.** "Les idées ambitieuses et exagérées qui inspirèrent *Corinne* à l'éloquente fille de Necker [Staël] exercèrent sur [Girardin] le plus funeste empire [. . .]. Mme de Girardin s'est ressentie dans toute sa vie littéraire de cette fatale prétention" (Molènes 71).

**8.** Desbordes-Valmore, *Œuvres poétiques,* ed. Bertrand, 2: 482–83. All further citations to Desbordes-Valmore's poetry refer to this edition (*OP*).

**9.** Cf. Barney: "Le cœur d'un savant est un puits ténébreux où sont engloutis bien des sentiments avortés qui remontent à la surface en guise d'arguments. Ces concepts qu'il croit atteindre par raisonnement témoignent d'instincts, éveillés à travers ce même esprit qui voulut les condamner au néant" (251–52).

**10.** *Œuvres complètes* 1: 40. Much later, Apollinaire penned this imperious alexandrine: "Hommes de l'avenir, souvenez-vous de moi" ("Vendémiaire" [149]).

**11.** Some prefaces are in the end accorded equal or greater importance than the work they precede (Gautier's preface to *Mlle de Maupin,* Hugo's to *Cromwell,* Maupassant's to *Pierre et Jean*).

**12.** See Derrida's "Parergon" (*La vérité en peinture* 19–168) on these apparently accessory, supposedly nonessential appendages (dedications, epigraphs, footnotes, etc.), which frame the text and complicate its boundaries. (See also Culler's commentary on Derrida's text in *On Deconstruction* 193–99.) Derrida examines the troublesome nature of these eccentric texts that reveal themselves, ultimately, to be infinitely interesting and informative. In the context of the poetic collection, they can obscure the moment of beginning, for it is not always clear where the frame of a collection ends and where its picture begins, nor what distinguishes the outside from the inside of the collection given a series of preliminary texts. This distinction becomes important when one notices how these preliminary texts mark the uncertain transition from the author of the collection to the speaking subject of its poems and in so doing are revelatory of both. Whether from a writer posturing as an apprentice, displaying self-effacement and indebtedness (as in Baudelaire's homage to his "très cher et très vénéré maître," Gautier), or offered as a measure and a gift of love (Verlaine opts for this formula in dedicating *La bonne chanson* to Mathilde Mauté, "ma bien aimée"), in either case, the dedication has not yet entered the realm of fiction. Regardless of the author's sincerity, in the dedication real people are addressed and sign their name.

**13.** Cf. Planté's essay "L'art sans art de Marceline Desbordes-Valmore."

**14.** Other poems to female poets include "À Madame Sophie Gay," *Poésies;* "Lucretia Davidson," *Les pleurs;* "Elisa Mercœur" and "À Madame A. Tastu," *Pauvres fleurs;* "La page blanche" (addressed to Desbordes-Valmore's daughter Ondine, also a poet), *Bouquets et prières;* and "Le soleil lointain, à Marie d'Agoult" and "Mme Émile [Delphine] de Girardin," *Poésies inédites.*

**15.** Cf. Vincent-Buffault's *Histoire des larmes.* While devoted to a study of the novel, it demonstrates with great clarity the unstable association of femininity and tears during Romanticism and beyond.

**16.** Woolf: "I would ask you [women] to write all kinds of books [. . .]. If you would please me [. . .] you would write books [of poetry and fiction,] of travel and adventure, and research and scholarship, and history and biography, and criticism and philosophy and science [. . .]" (*A Room of One's Own,* 1929). Cixous: "Il faut que la femme s'écrive: que la femme écrive de la femme et fasse venir les femmes à l'écriture, dont elles ont été éloignées aussi violemment qu'elles l'ont été de leurs corps [. . .]" ("Rire" 39).

**17.** This image played so forcefully on the poetic imagination that several writers chose to be buried facing the sea, as did Chateaubriand in a solitary tomb at Saint-Malo and Valéry in his "cimetière marin" at Sète, which, he wrote, "domine la mer" (Valéry 1: 1687).

**18.** Cf. Irigaray's work on the metaphor of fluidity in "La 'mécanique' des fluides" (*Ce sexe* 103–16).

**19.** See Bertrand's exhaustive study, *Les techniques de versification de Marceline Desbordes-Valmore*.

**20.** In passing, let me note that Desbordes-Valmore's poetic persona occupies roles of both daughter and mother in many of her poems; these positions are not simply interchangeable, but coexistent (the mother as daughter, the maternal daughter).

**21.** Desbordes-Valmore, *Lettres de Marceline Desbordes à Prosper Valmore* 1: 151.

**22.** See Baker, *The Subject of Desire: Petrarchan Poetics and the Female Voice in Louise Labé*.

**23.** A second sonnet, "À la voix de Mlle Mars," appears among the isolated poems collected in her *OP* (2: 634). Bertrand's notes (2: 798–99) explore the uncertain attribution of the latter sonnet. While his discussion remains inconclusive, I might point out that it is not unusual to find women's authorship questioned. This will become particularly clear in my discussion of Nina de Villard's poetry below.

**24.** Sainte-Beuve wrote several journal articles on Desbordes-Valmore and her work, which were later collected in his *Portraits contemporains* and *Causeries du lundi*. He also edited and introduced her *Choix de poésies* (Charpentier, 1842). In turn, Desbordes-Valmore addressed this sonnet and also "Au poète" to Sainte-Beuve.

## Part 2
## Parnassian Impassivity and Frozen Femininity

### Introduction

**1.** Most of the fifteen "Nouvelles fleurs du Mal" and Baudelaire''s contribution to the "Sonnets" section at the end of the first *Parnasse contemporain* ("Le couvercle") were subsequently included in the 1868 posthumous edition of *Les fleurs du Mal*.

**2.** "Romantisme, Parnasse, Symbolisme [. . .] c'est un effort continu" (Martino 4). "[L]e Parnasse [était une] étape indispensable dans l'*évolution* de la poésie entre le romantisme et le symbolisme" (Pakenham, "La réception" 4). "Art for Art's Sake and Parnassianism rose in open reaction to the types of social and utilitarian Romanticism that came to dominate the two decades of the July Monarchy" (Denommé 1). Souriau concurs with Denommé.

**3.** On Second Empire trials, see Leclerc (*Crimes écrits*), Matlock (*Scenes of Seduction*), and Wing (*Limits of Narrative*).

**4.** Nearly all of Desbordes-Valmore's collections contain poems in praise or defense of the poor and the oppressed. Here are some examples from *Pauvres fleurs* (1839), which, published shortly after the 1834 workers' uprising and subsequent crackdown in Lyon, contains many protest pieces: "Cantique des bannis," "Amnistie," "L'enfant et le pauvre," "L'agonie du mineur," etc. Similarly, in *Bouquets et prières* (1843), Desbordes-Valmore devotes numerous poems to the common people and the disenfranchised: "Croyance populaire," "Au jeune paralytique," "Au poète prolétaire," "Prison et printemps," "Dieu pleure avec les innocents," "Rahel la créole," "L'enfant abandonné," and so forth.

For Hugo see, for example, "Le poète et la Révolution" (*Odes et ballades*, 1826), "Pour les pauvres" (*Feuilles d'automne*, 1831), "À un riche" (*Voix intérieures*, 1837), "L'art et le peuple" (*Les châtiments*, 1853), "Le mendiant" (*Contemplations*, 1856). The monumental example of Hugo's defense of the disenfranchised is, of course, *Les misérables* (1862).

5. On proto-Parnassian publications, see Edwards ("La revue *L'artiste* et les poètes du Parnasse") and Schaffer ("Parnassians at Play").

6. Vol. 1 in 1866, 2 in 1871 (dated 1869, but suspended until the conclusion of the Franco-Prussian war), and 3 in 1876.

7. Mendès reproduces this poem in *Légende* 242–45.

8. 1: Leconte de Lisle, Ricard, and Mendès; 2: Leconte de Lisle and Lemerre; 3: Coppée, France, and Banville.

9. On Parnassian social communities, see Schaffer ("Parnassians at Play") and Zayed ("Un salon parnassien").

## Chapter Three
## Leconte de Lisle's Hardening Arteries

1. Baudelaire, *Œuvres complètes* 2: 176. See Christopher Miller's analysis of this article on Leconte de Lisle in the context of his discussion of Baudelaire's Africanist discourse (*Blank Darkness* 93 ff.). See also Lloyd's treatment (*Baudelaire's Literary Criticism* 229–39).

2. *Poèmes et poésies* was eventually incorporated into augmented editions of the *Poèmes antiques* (1872) and the *Poèmes barbares* (1874). *Poèmes tragiques* (1884) and the posthumous *Derniers poèmes* (1895) closed Leconte de Lisle's poetic career.

3. Baudelaire, *Œuvres complètes* 2: 177; emphasis mine. Cf. Schaffer, who blamed Leconte de Lisle's unreadability on an undereducated public, with contempt worthy of the poet himself: "Here, of course, is the reason for the fact that Leconte de Lisle has never been a popular poet; the average reader is a lazy fellow, and the concentration required for the complete understanding of this poetry is too exhausting for mental sluggards." Ironically, Schaffer shuns such a complete reading himself: "It would be idle to attempt here any analysis of Leconte de Lisle's Greek and Roman poems" (*Parnassus* 83).

4. Cf. Pich's note: "Leconte de Lisle considère la virilité comme l'un des caractères essentiels du vrai poète. La société où il vit lui paraît corrompue par les influences féminines" (Leconte de Lisle, *Articles* 171n13).

**5.** See *Articles* for Leconte de Lisle's contributions to such Fourierist journals as *La variété* and *La phalange*.

**6.** Pich is one of the most authoritative of very few contemporary scholars working on Leconte de Lisle (see *Leconte de Lisle et sa création poétique* [1975] and Pich's editions of Leconte de Lisle's poetry [Les Belles Lettres, 1976–78]). More recently, Gothot-Mersch has revisited the *Poèmes antiques* and the *Poèmes barbares,* offering new editions with pertinent introductions. I refer to the Gothot-Mersch editions in the following pages.

**7.** Leconte de Lisle's preface to *Poèmes et poésies,* his "discours de réception" before the Académie française, and an article entitled "Les femmes de Byron" (all in *Articles*).

**8.** "L'amour, c'est le goût de la prostitution. Il n'est même pas de plaisir noble qui ne puisse être ramené à la Prostitution. [. . .] Goût invincible de la prostitution dans le cœur de l'homme, d'où naît son horreur de la solitude. Il veut être *deux.* L'homme de génie veut être *un,* donc solitaire. La gloire, c'est rester *un,* et se prostituer d'une manière particulière" (Baudelaire, *Œuvres complètes* 1: 649, 700).

## Chapter Four
## Parnassian Obsessions

**1.** *American Heritage Dictionary* (Boston: Houghton Mifflin, 1975), 907.

**2.** Freud, "Further Remarks on the Neuro-Psychoses of Defence," *Standard Edition* 3: 169.

**3.** See Cassagne (*Théorie*) on the history of *l'art pour l'art* in nineteenth-century France. Lloyd questions how dedicated Gautier was to this position in the 1840s ("Gautier").

**4.** See, for example, "Lacenaire," "Coquetterie posthume," "Bûchers et tombeaux," and "Les joujoux de la morte" (Gautier, *Émaux et camées*).

**5.** The definitive edition of *Émaux et camées* (1872) consists of forty-seven poems, expanded from eighteen in the first edition.

**6.** Cf. Chambers's reading of this poem's pretense of neutrality in *Mélancolie et opposition* (55–61). See also Schick and David-Weill.

**7.** Houpoe, the crested bird that appears in Goethe's collection.

**8.** The French translation, under the title *Le divan occidental,* appeared in 1843.

**9.** See David-Weill on Gautier's aesthetic of hardness and its reliance on femininity. See also Johnson, "Dream of Stone."

**10.** Gautier, *Émaux et camées* 42–44. This poem elicited several responses from other poets. Cf. Krysinska, "Symphonie en gris" (discussed below) and Floupette's parodic "Symphonie en vert mineur," both published in the 1880s.

**11.** Mallarmé 67–68. "Tout son col secouera cette blanche agonie," etc.

**12.** All italics are mine, save the example from Deschamps.

**13.** Astarte is also assimilated with Artemis and the Great Mother.

**14.** While I focus on Venus in these pages, the huntress Diana or Artemis is another figure deserving of scrutiny in the Parnassian context. Heredia represented her in two sonnets: "Artémis" (*Parnasse contemporain* 1: 14–15) and "La chasse" (1: 274–75). Other references to her pepper the collection: " Et Diane la chasseresse / D'un vert amour du mois de mai" and "J'ai suivi trop souvent la pâle chasseresse" (Houssaye, 1: 146 and 155); "Tu m'as fait voir [. . .] Diane" (Gautier, 1: 273); "On ne va plus suivre la Chasseresse" (Banville, 2: 53).

**15.** Cf. Berger: "Le Parnasse adore moins en Vénus le corps idéal et matriciel de l'amour que la froide beauté d'un marbre désaffecté par elle" (*Le banquet* 27).

**16.** Indeed, the historical figures appearing in the *Parnasse contemporain* are predominantly male. Writers named range from antiquity (Homer) to medieval and Renaissance Italy (Dante, Petrarch) and the French Renaissance (Rabelais and d'Aubigné), through classicism (Racine, Corneille, Pascal) and up to Romanticism, both German (Goethe) and French (the big four and even a few minors, such as Nodier). With these references, the Parnassians place themselves at the center of a hallowed canon. Composers (Mozart, Meyerbeer) and painters (Michaelangelo, Titien, Raphael) appear too as models of creators. Men of state and of the church are also present in significant numbers. The omnipresent Joan of Arc stands fairly alone to represent historical women.

**17.** Gautier, *Histoire* 345. Banville, in his *Petit traité,* notes that Hugo finally wrote one (published in 1874) for Judith Gautier.

**18.** For example, see in vol. 1: José-Maria de Heredia ("Sonnets"), Louis Ménard ("Sonnets mystiques"), Baudelaire (including "Recueillement," "Le gouffre"), Ricard (two "sonnets estrambotes"), Houssaye (including "La beauté"), Mallarmé ("À celle qui est tranquille," "Vere novo," *et alia*), Deschamps ("Sonnets"), Albert Mérat ("Sonnets"), François Fertiault (including "Ô doctissime!"). In vol. 2: Nina de Callias [Villard] ("La jalousie du jeune Dieu," "Tristan et Iseult"), Alfred Des Essarts ("D'après Shakspeare"), Armand Silvestre ("Nouveaux sonnets païens"), Gabriel Marc ("Sonnets parisiens"), Gautier ("Sonnets," including "L'impassible" and "J'aimais autrefois la forme païenne"), Frédéric Plessis ("Sonnet gothique"), Auguste Barbier ("Deux vieux sonnets"). In vol. 3: Robert de Bonnières ("Sonnets russes"), Louise Colet ("Groupes d'Arabes"), B. de Fourcaud ("Sonnets hiératiques"), Heredia ("Sonnets héroïques"), Soulary ("Sonnets").

**19.** A translation of Petrarch's poem 272, from the *Rime sparse*.

**20.** J.-M. de Heredia, "La chasse" in *Les trophées;* Leconte de Lisle, "L'ecclésiaste" in *Poèmes barbares;* Baudelaire, "Le couvercle" in *Les fleurs du Mal;* Verlaine, "Angoisse" in *Poèmes saturniens;* Mallarmé, "Tristesse d'été" in *Poésies.*

## Chapter Five
## Moving Statues: *Les Parnassiennes*

**1.** Maurras also subscribed to the notion that a woman poet was necessarily Romantic, regardless of era or formal intent: his "Le romantisme féminin" in fact studies four *Symbolist* women poets.

**2.** The following periodicals attest to continued academic interest in Parnassian poetry: *Parnasse* (Oxford, 1982–87), *Bulletin des études parnassiennes* (Lyon, 1980–87), *Bulletin d'études parnassiennes et symbolistes* (Lyon, 1988–).

**3.** Denommé, for example, does not mention one woman in *The French Parnassian Poets* (1972).

**4.** Mendès, *La légende du "Parnasse contemporain"*; Ricard, *Petits mémoires d'un Parnassien*. See also Souriau, *Histoire du Parnasse;* Martino, *Parnasse et symbolisme.*

**5.** Schaffer discusses Ackermann and Guyon under the rubric of the "philosophic genre," and he associates Villard with "satanic" poetry.

**6.** Penquer published under the name Mme Auguste Penquer and Villard as Nina de Callias in the *Parnasse contemporain.* Colet's name appears misspelled as Collet in the third volume.

**7.** In defining the *Parnassiennes* as female contributors to the *Parnasse contemporain,* we must not forget other women poets, such as Judith Gautier, who published at the same time in other journals with a Parnassian slant.

**8.** For example, Schaffer tells us that "Penquer [. . .] had no social contacts whatsoever [. . .] with the main body of the Parnassian poets" (*Genres* 376).

**9.** Ackermann (*Poésies* [1874], *Œuvres* [1877], and *Pensées d'une solitaire* [1882]), Blanchecotte (*Les militantes* [1875]), Guyon (five collections between 1877 and 1905), Penquer (*Mes nuits* [posthumously, 1891]), and Siefert (four collections of poetry and one book of plays between 1868 and 1872).

**10.** While most Colet scholarship focuses on her relationship and correspondence with Flaubert, see the following recent works devoted more exclusively to her: Beizer's reading of the long poem *La servante* in *Ventriloquized Bodies;* biographies by Gray (*Rage and Fire*) and by Bood and Grand (*L'indomptable Louise Colet*); Bellet's *Femmes de lettres au XIXᵉ siècle: Autour de Louise Colet;* and Greenberg's article on mentoring. Bellet includes a comprehensive bibliography of Colet's works published between 1836 and 1879, and reprints *La servante.* Other than this and Gaddis Rose's translation of Colet's novel *Lui,* little of her work is available. See also "La femme du peuple" in Stanton, *The Defiant Muse.* I am indebted to Aaron Prevots for his meticulous bibliographic work on Colet.

**11.** See *L'Italie des Italiens* (1862), the product of her interest and travels in Italy. See also Gray's chapter "Attending a Revolution."

**12.** To add insult to injury, she was also ridiculed in her advancing age for her body's decline. During her trip to Egypt in the late 1860s, a fellow journalist described her as "a rather vulgar fat woman with a virile voice and masculine manners [. . .]. It was hard to recall that she had once been an ornament of Madame Récamier's salon" (qtd. in Gray 346).

**13.** *Les bas-bleus* 241. Barbey meant something entirely different, of course, from Leconte de Lisle's meaning in his reference to Hugo's "éruptions volcaniques."

**14.** On Villard's salon, in addition to Raynaud and Dufay, see Ricard, *Petits mémoires* (82–85); Schaffer, "Parnassians at Play"; Zayed, "Un salon parnassien."

**15.** Harismendy-Lony has provided an important exception with "De Nina de Villard au Cercle zutique: Violence et représentation," diss., 1995. See also her recent article "Nina de Villard."

**16.** Forestier 264. Other striking examples of Nina-bashing: Mendès, *La maison de la vieille,* a vicious *roman-à-clef* that ruthlessly satirized Villard, her mother, and their salon; and Bersaucourt, *Au temps des Parnassiens: Nina de Villard et ses amis.*

**17.** Vandegans suggests that "La jalousie du jeune Dieu" and "Tristan et Iseult," Villard's second Parnassian sonnet, were in fact written by Anatole France. His source is undoubtedly Ricard: "on soupçonna France non certes d'avoir tenu la plume de la poétesse, mais d'avoir guidé la main qui tenait la plume" (84).

**18.** This recalls not only Gautier's cold statues but Baudelaire's frigid beauty as well: "La froide majesté de la femme stérile" (*Œuvres complètes* 1: 29).

**19.** "Tout amoureux, de sa maîtresse, / Sur son cœur ou dans son tiroir, / Possède *un gage qu'il caresse . . .*" (Gautier, "Diamant du cœur," *Émaux et camées* 47; emphasis mine).

**20.** See "Étude de mains" and select passages of other poems, as the following from "Le poème de la femme": "Glissant de l'épaule à la hanche, / La chemise aux plis nonchalants, / Comme une tourterelle blanche / Vint s'abattre sur *ses pieds blancs*" (Gautier, *Émaux et camées* 29; emphasis mine). On feet in Gautier's oeuvre, see David-Weill (49). More generally on fetishization in turn-of-the-century narrative literature, see Apter, *Feminizing the Fetish.*

**21.** See also Gautier's *Le roman de la momie,* which recounts how a young English lord, accompanied by an Egyptologist, descends into an ancient tomb and plunders the remains of its mummified female inhabitant. Thanks to Rosemary Lloyd for pointing me to Gautier's prose texts as further targets of Villard's satire.

**22.** Ironically, Forestier attributes this line and the monologue containing it ("Le clown") to Cros (264–65).

**23.** "Le baiser de pierre" is not included in Villard's *Feuillets parisiens* and has to my knowledge not been published in a critical edition. The original manuscript, in Cros's hand, is housed in the Collection Lovenjoul at the Bibliothèque de l'Institut in Paris. Permission pending.

**24.** Two thoughts on these associations: first, Villard's formulation also recalls the poets or "chercheurs d'infini" of Marc's "Entresol du Parnasse" (see Mendès, *Légende* 242–45). Secondly, evocative of Baudelaire, there is a certain amount of lesbian tension in Villard's poem, since the gender of the statue is not revealed until the poem's final lines.

**25.** Villard's dizains appear also in her *Feuillets parisiens.*

**26.** See in particular Coppée's *Promenades et intérieurs.* Verlaine and Rimbaud helped inaugurate the sport of Coppée-bashing with their parodic dizains. See *L'album zutique* and Verlaine's "Vieux Coppées" (*Cellulairement*).

**27.** Cf. this quatrain, entitled "Madrigal":

> Fière comme Junon, comme Froufou vêtue,
> Vous me représentez, madame, une statue,
> Qui, prise par le spleen en l'olympe natal,
> Pour s'habiller chez Worth a fui son piédestal.
>
> (*Feuillets*)

**28.** Blanchecotte and Bourotte were dismissively referred to as "Cotte et Rotte" by the Parnassians.

**29.** I am grateful to my friend and colleague, biblical scholar Saul Olyan, for helping me work through Penquer's poem and its biblical allusions.

**30.** On Penquer, see Schaffer (*Genres* 374–76); Badesco (2: 1330–34); Somoff and Marfée (61–67 and 88–90).

**31.** One of Leconte de Lisle's few nods to the Bible is the epic "Kaïn," which first appeared in the second *Parnasse contemporain* and was later included in the *Poèmes barbares* as "Qaïn." The murderous brother becomes, for Leconte de Lisle, a misunderstood, outcast figure for the poet. Cf. also Baudelaire's "Abel et Caïn."

**32.** Cf. Baudelaire, who unites these two names under the sign of transcendental beauty: "La femme est non seulement un être d'une beauté suprême, comparable à celle d'Ève ou de Vénus, [. . .] mais encore faudrat-il doter la femme d'un genre de beauté tel que l'esprit ne peut le concevoir que comme existant dans un monde supérieur" (*Œuvres complètes* 2: 165).

## Part 3
## Symbolist Fluidity

### Introduction

**1.** Including the *Hirsutes, Jemenfoutistes, Zutistes, Décadents, Naturistes,* and the *École romaine.*

**2.** These poets were, perhaps not coincidentally, refused by the editorial committee (France, Banville, Coppée) of the final volume of the

*Parnasse contemporain.* A document describing the decisions of this committee sheds some light on the process (see Somoff and Marfée 69–76). While Mallarmé was refused because of the unacceptable opacity of "L'après-midi d'un faune," Verlaine's crime was more personal ("l'homme est indigne" [Somoff and Marfée 72]).

**3.** In Mallarmé's *Œuvres complètes:* "Crise de vers" (360–68), "Réponses à des enquêtes sur l'évolution littéraire" (866–72).

**4.** Valéry concurred: "Ce qui fut baptisé: le *Symbolisme,* se résume très simplement dans l'intention commune à plusieurs familles de poètes (d'ailleurs ennemis entre elles) de 'reprendre à la Musique leur bien'" (1: 1272).

**5.** Cf. Laforgue's "L'hiver qui vient" and Apollinaire's "Zone," two great free-verse poems that rely on passages in alexandrines.

**6.** See also Kahn's essay in the same volume, "L'art social et l'art pour l'art" (295–307).

**7.** See, for example: Barre, *Le symbolisme;* Cornell, *The Symbolist Movement;* Balakian, *The Symbolist Movement.*

## Chapter Six
## Baudelaire's Frontiers

**1.** In addition to Johnson's "Gender," Kamuf's article "Baudelaire au féminin" must be noted as a significant exception. Kamuf argues that Baudelaire both "gives and takes away" (80) the multiple voices of his feminine figures. Recently, an important dialogue has begun more specifically around the figure of the lesbian in *Les fleurs du Mal.* See Fisher's "The Silent Erotic/Rhetoric of Baudelaire's Mirrors," Morgan's "Male Lesbian Bodies," and my "Baudelaire's Lesbian Connections."

**2.** Michaud might be taken to represent the French school of Baudelairians (the author places himself in the tradition of Pichois, Richard, Milner) who, I would argue, have no sustained analysis of gender. Michaud's "Érotisme et cruauté: Le culte baudelairien de la femme-idole" predictably considers "woman" as a privileged site of (masculine) literary imagination.

**3.** See Benjamin, *Charles Baudelaire.* Among recent studies indebted to Benjamin's work on Baudelaire in the context of Paris as the capital of the nineteenth century are: Ferguson (*Paris as Revolution*), Prendergast (*Paris and the Nineteenth Century*), Sharpe (*Unreal Cities*), Terdiman (*Discourse/Counter-Discourse*), Buci-Glucksmann (*La raison baroque de Baudelaire à Benjamin*).

**4.** Again, I must note an important exception in Buci-Glucksmann's work, which proposes a feminist Benjaminian analysis of Baudelaire's identification with the "heroines of modernity" (the prostitute and the lesbian). While this is a rich and brilliantly argued book, I disagree with the notion of an androgynous Baudelaire and believe that any discussion of his identification with female outlaws needs serious problematization ("Baudelaire [est] un poète 'féminisé' en proie à sa propre andro-gynie, livré au marché tel une prostituée" [114]). My own sense is that embattled masculinity, rather than feminine identification, is behind Baudelaire's representations of women. Benjamin himself suggests that "L'impuissance est le fondement du chemin de croix de la sexualité mas-culine" (*Charles Baudelaire* 218).

**5.** Baudelaire's art criticism (and in particular his study of Constantin Guys, *Le peintre de la vie moderne*) has received considerable atten-tion from both literary and art critics (see Clark's groundbreaking study).

**6.** In response to Verlaine's article "Charles Baudelaire," Baudelaire writes in 1866: "Il y a du talent chez ces jeunes gens; mais que de folies! quelles exagérations et quelle infatuation de jeunesse! Depuis quelques années je surprenais, ça et là, des imitations et des tendances qui m'alar-maient. [. . .] je n'aime rien tant que d'être seul. Mais ce n'est pas pos-sible; et il paraît que *l'école Baudelaire* existe." And: "Pour dire la vérité, ils me font une peur de chien" (*Corr.* 2: 625, 626).

**7.** Baudelaire condemned "l'hérésie de la longueur" of the epic (*Œuvres complètes* 2: 332). All further citations refer to this edition.

**8.** Benjamin, *Charles Baudelaire* 9. The figure of the outcast Poet, whether exiled literally or intellectually, would become much more fa-miliar to readers after Hugo's exile during the Second Empire and Ver-laine's series of articles *Les poètes maudits,* published in the 1880s, which gave a new name to poetic alienation and isolation (*Œuvres en prose* 635–90). Although Verlaine does not include Baudelaire among the six poets he spotlights in these articles (Tristan Corbière, Rimbaud, Mallarmé, Desbordes-Valmore, Jean-Marie Villiers de l'Isle-Adam, and himself), his earlier article on Baudelaire (cited above) places him in the com-pany of these misunderstood poets.

**9.** Although elsewhere Baudelaire appeared to take pleasure in ridi-culing Staël as a *bas-bleu* (2: 465).

**10.** Baudelaire 2: 44–49. See Lloyd's analysis of this article in *Baude-laire's Literary Criticism* 39–47.

**11.** Cf. Baudelaire's dedication of *Les fleurs* to Gautier, "[le] poète impeccable [et le] parfait magicien ès lettres françaises," and his praise of Gautier's "goût inné de la forme et de la perfection dans la forme" (2: 122).

**12.** Cf. also "la froide cruauté" ("De profundis clamavi"); "[l]es froides prunelles [de la] reine des cruelles" (xxxii); "tes beaux yeux, mêlés de métal et d'agate" ("Le chat" [xxxiv]); "Statue aux yeux de jais" (xxxix); "dur fléau des âmes" ("Causerie"); "ma si froide Marguerite" ("Sonnet d'automne"); etc.

**13.** Cf. "Le masque: Statue allégorique": "beauté parfaite [. . .] elle pleure parce qu'elle a vécu!" (Baudelaire 1: 24).

**14.** Baudelaire quotes from Emerson's *Conduct of Life* (*Hygiène* [1: 674]).

**15.** *Fusées* (1: 649–67), *Hygiène* (1: 668–75), *Mon cœur* (1: 676–708).

**16.** Verlaine credits Baudelaire with liberating the poet from this stance: "le poète, trop longtemps réduit, par d'absurdes préjugés, à ce rôle humiliant d'un instrument au service de la *Muse*" (*Œuvres en prose* 606).

**17.** Cf. *Fusées:* "Il n'y a que deux endroits où l'on paye pour avoir le droit de dépenser, les latrines publiques et les femmes" (1: 661). Behind Baudelaire's ironic cynicism lurks the fear of psychic dispersal, metaphorically represented by the loss of bodily fluids. See Laurence Porter on sexualized fluids in Baudelaire (*Crisis* 136–67).

**18.** Flaubert mocked this *idée reçue* in *Madame Bovary,* in which the Yonvillais deride Emma for her "airs évaporés," "défaillances," and all "ces vapeurs-là" that result from her idleness (191).

**19.** As such, Baudelaire's conception of sexual difference and attributes confirms Irigaray's critique of the dominant ideological association of masculinity and oneness.

**20.** Baudelaire 1: 335–36; emphasis mine. For interesting readings of this prose poem from other vantage points, see Guerlac (78–85), Johnson (*Défigurations* 59–82), and Todorov (*Les genres du discours* 123–24).

**21.** It is, moreover, inspired by a similar passage in Thomas De Quincy's *Confessions of an Opium Eater,* and so can be read in the context of Baudelaire's *Paradis artificiels.* See Baudelaire 1: 1341.

**22.** "Avec ses vêtements ondoyants et nacrés" (xxvii, Baudelaire 1: 29); "Une femme passa, d'une main fastueuse / Soulevant, balançant le feston et l'ourlet" ("À une passante," Baudelaire 1: 92).

**23.** Hamon refers to "anti-architectural" elements (of which there are three in "La musique": "une mer," "le vaste ether," "l'immense gouffre"), which by their lack of definition are opposed to the differentiating, identity-constructing function of architecture (the stuff of city poetry) as referent and metaphor.

**24.** In *Civilization and Its Discontents,* Freud refers to an "oceanic feeling," jubilation resulting from a sense of limitlessness or continuity between the self and the external world (or more precisely, the maternal body), which he attributes to "an early phase of ego-feeling": "An infant at the breast does not as yet distinguish his ego from the external world as the source of the sensations flowing in upon him" (19, 13–14).

**25.** In *Baudelaire et la musique,* Loncke writes of the "alternance de pair et d'impair qui réussit à parodier le mouvement d'un bâteau soulevé par les vagues qui roulent quelquefois doucement, quelquefois irrégulièrement, mais toujours de manière rythmique" (202).

**26.** After Freud's "Mourning and Melancholia," Kristeva's *Soleil noir* identifies melancholy as a symptom of primal loss or separation (see in particular her reading of Nerval's "El desdichado"). The language of melancholy would retrieve the lost object, inscribe it with its rhythms and by the polyvalence of its signs. On depression and nineteenth-century poets, see also Chambers, *Mélancolie et opposition,* and Starobinski, *La mélancolie au miroir.*

**27.** See my reading of "La géante," "Feminine Proportions and Lyric Subjectivity."

**28.** It also, of course, brings to mind Lacan's essay on the acquisition of subjectivity, "Le stade du miroir comme formateur de la fonction du Je" (1: 89–97).

## Chapter Seven
## Loose Ends

**1.** For recent and engaging Verlaine criticism, see the *Revue Verlaine* (1993–). Cornulier and Ruwet have contributed rigorous metrical and linguistic analyses. Laurence Porter's chapter "Verlaine's Subversion of Language" is excellent (*Crisis*). To my mind, Zimmermann's 1967 study, *Magies,* remains one of the more important treatments of Verlaine to date. Moreover a number of important re-editions have recently appeared, including Corsetti and Giusto's of *Femmes; Hombres* and Steinmetz's of *Cellulairement* (the first publication of this 1875 manuscript).

**2.** Steve Murphy inaugurated the *Revue Verlaine* in 1993 by stating, "il paraît injuste que l'auteur des *Poètes maudits* [. . .] bénéficie aujourd'hui de si peu d'attention critique" ("Éditorial" 3). Zimmermann similarly has remarked that "on s'aperçoit que Verlaine retient bien moins l'attention des critiques que ne le font bien d'autres poètes du dix-neuvième siècle" ("Variété" 5). And Laurence Porter: "Verlaine has been neglected in recent years" (*Crisis* 76).

**3.** Raymond includes these two seemingly contradictory portraits in his *De Baudelaire au surréalisme,* where Verlaine appears both in the company of prison poets (in "la ligne idéale qui va de Villon à Verlaine, à Apollinaire" [358]) and as one predestined to "conduire à sa perfection le lyrisme intime et sentimental fondé par Desbordes-Valmore et par Lamartine" (28).

**4.** "[Si Verlaine] a ce culte de la force, ce n'est pas parce qu'il la sent en soi, c'est au contraire parce qu'elle lui manque, c'est parce qu'il est femme et qu'il a besoin de la virilité. [. . .] L'amour de Verlaine pour Rimbaud répondait bien [. . .] à ce besoin enfantin de sentir près de soi une force [. . .]" (Adam 42–43); "Pauvre Verlaine, à la fois si violent et si faible! Voici que sa violence est surpassée, et que sa faiblesse est vaincue. Il a trouvé son maître [dans Rimbaud]" (Porché 164).

**5.** Verlaine, *Œuvres poétiques,* ed. Dantec and Borel 22. All further references are to this edition (*OP*), unless otherwise noted. See also "Çavitrî" as an example of Leconte de Lisle's Orientalist and statuary influence: "Pour sauver son époux, Çavitrî fit le vœu / De se tenir trois jours entiers, trois nuits entières, / Debout, sans remuer jambes, buste ou paupières: / Rigide, ainsi que dit Vyaça, comme un pieu" (*OP* 78).

**6.** Décaudin writes of the "voix intérieure à peine personnalisée" in Verlaine's poetry ("Sur l'impressionnisme" 45).

**7.** Verlaine's article takes quite a different tone from that of Baudelaire and in so doing, it tells a different story about women's involvement in the world of letters. His impassioned appreciation responds directly to her poetry, rather than maintaining a critical distance, as did Baudelaire. Verlaine reacts in kind to the effusive tears of Desbordes-Valmore's poetry: "laissez-nous," he prefaces one of her poems, "les larmes littéralement aux yeux, vous réciter de la plume ceci" (*Œuvres en prose* 669). Baudelaire's recognition of the place of tears in her poetics comes instead in the form of denigration: he speaks of the "pleurs de l'hystérie" provoked by her work (2: 149).

**8.** On Verlaine's use of the hendecasyllable, see Fongaro, Cornulier, Victor, Deguy, and Bobillot.

**9.** Morier and Mazaleyrat also quote Verlaine with great frequency.

**10.** Novelists soon took up the lesbian theme, fueled by Naturalism for which, ostensibly, no subject was taboo, and by Decadent fascination with sexual transgression. On the subject of lesbian representations in nineteenth-century French literature, see DeJean (*Fictions of Sappho*) and Albert ("Sappho Mythified").

**11.** Raymond: "[Verlaine] naquit pour conduire à sa perfection le lyrisme intime et sentimental fondé par Marceline Desbordes-Valmore et par Lamartine" (28).

**12.** The fourth of the "Ariettes oubliées" (*Romances sans paroles*), "La tristesse, la langueur . . ." (*Sagesse*), "Vers pour être calomnié" and "Crimen Amoris" (*Jadis et naguère*), "Adieu" and "Lucien Létinois" (*Amour*). Victor's article catalogues Verlaine's ten hendecasyllabic poems (221–22).

**13.** Verlaine's "Sonnet boiteux," written in previously unimaginable thirteen-syllable lines, offers an interesting comparison not only for its limping meter, but for its antipoetic vocabulary as well, which includes a number of English words (*OP* 323–24).

**14.** See Bobillot's article on "regularity" and "irregularity" in Verlaine's hendecasyllablic poems.

**15.** Such as Schmidt ("Visions of Violence: Rimbaud and Verlaine") and Milech ("'This Kind': Pornographic Discourses, Lesbian Bodies and Paul Verlaine's *Les amies*"). However, see Minahen's recent "Homosexual Erotic Scripting in Verlaine's *Hombres,*" the first serious treatment of this collection to appear.

**16.** The editors sanitized this final line prosodically by changing the original "fesses" (which I restore) to "fesse" and adding this note: "L'édition originale [. . .] rompt ainsi la métrique de l'alexandrin" (*Femmes; Hombres* 119). Minahen justly criticized Corsetti and Giusto's disparaging attitude toward Verlaine's erotic poetry. The editors apparently found his rhythmic audacity equally as troubling as the content of his homosexual poetry. Moreover, I retain the heterometric disposition of the poem's lines, which Corsetti and Giusto flattened by justifying at the left margin.

**17.** This concession is both marginalized by the parentheses and centralized thanks to its position in the poem. Verlaine's equivocation, even the simple inclusion of this heterosexual digression, is not without precedent in *Hombres,* in which there are several other poems (e.g., poems I and X) that introduce a comparison between homosexual and heterosexual relationships. Is this a final acquiescence to compulsory heterosexuality?

**18.** Cornulier indicates the few free-verse poems written by Verlaine (223).

**19.** In reference, of course, to the violent homoerotic scene suggested in "Le cœur du pitre" (Rimbaud 249).

**20.** Very little has been written on female-authored Symbolist poetry. Older sources include Décaudin, *La crise des valeurs symbolistes,* especially "Le lyrisme féminin" (155–65); Billy, *L'époque 1900,* especially the chapter "Les femmes de lettres" (214–33); Moulin, *La poésie féminine,* vol. 2.

**21.** These English and American women living in France have received more critical attention than their French peers. See Benstock, *Women of the Left Bank;* Jay, *The Amazon and the Page: Barney and Vivien;* Marks, "'Sapho 1900': Imaginary Renée Viviens and the Rear of the Belle Époque."

**22.** For readers of Polish, however, see Szarama-Swolkieniowa's *Maria Krysinska: Poetka Francuskiego Symbolizmu,* which includes a thorough bibliography in French of (mostly nineteenth-century) sources mentioning Krysinska. And as my study goes to press, I learn of a recently defended dissertation and forthcoming articles on Krysinska by Goulesque.

**23.** Kahn recounts his reaction on seeing the poetry of Krysinska (whom he refuses to name) in print: "je vis un poème en vers libres [. . .] très ressemblant à mes essais. Il était signé d'une personne qui me connaissait bien, et voulait bien, moi absent, se conformer étroitement à mon esthétique" (29).

**24.** I am indebted to Scott's study, *Vers libre: The Emergence of Free Verse in France (1886–1914),* which includes a comprehensive list of free-verse poetry published in France beginning in 1886 (63–74).

**25.** Maurras labeled the four women poets (Delarue-Mardrus, d'Houville, Noailles, Vivien) at the heart of his study, "Le romantisme féminin," "[des] métèques indisciplinées" (181). Of course Vivien, an Englishwoman, was the only one not born in France. Xenophobia has long played a significant role in conservative French literary polemic.

**26.** Scott himself points to Grojnowski's article, "Poétique du vers libre." See also Mickel.

**27.** Oddly enough, Maurras supported her claims as well, although Delvaille suggests that he had ulterior motives for refuting Kahn's claim (28).

## Appendix

## Poems

**1.** See also anthologies of French women's poetry by Deforges, Moulin, Stanton. And as this book goes to press, Planté's *Femmes poètes du XIX^e siècle: Une anthologie* just appeared in France. Her volume will be an invaluable resource for work on women poets of the period.

# Bibliography

Ackermann, Louise. *Contes et poésies.* Paris: Hachette, 1863.

———. *Œuvres: Ma vie; Premières poésies; Poésies philosophiques.* Paris: Lemerre, 1885.

———. *Pensées d'une solitaire.* Paris: Lemerre, 1882.

Adam, Antoine. *Le vrai Verlaine: Essai psychanalytique.* 1936. Geneva: Slatkine, 1981.

Albert, Nicole. "Sappho Mythified, Sappho Mystified, or The Metamorphoses of Sappho in Fin de Siècle France." Mendès-Leite and Busscher 87–104.

Albistur, Maïté, and Daniel Armogathe. *Histoire du féminisme français.* 2 vols. Paris: des femmes, 1977.

Allen, James Smith. *Popular French Romanticism: Authors, Readers, and Books in the Nineteenth Century.* Syracuse, NY: Syracuse UP, 1981.

Ambrière, Francis. *Le siècle des Valmore.* 2 vols. Paris: Seuil, 1987.

Anderson, Jean. "Baudelaire Misogyne." *New Zealand Journal of French Studies* 8.1 (1987): 16–28.

Apollinaire, Guillaume. *Œuvres poétiques.* Pléiade. Paris: Gallimard, 1965.

Apter, Emily. *Feminizing the Fetish: Psychoanalysis and Narrative Obsession in Turn-of-the-Century France.* Ithaca: Cornell UP, 1991.

Aron, Jean-Paul, ed. *Misérable et glorieuse: La femme du XIXᵉ siècle.* Paris: Éditions Complexe, 1980.

Aynesworth, Donald. "A Face in the Crowd: A Baudelairian Vision of the Eternal Feminine." *Stanford French Review* 5.3 (1981): 327–39.

Baale-Uittenbosch, A[lexandrina] E[lisabeth] M[aria]. *Les poétesses dolantes du romantisme.* Haarlem: De Erven F. Bohn, 1928.

Bachelard, Gaston. *L'eau et les rêves.* Paris: Corti, 1942.

Badesco, Luc. *La génération poétique de 1860, la jeunesse des deux rives.* 2 vols. Paris: Éditions A.-G. Nizet, 1971.

Baker, Deborah Lesko. *The Subject of Desire: Petrarchan Poetics and the Female Voice in Louise Labé.* Purdue Studies in Romance Literatures 11. West Lafayette, IN: Purdue UP, 1996.

Balakian, Anna. *The Symbolist Movement: A Critical Appraisal.* New York: New York UP, 1977.

Balzac, Honoré de. *Les illusions perdues.* Paris: Flammarion, 1990.

Banville, Théodore de. *Les exilés*. 1867. N.p.: La Différence, 1991.

———. *Petit traité de poésie française*. 1872. Paris: Lemerre, 1891.

Barbey d'Aurevilly, Jules. *Le XIX^e siècle des œuvres et des hommes*. Comp. and ed. Jacques Petit. 2 vols. Paris: Mercure de France, 1966.

———. *Les bas-bleus*. 1878. *Les œuvres et les hommes*. Vol. 5.

———. *Les œuvres et les hommes*. 1860–1909. 26 vols. Geneva: Slatkine, 1968.

———. *Les poètes, deuxième série*. 1889. *Les œuvres et les hommes*. Vol. 11.

———. *Les poètes, première série*. 1862. *Les œuvres et les hommes*. Vol. 3.

Barney, Natalie Clifford. *Aventures de l'esprit*. Paris: Éditions Émile-Paul Frères, 1929.

Barre, André. *Le symbolisme: Essai historique sur le mouvement symboliste en France de 1885–1900*. 1911. New York: Burt Franklin, 1968.

Barthes, Roland. *Le bruissement de la langue*. Paris: Seuil, 1984.

———. *La chambre claire*. Paris: Seuil, 1980.

Bassim, Tamara. *La femme dans l'œuvre de Baudelaire*. Neuchatel: À la Baconnière, 1974.

Battersby, Christine. *Gender and Genius: Towards a Feminist Aesthetics*. Bloomington: Indiana UP, 1989.

Baudelaire, Charles. *Correspondance*. Ed. Claude Pichois. 2 vols. Pléiade. Paris: Gallimard, 1973.

———. *Les fleurs du Mal*. Ed. Antoine Adam. Paris: Garnier Frères, 1961.

———. *Œuvres complètes*. Ed. Claude Pichois. 2 vols. Pléiade. Paris: Gallimard, 1975–76.

Bedetti, Gabriella. "Henri Meschonnic: Rhythm as Pure Historicity." *New Literary History* 23 (1992): 431–50.

Beizer, Janet. *Ventriloquized Bodies: Narratives of Hysteria in Nineteenth-Century France*. Ithaca: Cornell UP, 1994.

Bellet, Roger, ed. *Femmes de lettres au XIX^e siècle: Autour de Louise Colet*. Lyon: PU de Lyon, 1982.

Bénichou, Paul. *L'école du désenchantement: Sainte-Beuve, Nodier, Musset, Nerval, Gautier*. Paris: Gallimard, 1992.

———. *Les mages romantiques*. Paris: Gallimard, 1988.

———. *Le sacre de l'écrivain, 1750–1830: Essai sur l'avènement d'un pouvoir spirituel laïque dans la France moderne.* Paris: Corti, 1973.

———. *Le temps des prophètes: Doctrines de l'âge romantique.* Paris: Gallimard, 1977.

Benjamin, Walter. *Charles Baudelaire: Un poète lyrique à l'apogée du capitalisme.* Paris: Payot, 1974.

———. *Illuminations.* Ed. Hannah Arendt. New York: Schocken, 1969.

Benstock, Shari. *Women of the Left Bank: Paris, 1900–1940.* Austin: U of Texas P, 1986.

Benveniste, Émile. *Problèmes de linguistique générale.* 2 vols. 1966. Paris: Gallimard, 1974.

Berger, Anne-Emmanuelle. *Le banquet de Rimbaud: Recherches sur l'oralité.* Seyssel: Champ Vallon, 1992.

———. "The Maternal Idol in a System of Bourgeois Poetics." *On the Feminine.* Ed. Mireille Calle. Atlantic Highlands, NJ: Humanities, 1996. 135–47.

———. "Le sexe du cœur: Essai de stéthoscopie de la poésie lyrique." *Lectures de la différence sexuelle.* Ed. Mara Négron. Paris: des femmes, 1994. 125–38.

Bermann, Sandra L. *The Sonnet over Time: A Study in the Sonnets of Petrarch, Shakespeare, and Baudelaire.* Chapel Hill: U of North Carolina P, 1988.

Bersani, Leo. *Baudelaire and Freud.* Berkeley: U of California P, 1977.

Bersaucourt, Albert de. *Au temps des Parnassiens: Nina de Villard et ses amis.* Paris: La Renaissance du livre, 1922.

Bertrand, Marc. *Les techniques de versification de Marceline Desbordes-Valmore.* Diss. Université de Grenoble III, 1977. Lille: Service de reproduction des thèses, 1981.

Bertrand-Jennings, Chantal. "Romantisme et exclusion des femmes." *Itinéraires du XIX$^e$ siècle.* Toronto: Centre d'Études Romantiques Joseph Sablé, 1996. 25–41.

Bibliothèque de la Ville de Metz. *Dédicaces à Paul Verlaine.* Metz: Éditions Serpenoise, 1996.

Billy, André. *L'époque 1900.* Paris: Tallandier, 1951.

Bishop, Lloyd. *The Romantic Hero and His Heirs in French Literature.* New York: Peter Lang, 1984.

Bloom, Harold. *The Anxiety of Influence: A Theory of Poetry.* Oxford and New York: Oxford UP, 1973.

Bobillot, Jean-Pierre. "De l'anti-nombre au quasi-mètre: Le 'hendéca-syllabe' chez Verlaine." *Revue Verlaine* 2 (1994): 66–86.

Boileau-Despréaux, Nicolas. *L'art poétique.* 1674. *Œuvres complètes.* Pléiade. Paris: Gallimard, 1966.

Bood, Micheline, and Serge Grand. *L'indomptable Louise Colet.* Paris: Horay, 1986.

Buci-Glucksmann, Christine. *La raison baroque de Baudelaire à Benjamin.* Paris: Galilée, 1984.

Buisine, Alain. *Verlaine: Histoire d'un corps.* Paris: Tallandier, 1995.

Butler, Judith. *Bodies That Matter.* New York: Routledge, 1993.

———. *Gender Trouble: Feminism and the Subversion of Identity.* New York: Routledge, 1990.

Byron, George Gordon, Lord. *Byron.* Ed. Jerome J. McGann. Oxford and New York: Oxford UP, 1986.

Calmettes, Fernand. *Leconte de Lisle et ses amis.* Paris: Librairies-Imprimeries réunies, n.d.

Carroll, David. *French Literary Fascism: Nationalism, Anti-Semitism, and the Ideology of Culture.* Princeton: Princeton UP, 1995.

Cassagne, Albert. *La théorie de l'art pour l'art en France.* Paris: Dorbon, 1959.

———. *Versification et métrique de Charles Baudelaire.* 1906. Geneva: Slatkine, 1982.

Chambers, Ross. "Literature Deterritorialized." Hollier 710–16.

———. *Mélancolie et opposition.* Paris: Corti, 1987.

Charlton, D. G. *Positivist Thought in France during the Second Empire.* Oxford: Clarendon, 1959.

Chase, Cynthia. Introduction. *Romanticism.* Ed. Chase. London and New York: Longman, 1993. 1–42.

Chateaubriand, François René de. *Atala; René.* Ed. Fernand Letessier. Paris: Garnier, 1958.

Chénier, André. *Poésies.* Ed. Louis Becq de Fouquières. Paris: Gallimard, 1994.

Cixous, Hélène. "Le rire de la méduse." *L'arc* 61 (1975): 39–54.

Cixous, Hélène, and Catherine Clément. *La jeune née.* Paris: Union Générale d'Éditions, 1975.

Clark, T. J. *The Painting of Modern Life.* Princeton: Princeton UP, 1984.

Collot, Michel. *La matière-émotion.* Paris: PUF, 1997.

Combes, Dominique. *Poésie et récit: Une rhétorique des genres.* Paris: Corti, 1989.

Coppée, François. *Poésies complètes.* 2 vols. Paris: Lemerre, 1885.

Cornea, Doina, and Livia Titieni. "Symboles de la féminité dans l'œuvre de Verlaine." *Studia Univ. Babes-Bolyai, Philologia* 25.1 (1980): 41–47.

Cornell, Kenneth. *The Symbolist Movement.* New Haven: Yale UP, 1951.

Cornulier, Benoît de. *Théorie du vers: Rimbaud, Verlaine, Mallarmé.* Paris: Seuil, 1982.

Courouve, Claude. *Vocabulaire de l'homosexualité masculine.* Paris: Payot, 1985.

Cranston, Maurice. *The Romantic Movement.* Oxford: Blackwell, 1994.

Crépet, M. Eugène, ed. *Les poètes français.* Paris: Maison Quantin, 1887.

Cros, Charles. *Œuvres complètes.* Ed. Louis Forestier and Pascal Pia. N.p.: J.-J. Pauvert, 1964.

Culler, Jonathan. *On Deconstruction.* Ithaca: Cornell UP, 1982.

———. *The Pursuit of Signs.* Ithaca: Cornell UP, 1981.

———. *Structuralist Poetics.* Ithaca: Cornell UP, 1975.

Danahy, Michael. *The Feminization of the Novel.* Gainesville: U of Florida P, 1991.

———. "Marceline Desbordes-Valmore." Sartori 121–33.

———. "Marceline Desbordes-Valmore and the Engendered Canon." *Yale French Studies* 75 (1988): 129–47.

———. "Marceline Desbordes-Valmore et la fraternité des poètes." *Nineteenth-Century French Studies* 19.3 (1991): 386–93.

———. "Poète maudite." Hollier 731–37.

David-Weill, Natalie. *Rêve de pierre: La quête de la femme chez Théophile Gautier.* Geneva: Droz, 1989.

Dean, Carolyn J. *The Self and Its Pleasures: Bataille, Lacan and the History of the Decentered Subject.* Ithaca: Cornell UP, 1992.

Décaudin, Michel. *La crise des valeurs symbolistes, 1895–1914.* Geneva: Slatkine, 1981.

———. "Sur l'impressionnisme de Verlaine." Société des études romantiques 45–48.

Deforges, Régine, ed. *Poèmes de femmes des origines à nos jours.* Paris: Le cherche midi, 1993.

Deguy, Michel. *Choses de la poésie et affaire culturelle.* Paris: Hachette, 1986.

DeJean, Joan. *Fictions of Sappho, 1546–1937.* Chicago: U of Chicago P, 1989.

———. *Tender Geographies: Women and the Origins of the Novel in France.* New York: Columbia UP, 1991.

DeJean, Joan, and Nancy K. Miller, eds. *Displacements: Women, Tradition, Literatures in French.* Baltimore: Johns Hopkins UP, 1991.

DeKoven, Marianne. *Rich and Strange: Gender, History, Modernism.* Princeton: Princeton UP, 1991.

Delvaille, Bernard, ed. *La poésie symboliste: Anthologie.* Paris: Seghers, 1971.

Denommé, Robert T. *The French Parnassian Poets.* Carbondale: Southern Illinois UP, 1972.

Derrida, Jacques. *De la grammatologie.* Paris: Éditions de Minuit, 1967.

———. *La vérité en peinture.* Paris: Flammarion, 1978.

Desbordes-Valmore, Marceline. *Contes.* Ed. Marc Bertrand. Lyon: PU de Lyon, 1989.

———. *Lettres de Marceline Desbordes à Prosper Valmore.* Ed. Boyer d'Agen. 2 vols. Paris: Éditions de la Sirène, 1924.

———. *Œuvres poétiques.* Ed. Marc Bertrand. 2 vols. Grenoble: PU de Grenoble, 1973.

———. *Œuvres poétiques.* Intro. Auguste Lacaussade. 4 vols. Paris: Lemerre, n.d.

———. *Poésies.* Ed. Yves Bonnefoy. Paris: Gallimard, 1983.

d'Houville, Gérard. *Poésies.* Paris: Grasset, 1931.

Diderot, Denis. "Génie." *Œuvres esthétiques.* Ed. Paul Vernière. Paris: Garnier, 1959. 9–20.

*Dixains réalistes.* Paris: Cochet, 1876.

Drillon, Jacques, ed. *Tombeau de Verlaine.* Paris: Promeneur-Gallimard, 1995.

Ducrot, Oswald, and Tzvetan Todorov. *Dictionnaire encyclopédique des sciences du langage.* Paris: Seuil, 1972.

Dufay, Pierre. "Chez Nina de Villard." *Mercure de France* 1 June 1927: 324–52.

Easthope, Antony. *Poetry as Discourse.* New York: Methuen, 1983.

Edwards, Peter J. "La revue *L'artiste* et les poètes du Parnasse." *Bulletin des études parnassiennes* 8 (1986): 15–25.

Ferguson, Priscilla. *Paris as Revolution: Writing the Nineteenth-Century City.* Berkeley: U of California P, 1994.

Filliolet, Jacques. "Problématique du vers libre." *Langue française* 23 (1974): 63–71.

Fisher, Dominique. "The Silent Erotic/Rhetoric of Baudelaire's Mirrors." Fisher and Schehr 34–51.

Fisher, Dominique, and Lawrence Schehr, eds. *Articulations of Difference: Gender Studies and Writing in French.* Stanford: Stanford UP, 1997.

Flaubert, Gustave. *Correspondance.* 9 vols. Paris: Conard, 1926–33.

———. *Le dictionnaire des idées reçues.* Bordeaux: Le Castor Astral, 1991.

———. *Madame Bovary.* Paris: Flammarion, 1986.

Floupette, Adoré [Gabriel Vicaire and Henri Beauclair]. *Les déliquescences: Poèmes décadents.* 1885. Milan: Cisalpino-Goliardica, 1972.

Fongaro, Antoine. "Verlaine et Marceline Desbordes-Valmore." *Studi francesi* 2.6 (1958): 442–45.

Fontanier, Pierre. *Les figures du discours.* 1830. Paris: Flammarion, 1977.

Forestier, Louis. *Charles Cros, l'homme et l'œuvre.* Paris: Minard, 1969.

Foucault, Michel. *La volonté de savoir.* Vol. 1 of *Histoire de la sexualité.* Paris: Gallimard, 1976.

———. "Qu'est-ce qu'un auteur?" *Bulletin de la Société française de Philosophie* 64.3 (1969): 73–104.

———. *Surveiller et punir: Naissance de la prison.* Paris: Gallimard, 1975.

Fraisse, Geneviève, and Michelle Perrot, eds. *Emerging Feminism from Revolution to World War.* Vol. 4 of *A History of Women.* Cambridge: Harvard UP, 1993.

France, Anatole. *Croquis féminins.* Pakenham, *Portraits* 3–17.

Freud, Sigmund. *Civilization and Its Discontents.* New York: Norton, 1961.

———. "Further Remarks on the Neuro-Psychoses of Defence." *The Standard Edition of the Complete Psychological Works.* Vol. 3. London: Hogarth, 1962. 162–85.

———. "Mourning and Melancholia." *The Standard Edition of the Complete Psychological Works.* Vol. 14. London: Hogarth, 1957. 239–58.

Friedrich, Hugo. *The Structure of Modern Poetry.* Evanston, IL: Northwestern UP, 1974.

Frye, Northrop. "Approaching the Lyric." Hosek and Parker 31–37.

Fuss, Diana. *Essentially Speaking: Feminism, Nature and Difference.* New York: Routledge, 1989.

Gans, Eric. "Naissance du Moi lyrique: Du féminin au masculin." *Poétique* 46 (1981): 129–39.

Gautier, Théophile. *Albertus.* Vol. 1 of *Poésies complètes.* Ed. René Jasinski. 3 vols. Paris: Nizet, 1970. 81–188.

———. *Émaux et camées.* 1852, 1872. Ed. Claudine Gothot-Mersch. Paris: Gallimard, 1981.

———. *Histoire du romantisme, suivie de Notices romantiques et d'une Étude sur la poésie française 1830–1868.* Paris: Charpentier, 1927.

———. *Mademoiselle de Maupin.* Ed. Jacques Robichez. Paris: Imprimerie nationale, 1979.

———. "Le pied de momie." *Romans et contes.* Paris: Lemerre, 1898. 433–52.

———. *Le roman de la momie.* 1858. Paris: Flammarion, 1966.

Gendre, André. *Évolution du sonnet français.* Paris: PUF, 1996.

Genette, Gérard. *Figures III.* Paris: Seuil, 1972.

———. *Introduction à l'architexte.* Paris: Seuil, 1979.

Genlis, Stéphanie-Félicité, Comtesse de. *De l'influence des femmes sur la littérature française.* Paris: Maradan, 1811.

Gilbert, Sandra, and Susan Gubar, eds. *Shakespeare's Sisters: Feminist Essays on Women Poets.* Bloomington: Indiana UP, 1979.

Gioia, Dana. *Can Poetry Matter? Essays on Poetry and American Culture.* Saint Paul: Graywolf, 1992.

Goncourt, Edmond de, and Jules de Goncourt. *La femme au dix-huitième siècle.* Paris: Flammarion, 1982.

———. *Journal: Mémoires de la vie littéraire.* 22 vols. Monaco: L'Imprimerie nationale, 1956.

Goulesque, Florence. "'Le Hibou' qui voulait danser: Marie Krysinska, innovatrice du vers libre et théoricienne de la poésie moderne." *Symposium* (1999). Forthcoming.

———. "Marie Krysinska (1864–1908), une femme poète symboliste: Quatuor pour quatre voix, impressionnisme, musique, danse et poésie." Diss. U of New Mexico, 1997.

———. "Une femme voyageuse dans les flous artistiques symbolistes: 'Devant le miroir' de Marie Krysinska, trio pour vers, prose, et vers libre métissé." *Chimères* (Spring 1999). Forthcoming.

Gourmont, Jean de. *Les muses d'aujourd'hui*. Paris: Mercure de France, 1910.

Gray, Francine du Plessix. *Rage and Fire: A Life of Louise Colet*. New York: Simon and Schuster, 1994.

Greenberg, Wendy. "An Aspect of Desbordes-Valmore's Life in Her Poetry." *Nineteenth-Century French Studies* 17.3–4 (1989): 299–306.

———. "Elisa Mercœur: The Poetics of Genius and the Sublime." *Nineteenth-Century French Studies* 24.1–2 (1995–96): 84–96.

———. "Mentoring in Four Nineteenth-Century Women Poets." *Nineteenth-Century French Studies* 22.3–4 (1994): 450–64.

Grimal, Pierre. *The Dictionary of Classical Mythology*. 1951. Trans. A. R. Maxwell-Hyslop. London: Blackwell, 1996.

Grojnowski, Daniel. "Poétique du vers libre." *Revue d'histoire littéraire de la France* 84 (1984): 390–413.

Guerlac, Suzanne. *The Impersonal Sublime: Hugo, Baudelaire, Lautréamont*. Stanford: Stanford UP, 1990.

Hamon, Philippe. *Expositions: Littérature et architecture au XIXe siècle*. Paris: Corti, 1989.

———. "Texte et architecture." *Poétique* 73 (1988): 3–26.

Harismendy-Lony, Sandrine. "De Nina de Villard au Cercle zutique: Violence et représentation." Diss. U of California Santa Barbara, 1995.

———. "Nina de Villard, *singulière* Parisienne." *Nineteenth-Century French Studies* 27.1–2 (1998–99): 200–13.

Hartman, Geoffrey. "Reflections on Romanticism in France." *Romanticism: Vistas, Instances, Continuities*. Ed. David Thorburn and Geoffrey Hartman. Ithaca: Cornell UP, 1973. 38–61.

Heredia, José-Maria de. *Les trophées*. 1893. Paris: Gallimard, 1981.

Hillery, David. *Verlaine: Fixing an Image*. Durham: U of Durham P, 1988.

Hollier, Denis, ed. *A New History of French Literature*. Cambridge: Harvard UP, 1989.

Homans, Margaret. *Women Writers and Poetic Identity*. Princeton: Princeton UP, 1980.

Hosek, Chaviva, and Patricia Parker, eds. *Lyric Poetry: Beyond New Criticism*. Ithaca: Cornell UP, 1985.

Hugo, Victor. *Hernani*. Paris: Larousse, 1971.

———. *Poésie*. 3 vols. Ed. Bernard Leuilliot. Paris: Seuil, 1972.

Huret, Jules. *Enquête sur l'évolution littéraire*. Paris: Charpentier, 1894.

Irigaray, Luce. *Ce sexe qui n'en est pas un*. Paris: Minuit, 1977.

# Bibliography

Irigaray, Luce. *Speculum de l'autre femme.* Paris: Minuit, 1974.

Jackson, John E. *La question du Moi: Un aspect de la modernité poétique européenne.* Neuchatel: À la Baconnière, 1978.

Jakobson, Roman. *Essais de linguistique générale.* Paris: Minuit, 1963.

Jasenas, Éliane. *Marceline Desbordes-Valmore devant la critique.* Geneva: Droz; Paris: Minard, 1962.

———. *Le poétique: Desbordes-Valmore et Nerval.* Paris: Delarge, 1975.

Jay, Karla. *The Amazon and the Page: Natalie Clifford Barney and Renée Vivien.* Bloomington: Indiana UP, 1988.

Jenny, Laurent. "Le poétique et le narratif." *Poétique* 28 (1976): 440–49.

Jenson, Deborah. "Gender and the Aesthetic of 'le Mal': Louise Ackermann's *Poésies philosophiques*, 1871." *Nineteenth-Century French Studies* 23.1–2 (1994–95): 175–93.

———. "Louise Ackermann's Monstrous Nature." *Symposium* (1999). Forthcoming.

Johnson, Barbara. *Défigurations du langage poétique.* Paris: Flammarion, 1979.

———. "The Dream of Stone." Hollier 743–48.

———. "*Les fleurs du mal armé*: Some Reflections on Intertextuality." Hosek and Parker 264–80.

———. "Gender and Poetry: Charles Baudelaire and Marceline Desbordes-Valmore." DeJean and Miller 163–81.

———. "The Lady in the Lake." Hollier 627–32.

Jones, Ann Rosalind. *The Currency of Eros: Women's Love Lyric in Europe, 1540–1620.* Bloomington: Indiana UP, 1990.

Juhasz, Suzanne. *Feminist Critics Read Emily Dickinson.* Bloomington: Indiana UP, 1983.

Kahn, Gustave. *Symbolistes et décadents.* Paris: Vanier, 1902.

Kamuf, Peggy. "Baudelaire au féminin." *Paragraph* 8 (1986): 75–93.

———. "Baudelaire's Modern Woman." *Qui Parle* 4.2 (1991): 1–7.

———. *Fictions of Feminine Desire.* Lincoln: U of Nebraska P, 1982.

———. *Signature Pieces: On the Institution of Authorship.* Ithaca: Cornell UP, 1988.

Keller, Lynn, and Cristanne Miller, eds. *Feminist Measures: Soundings in Poetry and Theory.* Ann Arbor: U of Michigan P, 1994.

Kelly, Dorothy. *Fictional Genders: Role and Representation in Nineteenth-Century French Narrative.* Lincoln: U of Nebraska P, 1989.

Kerbrat-Orecchioni, Catherine. *L'énonciation de la subjectivité dans le langage*. Paris: Colin, 1980.

Klein, Richard. "Straight Lines and Arabesques: Metaphors of Metaphor." *Yale French Studies* 45 (1970): 64–86.

Knight, Philip. *Flower Poetics in Nineteenth-Century France*. Oxford: Oxford UP, 1986.

Kristeva, Julia. *Desire in Language*. Ed. Leon S. Roudiez. New York: Columbia UP, 1980.

———. *The Kristeva Reader*. Ed. Toril Moi. New York: Columbia UP, 1986.

———. *Pouvoirs de l'horreur*. Paris: Seuil, 1980.

———. *La révolution du langage poétique*. Paris: Seuil, 1974.

———. *Soleil noir: Dépression et mélancolie*. Paris: Gallimard, 1987.

Krueger, Roberta L. *Women Readers and the Ideology of Gender in Old French Verse Romance*. Cambridge: Cambridge UP, 1993.

Krysinska, Marie. *Intermèdes: Nouveaux rythmes pittoresques*. Paris: Messein, 1903.

———. *Joies errantes: Nouveaux rythmes pittoresques*. Paris: Lemerre, 1894.

———. *Rythmes pittoresques: Mirages, symboles, femmes, contes, résurrections*. Paris: Lemerre, 1890.

Labé, Louise. *Élégies, sonnets*. In *Poètes du XVIe siècle*. Ed. Albert-Marie Schmidt. Pléiade. Paris: Gallimard, 1953.

Labitte, Charles. "Poetæ minores." *Revue des deux mondes* 3 (1843): 99–138.

Lacan, Jacques. *Écrits*. 2 vols. 1966. Collection "Points." Paris: Seuil, 1971.

Laforgue, Jules. *Les complaintes et les Premiers poèmes*. Ed. Pascal Pia. Paris: Gallimard, 1979.

———. *L'imitation de Notre-Dame la Lune; Des fleurs de bonne volonté*. Ed. Pascal Pia. Paris: Gallimard, 1979.

———. *Mélanges posthumes*. 1903. Paris and Geneva: Ressources, 1979.

Lamartine, Alphonse de. *Méditations poétiques; Nouvelles méditations poétiques; Poésies diverses*. Ed. Marius-François Guyard. Paris: Gallimard, 1981.

———. *Recueillements poétiques*. Paris: Garnier frères, 1966.

Lanser, Susan S. *Fictions of Authority: Women Writers and Narrative Voice*. Ithaca: Cornell UP, 1992.

Lanson, Gustave. *Histoire de la littérature française*. 1894. Paris: Hachette, 1964.

Larnac, Jean. *Histoire de la littérature féminine en France*. Paris: Kra, 1929.

Leclerc, Yvan. *Crimes écrits: La littérature en procès au dix-neuvième siècle*. Paris: Plon, 1991.

Leconte de Lisle, Charles de. *Articles, préfaces, discours*. Ed. Edgard Pich. Paris: Société d'édition "Les Belles Lettres," 1971.

———. *Œuvres*. Ed. Edgard Pich. 4 vols. Paris: Les Belles Lettres, 1976–78.

———. *Poèmes antiques*. 1852. Ed. Claudine Gothot-Mersch. Paris: Gallimard, 1994.

———. *Poèmes barbares*. 1862. Ed. Claudine Gothot-Mersch. Paris: Gallimard, 1985.

Lepelletier, Edmond. *Paul Verlaine, sa vie et son œuvre*. Paris: Mercure de France, 1907.

Le Rouge, Gustave. *Verlainiens et décadents*. Paris: Julliard, 1993.

Littré, Émile. *Dictionnaire de la langue française*. 5 vols. Paris: Hachette, 1874–77.

Lloyd, Rosemary. "Baudelaire, Marceline Desbordes-Valmore et la fraternité des poètes." *Bulletin baudelairien* 26.2 (Dec. 1991): 65–74.

———. *Baudelaire's Literary Criticism*. Cambridge: Cambridge UP, 1981.

———. "Gautier est-il aussi partisan de la doctrine de l'art pour l'art qu'on veut nous le faire croire?" *Bulletin des études parnassiennes* 7 (1985): 1–13.

Loncke, Joycelynne. *Baudelaire et la musique*. Paris: Nizet, 1975.

Majewski, Henry. *Paradigm and Parody: Images of Creativity in French Romanticism*. Charlottesville: UP of Virginia, 1989.

Mallarmé, Stéphane. *Œuvres complètes*. Ed. Henri Mondor. Pléiade. Paris: Gallimard, 1945.

Marks, Elaine. "'Sapho 1900': Imaginary Renée Viviens and the Rear of the Belle Époque." DeJean and Miller 211–27.

Martino, Pierre. *Parnasse et symbolisme*. Paris: A. Colin, 1967.

Matlock, Jann. *Scenes of Seduction: Prostitution, Hysteria, and Reading Difference in Nineteenth-Century France*. New York: Columbia UP, 1994.

Maurras, Charles. *Pages littéraires choisies*. Paris: Champion, 1922.

———. "Le romantisme féminin: Allégorie du sentiment désordonné." 1904. *Romantisme et révolution*. Paris: Nouvelle librairie nationale, 1925. 131–203.

Mazaleyrat, Jean. *Éléments de métrique française*. Paris: Colin, 1974.

Mendès, Catulle. *Figurines des poètes*. Pakenham, *Portraits* 19–39.

———. *La légende du "Parnasse contemporain."* Brussels: Brancart, 1884.

———. *La maison de la vieille*. Paris: Charpentier, 1894.

Mendès-Leite, Rommel, and Pierre-Olivier de Busscher, eds. *Gay Studies from the French Cultures*. New York: Haworth, 1993.

Meschonnic, Henri. *Critique du rythme: Anthropologie historique du langage*. Paris: Verdier, 1982.

———. *Modernité modernité*. Paris: Verdier, 1988.

———. "Qu'entendez-vous par oralité?" *Langue française* 56 (1982): 6–23.

Michaud, Stéphane. "Érotisme et cruauté: Le culte baudelairien de la femme-idole." *Études baudelairiennes* 12 (1987): 23–53.

Mickel, Emanuel J., Jr. "Darío and Krysinska's 'Symphonie en gris': The Gautier-Verlaine Legacy." *Latin American Literary Review* 15 (1979): 12–24.

Middlebrook, Diane, and Marilyn Yalom, eds. *Coming to Light: American Women Poets of the Twentieth Century*. Ann Arbor: U of Michigan P, 1985.

Milech, Barbara. "'This Kind': Pornographic Discourses, Lesbian Bodies and Paul Verlaine's *Les amies*." Morgan 107–22.

Miller, Christopher L. *Blank Darkness: Africanist Discourse in French*. Chicago: U of Chicago P, 1985.

Miller, Nancy K. *The Heroine's Text: Readings in the French and English Novel, 1722–1782*. New York: Columbia UP, 1980.

———. "Men's Reading, Women's Writing: Gender and the Rise of the Novel." DeJean and Miller 40–55.

———. *Subject to Change: Reading Feminist Writing*. New York: Columbia UP, 1988.

Miller Frank, Felicia. *The Mechanical Song: Women, Voice, and the Artificial in Nineteenth-Century French Narrative*. Stanford: Stanford UP, 1995.

Milner, Max, ed. *Les fleurs du Mal: L'intériorité de la forme*. Paris: SEDES, 1989.

Milton, John. *Paradise Lost*. Ed. Merritt Y. Hughes. New York: Macmillan, 1962.

Minahen, Charles. "Homosexual Erotic Scripting in Verlaine's *Hombres*." Fisher and Schehr 119–35.

Moi, Toril. *Sexual/Textual Politics: Feminist Literary Theory*. London and New York: Methuen, 1985.

Molènes, Paul Gaston de. "Les femmes poètes." *Revue des deux mondes* July 1842: 48–76.

Monneyron, Frédéric. *L'androgyne romantique: Du mythe au mythe littéraire*. Grenoble: ELLUG, 1994.

Montefiore, Jan. *Feminism and Poetry*. 1987. London: Pandora, 1994.

Montrelay, Michèle. *L'ombre et le nom: Sur la féminité*. Paris: Minuit, 1977.

Moréas, Jean. *Les premières armes du symbolisme*. 1889. Ed. Michael Pakenham. Exeter: U of Exeter, 1973.

Morgan, Thaïs E. "Male Lesbian Bodies." *Genders* 15 (1992): 37–57.

———, ed. *Men Writing the Feminine*. Albany: State U of New York P, 1994.

Morier, Henri. *Dictionnaire de poétique et de rhétorique*. Paris: PUF, 1961.

Moses, Claire Goldberg. *French Feminism in the Nineteenth Century*. Albany: State U of New York P, 1984.

Moses, Claire Goldberg, and Leslie Wahl Rabine, eds. *Feminism, Socialism, and French Romanticism*. Bloomington: Indiana UP, 1993.

Moulin, Jeanine. *Marceline Desbordes-Valmore*. Paris: Seghers, 1955.

———, ed. *La poésie féminine du XII$^e$ au XIX$^e$ siècle*. 2 vols. Paris: Seghers, 1966.

Murger, Henry. *Scènes de la vie de bohème*. 1851. Paris: Calmann-Lévy, 1909.

Murphy, Steve. "Éditorial." *Revue Verlaine* 1 (1993): 3.

———. Rev. of *Femmes; Hombres*, ed. J.-P. Corsetti and J.-P. Giusto. *Revue Verlaine* 1 (1993): 211–12.

Musset, Alfred de. *Poésies nouvelles*. Paris: Garnier, 1962.

Nadal, Octave. *Paul Verlaine*. Paris: Mercure de France, 1961.

Nash, Suzanne, ed. *Home and Its Dislocations in Nineteenth-Century France*. Albany: State U of New York P, 1993.

Newmark, Kevin. *Beyond Symbolism: Textual History and the Future of Reading*. Ithaca: Cornell UP, 1991.

Noailles, Anna de. *Choix de poésies*. Paris: Charpentier, 1930.

———. *L'offrande*. N.p.: La Différence, 1991.

Ong, Walter. *The Presence of the Word*. New Haven: Yale UP, 1967.

Ostriker, Alicia. *Stealing the Language: The Emergence of Women's Poetry in America*. Boston: Beacon, 1986.

Ovid. *Metamorphoses*. Trans. Rolfe Humphries. Bloomington: Indiana UP, 1974.

Pakenham, Michael. "La réception du premier *Parnasse*." *Bulletin des études parnassiennes* 8 (1986): 3–13.

———, ed. *Portraits littéraires*. Exeter: U of Exeter, 1979.

Paliyenko, Adriana M. "Is a Woman Poet Born or Made? Discourse of Maternity in Louisa Siefert and Louise Ackermann." *Esprit Créateur* 39.2 (1999). Forthcoming.

———. "Re-reading *la femme poète*: Rimbaud and Louisa Siefert." *Nineteenth-Century French Studies* 26.1–2 (1995–96): 146–60.

———. "(Re)placing Women in French Poetic History: The Romantic Fallacy." *Symposium* (1999). Forthcoming.

*Le Parnasse contemporain*. Vols. 1–3. Paris: Lemerre, 1866, 1869/71, 1876.

*Le Parnassiculet contemporain*. 1872. Bassac: Plein chant, 1993.

Petrarch. *Lyric Poems*. Trans. Robert M. Durling. Cambridge: Harvard UP, 1976.

Peyre, Henri. *Literature and Sincerity*. New Haven: Yale UP, 1963.

———. *Qu'est-ce que le romantisme?* Paris: PUF, 1971.

———. *Rimbaud vu par Verlaine*. Paris: Nizet, 1975.

Pich, Edgard. "Pour une relecture des textes parnassiens." *Bulletin des études parnassiennes* 8 (1986): 87–92.

———. *Leconte de Lisle et sa création poétique*. N.p.: Chirat, 1975.

Planté, Christine. "L'art sans art de Marceline Desbordes-Valmore." *Europe* 65 (1987): 164–75.

———, ed. *Femmes poètes du XIXe siècle: Une anthologie*. Lyon: Presses Universitaires de Lyon, 1998.

———. "Marceline Desbordes-Valmore: L'autobiographie indéfinie." *Romantisme* 56 (1987): 47–58.

———. "Marceline Desbordes-Valmore: Ni poésie féminine, ni poésie féministe." *French Literature Series* 16 (1989): 78–93.

———. "Un monstre du XIXe siècle: Essai sur la femme auteur." *Sources* 12 (1987): 45–53.

Planté, Christine. "'Ondine,' ondines—femme, amour et individuation." *Romantisme* 62 (1988): 89–102.

———. *La petite sœur de Balzac: Essai sur la femme auteur.* Paris: Seuil, 1989.

Poe, Edgar Allen. "The Poetic Principle." *Poems and Essays.* New York: Dutton, 1979.

Porché, François. *Verlaine tel qu'il fut.* Paris: Flammarion, 1933.

Porter, Dennis. *Rousseau's Legacy: Emergence and Eclipse of the Writer in France.* New York and Oxford: Oxford UP, 1995.

Porter, Laurence M. *The Crisis of French Symbolism.* Ithaca: Cornell UP, 1990.

———. "Poetess or Strong Poet? Gender Stereotypes and the Elegies of Marceline Desbordes-Valmore." *French Forum* 18.2 (1993): 185–94.

———. *The Renaissance of the Lyric in French Romanticism: Elegy, "Poëme" and Ode.* Lexington, KY: French Forum, 1978.

Praz, Mario. *The Romantic Agony.* 1933. London: Oxford UP, 1951.

Preminger, Alex, and T. V. F. Brogan, eds. *The New Princeton Encyclopedia of Poetry and Poetics.* Princeton: Princeton UP, 1993.

Prendergast, Christopher, ed. *Nineteenth-Century French Poetry.* Cambridge UP, 1990.

———. *Paris and the Nineteenth Century.* Oxford and Cambridge: Blackwell, 1992.

Prins, Yopie, and Maeera Shreiber, eds. *Dwelling in Possibility: Women Poets and Critics on Poetry.* Ithaca: Cornell UP, 1997.

Rabaté, Dominique, ed. *Figures du sujet lyrique.* Paris: PUF, 1996.

Racot, Adolphe. *Portraits-cartes.* Pakenham, *Portraits* 41–62.

Raymond, Marcel. *De Baudelaire au surréalisme.* 1940. Paris: Corti, 1985.

Raynaud, Ernest. "La jeunesse de Nina." *Cahiers de la quinzaine* 19.15 (1930): 71–141.

Ricard, Louis-Xavier de. *Petits mémoires d'un Parnassien.* Ed. Michael Pakenham. Paris: Minard, 1967.

Rich, Adrienne. "Compulsory Heterosexuality and Lesbian Existence." *Signs: Journal of Women in Culture and Society* 5.4 (1980): 631–60.

Richard, Jean-Pierre. *Poésie et profondeur.* Paris: Seuil, 1955.

Riffaterre, Michael. *Semiotics of Poetry.* Bloomington: Indiana UP, 1978.

Rimbaud, Arthur. *Œuvres complètes.* Ed. Antoine Adam. Pléiade. Paris: Gallimard, 1972.

Rudrauf, Lucien. *Rime et sexe: Une nouvelle théorie de l'alternance des rimes masculines et féminines dans la poésie française.* Tartu: Akadeemilise Kooperatiivi Kirjastus, 1936.

Ruwet, Nicolas. *Langage, musique, poésie.* Paris: Seuil, 1972.

Sainte-Beuve, Charles. "Marceline Desbordes-Valmore." *XIX$^e$ siècle: Les poètes.* Ed. Maurice Allem. Vol. 3 of *Les grands écrivains français.* Paris: Garnier frères, 1932. 1–52.

Sartori, Eva, and Dorothy Zimmerman, eds. *French Women Writers.* Lincoln: U of Nebraska P, 1991.

Schaffer, Aaron. *The Genres of Parnassian Poetry: A Study of the Parnassian Minors.* Baltimore: Johns Hopkins UP, 1944.

——. "The Parnassians at Play: Their Reviews and Their Salons." *Romanic Review* 21 (1930): 49–59.

——. *Parnassus in France.* Austin: U of Texas P, 1929.

Schick, Constance Gosselin. *Seductive Resistance: The Poetry of Théophile Gautier.* Amsterdam: Rodopi, 1994.

Schmidt, Paul. "Visions of Violence: Rimbaud and Verlaine." Stambolian and Marks 228–42.

Schor, Naomi. *Breaking the Chain: Women, Theory, and French Realist Fiction.* New York: Columbia UP, 1985.

——. *George Sand and Idealism.* New York: Columbia UP, 1993.

Schultz, Gretchen. "Baudelaire's Lesbian Connections." *Approaches to Teaching Baudelaire's "Les fleurs du Mal."* Ed. Laurence Porter. New York: MLA. Forthcoming.

——. "'La géante': Feminine Proportions and Lyric Subjectivity." *Understanding "Les fleurs du Mal": Critical Readings.* Ed. William Thompson. Nashville and London: Vanderbilt UP, 1997. 35–48.

——. "Gender and the Sonnet: Marceline Desbordes-Valmore and Paul Verlaine." *Cincinnati Romance Review* 10 (1991): 190–99.

——. "Loathsome Movement: Parnassian Politics and Villard's Revenge." *Moving Forward, Holding Fast: The Dynamics of Nineteenth-Century French Culture.* Ed. B. Cooper and M. Donaldson-Evans. Amsterdam: Rodopi, 1997. 169–81.

——. "Lyric Itineraries in Verlaine's 'Almanach pour l'année passée.'" *Romance Quarterly* 38.2 (1991): 139–55.

——. "Sexualités de Verlaine." *Revue Verlaine* 5 (1997): 46–59.

Scott, Clive. *French Verse-Art.* Cambridge: Cambridge UP, 1980.

———. *A Question of Syllables: Essays in Nineteenth-Century French Verse.* Cambridge: Cambridge UP, 1986.

———. *The Riches of Rhyme: Studies in French Verse.* Oxford: Clarendon, 1988.

———. *Vers libre: The Emergence of Free Verse in France, 1886–1914.* Oxford: Clarendon, 1990.

Sedgwick, Eve Kosofsky. *Epistemology of the Closet.* Berkeley: U of California P, 1990.

Ségal, Naomi. "La première vierge folle avec son époux infernal." *Revue Verlaine* 2 (1994): 56–62.

Sharpe, William. *Unreal Cities: Urban Figuration in Wordsworth, Baudelaire, Whitman, Eliot, and Williams.* Baltimore: Johns Hopkins UP, 1990.

Shaw, Annette. "Baudelaire's 'Femmes damnées': The Androgynous Space." *Counterpoint* 11 (1980): 57–65.

Slama, Béatrice. "Femmes écrivains." Aron 213–43.

Smith, Paul. *Discerning the Subject.* Minneapolis: U of Minnesota P, 1988.

Société des études romantiques. *La petite ·musique de Verlaine: "Romances sans paroles"; "Sagesse."* Paris: SEDES, 1982.

Somoff, J.-P., and A. Marfée. *Les muses du Parnasse.* Paris: À Rebours, 1979.

Soulary, Joséphin. *Sonnets humouristiques.* Lyon: N. Scheuring, 1859.

Soulié-Lapeyre, Paule. *Le vague et l'aigu dans la perception verlainienne.* Nice: Annales de la Faculté des Lettres et Sciences Humaines, 1969.

Souriau, Maurice. *Histoire du Parnasse.* Paris: Spès, 1929.

Spivak, Gayatri Chakravorty. "Imperialism and Sexual Difference." *Oxford Literary Review* 8.1–2 (1986): 225–40.

Staël, Germaine de. *Corinne ou l'Italie.* Paris: Gallimard, 1985.

———. *De la littérature.* 1800. Paris: Flammarion, 1991.

———. *De l'Allemagne.* 1813. Ed. J. de Pange. 5 vols. Paris: Hachette, 1958.

Stambolian, George, and Elaine Marks, eds. *Homosexualities and French Literature: Cultural Contexts, Critical Texts.* Ithaca: Cornell UP, 1979.

Stanton, Domna, ed. *The Defiant Muse: French Feminist Poems from the Middle Ages to the Present: A Bilingual Anthology.* New York: Feminist, 1986.

Starobinski, Jean. *La mélancolie au miroir: Trois lectures de Baudelaire.* N.p.: Julliard, 1989.

Stewart, Joan Hinde. *Gynographs: French Novels by Women of the Late Eighteenth Century.* Lincoln: U of Nebraska P, 1993.

Sullerot, Evelyne. *Histoire de la presse féminine en France des origines à 1848.* Paris: Colin, 1966.

Szarama-Swolkieniowa, Maria. *Maria Krysinska: Poetka Francuskiego Symbolizmu.* Krakow: Nakladem Uniwersytetu Jagiellonskiego, 1972.

Tastu, Amable. *Poésies complètes.* Paris: Didier, 1858.

Terdiman, Richard. "Class Struggles in France." Hollier 705–10.

———. *Discourse/Counter-Discourse: The Theory and Practice of Symbolic Resistance in Nineteenth-Century France.* Ithaca: Cornell UP, 1985.

Todorov, Tzvetan. *Les genres du discours.* Paris: Seuil, 1978.

———. *Qu'est-ce que le structuralisme? 2: Poétique.* Paris: Seuil, 1968.

Valéry, Paul. *Œuvres.* 2 vols. Pléiade. Paris: Gallimard, 1957.

Vandegans, André. "Sur deux sonnets de Nina de Callias." *Rivista de letterature moderne* Oct.–Dec. 1953: 302–08.

Vannier, Gilles. *Paul Verlaine ou l'enfance de l'art.* Seyssel: Champ Vallon, 1993.

Verlaine, Paul. *Cellulairement.* Ed. Jean-Luc Steinmetz. Talence: Le Castor Astral, 1992.

———. *Correspondance.* Ed. Ad. van Bever. 3 vols. Paris: Messein, 1922–29.

———. *Femmes; Hombres.* Ed. Jean-Paul Corsetti and Jean-Pierre Giusto. Paris: Terrain vague, 1990.

———. *Œuvres en prose complètes.* Ed. Jacques Borel. Pléiade. Paris: Gallimard, 1972.

———. *Œuvres poétiques complètes.* Ed. Y.-G. Dantec and Jacques Borel. Pléiade. Paris: Gallimard, 1962

Velter, André. *Les poètes du Chat noir.* Paris: Gallimard, 1996.

Vickers, Nancy. "Diana Described: Scattered Women and Scattered Rhyme." *Critical Inquiry* (1981): 265–79.

Victor, Lucien. "À propos de vers: L'impair de onze syllabes (et le statut de l'impair long dans la poésie de Verlaine)." *Le Français moderne* 53.3–4 (1985): 217–30.

Vigny, Alfred de. *Chatterton.* 1835. Paris: Larousse, 1973.

———. *Poèmes antiques et modernes: Les destinées.* Ed. André Jarry. Paris: Gallimard, 1973.

Viguié, Pierre. "Louise Colet: La Vénus en marbre chaud." *Revue de Paris* 74.9 (1967): 95–100.

Villard, Nina de. *Feuillets parisiens.* Paris: Messager, 1885.

Vincent-Buffault, Anne. *Histoire des larmes.* Paris: Rivages, 1986.

Vivien, Renée. *Poèmes.* New York: Arno, 1975.

Waelti-Walters, Jennifer. *Feminist Novels of the Belle Époque.* Bloomington: Indiana UP, 1990.

Waller, Margaret. *The Male Malady: Fictions of Impotence in the French Romantic Novel.* New Brunswick, NJ: Rutgers UP, 1993.

Weil, Kari. *Androgyny and the Denial of Difference.* Charlottesville: UP of Virginia, 1992.

Wesling, Donald, and Tadeusz Slawek, eds. *Literary Voice: The Calling of Jonah.* Albany: State U of New York P, 1995.

Wing, Nathaniel. "Dialogues with the Muse." Hollier 666–71.

——. *The Limits of Narrative: Essays on Baudelaire, Flaubert, Rimbaud, and Mallarmé.* Cambridge: Cambridge UP, 1986.

Wood, Kathryn L. *Criticism of French Romantic Literature in the "Gazette de France," 1830–1848.* Philadelphia: Bryn Mawr College, 1934.

Woolf, Virginia. *A Room of One's Own.* 1929. New York: Harcourt, 1957.

Zayed, Georges. *La formation littéraire de Verlaine.* Paris: Minard, 1962.

——. "Un salon parnassien d'avant-garde: Nina de Villard et ses hôtes." *Aquila-Chestnut Hill Studies in Modern Languages and Literatures* 2 (1973): 177–229.

Zimmermann, Éléonore. *Magies de Verlaine.* Paris: Corti, 1967. Geneva: Slatkine, 1981.

——. "Variété de Verlaine." Société des études romantiques 5–16.

Zola, Émile. "Le solitaire." Drillon 71–75.

——. "Les poètes contemporains." *Documents littéraires.* Vol. 45 of *Les œuvres complètes.* Paris: Bernouard, 1927. 129–52.

Zumthor, Paul. *Introduction à la poésie orale.* Paris: Seuil, 1983.

# Index

# Index